RELIABLE JAVASCRIPT®

Reliable JavaScript®

Lawrence D. Spencer
Seth H. Richards

wrox™
A Wiley Brand

Reliable JavaScript®

Published by
John Wiley & Sons, Inc.
10475 Crosspoint Boulevard
Indianapolis, IN 46256
www.wiley.com

Copyright © 2015 by John Wiley & Sons, Inc., Indianapolis, Indiana

Published simultaneously in Canada

ISBN: 978-1-119-02872-7

ISBN: 978-1-119-02873-4 (ebk)

ISBN: 978-1-119-02874-1 (ebk)

Manufactured in the United States of America

10 9 8 7 6 5 4 3 2 1

We dedicate this book to all JavaScript developers who work hard to hone their craft. You are making the world a more beautiful place.

CREDITS

PROJECT EDITOR
Christina Haviland

TECHNICAL EDITORS
Keith Pepin
John Peloquin

PRODUCTION MANAGER
Kathleen Wisor

COPY EDITOR
Nancy Rapoport

**MANAGER OF CONTENT DEVELOPMENT
& ASSEMBLY**
Mary Beth Wakefield

MARKETING DIRECTOR
David Mayhew

MARKETING MANAGER
Carrie Sherrill

**PROFESSIONAL TECHNOLOGY & STRATEGY
DIRECTOR**
Barry Pruett

BUSINESS MANAGER
Amy Knies

ASSOCIATE PUBLISHER
Jim Minatel

PROJECT COORDINATOR, COVER
Brent Savage

PROOFREADER
Nancy Carrasco

INDEXER
Johnna VanHoose Dinse

COVER DESIGNER
Wiley

COVER IMAGE
© Getty Images/Andrew Rich

ABOUT THE AUTHORS

LARRY SPENCER is Vice President of Application Development at ScerIS, a software and services company in Sudbury, Massachusetts. He and his team create browser-based applications in AngularJS, with a C#/Web API/SQL Server back end. Larry's 35-year career has included stints programming in COBOL, C, C++, C#, and even mainframe assembly language, but he says JavaScript is the most fun. A frequent speaker at Code Camps and other gatherings, Larry enjoys sharing his love of software with the development community. You can find his blog at `http://FascinatedWithSoftware.com`.

Larry's outside interests include philosophy, chess, and classical guitar. He lives in Marlborough, Massachusetts.

SETH RICHARDS has been crafting software professionally since 2002. He got his start programming embedded devices for the bar and nightclub industry and transitioned to web application development in 2007. He has worked on numerous web-based applications ranging from an enterprise-class geographic information system–centric physical asset management system to a social network for product discovery and recommendation.

Seth graduated from Plymouth State College (now University) in Plymouth, New Hampshire, where he studied computer science and mathematics. He is currently pursuing his M.S. in Computer Science from the Georgia Institute of Technology. Seth's blog can be found at `http://blog.shrichards.com`, and he can be followed on Twitter at @shrichards.

ABOUT THE TECHNICAL EDITORS

KEITH PEPIN has been developing sites and applications on the web for over 17 years. Early in his career, he fell in love with JavaScript and has been passionately building dynamic user experiences ever since. He is currently a Senior Software Engineer at Meltwater, and is using HTML5, CSS3, JavaScript, AngularJS, Node.js, and MongoDB to build the next generation of their online marketing intelligence platform. When not coding or spending time with his family, he enjoys other geeky pursuits, including all forms of games, comic books, painting, and sketching.

JOHN PELOQUIN is a software engineer with over 10 years of JavaScript experience ranging across applications of all sizes. John earned his B.A. in Mathematics from U.C. Berkeley and is currently a lead engineer at Spreemo, a healthcare technology startup in NYC. Prior to editing this volume, John edited *Professional Website Performance* by Peter Smith (Wiley 2012) and *Professional JavaScript for Web Developers*, 3rd ed. by Nicholas Zakas (Wiley 2012). When he is not coding or collecting errata, John can occasionally be found doing stand-up comedy at an open mic.

ACKNOWLEDGMENTS

Thank you to my wife, Bethany, for her love and support while we wrote this book, and for enduring (or enjoying?) many husband-less nights and weekends while I worked to meet a deadline.

−SETH RICHARDS

Thanks to my family for encouraging me to pursue my dreams. My dreams may include writing a book, but they begin and end with you.

−LARRY SPENCER

This book would not have been possible without the willingness of others to share their knowledge and expertise with us and the community at large in book, blog, and source-code format. Together, we'd like to acknowledge and thank:

➤ Douglas Crockford, for his exposure of good parts of JavaScript and his work on jsLint.

➤ Nicolas Zakas, for the numerous books and blog posts he wrote that acted as guides through JavaScript's sometimes-treacherous waters, and also his maintenance of and contributions to ESLint.

➤ Stoyan Stefanov, for his instruction on applying pattern-based development to JavaScript.

➤ Robert C. Martin, for instilling in us the desire to write clean code.

➤ Fredrik Appelberg, for his creation of, and Dave Clayton for his contributions to, the AOP.js aspect-oriented programming framework.

➤ Mike Bostock, for inspiring us with the D3 library for SVG graphics.

➤ The folks at Pivotal Labs, for the creation of the open-source JavaScript framework Jasmine, and members of the community that have contributed to the framework.

➤ The AngularJS team, for showing the world a great way to build single-page applications.

➤ The vast and growing network of generous people on sites such as Stack Overflow and GitHub. Without you, we'd still be thumbing through manuals.

We would also like to express our appreciation to our project editor, Chris Haviland, who deftly maneuvered us through the writing process from beginning to end. Our copy editor, Nancy Rapoport, has read our book more carefully, and more times, than anyone else ever will. For her dedication and suggestions we offer heartfelt thanks. We would also like to express our sincerest thanks to our technical editors, Keith Pepin and John Peloquin. Their JavaScript prowess helped us avoid more than a few technical errors. Should any errors still exist, it's likely because we didn't follow some of their advice. Our hats are off to you, gentlemen.

Finally, we'd like to thank Carol Long, the Executive Acquisitions Editor at Wiley, who gave us the opportunity to write this book. Without her, we'd still just be a couple of guys that write software for a living. We're still that, but now we're authors, too. Carol announced her retirement from the publishing industry just before we finished the book. We sure hope we weren't the straw that broke the camel's back! Thank you, Carol, and we wish you nothing but sunny days and margaritas in your retirement.

—LARRY AND SETH

CONTENTS

PART II: TESTING PATTERN-BASED CODE

INTRODUCTION

WHEN WE SHARED THE TITLE OF THIS BOOK, *Reliable JavaScript*, with fellow developers, we received feedback such as:

> "Now *there's* a juxtaposition!"

> "It must be a very short book."

> "Will I find it next to the latest John Grisham thriller in the fiction section of the bookstore?"

No, this book is not a work of fiction.

The feedback we received about the title of the book illustrates a broader perception about JavaScript that some developers with experience in classical, compiled languages have: JavaScript is used to create flashy portfolio websites or simple to-do apps; it has no business in my mission-critical enterprise application.

In the past that was true, but no more.

THE RISE OF JAVASCRIPT AS A FIRST-CLASS LANGUAGE

JavaScript's reputation as a wild child is well-deserved, and we hope to amuse you with some of its exploits in the next two sections. However, like a spoiled heiress who inherits the family business and surprises everyone by rising to the challenge, she has turned serious and responsible, lately showing herself capable of true greatness.

Her early life was as a dilettante, rarely entrusted with anything more than short "scripting" tasks. The decisions she made were simple: If a required field was not filled in, she should color it red; if a button was clicked, she should bring another page into view. Although her responsibilities were limited, she was easy to get along with and made many friends. To this day, most programmers' experience of her is primarily of this sort.

Then, in the shift that was to redefine her life, the world turned to the web. This had been her playground, her little place to amuse herself while members of The Old Boys Club did the real work on the server.

The wave started to break in the late 1990s when Microsoft introduced first iframes and then XMLHTTP. When Google made Ajax part of its Gmail application in 2004 and Google Maps in 2005, the wave came crashing down. The world was suddenly aware of just how much richer the web experience could be when the browser was entrusted with more than just displaying whatever the server dispensed.

So it was that our princess was given more responsibility than anyone had ever intended. She would need help.

And help did come, in the form of toolkits and frameworks like jQuery, Ext JS, Ember.js, Knockout, Backbone, and AngularJS. These worthy advisors did everything they could to bring discipline and structure to JavaScript. However, they never quite tamed her youthful exuberance. In spite of her advisors and her good intentions, she was always getting into trouble.

THE EASE OF WRITING TRULY DISASTROUS CODE IN JAVASCRIPT

Part of the problem, which she has only recently begun to outgrow, was her years spent as a page-scripting language. In that limited sphere, there was no harm in making a variable or function global. If a variable was misspelled, the effects were limited and easy to track down. (By the way, the effect would likely be to create yet another global.) If the architecture was sloppy . . . well, how much architecture can there even *be* on just one web page?

Compounding the potential for error was the lack of a compiler. Server-side programs in C# or Java are guaranteed to be at least syntactically correct before they are run. JavaScript must start and hope for the best. A misspelled variable, or a call to a non-existent function, can lurk in the code for months until a particular execution path is followed.

And then there are the quirks. Ah, those endearing, maddening quirks.

At the top of the list must be the distinction between == (equality with type coercion) and === (without). A great idea, but so hard for programmers primarily trained in other languages to get used to!

Never is JavaScript more coquettish than when it comes to truth and falsehood. She has a notion of "truthy" and "falsy" that confuses all but the most determined suitors. Zero is a falsy value so, thanks to type coercion, the expression

```
false == '0'
```

is true. But not for the reason you think. The value false is coerced to a number, which is 0 (true would convert to 1). Next, the string '0' is also coerced to a number. That is also 0, so the result is true.

However,

```
false == 'false'
```

evaluates to false because the left-hand false, again coerced to the number 0, is compared to the string 'false', also coerced to a number. Except 'false' is not a number at all so the second conversion yields NaN (Not a Number) and the equality fails. Ah, JavaScript.

She is always up for a little fun. If you declare the function

```
function letsHaveFun(me, you) {
  // Fun things happening between me and you
}
```

and call it thus:

```
letsHaveFun(me);
```

JavaScript will let the call proceed with the variable *you* undefined, just for the fun of watching you try to play with someone who isn't there.

We could go on and on. There are surprising scoping rules, a unique "prototypal" inheritance mechanism, automatic and sometimes incorrect semicolon insertion, the ability of one object to borrow a function from a totally unrelated object, *et cetera, et cetera*.

With globals popping into existence unbidden, an almost total lack of architectural tradition, a questionable relationship to the truth, and more quirkiness than you'd find at a cosplay convention, it's a wonder that JavaScript has done as well as she has in the world.

Believe it or not, it gets worse before it gets better. Even if you get it right, it can go wrong oh so easily.

THE EASE OF UNINTENTIONALLY BREAKING JAVASCRIPT CODE

JavaScript has a perverse sense of humor. In a staid, compiled language, if you have a line of perfectly correct, debugged code running flawlessly in production like this one

```
myVariable = myObject.myProperty;
```

and then accidentally bump the x key on your keyboard so that you now have

```
myVariable = myObject.myPropxerty;
```

the compiler will emit a stern message that you should be more careful next time. JavaScript will happily run the code and give the value of `undefined` to `myVariable`. "Let's have fun and see what happens!" she says.

When you want to change the name of a property, JavaScript likes to play hide-and-seek. You might think that searching your entire source tree for

```
.myProperty
```

would turn up all the places to change. "No, no, no!" JavaScript says with a grin. "You forgot to search for `['myProperty']`."

Actually, you should search with a regular expression that allows spaces between the brackets and the quotes. Have you ever done that? Neither have we.

And then, depending on her mood, she may or may not let it come to your mind that you should also search for constructs like this:

```
var prop = 'myProperty';
// . . .
myObject[prop] = something;
```

When it is so hard to accomplish even such a trivial refactoring, you can imagine how easily mistakes can find their way into your code. Code that is not amenable to refactoring almost defines the word "brittle."

How can you avoid these problems? If there is one concept that we hope to preach *and* practice in this book, it is test-driven development. In the absence of a compiler, tests are your best defense against error.

JavaScript is also more than amenable to playing by the rules of software engineering. In fact, because of her extremely. . .um. . .creative nature, JavaScript may need them more than most languages.

We have met many developers who are open to this message and would like to learn more about how to proceed. We hope you are one of them.

THIS BOOK'S INTENDED AUDIENCE

Because this book isn't a JavaScript primer, we assume you have some JavaScript experience. The following sections outline the attributes of the book's ideal audience.

Developers Who Come to JavaScript from Other Languages

Neither of us started his career as a JavaScript developer, and it's likely you didn't either: JavaScript is a relatively new kid on the block when it comes to large-scale application development.

JavaScript is also quite different from any of the languages that we did have experience in. We come from the comfortable world of the compiled, statically typed language C#.

Our JavaScript got a lot better when we embraced its dynamic nature while maintaining a C# programmer's sense of architecture and discipline.

If you're like us and have a background thinking and programming in a language other than JavaScript, such as C# or Java, this book is for you. Your knowledge of data structures and architecture provide a solid base on which to master JavaScript for large-scale development.

Many of the sections illustrate how language features in C# and Java, such as inheritance and interfaces, correspond to the capabilities in JavaScript. We also highlight many of the major differences between JavaScript and other languages, such as scoping rules and type-coercing equality comparisons. Knowledge of its capabilities and features will improve your ability to think in JavaScript.

Another major focus of this book is how software engineering concepts and practices more commonly associated with C# and Java development, such as design patterns, unit-testing, and test-driven development, may be applied to JavaScript. Sound engineering will temper JavaScript's wild nature, creating reliable and maintainable code.

Developers with Small-Scale JavaScript Experience

In our endeavor to add developers with JavaScript experience to our team, we've encountered many candidates who feel small-scale JavaScript experience, such as input field validation or jQuery element transitions, warrants listing "JavaScript" prominently on a résumé.

In an interview, it doesn't take much time to determine such a candidate has no problem hooking up a button handler, perhaps in the context of an ASP.NET Web Forms application, but would be hard-pressed to create a JavaScript module that has variables that are protected from external manipulation.

As our organization's use of JavaScript has evolved, our definition of what it means to have JavaScript experience has evolved as well. A few years ago, if a developer had a bit of experience with jQuery, we would check our "JavaScript" box with satisfaction.

Now, however, we're looking for a lot more. And we're not alone. It's no longer uncommon for entire applications to be written in JavaScript. In so-called single-page applications (SPAs), the JavaScript code organizes the entire application, bearing vastly more responsibility than the ephemeral click-handlers of the past. In order to participate in the development of a large-scale JavaScript application, developers must know how to use the language in a structured and disciplined way while simultaneously taking advantage of its many unique capabilities and quirks.

Through the examples in this book, we hope to help you, the small-scale JavaScript developer, make it big.

Developers Responsible for Choosing Programming Languages for a New Project

Perhaps you've heard the adage "No one ever gets fired for buying IBM." The statement reflects the feeling that, when faced with choosing a technology partner for an IT project, it's unlikely that the decision to pick an established, reputable company such as IBM will be second-guessed. The statement implies that IBM is the *safe* choice. Even if the project experiences cost over-runs, missed deadlines, or complete failure, the choice of IBM is above reproach.

If you're in a position to choose the language or languages used for the development of a new application, you're in the same position as the IT manager choosing a technology partner. There are many tried-and-true programming languages with long histories. For instance, C# and Java, each backed by a large, established technology company, have been used to build both web and desktop applications for over a decade. No one would be fired for choosing C#.

In terms of being a safe choice for a new programming project, especially in the enterprise, JavaScript is decidedly not like C#. JavaScript is not a mature, staid, starched-shirt-wearing programming language. She is young, daring, and free-spirited.

She doesn't have the same long track record of success for large-scale software projects that languages such as C# and Java have. That's not to say that projects using C# and Java are guaranteed to succeed. If a project using one of those languages isn't successful, however, language choice probably wouldn't be included as a factor contributing to failure.

As we mentioned in the previous section, JavaScript makes it all too easy to write disastrous code. This has given her a bit of a reputation, reducing the likelihood you'd want to bring her home to meet mom and dad.

JavaScript's reputation should not automatically exclude her for consideration for projects that could benefit from her strengths. Node.js, a server-side JavaScript engine, is lightweight and highly scalable; perfect for real-time and data-intensive applications. JavaScript may be used to create rich user interfaces in the browser. Client-side frameworks such as Ember and AngularJS may be used to build complete browser-based applications that can help reduce the load on the web server by off-loading presentation logic to the client.

While we can't guarantee it will succeed, the upcoming chapters will show ways to mitigate the risk of choosing JavaScript for your next project by applying the lessons we've learned while working on our own projects.

Success will not happen by accident, especially with JavaScript. It requires a firm grasp of engineering principles, which are the subject of the first chapter.

HOW THIS BOOK IS STRUCTURED

We've organized the book into five parts.

Part I, "Laying a Solid Foundation," covers key concepts of software engineering such as the SOLID and DRY principles. It also discusses the benefits of unit-testing and test-driven development. Part I also introduces the tools and JavaScript libraries that will be used throughout the book. Finally, it discusses objects in JavaScript and their testability.

In Part II, "Testing Pattern-Based Code," we describe and use test-driven development to create several useful code patterns. Some of the patterns, such as the Singleton, may be familiar from other languages you're familiar with. Others, such as Promises, are associated primarily with JavaScript.

Part III, "Testing and Writing with Advanced JavaScript Features," describes how to leverage and test more advanced features of the JavaScript language. It also covers creation and testing of applications that use advanced program architectures, such as the Mediator and Observer Patterns.

Part IV, "Special Subjects in Testing," provides examples of testing DOM manipulation, and it also illustrates the use of static analysis tools to enforce coding standards.

Finally, Part V, "Summary," reviews the concepts of test-driven development, and also presents a collection of JavaScript idioms that you will have encountered in the book.

WHAT YOU NEED TO USE THIS BOOK

To run the samples in the book, you need the following:

- ➤ A text editor
- ➤ A web browser

The source code for the samples is available for download from the Wrox website at:

www.wrox.com/go/reliablejavascript

Open-source software based on the book can be found on GitHub at
www.github.com/reliablejavascript.

CONVENTIONS

To help you get the most from the text and keep track of what's happening, we've used a number of conventions throughout the book.

> **NOTE** *Notes indicate notes, tips, hints, tricks, and asides to the current discussion.*

As for styles in the text:

➤ We *italicize* new terms and important words when we introduce them.

➤ We present keyboard strokes like this: Ctrl+A.

➤ We show filenames, URLs, and code within the text like so: persistence.properties.

We present code in two different ways:

```
We use a monofont type with no highlighting for most code examples.
```

We use bold to emphasize code that is particularly important in the present context or to show changes from a previous code snippet.

SOURCE CODE

As you work through the examples in this book, you may choose either to type in all the code manually, or to use the source code files that accompany the book. All the source code used in this book is available for download at www.wrox.com. Specifically for this book, the code download is on the Download Code tab at:

www.wrox.com/go/reliablejavascript

You can also search for the book at www.wrox.com by ISBN (the ISBN for this book is 978-1-119-02872-7) to find the code. A complete list of code downloads for all current Wrox books is available at www.wrox.com/dynamic/books/download.aspx.

Most of the code on www.wrox.com is compressed in a .ZIP, .RAR, or similar archive format appropriate to the platform. Once you download the code, just decompress it with an appropriate compression tool.

> **NOTE** *Because many books have similar titles, you may find it easiest to search by ISBN; this book's ISBN is 978-1-119-02872-7.*

ERRATA

We make every effort to ensure that there are no errors in the text or in the code. However, no one is perfect, and mistakes do occur. If you find an error in one of our books, like a spelling mistake or faulty piece of code, we would be very grateful for your feedback. By sending in errata, you may save another reader hours of frustration, and at the same time, you will be helping us provide even higher quality information.

To find the errata page for this book, go to

`www.wrox.com/go/reliablejavascript`

and click the Errata link. On this page, you can view all errata that has been submitted for this book and posted by Wrox editors.

If you don't spot "your" error on the Book Errata page, go to `www.wrox.com/contact/techsupport.shtml` and complete the form there to send us the error you have found. We'll check the information and, if appropriate, post a message to the book's errata page and fix the problem in subsequent editions of the book.

P2P.WROX.COM

For author and peer discussion, join the P2P forums at `http://p2p.wrox.com`. The forums are a web-based system for you to post messages relating to Wrox books and related technologies and interact with other readers and technology users. The forums offer a subscription feature to e-mail you topics of interest of your choosing when new posts are made to the forums. Wrox authors, editors, other industry experts, and your fellow readers are present on these forums.

At `http://p2p.wrox.com`, you will find a number of different forums that will help you, not only as you read this book, but also as you develop your own applications. To join the forums, just follow these steps:

1. Go to `http://p2p.wrox.com` and click the Register link.

2. Read the terms of use and click Agree.

3. Complete the required information to join, as well as any optional information you wish to provide, and click Submit.

4. You will receive an e-mail with information describing how to verify your account and complete the joining process.

> **NOTE** *You can read messages in the forums without joining P2P, but in order to post your own messages, you must join.*

Once you join, you can post new messages and respond to messages other users post. You can read messages at any time on the web. If you would like to have new messages from a particular forum e-mailed to you, click the *Subscribe to This Forum* icon by the forum name in the forum listing.

For more information about how to use the Wrox P2P, be sure to read the P2P FAQs for answers to questions about how the forum software works, as well as many common questions specific to P2P and Wrox books. To read the FAQs, click the FAQ link on any P2P page.

PART I
Laying a Solid Foundation

Practicing Skillful Software Engineering

WHAT'S IN THIS CHAPTER?

➤ Writing code that starts correct

➤ Writing code that stays correct

WROX.COM CODE DOWNLOADS FOR THIS CHAPTER

You can find the wrox.com code downloads for this chapter at www.wrox.com/go/ reliablejavascript on the Download Code tab. The code is in the Chapter 1 download and organized in directories according to this chapter's topics, with each directory holding one sample. You can run a sample by copying its directory to your hard drive and double-clicking on the index.html file.

Few professions are more humbling than computer programming. If we did things right the first time, we could accomplish a day's work in about 20 minutes. That's how long it would take to type the debugged lines of code most of us pump out in a day.

We spend the rest of our time correcting our mistakes as brought to our attention by the compiler, the QA staff, our bosses, and our customers.

As anyone who has worked on a "mature" system knows, we also waste a lot of time refactoring (or wishing it were possible to refactor) code that has grown brittle and unmaintainable over the years, thanks to poor design decisions by our fellow programmers or even ourselves.

Yet somehow, we continue to think we're pretty smart, and that only makes things worse. All our lives, we've been the ones who can figure stuff out. We love puzzles and problems. We're the guys (most of us *are* guys, and that probably also makes things worse) who don't like to ask for directions and don't like to read instructions.

Plunk us down in the middle of a problem, and we're optimistic that we can find the way out. On our own.

This chapter brings good news. Software developers *are* smart, and some of them have developed techniques that will help us create a lot more than 20 minutes' worth of code in a day, and with vastly increased aesthetic satisfaction.

These techniques are not new. Every idea in this chapter is at least a decade old. However, as we have interviewed dozens of candidates for developer positions for our team, from both the United States and abroad, very few have heard of the principles behind the SOLID acronym (let alone the acronym itself). They may have heard of DRY code, but they do not appreciate its absolutely central role in good software development. Misconceptions about unit-testing abound, with many developers unaware of the benefits of letting tests drive the development process.

When you have mastered these ideas, you will be among the elite. Most developers know about object-oriented programming. Only a few also know about dependency inversion and the Liskov Substitution Principle. Fewer still have mastered test-driven development.

WRITING CODE THAT STARTS CORRECT

What Johann Sebastian Bach said about playing a keyboard instrument applies equally to programming a computer: There's nothing remarkable about it. All one has to do is hit the right keys at the right time and the instrument plays itself.

This section is about hitting the right keys at the right time. As you might guess, there's more to it than the uninitiated might think.

But first, a story.

Mastering the Features of JavaScript

Have you ever seen someone get his head chopped off on a squash court? One of us nearly did. It was during an introductory college course in the sport, but the episode had a lot to teach about writing reliable JavaScript.

In case you're not familiar with the game, it's played in a court that is like a large room. Two players alternate hitting a ball with their rackets toward the back wall, which they both face. In the most basic scenario, you hit the ball at the wall; it bounces off and then bounces off the floor toward your opponent, who is standing next to you. Then *he* smashes it toward the back wall for *you* to try to hit.

Anyway, it was the first day of the course. The instructor was standing to the student's left and a little behind him, and the rest of us were watching through the glass front wall. The instructor directed the student to hit the ball toward the back wall.

The student, who was a tennis player, hit a forehand as he would in tennis, stroking from low to high, with a high follow-through that wrapped around his body. That is how you hit with topspin in tennis. It's also how you chop off the head of whoever happens to be standing to your left and a little behind you.

Fortunately, the instructor knew this would happen and had positioned his racket in front of his face to defend himself.

The student's racket crashed against the instructor's, making a lot of noise and causing the student some embarrassment, but no harm was done.

The instructor pointed out that in tennis, you generally hit with topspin so the ball dives down and bounces up with a kick toward your opponent. However, that same stroke in squash does the opposite. If you hit with topspin, the squash ball will kick up off the wall, making an easy, looping arc, and then bounce in a lazy manner off the floor, whence your opponent will crush it. In squash, you want to hit with *back*spin. The ball will then kick *down* off the wall, and kick off the floor toward your opponent with increased velocity.

The normal stroke in squash, then, is a chopping, downward motion to impart backspin—just the opposite of the typical stroke in tennis.

Even though the two sports have basic features in common (two players, rackets, and a ball) as well as common demands (good hand-eye coordination, good anticipation and movement on your feet), you won't play squash well if you try to hit the ball as you would in tennis.

In the same way, JavaScript makes its particular demands on the programmer. If you come to large-scale JavaScript development with primary experience in another language, you will do well to attune yourself to the differences in technique.

The differences are at both the small scale of syntax and the large scale of architecture and engineering.

Throughout this book, you will encounter JavaScript's unique syntactic delights. Many of them are summarized in Chapter 25. This chapter looks at the larger issues of how JavaScript's peculiarities make certain engineering techniques possible.

By employing these techniques, you will write JavaScript with kick. Your game will improve. You will "win" more often because you will be working *with* the language instead of contrary to it.

Case Study: D3.js

Mike Bostock's JavaScript masterpiece, `D3.js`, is a perfect example.

D3 stands for Data-Driven Documents, so called because it lets you create beautiful SVG graphics from data. For example, Figure 1-1 is a D3 diagram that shows class dependencies in a software system (from `http://bl.ocks.org/mbostock/4341134`).

Figure 1-2 presents the same data in a radial layout (`http://bl.ocks.org/mbostock/1044242`). D3 is *very* flexible. It is also very concise; each diagram takes just a few dozen lines of pleasingly formatted JavaScript to create.

D3's home page is `http://d3js.org`, with source code available at `https://github.com/mbostock/d3`. This is *real* JavaScript, not for the faint of heart and orders of magnitude more artful than the field-validators and button-handlers that are sprinkled through a typical website.

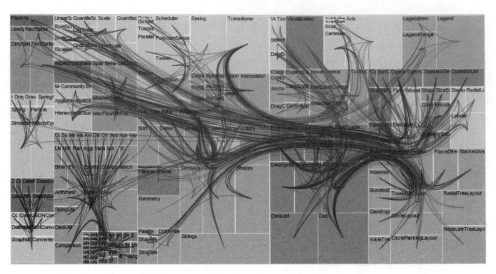

FIGURE 1-1

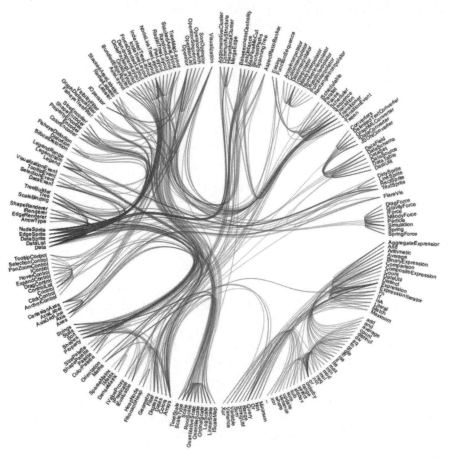

FIGURE 1-2

In fact, it's so artful as to be overwhelming at first read, so we have simplified just one corner of it for discussion. Listing 1-1 is an abridged version of d3.svg.line, a function that creates an SVG line generator. An explanation follows the listing.

LISTING 1-1: A function to create an SVG line (code filename: rj3\rj3.js)

```
// Create a namespace to avoid creating many global variables.
var rj3 = {};

// Make a sub-namespace called svg.
rj3.svg = {};

// Put a line function in the rj3.svg namespace.
rj3.svg.line = function() {
  var getX = function(point) {
      return point[0];
    },
      getY = function(point) {
      return point[1];
    },
      interpolate = function(points) {
      return points.join("L");
    };

  function line(data) {
    var segments = [],
        points = [],
        i = -1,
        n = data.length,
        d;

    function segment() {
      segments.push("M",interpolate(points));
    }

    while (++i < n) {
      d = data[i];
      points.push([+getX.call(this,d,i), +getY.call(this,d,i)]);
    }

    if (points.length) {
      segment();
    }

    return segments.length ? segments.join("") : null;
  }

  line.x = function(funcToGetX) {
    if (!arguments.length) return getX;
    getX = funcToGetX;
    return line;
  };

  line.y = function(funcToGetY) {
    if (!arguments.length) return getY;
```

continues

LISTING 1-1 *(continued)*

```
    getY = funcToGetY;
    return line;
};

  return line;
};
```

You would use this function to turn an array of data into an SVG path. SVG paths are just strings in the small language of SVG. Suppose you wanted to draw a line like the one in Figure 1-3.

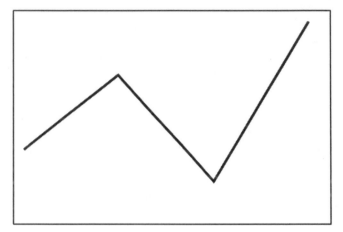

FIGURE 1-3

The SVG `<path>` element would be

```
<path d="M10,130L100,60L190,160L280,10"></path>
```

In English, that says to pick up the pen and move it ("M") to the (x, y) coordinate (10, 130), and then draw a line ("L") to (100, 60), and then draw another line to (190, 160), and then finish with a line to (280, 10).

So how does the code in Listing 1-1 create a path like that? Consider Listing 1-2, which contains a sample call.

LISTING 1-2: Sample call to rj3.svg.line() (code filename: rj3\pathFromArrays.js)

```
var arrayData = [
      [10,130],
      [100,60],
      [190,160],
      [280,10]
    ],
    lineGenerator = rj3.svg.line(),
    path = lineGenerator(arrayData);

document.getElementById('pathFromArrays').setAttribute('d',path);
```

On the highlighted line, what ends up in *lineGenerator*? Well, according to the last line of Listing 1-1, a call to `rj3.svg.line()` will return something called `line`. What is that? It is a function *nested inside* the outer function `rj3.svg.line`!

> **NOTE** *In JavaScript, functions can nest inside other functions. This becomes an important way to control scope.*

By the way, we have retained D3's names for most properties and variables so you can study the full listing at `https://github.com/mbostock/d3/blob/master/src/svg/line.js` if you wish, and be as well-oriented to it as possible. In only a few cases have we attempted to clarify things by changing a variable's name. If you find it confusing that both the outer and inner functions are named `line`, well, this is very much in the spirit of all the D3 source code so you might as well learn to enjoy it.

Yes, the function returns a function. This is a confusing no-no in most languages, but in JavaScript it's a very idiomatic yes-yes that broadens your architectural options. If you're going to code industrial-strength JavaScript, get used to functions being first-class objects that are passed as arguments, sent back as return values and just about anything else you can imagine. As first-class citizens of JavaScript, they can even have properties and methods of their own.

> **NOTE** *In JavaScript, functions are objects that can have methods and properties. Your functions can have more flexibility and power than they might in other languages.*

You can see an example of attaching a method to a function in this part of Listing 1-1:

```
line.x = function(funcToGetX) {
  if (!arguments.length) return getX;
  getX = funcToGetX;
  return line;
};
```

It creates a function, x, that is a member of the returned function, `line`. Shortly, you will see how x and its twin, y, are used, and learn the very JavaScript-ey peculiarities of what's inside them.

So the call `rj3.svg.line()` returns a function. Continuing with Listing 1-2, the function is called with *arrayData*, which becomes the *data* argument to that inner `line` function from Listing 1-1. From there, the `while` loop fills the *points* array from the incoming *data*:

```
while (++i < n) {
  d = data[i];
  points.push([+getX.call(this,d,i), +getY.call(this,d,i)]);
}
```

Each element of *data*, held in the variable *d*, is passed to the getX and getY functions, which extract the *x* and *y* coordinates. (The use of `call` to invoke getX and getY will be covered at the end of this Case Study, as well as in Chapter 18. The + in front of getX and getY is a little trick to ensure that actual numbers, not numeric strings, go in the points array.) By default, those coordinates are the first and second elements of the 2-element array that comprises each element of *arrayData*. This occurs in the following snippet of Listing 1-1.

```
var getX = function(point) {
    return point[0];
},
getY = function(point) {
    return point[1];
}
```

Next, the `segment` function is called. This is a function at yet another level of nesting, private to the `line` function. It fills the *segments* variable, putting the SVG `"M"` command in the first element and the path in the second. From Listing 1-1 again:

```
function segment() {
  segments.push("M",interpolate(points))
}

// . . .

if (points.legth) {
  segment();
}
```

The path is produced by the `interpolate` function, which in the default implementation just joins the points (each implicitly converted to a string), putting an `"L"` between them. (We'll cover `interpolate` in more detail later in this chapter.)

```
var interpolate = function(points) {
    return points.join("L");
};
```

Thus, the array

```
var arrayData = [
    [10,130],
    [100,60],
    [190,160],
    [280,10]
    ],
```

becomes

```
"10,130L100,60L190,160L280,10"
```

As a final step, the two elements of *segments* (`"M"` and the points-as-string) are joined in the `return` statement to produce the SVG path

```
"M10,130L100,60L190,160L280,10"
```

That's the basic operation. Now for some complications that will illustrate additional ways that you can use JavaScript idiomatically.

Suppose that each point in your data were an object instead of an `[x,y]` coordinate pair in array form. It might look something like this:

```
{ x: 10, y: 130 }
```

How could you use `rj3.svg.line` to draw it? One way would be to transform the data on the way in, as in Listing 1-3.

LISTING 1-3: Transforming the data on the way in (code filename: rj3\
pathFromTransformedObjects.js)

```javascript
(function() {
  var objectData = [
        { x: 10, y: 130 },
        { x: 100, y: 60 },
        { x: 190, y: 160 },
        { x: 280, y: 10 }
      ],
      arrayData = objectData.map(function(d) {
        return [ +d.x, +d.y];
      }),
      lineGenerator = rj3.svg.line(),
      path = lineGenerator(arrayData);

  document.getElementById('pathFromTransformedObjects')
      .setAttribute('d',path);
}());
```

However, that would be wasteful, as it creates a second, complete copy of the data. It's the sort of thing a C# programmer accustomed to the efficiencies of LINQ would do. (LINQ peels off just one element at a time from an array as requested, without making a second copy of the whole array.)

The strategy in Listing 1-3 would also limit your possibilities in the user interface. You probably want your line to change dynamically if the data change. Thanks to the design decision that you're going to see in a moment, D3 does this for you with no effort—but only with the data it knows about. If you have called its functions with only a one-time copy of the real data, you don't get this benefit.

The design decision is exemplified by the little functions, line.x and line.y. Listing 1-4 shows how to use them.

LISTING 1-4: Using line.x and line.y (code filename: rj3\pathFromObjects.js)

```javascript
(function() {
  var objectData = [
        { x: 10, y: 130 },
        { x: 100, y: 60 },
        { x: 190, y: 160 },
        { x: 280, y: 10 }
      ],
      lineGenerator = rj3.svg.line()
        .x(function(d) { return d.x; })
        .y(function(d) { return d.y; }),
      path = lineGenerator(objectData);

  document.getElementById('pathFromObjects').setAttribute('d',path);
}());
```

The call

```javascript
x(function(d) { return d.x; })
```

replaces the default value of Listing 1-1's *getX* variable with your new function. Now, when the `while` loop calls

```
points.push([+getX.call(this,d,i), +getY.call(this,d,i)]);
```

the `getX.call` will invoke your function, which returns the x property of your objects—the original, authoritative objects, and not copies of them.

There's something else worth noting about those `calls`. Without stealing all the thunder from Chapter 18, we'll state that whatever function is installed to get the x coordinate is actually called with *two* arguments, even though your `function(d){return d.x;}` only took one. The second argument, *i*, is the index of the datum, *d*, in the array. You didn't use *i*, but you could have. This is how the object-oriented concept of function overloading works in JavaScript.

Another example of JavaScript's function overloading is in the `line.x` function itself. Did you notice the `if` test of *arguments*?

```
line.x = function(funcToGetX) {
    if (!arguments.length) return getX;
    getX = funcToGetX;
    return line;
};
```

In JavaScript, *arguments* is an array-like object that is available inside every function, containing the arguments the function was called with. Here, the test inspects the length of that pseudo-array. Zero is a "falsy" value in JavaScript (see "Values May Be Truthy or Falsy" in Chapter 25) so if there are no arguments, the function just returns the current value of *getX*.

To recap, if `line.x` is called with no arguments, it returns the current accessor for x-coordinates. If it is called *with* an argument, it sets the x-coordinate accessor to it and returns something else entirely, namely the `line` function-object. This, and the possibility of the extra argument, *i*, exemplify function overloading in JavaScript.

> **NOTE** *In JavaScript, the object-oriented concept of function overloading is done by inspecting the function's arguments and adjusting accordingly.*

Now why would a function that sets the x-accessor return the `line`? You probably know the answer: It allows you to chain the calls as you saw in Listing 1-4:

```
lineGenerator = rj3.svg.line()
    .x(function(d) { return d.x; })
    .y(function(d) { return d.y; }),
```

The design possibilities of call-chaining are explored at length in Chapter 15.

Now here's a question for you. What do you suppose would happen if you were to add a z-coordinate to each data point?

```
var objectData = [
        { x: 10,  y: 130, z: 99  },
        { x: 100, y: 60,  z: 202 },
        { x: 190, y: 160, z: 150 },
        { x: 280, y: 10,  z: 175 }
    ],
```

If you guessed that the program would happily produce exactly the same result, you are right. In JavaScript, an object with x, y, and z properties can also function as an object with x and y properties.

You could also produce the objects with a constructor function, which looks completely different but has the same result:

```
function XYPair(x,y) {
   this.x = x;
   this.y = y;
}

var objectData = [
    new XYPair(10, 130),
    new XYPair(100, 60),
    new XYPair(190, 160),
    new XYPair(280, 10)
    ],
```

This is called duck typing, after the saying, "If it looks like a duck, walks like a duck and quacks like a duck, it is a duck." In JavaScript, ducks are some of your best friends. It is possible to distinguish the cases thus:

```
if (something instanceof XYPair)
```

However, there is almost never a reason to do so. A C# or Java programmer might attempt to learn whether an object is up to snuff through such inspections, but the JavaScript way is to simply check for the existence of the properties:

```
if ('x' in something) // something has or inherits a property x.
```
or
```
if (something.hasOwnProperty('x')) // something has x without inheriting it
```

Duck typing is not sloppiness. It is an important way to give a component more reach.

> **NOTE** *Embrace duck typing. It allows a little code to accommodate a wide range of objects.*

If you read Listing 1-1 with unusual attention, you might have wondered how the inner `line` function manages to access the private variables of the outer `rj3.svg.line` after the outer function has returned. Programmers from other languages might expect the variables *getX*, *getY*, and *interpolate* to pop off the stack once control exits the function that declared them. And so they would, except for one thing: JavaScript's concept of *closures*.

We said earlier that when you call `rj3.svg.line()`, it returns the inner `line` function. There's more to it than that. It actually returns a closure, which you can think of as an object that from the outside looks like the function (inner `line`), but on the inside also remembers the environment that prevailed when the function was created (the variables *getX*, *getY* and *interpolate*). You call inner `line`'s functions as you normally would, but they are aware of `line`'s original environment.

> **NOTE** *Closures are a very powerful design element in JavaScript. Every function is a closure.*

Consider once more the `call` statements in the `while` loop:

```
while (++i < n) {
  d = data[i];
  points.push([+getX.call(this,d,i), +getY.call(this,d,i)]);
}
```

What does `getX.call(this,d,i)` really do? In English, it calls the `getX` function, pretending that it is a member of the object *this* (more on that in a moment) and passing the arguments *d* and *i*. The special variable *this* is, loosely speaking, the "object before the dot" when you call the function in which *this* appears.

Why all this fuss and bother? Why not just say `getX(d,i)` and be done with it? In JavaScript, the ability to specify *this* is an important design opportunity.

> **NOTE** *In JavaScript,* `this` *offers a design opportunity. Use it!*

Listing 1-5 shows the power of this language feature. Here, the data are just an array of years. The function `line.x` computes the desired x coordinate based on the index, *i* (now we're using *i*!), but what's going on with `line.y`? It appears to be calling a function, `getValue`, that is nowhere in scope.

LISTING 1-5: Extending the line generator to get values from an outer object (code filename rj3\pathFromFunction.js)

```
rj3.svg.samples = {};

rj3.svg.samples.functionBasedLine = function functionBasedLine() {
  var firstXCoord = 10,
      xDistanceBetweenPoints = 50,
      lineGenerator,
      svgHeight = 200; // Yes, this is cheating.

  lineGenerator = rj3.svg.line()
    .x(function(d,i) { return firstXCoord + i * xDistanceBetweenPoints; })
    .y(function(d) { return svgHeight - this.getValue(d); });

  return lineGenerator;
};

(function() {
  var yearlyPriceGrapher = {
      lineGenerator: rj3.svg.samples.functionBasedLine(),

      getValue: function getValue(year) {
        // Pretend this is a call to a web service!
        return 10 * Math.pow(1.8, year-2010);
      }
    },
    years = [2010, 2011, 2012, 2013, 2014, 2015],
```

```
        path = yearlyPriceGrapher.lineGenerator(years);

    document.getElementById('pathFromFunction').setAttribute('d',path);
}());
```

So where does getValue come from? In the second part of the listing, a *yearlyPriceGrapher* object is instantiated that combines a line generator with a function, getValue, that returns the value for a given year. In the call

```
    path = yearlyPriceGrapher.lineGenerator(years);
```

the *yearlyPriceGrapher* is "dotted with" *lineGenerator*. That means that *yearlyPriceGrapher* becomes *this* in the y-accessor, which causes its getValue to be invoked properly. The result is in Figure 1-4.

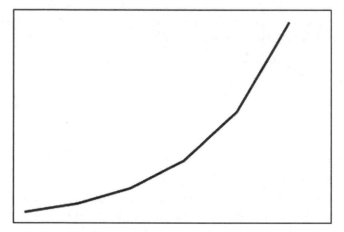

FIGURE 1-4

It is natural to think that *this* refers to the function in which it appears, or maybe the object enclosing the function. Not so. It refers to the object on which the function is called.

JavaScript Is Single-Threaded

Just one more thing to close out this section about language features: JavaScript is single-threaded. That doesn't mean it uses a blocking model—far from it. It just means that you do asynchronous programming differently.

Where a multi-threaded language would allow you to start a task that runs in parallel to the code that spawned it, in JavaScript you merely enqueue a function to execute as soon after a certain event as possible. The triggering event may be the passage of a certain amount of time (in the case of setTimeout), the arrival of data from a website (in the case of XMLHttpRequest.send), or the click of a mouse, among many possibilities. JavaScript has an event loop that consumes the functions thus enqueued one at a time.

From a design point of view, this makes your life easier than it would be in a true multi-threaded environment. You never have to worry about getting interrupted, or about other objects accessing your variables when you think you have control.

It also means you shouldn't hog the processor!

In Chapter 6, you will see how JavaScript `Promises` let you write code that does not block, yet is not a confusing scatter of event-handlers awkwardly connected by variables.

Avoiding JavaScript's Pitfalls in Larger Systems

Why is a system that contains 50 classes (or objects, in JavaScript) *more than* ten times as challenging to write and maintain as a system that contains five? With five objects, even if each one draws on the services of all the others, there are at most 20 channels of communication (each of 5 objects calling 4 others—allowing ourselves to count A calling B as well as B calling A). With 50, there are 2450 (50 times 49)—more than 100 times as many.

With the advent of Single-Page Applications, `node.js`, and other ways of making JavaScript shoulder the burdens of larger and larger systems on both client and server, the best JavaScript developers get serious about trimming those channels of communication to a bare minimum.

Where an object must interface with others to do its job, the connections are managed assiduously to ensure that they function properly in all circumstances.

This section will suggest ways to meet these goals.

Scripts Are Not Modules

Just last week, we were on the website of a company that makes a certain specialized device for user input. They had helpfully provided sample JavaScript code for using their device.

Argh! Their JavaScript library, suggested for all programmers to use, was over 1900 lines of one global variable or function after another—over 200 global functions in all. Most of the global functions were at least named so that collisions with other libraries were unlikely, but some, such as `makeUri` or `toHex`, were not.

This is the "scripting" heritage of JavaScript at work. In the old days, when your script was probably the only one on the page, there was little harm in adding to the global namespace. With today's JavaScript applications, that is never the case.

Your script is in no way isolated because it is in its own `.js` file. If your file starts with

```
var myVariable = makeValue();
```

as this one did (the names have been changed to protect the guilty), then `myVariable` is visible to all the other scripts in your application, and the `makeValue` function evidently is, too.

JavaScript presents an unusually diverse menu of choices for creating modules that properly encapsulate their data and functions. Script files are not one of them! (You will read more about data encapsulation in Chapter 3.)

Nested Functions Control Scope

In C# or Java, one class can contain another. However, this practice is not widespread. Microsoft even cautions against it. Code Analysis warning 1034 is "Nested types should not be visible" and their rationale is "Nested types include the notion of member accessibility, which some programmers do not understand clearly" (`https://msdn.microsoft.com/en-us/library/ms182162.aspx`).

JavaScript does not have classes, but nested *functions* serve the same purpose of organizing the code hierarchically. Crucially, the hierarchy not only helps the programmer find what he's looking for; it also helps the program minimize the scope of its variables and functions. That's key to keeping a large system under control, and it is the warp and woof of the best JavaScript code.

Recall this snippet from Listing 1-1:

```
rj3.svg.line = function() {
  var getX = function(point) {
      return point[0];
    },
    /*** Other vars omitted for clarity. ***/

  function line(data) {
    var segments = [],
      /*** Other variables omitted. ***/

    function segment() {
      segments.push("M",interpolate(points));
    }

    while (++i < n) {
      d = data[i];
      points.push([+getX.call(this,d,i), +getY.call(this,d,i)]);
    }

    if (points.length) {
      segment();
    }

    return segments.length ? segments.join("") : null;
  }

  line.x = function(funcToGetX) {
    if (!arguments.length) return getX;
    getX = funcToGetX;
    return line;
  };
```

The inner `line` function has a member function, `line.x`. Although x is a member of `line`, it cannot see `line`'s local variables, such as *segments*. Both `line` and `line.x` can see the `getX` variable in the enclosing function. Combine this sort of artfulness with closures, and you have some very powerful tools for keeping large JavaScript systems under control.

Coding by Contract

There is no better way to make a large system more manageable than to make it smaller. JavaScript, with the extraordinary flexibility of pervasive duck-typing, lets you write a little code that can do a lot. (Recall the variety of inputs handled in the D3 case study earlier in the chapter.)

The flip side is that you never know what someone is going to throw at your software.

If your function expects its arguments to meet certain requirements, consider validating them. In Chapters 16 through 21, you will see one way to do this as unobtrusively as possible: the `ContractRegistry`.

In a nutshell, the registry allows you to verify anything you wish about an argument or return value, without adding any code to your function. It does this through the magic of aspect-oriented programming (covered in Chapter 2) and in such a way that the overhead of validation can be eliminated in the shipped version.

Applying the Principles of Software Engineering

Have you ever been to a concert by a virtuoso musician? Maybe you play the same instrument, and you've marveled that the performer makes it look so easy. The truth is, he makes it *look* easy because it *is* easy—for him. And the reason it's easy for him is that he has trained his fingers to move efficiently, trained his body to relax and breathe, trained his mind to listen to the music rather than be distracted by anxiety.

He probably learned the piece by playing it very, very slowly at first. Only when he had mastered it completely at that pace did he take the metronome up one notch. Thus, he did not practice-in any mistakes. One of us, a classical guitarist, went to a masterclass taught by one of the world's best. The teacher boasted, "I bet I can play this piece slower than any of you." He has learned that the *quickest* way to learn to play a piece flawlessly is to play it slowly.

When you have mastered the principles in this section, you will write flawless software more quickly and with less effort. Your fellow developers will look at your code and say, "He makes it look so easy!"

The SOLID Principles

The acronym SOLID was coined by Michael Feathers as a way to remember the five principles of object-oriented design that Robert Martin set forth in the late 1990s (summarized at http://www .objectmentor.com/resources/articles/Principles_and_Patterns.pdf). They are:

- ➤ The **Single Responsibility** Principle
- ➤ The **Open/Closed** Principle
- ➤ The **Liskov Substitution** Principle
- ➤ The **Interface Segregation** Principle
- ➤ The **Dependency Inversion** Principle

The Single Responsibility Principle

Stated in its most extreme form, the Single Responsibility Principle is that *a class (or function, in JavaScript) should have only one reason to change.*

That is a very tall order. Surely every line of code represents something that could change. Must every function consist of just one line of code?

No, but don't give up on this principle too quickly. Consider once more the `rj3.svg.line` function in Listing 1-1. As you saw, it is able to generate SVG line paths from just about any data source you can imagine, but what about it might change? It takes almost every cue from outside, even down to how it obtains the x and y coordinates for each data point.

By the way, one of the casualties of our abridgement of D3's code was the `interpolate` function. In the full version, D3 lets you specify this just as you can specify the functions that obtain x and y. And what does `interpolate` do? It connects the points in an SVG path. The default is to connect the points with straight line segments, but you could plug in an interpolator that constructs graceful curves instead, and D3 supplies several such interpolators.

Thus, when it comes right down to it, `rj3.svg.line` really doesn't "know" much. All it does is return a function (the inner `line`) that can create an SVG path out of an array of data points—somehow.

What reasons could there be for `rj3.svg.line` to change? Its one responsibility is to produce an SVG path from an array. *Everything* about how it carries out that responsibility is external to the function and therefore not a reason for it to change!

All together now: "Mike Bostock, you make it look so easy!"

The Open/Closed Principle

This principle states that "Software entities should be open for extension, but closed for modification" (http://www.objectmentor.com/resources/articles/ocp.pdf).

In other words, you should never change working code. Instead, reuse it somehow (for example, by inheritance) and extend it.

This, too, is a tall order. Robert Martin even admits in the same article, "In general, no matter how 'closed' a module is, there will always be some kind of change against which it is not closed. Since closure cannot be complete, it must be strategic. That is, the designer must choose the kinds of changes against which to close his design. This takes a certain amount of prescience derived from experience."

When Mike Bostock designed his `d3.svg.line` function, he anticipated changes in the way coordinates might be plucked from data and how the points might be joined (interpolated), and he wisely abstracted those features out of his function.

What he did *not* think would change (at least not in a backward-incompatible way) was the SVG path specification. He dared to hard-code that a path could always start with `"M"` and continue with the points in order, as a text string.

Short of a breaking change to the SVG spec, it is hard to imagine how `d3.svg.line` would ever have to change.

The Liskov Substitution Principle

"The what??" you ask!

Coined by Barbara Liskov in a formal way in *Data Abstraction and Hierarchy* (SIGPLAN Notices 23, 5 [May, 1988]), this principle might be stated more colloquially for a JavaScript context as follows:

Code written to use an object of a certain type should not have to change if provided with an object of a derived type.

Another way of saying this is that when you derive one object from another, the base-level semantics should not change.

If you find yourself writing branching logic so that your function does one thing if provided with a base class, but something else for a derived class, you have violated this principle.

This does *not* apply to types that do not derive from each other. For example, it is a common and good practice in JavaScript for a function to branch one way if an argument is a Number, another way if it's a String, and a third way if it's not there at all and therefore of the Undefined type. As discussed previously, that's how JavaScript fulfills the object-oriented idea of function overloading.

Incidentally, the use of duck-typing, while not the same as derivation, is very much in the spirit of this principle!

The Interface Segregation Principle

This principle arose in a milieu of interface-based languages such as C++ and Java. In those languages, an interface is a piece of code that *describes* the functions in a class (names, parameters, and return types) without *implementing* those functions.

The idea is that *an interface with many functions should be broken up into smaller, cohesive parts. Consumers should rely on only one of the mini-interfaces, not on the "fat" whole.*

Of course, this is in the service of minimizing the width of the connections between modules. As stated previously, trimming the channels of communication is critical to making large JavaScript systems manageable.

But wait a minute! In JavaScript, there are neither classes nor interfaces. Does that mean JavaScript programmers cannot experience the benefits of following this principle?

Not at all. In fact, we will devote all of Chapter 16 to how to implement this principle in JavaScript. In the meantime, here's a preview: To follow the spirit of the Interface Segregation Principle, a function can make clear what it expects of its arguments, and those expectations should be minimized. As stated earlier, duck typing is your friend here. Rather than expecting an argument of a certain type, just expect it to have the few properties of that type that you actually need. The ContractRegistry that will be developed in Chapters 16 through 21 provides a formal way to make the expectations clear and to enforce them. If the ContractRegistry is not to your taste, you can always write argument-validation code or even write comments!

The Dependency Inversion Principle

This principle, too, was developed with interfaces in mind. Robert Martin states it thus: "High-level modules should not depend upon low-level modules. Both should depend upon abstractions" (http://www.objectmentor.com/resources/articles/dip.pdf).

In an interface-based language, this principle usually finds its expression in the related idea of dependency *injection*. If class A needs the services of B, it does not construct B. Instead, one parameter to A's constructor is an interface that describes B. A no longer depends on B, but on its interface. When A is constructed, a concrete B is passed in. B, too, depends on its interface.

The benefit is that a derived version of B, which also fulfills the interface, can be supplied instead thanks to the Liskov Substitution Principle. Furthermore, if B does need to change (in spite of the

Open/Closed Principle), the interface concisely describes how it must continue to behave in order to be backward-compatible.

Once again, in JavaScript there are no abstractions, but JavaScript programmers can still program in the spirit of this principle and enjoy its benefits.

The full version of D3's `d3.svg.line` function starts like this (from `https://github.com/mbostock/d3/blob/master/src/svg/line.js`):

```
d3.svg.line = function() {
  return d3_svg_line(d3_identity);
};

function d3_svg_line(projection) {
  /*** vars omitted for clarity ***/

  function line(data) {
    /*** vars omitted for clarity ***/

    function segment() {
      segments.push("M", interpolate(projection(points), tension));
    }
```

The *projection* parameter of `d3_svg_line` is used to possibly project the data points to another coordinate space. By default, *projection* is `d3_identity`, which makes no changes to the points at all. However, other projections are possible. For example, `d3.svg.line.radial` uses polar coordinates (an angle and distance from the origin) by injecting the `d3_svg_lineRadial` projection (`https://github.com/mbostock/d3/blob/master/src/svg/line-radial.js`):

```
d3.svg.line.radial = function() {
  var line = d3_svg_line(d3_svg_lineRadial);
  /*** Code omitted for clarity. ***/
  return line;
};

function d3_svg_lineRadial(points) {
  /*** Transform points to polar coordinates. ***/
  return points;
}
```

By injecting the dependency on the coordinate space, D3's line-generator becomes as flexible as possible.

The DRY Principle

Many sages have said that all of ethics is contained in the statement, "Do to others as you want them to do to you." If you just follow the Golden Rule, everything else will fall into place.

The DRY Principle, Don't Repeat Yourself, is likewise the wellspring of all good conduct in software development. It says, "Every piece of knowledge must appear only once."

How does this little maxim have such great effect? For one thing, some of the most important SOLID principles are nothing more than corollaries of this one.

Take the Single Responsibility Principle. You have surely seen code that violates it and, as a result, is not reusable. A module does X *and* Y. You need some code that also does X, but you can't reuse the module without dragging in behavior Y, so you code X all over again. You have just violated the DRY Principle.

You can fix the situation by injecting functions that do X and Y into the module, giving it the single responsibility of relating X to Y. Presto! In the process of making your code DRY, you got both dependency injection and a single responsibility.

`d3.svg.line` is very DRY. It does not repeat anything that might be coded elsewhere—not even the extraction of coordinates from data.

DRYness can occur even within a function. Our exemplary friend the `line` function did this:

```
var d;

while (++i < n) {
  d = data[i];
  points.push([+getX.call(this,d,i), +getY.call(this,d,i)]);
}
```

instead of this:

```
while (++i < n) {
  points.push([+getX.call(this, data[i],i),
              +getY.call(this, data[i],i)]);
}
```

Although the second version is a little shorter, it is not DRY because the "piece of knowledge" that `data[i]` is the datum being processed is repeated. It appears once in the call to `getX` and again in the call to `getY`.

In JavaScript, DRYness is even more important than in other languages. Every time you type something, there is a chance you'll make a mistake. Because JavaScript has no compiler to catch certain classes of mistakes, such mistakes have a better chance of getting out to your customers. An important way to prevent these catastrophes is to make your mistakes as noticeable as possible. If you enter a "piece of knowledge" just once, then an error will show up *everywhere*. That's a very, very good thing!

WRITING CODE THAT STAYS CORRECT

We said that programming is easy in the same way that playing a keyboard instrument is easy: "All one has to do is hit the right keys at the right time." But there is one difference. If you play a perfect concert on the piano, nobody can take it away from you. If you write a program that fulfills business requirements to the letter, well, return to it after five years of maintenance. You may hear the development team muttering that it would be easier to rewrite it than to continue maintaining it. "Time to put it out of its misery," they will say.

This section is about how to prevent that sorry state of affairs so your code can live a long and healthy life!

Investing for the Future with Unit Tests

Unit tests help your perfect program weather the storm of changes that you and others make to it over time. A unit test is a piece of code that verifies a small portion of your application. The *unit* in unit test behaves as if it should be given a specific set of conditions. More often than not, the unit under test will be a function, but that's not always the case.

The code in the body of a unit test generally follows the pattern *arrange, act, assert*.

First, the test *arranges*: It establishes the conditions under which it will exercise the unit, perhaps configuring dependencies or setting up inputs to a function.

Next, the test *acts*: It exercises the unit under test. If the unit is a function, for instance, the test will execute the function with the inputs configured during the arrange stage.

Finally, the test *asserts*: It verifies that the unit behaved as expected when exercised under the established conditions. If the unit under test is a function, the assert phase may verify that the function returned the expected value.

Investing in the creation of a full suite of unit tests is insurance against future breaking changes to your program, and is the best investment that you can make to ensure that your application remains reliable. A failing unit test is a red flag that a change has altered the functionality of your program and that the change that caused the failure warrants close inspection.

The section *Using a Testing Framework* in Chapter 2 covers, in detail, how to use the Jasmine unit test framework to create a JavaScript unit test suite.

Practicing Test-Driven Development

Test-driven development (TDD) helps ensure that the program you write is perfect in the first place. TDD is the practice of writing a unit test *before* you write the application code that allows the test to pass. Along with creating a full suite of unit tests as you develop your application, TDD helps you design the interfaces to the units as you create them.

The following sections describe the practice of TDD, and concepts to keep in mind while writing code in order to make the code testable.

A developer practicing test-driven development performs the following steps for each and every change he or she makes to an application. The change may be adding a completely new feature, tweaking an existing one, or fixing a bug.

1. Write a unit test that will succeed if the change is made correctly, but fails until then.

2. Write the *minimum* amount of application code that allows the test to pass.

3. Refactor the application code to remove any duplication.

The preceding steps are commonly summarized as *red, green, refactor*, where red and green signify the failing and passing state of the new unit test.

The most important aspect of TDD is that the test is written before the code that satisfies it. It is also one of the most difficult aspects to adjust to when starting out with TDD. Writing the test first feels just a bit uncomfortable, especially if the change you are testing is minor.

Before the practice of TDD is etched into your programmer-brain, it's all too tempting to just slightly tweak the application code and move on to the next task on your never-ending list of things to do.

If you want the application you're developing to be reliable, you must overcome the urge to not write the test. If you skip writing tests for even "minor" changes (if there really is such a thing), the net effect is an application with a lot of untested code. Your unit test suite, once a reliable safety net ensuring proper behavior of your application, quickly becomes nothing more than a source of a false sense of security.

You may also be tempted to write the test *after* you change the application code. Again, you must not succumb to the temptation. You really can't be sure that the change you made causes a test written after the fact to pass. It's possible that the new test passes because it's faulty, adding no additional value to your unit test suite. Also, writing the test after the fact ensures that the application code behaves *as it was written*, which is not necessarily *as it should behave*.

We can't overstate how important we feel the practice of TDD is when developing reliable JavaScript applications. This book contains countless examples of TDD, and Chapter 24, "Summary of the Principles of Test-Driven Development," is devoted entirely to the topic.

Engineering Your Code to Be Easy to Test

One of the—if not *the*—most significant steps that you can take to create code that is easy to test is to properly separate concerns. (See "The Single Responsibility Principle," earlier in this chapter.)

For example, the following code sample defines the function `valididateAndRegisterUser`, which has multiple concerns. Can you identify them?

```
var Users = Users || {};
Users.registration = function(){
  return {
    validateAndRegisterUser: function validateAndDisplayUser(user){
      if(!user ||
        user.name === "" ||
        user.password === "" ||
        user.password.length < 6)
      {
        throw new Error("The user is not valid");
      }

      $.post("http://yourapplication.com/user", user);

      $("#user-message").text("Thanks for registering, " + user.name);
    }
  };
};
```

The function is doing three things:

➤ It verifies that the *user* object is populated correctly.

➤ It sends the validated *user* object to the server.

➤ It displays a message in the UI.

Accordingly, we can enumerate three separate concerns at work:

➤ User verification

➤ Direct server communication

➤   Direct UI manipulation

Now try to come up with all the conditions that must be tested to ensure that the validateAndRegisterUser function operates correctly. Take your time; we're not going anywhere.

How many did you come up with? Probably quite a few. Here are some of the conditions we came up with:

➤   An Error is thrown if *user* is null.

➤   A null *user* is not posted to the server.

➤   The UI isn't updated if *user* is null.

➤   An Error is thrown if *user* is undefined.

➤   An undefined *user* is not posted to the server.

➤   The UI isn't updated if *user* is undefined.

➤   An Error is thrown if *user* has an empty name property.

➤   A *user* with an empty name property is not posted to the server.

➤   The UI isn't updated if the *user* has an empty name property.

And so on and so forth. Those are just *some* of the invalid conditions that must be tested; there are many more. Additionally, tests that ensure valid conditions behave properly must be written as well, including tests that make sure the UI has been properly updated.

"But," you may be wondering, "if I write a test that ensures an Error is thrown when *user* is provided without a name, why do I also need to write tests to make sure the nameless *user* isn't posted to the server and used to update the UI? After all, the Error is thrown before those other things happen."

The logic behind the question is sound, given the way that the code is written *today*. If you omit those seemingly irrelevant tests, however, what happens when someone comes along *tomorrow* and changes the function so that the verification of *user* happens at the end?

```
var Users = Users || {};
Users.registration = function(){
  return {
    validateAndRegisterUser: function validateAndDisplayUser(user){
      $.post("http://yourapplication.com/user", user);

      $("#user-message").text("Thanks for registering, " + user.name);

      if(!user ||
        user.name === "" ||
        user.password === "" ||
        user.password.length < 6)
      {
          throw new Error("The user is not valid");
      }
    }
  };
};
```

The test that you wrote to ensure an `Error` is generated still passes, but the function is now significantly broken. Those additional tests don't seem so irrelevant now, do they? Admittedly, that change is not likely one someone would make intentionally, but accidents do happen.

Make no mistake, this code *is* testable, it's just not *easy to test*. There are so many permutations of conditions that must be tested, both valid and invalid, it's unlikely that they will all be covered. If all of the code in an application is written in this manner, we can all but guarantee that application won't have proper unit test coverage.

Suppose, however, that instead of working with the three separate concerns in the `validateAndRegisterUser` function, each of those concerns was extracted into a separate object with that concern as its single responsibility. For the purpose of this example, assume that each of the new objects has its own, complete test suite. The code for `validateAndRegisterUser` may then look something like this:

```
var Users = Users || {};
Users.registration = function(userValidator, userRegistrar, userDisplay){
  return {
    validateAndRegisterUser: function validateAndDisplayUser(user){
      if(!userValidator.userIsValid(user)){
        throw new Error("The user is not valid");
      }
      userRegistrar.registerUser(user);
      userDisplay.showRegistrationThankYou(user);
    }
  };
};
```

The new version of the `registration` module leverages dependency injection to provide instances of the objects that are responsible for user validation, registration, and display. In turn, `validateAndRegisterUser` uses the injected objects in place of the code that directly interacted with the different concerns.

In essence, `validateAndRegisterUser` has transformed from a function that does work to a function that coordinates work done by others. The transformation has made the function much easier to test. In fact, the following six conditions are the only ones that must be tested in order to completely test the function:

➤ An `Error` is thrown if *user* is invalid.

➤ An invalid *user* is not registered.

➤ An invalid *user* is not displayed.

➤ The `userRegistrar.registerUser` function is invoked with *user* if *user* is valid.

➤ The `userDisplay.showRegistrationThankYou` function is not executed if `userRegistrar.registerUser` throws an `Error`.

➤ The `userDisplay.showRegistrationThankYou` function is executed with *user* as an argument if *user* has been successfully registered.

Six tests. That's it. We listed *nine* tests for the original version of the function, and we didn't even finish all of the error conditions.

Creating small, simple modules that isolate separate concerns leads to code that is easy to write, test, and understand. Code with those properties is more likely to remain correct in the long term.

You might think that test-driven development would slow you down. If you write the tests *after* the code and the code does not properly separate its concerns, that will be true. You will have baked in many mistakes, and writing unit tests will be just about the slowest possible way to find them.

However, if you follow the red-green-refactor cycle to produce small increments of code, you will actually go faster, just as the musician who practices slowly and carefully at first actually masters the piece more quickly. First of all, because each increment is simple, you will be less likely to make a mistake, so you will save a lot of debugging time. Second, because your code will be completely covered by tests, you will be able to refactor without fear. That will enable you to keep your code DRY, which generally means your code base is smaller, presenting fewer places where things can go wrong. DRY also means reusable, and we all know that reusable code saves time.

SUMMARY

JavaScript presents unique design opportunities to the developer. In this chapter, you saw many of these via an abridged version of a function in D3. Although the `rj3.svg.line` function was quite small, it showcased JavaScript's nested functions, functions-as-objects, function overloading, duck typing, closures, and power of `this`.

As JavaScript moves into larger systems, it becomes increasingly important to control this somewhat wild language. You saw that segregating code into separate script files, while a good idea for other reasons, does not truly modularize your code. Instead, rely on the design possibilities exemplified by the D3 case study, as well as the tried-and true principles of software engineering. Those include the five SOLID principles and the DRY principle: Don't Repeat Yourself.

Unit tests are the best investment you can make in long-term application reliability. Without them, the only thing you have to ensure your application functions properly is hope.

Practicing test-driven development provides multiple benefits. First, it builds the unit test suite that ensures long-term reliability. Second, it helps you design the correct interfaces for your application's objects. This book is chock full of examples of test-driven development, and Chapter 24 is dedicated to TDD. Third and surprisingly, it helps you produce working code faster.

One of the key actions you can take to improve testability is to pay close attention to separation of concerns and make use of software engineering concepts such as the Single Responsibility Principle and dependency injection.

With these ideas in hand, you are ready to meet the challenges of software craftsmanship. It's time to pick up some tools.

2

Tooling Up

WHAT'S IN THIS CHAPTER?

➤ Using the Jasmine unit-testing framework to prove the reliability of each component of your code

➤ Using a dependency-injection (DI) container to promote modularity, reusability, and testability

➤ Exploring how aspect-oriented programming (AOP) can make your code simpler and more reliable

➤ Exploring case studies in test-driven development

➤ Using JSLint to detect problems in your code before it ships

WROX.COM CODE DOWNLOADS FOR THIS CHAPTER

The wrox.com code downloads for this chapter are found at www.wrox.com/go/reliablejavascript on the Download Code tab. The code is in the Chapter 2 download and organized in directories according to this chapter's topics, with each directory holding one sample.

You can run a sample by copying its directory to your hard drive and double-clicking on the index.html file. Each sample's ReadMe.txt file contains further instructions.

USING A TESTING FRAMEWORK

Assume for a moment that you're working on a large team that's building a travel reservation system. You're responsible for the module that creates flight reservations, and one of the module functions should behave as follows: Given a passenger object and a flight object, createReservation will return a new object with the passengerInformation property set to the provided passenger object and the `flightInformation` property set to the provided flight object.

Simple enough, right? So simple, in fact, that there's no harm in just going ahead and implementing the function, as shown in Listing 2-1.

LISTING 2-1: Implementation of createReservation without using TDD (code filename: Test Frameworks\TestFrameworks_01.js)

```
function createReservation(passenger, flight){
  return {
    passengerInfo: passenger,
    flightInfo: flight
  };
}
```

> **NOTE** *This example uses the object literal mechanism of object creation. You'll learn many other ways to create instances of objects, along with their benefits and drawbacks, in Chapter 3.*

Since your team has a requirement that no production code should be checked in without the appropriate (passing) unit tests, you'd write those now. You have the implementation of the function to refer to, so writing the tests for it is trivial. Listing 2-2 shows the tests that you might write with the code at hand.

LISTING 2-2: Unit tests for createReservation written after the subject under test is complete (code filename: Test Frameworks\TestFrameworks_01_tests.js)

```
describe('createReservation(passenger, flight)', function(){
  it('assigns the provided passenger to the passengerInfo property', function(){
    var testPassenger = {
      firstName: 'Pete',
      lastName: 'Mitchell'
    };

    var testFlight = {
      number: '3443',
      carrier: 'AceAir',
      destination: 'Miramar, CA'
    };

    var reservation = createReservation(testPassenger, testFlight);
    expect(reservation.passengerInfo).toBe(testPassenger);
  });

  it('assigns the provided flight to the flightInfo property', function(){
```

```
        var testPassenger = {
          firstName: 'Pete',
          lastName: 'Mitchell'
        };

        var testFlight = {
          number: '3443',
          carrier: 'AceAir',
          destination: 'Miramar, CA'
        };

        var reservation = createReservation(testPassenger, testFlight);
        expect(reservation.flightInfo).toBe(testFlight);
      });
    });
```

These unit tests are written using the Jasmine testing framework. This book will feature Jasmine throughout, and you will see a more extensive introduction later in this chapter.

For the time being, all you have to keep in mind is that each `it` function call is an individual unit test (this example has two), and that each of those unit tests verifies that a single attribute of the object returned by the function has the proper value. The tests each verify the attribute value via a call to `expect`.

> **NOTE** *There's a bit of repeated setup code in the two unit tests, a blatant violation of the Don't Repeat Yourself (DRY) principle. Later in this chapter, you'll see how the Jasmine framework allows you to remove that repetition.*

As you can see in Figure 2-1, the unit tests pass.

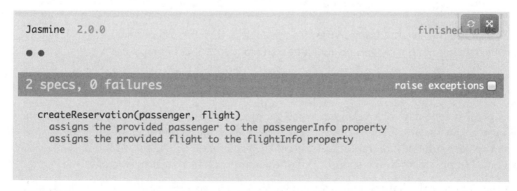

FIGURE 2-1

RUNNING JASMINE UNIT TESTS

While there are automated test runners for Jasmine unit tests, such as Karma (`http://karma-runner.github.io/`), in this book you'll leverage Jasmine's ability to run on-demand in the browser. To do so, simply create a plain HTML file and add references to the Jasmine library JavaScript and CSS files. Then, add a reference for each of the JavaScript files containing code you would like to test. Finally, add a script reference for each of the Jasmine unit test files that contains tests you would like to execute.

The HTML file to test the code from Listing 2-1 using the tests in Listing 2-2 looks like this:

```html
<!DOCTYPE html>
<html>
  <head>
    <!-- Jasmine Library Files -->
    <link data-require="jasmine@*" data-semver="2.0.0"
        rel="stylesheet"
        href="http://cdn.jsdelivr.net/jasmine/2.0.0/jasmine.css" />
    <script data-require="jasmine@*" data-semver="2.0.0"
        src="http://cdn.jsdelivr.net/jasmine/2.0.0/jasmine.js">
        </script>
    <script data-require="jasmine@*" data-semver="2.0.0"
        src="http://cdn.jsdelivr.net/jasmine/2.0.0/jasmine-html.js">
        </script>
    <script data-require="jasmine@*" data-semver="2.0.0"
        src="http://cdn.jsdelivr.net/jasmine/2.0.0/boot.js">
        </script>

    <!-- Code Under Test -->
    <script src="TestFrameworks_01.js"></script>

    <!-- Unit Tests -->
    <script src="TestFrameworks_01_tests.js"></script>
  </head>
</html>
```

All of our samples retrieve the Jasmine files from a content distribution network (CDN), but it is also possible to download the files and include them from your local computer.

You've satisfied your team's unit test requirement, so you check in the code and confidently move on to the next piece of functionality.

A few hours (or maybe days or weeks) later, you get an e-mail from Charlotte, a fellow team member, who is integrating your `createReservation` function into another area of the application. When she runs her suite of integration tests, all of the tests that exercise the `createReservation` function fail. "Impossible," you respond, "All of the unit tests for that function pass!"

Closer inspection reveals that the unit tests are incorrect. The specification says that the attribute names of the returned reservation object should be `passengerInformation` and `flightInformation`, and Charlotte wrote her code expecting those attributes to be present.

Unfortunately, in our hasty implementation of `createReservation` we used the attribute names `passengerInfo` and `flightInfo`.

Because the tests were written according to the function's implementation rather than its specification, they verify the actual—incorrect—behavior of the function rather than the expected behavior of the function. Had they been written first, based solely on the specification, the attribute names probably would have been correct the first time.

We won't dispute that the same mistake could happen if the function had been written using TDD, which would base the tests on the specification rather than the existing code. Our experience has shown that it is far less likely, however.

> **NOTE** *When working with existing code without unit tests, it is usually necessary to write tests that verify actual functionality. Doing so allows you to refactor the code while ensuring that its outward functionality does not change.*

Identifying Incorrect Code

TDD identifies defects in code at the earliest possible time: the moment after they're created. When following TDD, a test is written to verify a small piece of functionality, and then the functionality is implemented with the minimum amount of code possible.

Returning now to the `createReservation` function, you will see how a different outcome is assured by writing the tests first. As a reminder, the specification for the function as described earlier in the chapter is:

> Given a passenger object and a flight object, `createReservation` will return a new object with the `passengerInformation` property set to the provided passenger object and the `flightInformation` property set to the provided flight object.

Listing 2-3 shows the first test to verify that the `passengerInformation` property is properly assigned.

LISTING 2-3: First TDD unit test for createReservation (code filename: Test Frameworks\ TestFrameworks_02_tests.js)

```
describe('createReservation(passenger, flight)', function(){
  it('assigns the provided passenger to the passengerInfo property',
  function(){
    var testPassenger = {
      firstName: 'Pete',
      lastName: 'Mitchell'
```

continues

LISTING 2-3 *(continued)*

```
    };

    var testFlight = {
      number: '3443',
      carrier: 'AceAir',
      destination: 'Miramar, CA'
    };

    var reservation = createReservation(testPassenger, testFlight);
    expect(reservation.passengerInformation).toBe(testPassenger);
  });
});
```

Listing 2-4 shows your minimum implementation of `createReservation` that will cause the test to pass.

LISTING 2-4: Initial TDD implementation of createReservation (code filename: Test Frameworks\TestFrameworks_02.js)

```
function createReservation(passenger, flight){
  return {
    passengerInfo: passenger,
    flightInformation: flight
  };
}
```

You then immediately execute the unit test and it fails (Figure 2-2). How did that happen?

```
Jasmine  2.0.0                                                                    finished in 0.004s

X

1 spec, 1 failure                                                           raise exceptions ■

Spec List | Failures

createReservation(passenger, flight) assigns the provided passenger to the passengerInformation property

Expected undefined to be { firstName : 'Pete', lastName : 'Mitchell' }.

Error: Expected undefined to be { firstName : 'Pete', lastName : 'Mitchell' }.
    at stack (http://cdnjs.cloudflare.com/ajax/libs/jasmine/2.0.0/jasmine.js:1293:17)
    at buildExpectationResult (http://cdnjs.cloudflare.com/ajax/libs/jasmine/2.0.0/jasmine.js:1270:14)
    at Spec.Env.expectationResultFactory (http://cdnjs.cloudflare.com/ajax/libs/jasmine/2.0.0/jasmine.js:484:18)
    at Spec.addExpectationResult (http://cdnjs.cloudflare.com/ajax/libs/jasmine/2.0.0/jasmine.js:260:46)
    at Expectation.addExpectationResult (http://cdnjs.cloudflare.com/ajax/libs/jasmine/2.0.0/jasmine.js:442:21)
    at Expectation.toBe (http://cdnjs.cloudflare.com/ajax/libs/jasmine/2.0.0/jasmine.js:1209:12)
    at Object.<anonymous> (http://run.plnkr.co/plunks/iumNgRwEtpS7pwIyytPI/script.js:23:46)
    at attemptSync (http://cdnjs.cloudflare.com/ajax/libs/jasmine/2.0.0/jasmine.js:1510:12)
    at QueueRunner.run (http://cdnjs.cloudflare.com/ajax/libs/jasmine/2.0.0/jasmine.js:1498:9)
    at QueueRunner.execute (http://cdnjs.cloudflare.com/ajax/libs/jasmine/2.0.0/jasmine.js:1485:10)
```

FIGURE 2-2

Ah! The attribute name in the returned object was incorrect; it was called `passengerInfo` instead of `passengerInformation`. You quickly change the name of the attribute to the specified `passengerInformation`, and now your test passes (Figure 2-3). Note that the figure also reflects a change to the `it` statement: You changed the `it` statement to also indicate that the `passengerInformation` property is being tested.

FIGURE 2-3

You can then follow the same process for assignment of the flightInformation attribute, yielding a createReservation function that is verified correct via unit tests.

The error of incorrectly naming an attribute in the returned object once again made its way into the implementation of the createReservation function. This time, however, you wrote your test first and based the test on the specification. This allowed you to immediately identify and address the error rather than waiting hours (or days, or weeks) for another developer running integration tests to alert you to the problem.

For a trivial function such as createReservation, this piecewise creation of tests and addition of functionality admittedly feels like a bit of overkill. It is easy to imagine other cases, however, where the iterative process of TDD could end up saving a significant amount of debugging time.

Suppose that you have to write a function that performs a multitude of computations on an array of data. You attempt to implement a large portion of the function all at once, and that portion contains an off-by-one error such that you omit the last piece of data from the computations.

When you verify the output of your function, the computed value will be incorrect, but you won't know why it's incorrect. It could be a mathematical error in one of the computations, or perhaps you're not handling a case of numeric overflow. Had you written a simple test early on to verify that each and every element of the array is involved in the computation, you would have immediately caught the off-by-one error and likely would have had a working solution much sooner.

Designing for Testability

Writing tests first makes the testability of your code a primary concern rather than an afterthought. In our experience working with developers at all skill levels, there is a direct correlation between how easy code is to test and how well that code is tested. Additionally, we've found that code that is easy to test tends to be easier to maintain and extend. As we proposed in the first chapter, code that follows the principles of SOLID development lends itself quite well to testing. If you make testability a goal of your designs you will tend to write SOLID code.

For example, suppose every reservation created with the createReservation function should be submitted to a web service to be stored in a database.

If you're not practicing TDD, you may simply extend createReservation by adding a call to jQuery.ajax(...) which sends the reservation to a web service endpoint via asynchronous JavaScript and XML (AJAX). The addition of this one simple function call, though, has increased the number of responsibilities the humble little createReservation function has, and has increased the effort required to properly unit test it.

> **NOTE** *Testing interactions with web services is not trivial, but it is both possible and necessary when building a reliable code base.*

You've already added the `jQuery.ajax(...)` call, you already have tests for *some* of the things the `createReservation` function does, and maybe you manually tested and verified that the reservation ends up in the database. It's easy to decide that it's just too much effort to write unit tests for that one little bit of functionality and move on to your next task. We've seen it happen many times, and admit to doing it many times ourselves.

Assuming you have committed yourself to TDD, instead of steaming ahead and updating `createReservation`, you would write a test to verify the new functionality. The first test verifies that the reservation is sent to the correct web service endpoint.

You probably wouldn't get much further than defining the behavior before you would ask yourself the question, "Should createReservation be responsible for communicating with a web service?"

```
describe('createReservation(passenger, flight)', {
  // Existing tests
  it('submits the reservation to a web service endpoint', function(){

    // should createReservation be responsible for
    // communicating with a web service?

  });
});
```

The answer to the question is: No, most likely not. If one doesn't exist already, you would benefit from creating (and testing!) an object with the sole responsibility of web service communication.

By maximizing the testability of your code, you are able to identify violations of the SOLID principles. Many times, as in the example above, you can avoid violating them altogether.

Writing the Minimum Required Code

To review the basic TDD workflow, you write a test that will fail in order to verify a small piece of functionality, and then you write the minimum amount of code possible to make that new test pass. You then change the internal implementation details of the code under development, known as *refactoring*, to remove duplication.

Between only adding the minimum lines of code, and then refactoring to remove duplicate code, you can be certain that at the end of the process you have added the fewest lines of code possible. This is perfect, because there can be no defects in code you don't write!

Safe Maintenance and Refactoring

Practicing TDD guarantees that you will have a robust unit test suite for the production code in your project. Up-to-date unit tests are an insurance policy against future regression defects. A regression defect is a defect that appears in code that worked correctly at some time in the past, but is no longer working properly; the quality and reliability of the code has regressed.

Like any other insurance policy, there's a recurring cost that seems like a burden without benefit. In the case of unit-testing, the recurring cost is the development and maintenance of the unit test suite. Also like any other insurance policy, there comes a point when you are relieved that you paid that recurring cost. If you're a homeowner, it may be a violent storm that knocks a tree onto your house causing a significant amount of damage (as happened to one of us).

You will feel a similar sense of relief when it comes time to extend or maintain production code that has a comprehensive unit test suite. You can make changes to a portion of the code (still following TDD, of course) and be confident that you have not unintentionally changed the behavior of other portions of the code.

Runnable Specification

A robust unit test suite, like one generated when practicing TDD, also acts as a runnable specification for the code that the suite tests. Jasmine, the unit test framework that we'll introduce in a following section (and use throughout this book) uses a behavior-based test organization. Each individual test, or *specification* as Jasmine refers to them, begins with a natural-text statement about the behavior that the test is exercising and verifying. The default Jasmine test result formatter shows these statements to us for each test.

Once again using the `createReservation` function as an example, you can see that it's possible to read the output of the Jasmine unit tests to get a complete picture of how the function behaves. It isn't necessary to read the `createReservation` function to determine what it's doing; the unit tests tell you! The sort of "runnable documentation" that unit tests provide is invaluable when adding developers to a project, or even when revisiting code that you wrote in the past.

Current Open-Source and Commercial Frameworks

While Jasmine is the JavaScript test framework that we prefer, it isn't the only one out there. This section explores two popular alternatives: QUnit and D.O.H.

QUnit

The open-source QUnit framework was developed by the team that wrote the jQuery, jQuery UI, and jQuery Mobile JavaScript frameworks. QUnit may be run within non-browser environments, such as the `node.js` or Rhino JavaScript engines. QUnit tests may also be executed in the browser after including the requisite library JavaScript and CSS files in an HTML file.

Defining a QUnit test is a low-friction affair:

```
QUnit.test("This is a test", function(assert){
    assert.equal(true, true, "Oh no, true is not true!");
});
```

The only argument to a QUnit test function is a reference to the QUnit assertion object, which exposes eight assertions—including `equal`, as you can see in the preceding code snippet—for use within tests.

Tests can be grouped via the `QUnit.module` function, which causes the tests that follow to be grouped in the test results. All the tests that follow are in the module until another `QUnit.module` call is encountered or the end of the file is reached. We prefer Jasmine's nesting of tests within a suite because we find it more explicit and intuitive.

```
QUnit.module("module 1");
QUnit.test("I'm in module 1", function(assert){
  // Test logic
});
QUnit.module("module 2");
QUnit.test("I'm in module 2", function(assert){
  // Test logic
});
```

You can find out more about QUnit at `http://qunitjs.com/`.

D.O.H.

D.O.H., the Dojo Objective Harness, was created to help the creators and maintainers of the Dojo JavaScript Framework. D.O.H. does not have any dependencies on Dojo, however, so it may be used as a general-purpose JavaScript testing framework.

Like Jasmine and QUnit, D.O.H. supports browser-based test execution and non-browser–based execution (such as within the `node.js` or Rhino JavaScript engines).

D.O.H. unit tests are defined using the `register` function of the `doh` object. The `register` function accepts an array of JavaScript functions, which define simple tests, or objects, which define more complex tests that include setup and tear down (analogous to Jasmine's `beforeEach` and `afterEach`, which you will see in the next section).

```
doh.register("Test Module", [
  function simpleTest(){
    doh.assertTrue(true)
  },
  {
    name: "more complex",
    setup: function(){
      // code to set up the test before it runs
    },
    runTest: function(){
      doh.assertFalse(false);
    },
    tearDown: function(){
      // Code to clean up after the test executes
    }
  }
]);
```

D.O.H. provides four built-in assertions (such as `assertFalse`).

While we enjoy the framework's name (D'oh!), we find the Jasmine syntax for test organization and definition to be more clear and expressive.

You can explore the D.O.H. framework at `http://dojotoolkit.org/reference-guide/1.10/util/doh.html#util-doh`.

> **NOTE** *Unlike the Jasmine framework, neither QUnit nor D.O.H place library functions in the global scope; they're accessed via the* QUnit *and* doh *objects, respectively.*

Introducing Jasmine

Jasmine is a library for creating JavaScript unit tests in a behavior-driven development (BDD) style.

> **NOTE** *BDD? Aren't we doing TDD? Behavior-driven development and test-driven development are not mutually exclusive. Behavior-driven development uses natural-language descriptions to define the functionality, or behavior, that a particular unit test is exercising. We think that defining tests in this way helps us write tests that describe what the code we're writing should do, rather than how it does what it does. Also, as we noted previously, tests that are defined and organized in a behavior-driven manner have the benefit of generating a specification of functionality that is described in plain terms.*

In this section, we'll describe the basics of the framework, but we highly recommend that you visit the Jasmine homepage at http://jasmine.github.io where you can find the library's documentation—which is a runnable Jasmine test suite—for in-depth exposure.

Suites and Specs

Jasmine test suites are defined using the global describe function. The describe function accepts two arguments:

➤ A string, usually one that describes what is being tested

➤ A function, containing the implementation of the test suite

Test suites are implemented using specs, or individual tests. Each spec is defined using the global it function. Like the describe function, the it function takes two arguments:

➤ A string, usually one that describes the behavior being tested

➤ A function containing at least one expectation: an assertion that a state of the code is either true or false

Test suite implementations may also make use of the global beforeEach and afterEach functions. When included within a suite implementation, the beforeEach is executed before each of the tests in the suite. Conversely, the afterEach function is executed after each of the tests in the suite. The beforeEach and afterEach functions are useful for performing common setup and teardown, reducing duplication within a test suite.

NOTE *Test suites should be SOLID and DRY, too!*

In Listing 2-2, there were two tests that had exactly the same setup step. We noted at the time that we'd show how to remove this blatant violation of the DRY principle. Listing 2-5 shows how to do that using the `beforeEach` function.

LISTING 2-5: Jasmine's beforeEach and afterEach (code filename: Test Frameworks\ TestFrameworks_03_tests.js)

```
describe('createReservation(passenger, flight)', function(){
  var testPassenger = null,
    testFlight = null,
    testReservation = null;

  beforeEach(function(){
    testPassenger = {
      firstName: 'Pete',
      lastName: 'Mitchell'
    };

    testFlight = {
      number: '3443',
      carrier: 'AceAir',
      destination: 'Miramar, CA'
    };

    testReservation = createReservation(testPassenger, testFlight);
  });

  it('assigns passenger to the passengerInformation property', function(){
    expect(testReservation.passengerInformation).toBe(testPassenger);
  });

  it('assigns flight to the flightInformation property', function(){
    expect(testReservation.flightInformation).toBe(testFlight);
  });
});
```

For completeness, Listing 2-6 shows the implementation of `createReservation` that allows the refactored unit tests to pass.

LISTING 2-6: Complete implementation of createReservation (code filename: Test Frameworks\TestFrameworks_03.js)

```
function createReservation(passenger, flight){
  return {
    passengerInformation: passenger,
    flightInformation: flight
  };
}
```

Expectations and Matchers

Each of the tests contains an `expect` statement. Here's the `expect` from the first `createReservation` unit test:

```
expect(testReservation.passengerInformation).toBe(testPassenger);
```

The `expect` function takes the actual value generated by the code under test, in this case `testReservation.passengerInformation`, and compares it with the value that is expected. The expected value in the first unit test is *testPassenger*.

The comparison between the actual value and the expected value is performed using a matcher function. Matchers return either `true` to indicate that the comparison was successful, or `false` to indicate the comparison was not successful. A spec that contains one or more expectations with an unsuccessful matcher is considered failing. Conversely, a spec that contains only expectations with successful matchers is considered passing.

The example above used the `toBe` matcher, meaning—you guessed it—you expect `testReservation.passengerInformation` to be the same object as *testPassenger*.

Jasmine includes many built-in matchers, but if it doesn't have the exact matcher you need, Jasmine supports creating custom matchers. Creating custom matchers can be an excellent way to DRY out the test code.

> **NOTE** *There are also matcher libraries, such as jasmine-jquery (*`https://github.com/velesin/jasmine-jquery`*) that can increase your matching capabilities.*

Spies

Jasmine's spies are JavaScript functions that act as *test doubles*. A test double replaces the default implementation of a function or object with another, usually simpler, implementation during a test. Test doubles commonly reduce the complexity of unit-testing by removing dependency on external resources, such as web services.

Earlier in this section, you briefly contemplated extending the capabilities of the `createReservation` function to include direct communication with a web service to save the created reservation in a database. At the time, it was decided that web service communication did not fall within the responsibility of the function.

Charlotte, one of the other members on your team, has created a `ReservationSaver` JavaScript object encapsulating the ability to submit a reservation to a web service via a call to its `saveReservation` function. You'd like to extend the `createReservation` function to accept an instance of `ReservationSaver` as an argument and ensure the `ReservationSaver`'s `saveReservation` function is executed.

Because the `saveReservation` function communicates with a web service, your test needs to save the reservation and then somehow query the database and ensure that the reservation was added, right? Thankfully, no; you don't have to do that, nor would you want to. Doing so would make your unit tests depend on the presence and correct functionality of external systems: the web service and the database.

> **NOTE** *Tests that ensure the correctness of code that interacts with external systems are called* integration tests *and are important when writing reliable software, but they are distinct from unit tests. We'll assume that Charlotte has created the appropriate integration tests for the* ReservationSaver *object.*

Jasmine spies allow you to replace the complex implementation of saveReservation with a simpler version that removes the dependence on the external systems. For reference, here's the ReservationSaver object that Charlotte created:

```
function ReservationSaver(){
  this.saveReservation = function(reservation){
    // Complex code that interacts with a web service
    // to save the reservation
  }
}
```

> **NOTE** *Charlotte used the* Constructor-Function *Pattern of JavaScript object creation such that new instances of the* ReservationSaver *are made with the* new ReservationSaver() *statement. Chapter 3 covers this creation pattern, and others, in depth.*

For reasons that will become clear in the next section, "Using a Dependency-Injection Framework," the createReservation function has been updated to accept an instance of a ReservationSaver. Providing the ReservationSaver as an argument allows you to write the test that ensures that the reservation is saved like this:

```
describe('createReservation', function(){
  it('saves the reservation', function(){
    var saver = new ReservationSaver();
    // testPassenger and testFlight have been set up
    // in the beforeEach for this suite.
    createReservation(testPassenger, testFlight, saver);

    // How do we make sure saver.saveReservation(...) was called?
  });
});
```

As it's currently written, the test is providing the default, complex implementation of the ReservationSaver object to the createReservation function. However, you *don't* want to do this because doing so adds a dependency on an external system and makes the present function difficult to test. Here's where the power of Jasmine spies becomes evident.

Before calling createReservation, you can create a spy on the saveReservation function. Spies, among other things, allow you to verify that a particular function was executed. This capability is perfect for this first test.

You tell Jasmine to spy on a particular function using the spyOn global function. The spyOn function accepts an instance of an object as its first argument and the name of the function that should be spied on as its second argument. Thus, to create a spy on the saveReservation, you update the test like this:

```
it('saves the reservation', function(){
  var saver = new ReservationSaver();
  spyOn(saver, 'saveReservation');
  // testPassenger and testFlight have been set up
  // in the beforeEach for this suite.
  createReservation(testPassenger, testFlight, saver);

  // How do we make sure saveReservation was called?
});
```

By creating the spy, you've replaced the saver object's implementation of saveReservation with a function that does nothing related to the saving of a reservation at all. It does, however, keep track of each time the function is called as well as the arguments provided with each invocation. Jasmine also provides matchers for spies that can be used to create expectations that, among other things, verify that a particular spy was invoked one or more times. Adding that expectation to your test makes it complete:

```
it('saves the reservation', function(){
  var saver = new ReservationSaver();
  spyOn(saver, 'saveReservation');
  // testPassenger and testFlight have been set up
  // in the beforeEach for this suite.
  createReservation(testPassenger, testFlight, saver);

  expect(saver.saveReservation).toHaveBeenCalled();
});
```

Because you've added an argument to the createReservation function, you must update the two existing tests. You don't want *any* of your tests to execute the default implementation of the saveReservation function, so in Listing 2-7, you'll refactor the new test to move creation of the ReservationSaver and its associated spy into the suite's beforeEach function.

LISTING 2-7: Tests with introduction of the ReservationSaver (code filename: Test Frameworks\TestFrameworks_04_tests.js)

```
describe('createReservation', function(){
  var testPassenger = null,
    testFlight = null,
    testReservation = null,
    testSaver = null;

  beforeEach(function(){
    testPassenger = {
      firstName: 'Pete',
      lastName: 'Mitchell'
```

continues

```
    };

    testFlight = {
      number: '3443',
      carrier: 'AceAir',
      destination: 'Miramar, CA'
    };

    testSaver = new ReservationSaver();
    spyOn(testSaver, 'saveReservation');

    testReservation = createReservation(testPassenger, testFlight, testSaver);
  });

  it('assigns passenger to the passengerInformation property', function(){
    expect(testReservation.passengerInformation).toBe(testPassenger);
  });

  it('assigns flight to the flightInformation property', function(){
    expect(testReservation.flightInformation).toBe(testFlight);
  });

  it('saves the reservation', function(){
    expect(testSaver.saveReservation).toHaveBeenCalled();
  });
});
```

At this point, only the new test is failing. A minor refactor of the createReservation function yields a passing test suite in Listing 2-8.

LISTING 2-8: Implementation of createReservation using a ReservationSaver (code filename: Test Frameworks\TestFrameworks_04.js)

```
function createReservation(passenger, flight, saver){
  var reservation = {
    passengerInformation: passenger,
    flightInformation: flight
  };

  saver.saveReservation(reservation);
  return reservation;
}

// ReservationSaver created by Charlotte
function ReservationSaver(){
  this.saveReservation = function(reservation){
    // Complex code that interacts with a web service
    // to save the reservation
  };
}
```

USING A DEPENDENCY-INJECTION FRAMEWORK

You may remember from Chapter 1 that dependency *inversion* is one of the five pillars of SOLID development, and that dependency *injection* is part of the mechanism of bringing it about. In this section, you will develop a framework that brings both flexibility and discipline to dependency injection.

What Is Dependency Injection?

There's a JavaScript conference coming up, and you've volunteered to help construct its website. This will be the biggest JavaScript conference ever, with every session so jam-packed that attendees must reserve their seats. Your job is to write the client-side code to make reservations possible.

You'll need to call the conference's web service to work with the database. Being well-versed in the principles of object-oriented programming, your first step was to encapsulate that service in a ConferenceWebSvc object. You have also created a JavaScript object, Messenger, that shows fancy popup messages. We pick up the story from there.

Each attendee is allowed to register for 10 sessions. Your next task is to write a function that lets the attendee attempt to register for one session, and then display either a success message or a failure message. Your first version might look something like Listing 2-9. (We apologize for the synchronous nature of the calls to ConferenceWebSvc. Better ideas are coming in Chapters 5 and 6. Also, we are using the "new" keyword to create objects even though some authorities don't like it, so we cover the worst case.)

LISTING 2-9: Basic Attendee object (code filename: DI\Attendee_01.js)

```javascript
Attendee = function(attendeeId) {

  // Ensure created with 'new'
  if (!(this instanceof Attendee)) {
    return new Attendee(attendeeId);
  }

  this.attendeeId = attendeeId;

  this.service = new ConferenceWebSvc();
  this.messenger = new Messenger();
};

// Attempt to reserve a seat at the given session.
// Give a message about success or failure.
Attendee.prototype.reserve = function(sessionId) {
  if (this.service.reserve(this.attendeeId, sessionId)) {
    this.messenger.success('Your seat has been reserved!' +
      ' You may make up to ' + this.service.getRemainingReservations()+
      ' additional reservations.');
  } else {
```

continues

LISTING 2-9 *(continued)*

```
    this.messenger.failure('Sorry; your seat could not be reserved.');
  }
};
```

This code appears to be beautifully modular, with `ConferenceWebSvc`, `Messenger`, and `Attendee` each having a single responsibility. `Attendee.reserve` is so simple that it hardly needs to be unit-tested, which is a good thing because it *can't* be unit-tested! Behind `ConferenceWebSvc` sit HTTP calls. How can you unit-test something that requires HTTP? Remember that unit tests are supposed to be fast and stand on their own. Also, `Messenger` will require the OK button on each message to be pressed. That is not supposed to be the job of a *unit* test on your module. *Unit*-testing is one of the keys to creating reliable JavaScript, and you don't want to drift into *system* testing until all the units are ready.

The problem here is not with the `Attendee` object, but with the code it depends upon. The solution is dependency injection. Instead of burdening the code with hard-coded dependencies on `ConferenceWebSvc` and `Messenger`, you can inject them into `Attendee`. In production, you will inject the real ones, but for unit-testing you can inject substitutes, which could be fakes (objects with the appropriate methods but fake processing) or Jasmine spies.

```
// Production:
var attendee = new Attendee(new ConferenceWebSvc(), new Messenger(), id);

// Testing:
var attendee = new Attendee(fakeService, fakeMessenger, id);
```

This style of dependency injection (DI), which does not use a DI framework, is called "poor man's dependency injection," which is ironic because the best professional DI frameworks are actually free. Listing 2-10 shows the `Attendee` object with poor man's dependency injection.

LISTING 2-10: Attendee object with poor man's dependency injection (code filename: DI\Attendee_02.js)

```
Attendee = function(service, messenger, attendeeId) {
   // Ensure created with 'new'
  if (!(this instanceof Attendee)) {
    return new Attendee(attendeeId);
  }

  this.attendeeId = attendeeId;

  this.service = service;
  this.messenger = messenger;
};
```

Making Your Code More Reliable with Dependency Injection

You have just seen how dependency injection allows unit-testing that would otherwise be impossible. Code that has been tested, and can continue to be tested in an automated test suite, will obviously be more reliable.

There is another, more subtle benefit to DI. You typically have more control over injected spies or fakes than over real objects. Thus, it is easier to produce error conditions and other exotica. What's easier is more likely to get done, so you'll find that your tests cover more contingencies.

Finally, DI promotes code reuse. Modules that have hard-coded dependencies tend not to be reused because they drag in too much baggage. The original `Attendee` module could never have been reused on the server side because of its hard-coded use of `Messenger`. The DI version allows you to use *any* messenger that has `success` and `failure` methods.

Mastering Dependency Injection

Dependency injection is not difficult. In fact, it makes life much easier. To become a DI Jedi, just keep these things in mind.

Whenever you're coding an object, and it creates a new object, ask yourself the following questions. If the answer to any one of them is "Yes," then consider injecting it instead of directly instantiating it.

> ➤ Does the object or any of *its* dependencies rely on an external resource such as a database, a configuration file, HTTP, or other infrastructure?

> ➤ Should my tests account for possible errors in the object?

> ➤ Will some of my tests want the object to behave in particular ways?

> ➤ Is the object one of my own, as opposed to one from a third-party library?

Choose a good dependency-injection framework to help you and become intimately familiar with its API. The next section will help you get started.

Case Study: Writing a Lightweight Dependency-Injection Framework

The dependency injection you've seen so far is hard-coded. It's an improvement on the Big Ball of Mud style of programming, but still not ideal. Professional dependency-injection frameworks work like this:

1. Soon after application startup, you register your injectables with a DI container, identifying each one by name and naming the dependencies it has, in turn.

2. When you need an object, you ask the container to supply it.

3. The container instantiates the object you requested, but first it recursively instantiates all its dependencies, injecting them into the respective objects as required.

In frameworks that use dependency injection heavily, such as AngularJS, the process can seem almost magic and too good to be true. In fact, it's so magic that it can be hard to understand. To learn how these frameworks function, let's build a DI container.

This will also serve as a case study in test-driven development. You will see how building the code bit by bit, in response to tests, makes for reliable JavaScript.

You want your container to do just two things: accept registrations for injectables and their dependencies, and supply objects on request. Suppose you code the `register` function first. It will take three arguments:

- The name of the injectable.

- An array of the names of its dependencies.

- A function whose return value is the injectable object. In other words, when you ask the container for an instance of the injectable, it will call this function and return whatever the function returns. The container will also pass instances of the requested object's dependencies to this function, but you can hold off on figuring this out until later tests.

TDD works best when you code the absolute minimum at every stage, so you might start by coding only an empty version of `register`. Because this function is an asset that can be shared by all instances of DiContainer, you would make it part of DiContainer's prototype. (See Listing 2-11.)

LISTING 2-11: Empty DiContainer.register function (code filename: DI\DiContainer_00.js)

```
DiContainer = function() {
};

DiContainer.prototype.register = function(name, dependencies, func) {
};
```

To make the code as reliable as possible, you'd want to verify that those arguments were passed and are of the right types. Laying that solid foundation is often a good first test, for then your subsequent tests can rely on it. Listing 2-12 shows such a test.

LISTING 2-12: Test for verifying arguments (code filename: DI\DiContainer_01_tests.js)

```
describe('DiContainer', function() {
  var container;
  beforeEach(function(){
    container = new DiContainer();
  });
  describe('register(name, dependencies, func)', function() {

    it('throws if any argument is missing or the wrong type', function() {
      var badArgs = [
        // No args at all
        [],
        // Just the name
        ['Name'],
        // Just name and dependencies
        ['Name', ['Dependency1', 'Dependency2']],
        // Missing the dependencies.
        // (Commercial frameworks support this, but DiContainer does not.)
        ['Name', function() {}],
        // Various examples of wrong types
```

```
        [1, ['a', 'b'], function() {}],
        ['Name', [1,2], function() {}],
        ['Name', ['a', 'b'], 'should be a function']
      ];
      badArgs.forEach(function(args) {
        expect(function() {
          container.register.apply(container,args);
        }).toThrow();
      });
    });
  });
});
```

A few things to note about the test so far:

> The "subject under test," container, is created in a beforeEach. This gives you a fresh instance for each test, so one test cannot pollute the results of another.

> The text arguments to the two nested describes and the it concatenate to form something that reads like a sentence: "DiContainer register (name,dependencies,func) throws if any argument is missing or the wrong type."

> Although TDD purists might insist on a separate test for each of the elements of badArgs, in practice placing such a burden on the developer will mean that he will test fewer conditions than he ought. If one expectation and one description cover all the tests, then it might be acceptable to group them like this.

> **NOTE** *In case you're not familiar with the* apply *function in the expectation, it's just a way of calling a given function (*register*) on a given 'this' (*container*), passing the arguments (*args*) in the form of an array rather than comma-separated as in a normal call. For more on* call, *see the "Case Study: Building the Aop.js Module" section later in this chapter.*

When you run the test, it fails (Figure 2-4).

You can remedy the failure by adding the argument-checking functionality to DiContainer .register. Instead of the empty function, you now have the code in Listing 2-13.

LISTING 2-13: DiContainer.register with argument checking (code filename: DI\ DiContainer_01.js)

```
DiContainer.prototype.messages = {
  registerRequiresArgs: 'The register function requires three arguments: ' +
    'a string, an array of strings, and a function.'
```

continues

LISTING 2-13 *(continued)*

```
  };

  DiContainer.prototype.register = function(name, dependencies, func) {
    var ix;

    if (typeof name !== 'string'
    || !Array.isArray(dependencies)
    || typeof func !== 'function') {
      throw new Error(this.messages.registerRequiresArgs);
    }
    for (ix = 0; ix < dependencies.length; ++ix) {
      if (typeof dependencies[ix] !== 'string') {
        throw new Error (container.messages.registerRequiresArgs);
      }
    }
  };
```

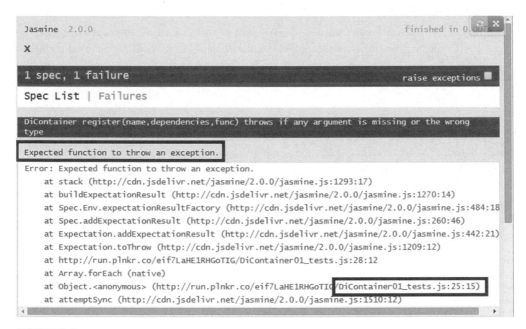

FIGURE 2-4

The test now passes (Figure 2-5).

If you read the listing closely, you may have noticed that the message is placed in the prototype, exposing it to the public. This technique allows you to make your tests tighter. Instead of just expecting the function `toThrow()`, you can make it more exact and therefore more reliable by changing the `.toThrow()` expectation to the following:

```
.toThrowError(container.messages.registerRequiresArgs);
```

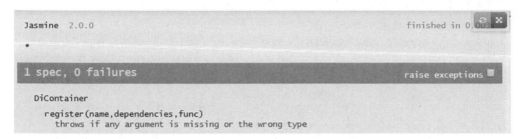

FIGURE 2-5

> **NOTE** *For the most reliable negative tests, verify the actual error message, not just the existence of an error. Often, this will mean exposing the messages of the subject under test, either on the prototype or through a function.*

The `register` function still doesn't do anything, but it will be hard to test how well it puts things in the container if you can't get them out again, so you turn your attention to the other half of the picture: the `get` function. It needs only one parameter: the name of what it's getting.

Again, it's a good idea to start with the argument-checking. We find that code is more reliable if the error-checking tests are done as early as possible. If they're left until "all the real code is done" it's too easy to move on to other things. Listing 2-14 is a good start.

> **NOTE** *Test error handling* first, *when you're not itching to move on to other things.*

LISTING 2-14: Testing get of a non-registered name (code filename: DI\DiContainer_02_tests.js)

```
describe('get(name)', function() {
  it('returns undefined if name was not registered', function() {
    expect(container.get('notDefined')).toBeUndefined();
  });
});
```

The test fails spectacularly because you don't even have a `get` function yet. As always with TDD, you code the absolute minimum to remedy the present error, as you can see in Listing 2-15.

LISTING 2-15: Minimal DiContainer.get function (code filename: DI\DiContainer_02.js)

```
DiContainer.prototype.get = function(name) {
};
```

What do you know!? The test passes! In TDD, it's okay for a test to pass "by coincidence." If you're thorough with your future tests, the situation will rectify itself. This is where you must have the courage of your TDD convictions. If you were to code anything now, your code would be ahead of your tests.

> **NOTE** *Code the absolute minimum to pass a test, even if that's nothing at all. Don't let your code get ahead of your tests.*

At last you're ready to make get (name) fulfill its destiny, as expressed in the test in Listing 2-16.

LISTING 2-16: Positive test of DiContainer.get (code filename: DI\DiContainer_03_tests.js)

```
it('returns the result of executing the registered function', function() {
  var name = 'MyName',
      returnFromRegisteredFunction = "something";
  container.register(name, [], function() {
    return returnFromRegisteredFunction;
  });
  expect(container.get(name)).toBe(returnFromRegisteredFunction);
});
```

The test also demonstrates a minor point of technique. By using the variables *name* and *returnFromRegisteredFunction*, you keep the test DRY (their values being represented only once) and make the expectation self-documenting.

> **NOTE** *Make your tests DRY and self-documenting by using well-named variables instead of literals.*

For the test to pass, you must make register store the registration and make get retrieve it. The relevant parts of DiContainer are now as in Listing 2-17. For clarity, we have replaced what we've already discussed with ellipses comments.

LISTING 2-17: DiContainer.get can get a registered function (code filename: DI\ DiContainer_03.js)

```
DiContainer = function() {
  // . . .
  this.registrations = [];
```

```
  };

  DiContainer.prototype.register = function(name,dependencies,func) {
    // . . .
    this.registrations[name] = { func: func };
  };

  DiContainer.prototype.get = function(name) {
    return this.registrations[name].func();
  };
```

The new test passes (Figure 2-6), but now the earlier test, which passed without writing any code, fails. In TDD, it is not unusual for these supposedly lucky breaks to quickly rectify themselves.

You can make all the tests pass by making get handle the undefined case more intelligently (Listing 2-18).

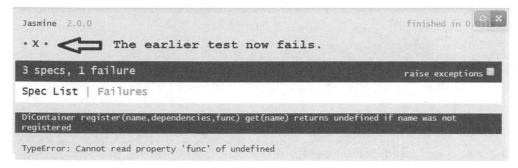

FIGURE 2-6

LISTING 2-18: Code catching up to the earlier test (code filename: DI\DiContainer_03b.js)

```
  DiContainer.prototype.get = function(name) {
    var registration = this.registrations[name];
    if (registration === undefined) {
      return undefined;
    }
    return registration.func();
  };
```

Now you are in a position to make get supply dependencies to the object it returns (Listing 2-19). Your test consists of registering a main object and two dependencies. The main object will return the sum of its dependencies' return values.

LISTING 2-19: Testing the supply of dependencies (code filename: DI\DiContainer_tests.js)

```
  describe('get(name)', function() {

    it('supplies dependencies to the registered function', function() {
      var main = 'main',
          mainFunc,
```

continues

LISTING 2-19 *(continued)*

```
            dep1 = 'dep1',
            dep2 = 'dep2';
        container.register(main, [dep1, dep2], function(dep1Func, dep2Func) {
          return function() {
            return dep1Func() + dep2Func();
          };
        });
        container.register(dep1, [], function() {
          return function() {
            return 1;
          };
        });
        container.register(dep2, [], function() {
          return function() {
            return 2;
          };
        });
        mainFunc = container.get(main);
        expect(mainFunc()).toBe(3);
      });
    });
```

And the implementation to make the test pass is in Listing 2-20.

LISTING 2-20: Supplying dependencies (code filename: DI\DiContainer.js)

```
DiContainer.prototype.register = function(name,dependencies,func) {

  var ix;

  if (typeof name !== 'string' ||
      !Array.isArray(dependencies) ||
      typeof func !== 'function') {
    throw new Error(this.messages.registerRequiresArgs);
  }
  for (ix=0; ix<dependencies.length; ++ix) {
    if (typeof dependencies[ix] !== 'string') {
      throw new Error(this.messages.registerRequiresArgs);
    }
  }

  this.registrations[name] =
      { dependencies: dependencies, func: func };
};

DiContainer.prototype.get = function(name) {
  var self = this,
      registration = this.registrations[name],
      dependencies = [];
  if (registration===undefined) {
    return undefined;
```

```
      }

    registration.dependencies.forEach(function(dependencyName) {
      var dependency = self.get(dependencyName);
      dependencies.push( dependency===undefined ? undefined : dependency);
    });
    return registration.func.apply(undefined, dependencies);
  };
```

The change was to add *dependencies* to the *registrations[name]* object in the `register` function, and then access `registration.dependencies` in the `get` function.

The final requirement is to supply dependencies recursively. Although you might suspect this works already, the wise test-driven developer takes nothing for granted. This final test is in `DiContainer_tests.js`, in this chapter's downloads. The completed library is `DiContainer.js`.

We hope this exercise has communicated the spirit of test-driven development, as well as given some insight into how typical JavaScript DI containers work.

Using a Dependency-Injection Framework

Earlier in this chapter, you developed a module that allowed an attendee to reserve a seat at a JavaScript conference. You got it to the point where you were injecting `Attendee`'s dependencies into its constructor, but in a hard-coded manner:

```
var attendee = new Attendee(new ConferenceWebSvc(), new Messenger(), id);
```

Now that you have a proper DI container, you can avoid hard-coding the dependencies each time you construct an object. Most large JavaScript applications start with a setup (configuration) routine. That is a good place to set up the dependency injection as well.

Suppose your application is managed under a global called `MyApp`. In the configuration, you would find something that looks like Listing 2-21.

LISTING 2-21: Using DiContainer with Attendee

```
MyApp = {};

MyApp.diContainer = new DiContainer();

MyApp.diContainer.register(
  'Service',       // DI tag for the web service
  [],              // No dependencies
                   // Function that returns an instance
  function() {
    return new ConferenceWebSvc();
  }
);

MyApp.diContainer.register(
  'Messenger',
```

continues

LISTING 2-21 *(continued)*

```
    [],
    function() {
      return new Messenger();
    }
);

MyApp.diContainer.register(
  'AttendeeFactory',
  ['Service','Messenger'], // Attendee depends on service and messenger.
  function(service, messenger){
    return function(attendeeId) {
      return new Attendee(service, messenger, attendeeId);
    }
  }
);
```

There is an advanced but important point in the way `Attendee` is placed in `DiContainer`. The registration is not for a function to produce an `Attendee`, but for a function to produce a *factory* that produces an `Attendee`. This is because `Attendee` requires a parameter in addition to its dependencies, namely the *attendeeId*. It would be possible to code the DI container so that you could do this:

```
var attendee = MyApp.diContainer.get('Attendee', attendeeId);
```

but then `Attendees` could not be supplied as recursive dependencies of other objects. (Those other objects could not, in general, be expected to pass an *attendeeId* all the way from the top of the chain, which is where it would have to originate.)

With that factory in place you can, deep in the application, get an `Attendee` from the DI container, as you see in Listing 2-22.

LISTING 2-22: Instantiating an Attendee from the factory

```
var attendeeId = 123;
var sessionId = 1;

// Instate an Attendee from the DI container, passing the attendee ID.
var attendee = MyApp.diContainer.get('AttendeeFactory')(attendeeId);

attendee.reserve(sessionId)
```

Current Dependency-Injection Frameworks

There are two dependency-injection frameworks that enjoy widespread adoption and are being kept current: AngularJS and RequireJS. Each is free and open source, and each has its unique strengths.

RequireJS

RequireJS uses a syntax very much like the `DiContainer` in this chapter. (Yes, we cheated.) Where `DiContainer` has a `register` function, RequireJS has `define`, which it supplies as a global. The `DiContainer` `get(moduleName)` becomes RequireJS's `require(moduleUrl)`.

"*ModuleUrl*??" you say. Yes—what makes RequireJS special is that you use the locations of your scripts as module names. For example, you could put your `AttendeeFactory` in the RequireJS container like this:

```
define(['./Service', './Messenger'], function(service, messenger) {
    return function(attendeeId) {
        return new Attendee(service, messenger, attendeeId);
    }
});
```

Instead of depending on the module names (`['Service', 'Messenger']`), `AttendeeFactory` depends on the relative URLs (`['./Service', './Messenger']`).

So how about the name of the thing we're defining (`'AttendeeFactory'`)? There's no need for it because the URL of the file in which this code appears (probably `./AttendeeFactory.js`) doubles as the module name. This feature of RequireJS has the added benefit of automatically avoiding naming collisions. It also implies that "one module per file" is the normal way of doing things in RequireJS.

It is possible to explicitly name your modules (using the same syntax as `DiContainer.register`), but to do so is not in the full spirit of this library.

RequireJS ties DI modules to URLs to allow it to optimize how it loads your scripts. In fact, RequireJS started out as just one of several proposals before the CommonJS committee to solve the problem of how to get modules from the server to the browser (Transport C at `http://wiki.commonjs.org/wiki/Modules/Transport`). Their proposal was never formally accepted by CommonJS, but it seems to be the only one left standing and is widely used.

You can check out its many additional features at `http://requirejs.org`.

AngularJS

Compared to RequireJS, Google's AngularJS is the new kid on the block, but it is taking the JavaScript world by storm. Although DI is at the very center of AngularJS, AngularJS is much more than a DI container. It is a complete, "opinionated" framework for building single-page applications (SPAs).

Dependency injection appears in AngularJS in a variety of ways. There are many functions along the lines of `DiContainer.register`, each suitable for different types of objects. For example, some AngularJS objects, called *services*, are by nature singletons, and the AngularJS framework ensures this with a `service` registration function that causes the same identical object to be injected each time one is requested. If that's not the behavior you want, there's a `factory` function that does just what the name implies. You can even register constants for dependency injection with the `constant` function.

Although AngularJS is an opinionated framework, many of its important features are under your control. In fact, if you don't like the dependency injector, you can inject one of your own.

Not that you'll have any time left to learn how to do that! Compared to RequireJS, Knockout, JQuery, or most other JavaScript libraries, AngularJS has a very long learning curve. However, once you've ascended most of it, everything will make complete sense and you will wonder what took you so long. AngularJS is very well designed, and if you're looking for a total solution for your SPA, you couldn't do much better.

The goodness is at `https://angularjs.org`.

USING AN ASPECT TOOLKIT

Aspect-oriented programming (AOP) is a way of gathering code that will be useful to more than one object (although it is not within the Single Responsibility of any of them) and distributing that code to the objects in a non-obtrusive way.

In the lingo of AOP, the pieces of code thus distributed are called *advices*, and the issues the advices address are called *aspects* or *cross-cutting concerns*. For an example, let's return to the JavaScript conference from the last section.

Case Study: Caching with and without AOP

You'll recall that you had volunteered to help write the conference's website. To help defer costs, the organizers of the conference have partnered with a travel-services company to sell airplane tickets. Your job is to call their web service to obtain a bargain airfare based on the logged-in attendee's preferred home airport. The ticket will be featured in an ad on the website.

You want the ad to appear without delay, but it involves a relatively time-consuming call to the web service. You decide to cache the featured ticket as long as the user does not change his preferred airport.

In fact, there may be a lot of things you want to cache on this website. Caching has become a *cross cutting concern*—a prime candidate for aspect-oriented programming. Let's see how it plays out.

Implementing Caching without AOP

First, Listing 2-23 shows the function without caching. To increase the happiness of readers who prefer not to use the "`new`" keyword, we have used a different module-creation pattern than in the previous section.

LISTING 2-23: TravelService module without caching

```
// Wraps the travel services company's raw web service,
// supplying parameters relevant to the conference.
TravelService = (function(rawWebService) {
  var conferenceAirport = 'BOS';
  var maxArrival = new Date(/* some date */);
  var minDeparture = new Date(/* some date */);

  return {
    getSuggestedTicket: function(homeAirport) {
      // Gets the cheapest ticket from the home airport that
      // will allow the user to attend the entire conference.
      return rawWebService.getCheapestRoundTrip(
        homeAirport, conferenceAirport,
        maxArrival, minDeparture);
    }
```

```
    };
})();

// To get the info for your ad:

TravelService.getSuggestedTicket(attendee.homeAirport);
```

Now you want to add caching. You could do so as in Listing 2-24 (without AOP).

LISTING 2-24: Caching without AOP

```
TravelService = (function(rawWebService) {
  var conferenceAirport = 'BOS';
  var maxArrival = new Date(/* some date */);
  var minDeparture = new Date(/* some date */);

  // Simple caching: The index is the airport and the object is the ticket.
  var cache = [];

  return {
    getSuggestedTicket: function(homeAirport) {
      var ticket;
      if (cache[homeAirport]) {
        return cache[homeAirport];
      }

      ticket = rawWebService.getCheapestRoundTrip(
        homeAirport, conferenceAirport,
        maxArrival, minDeparture);

      cache[homeAirport] = ticket;

      return ticket;
    }
  };
})();
```

That works, but you have more than doubled the lines of code in `getSuggestedTicket`. What's more, the new code has nothing to do with the function's core responsibility.

Wouldn't it be nice if you could add the feature without modifying `getSuggestedTicket` at all? And even change the caching strategy later—expiring the cached result after 10 minutes, for example? Wouldn't it be even better if you could chain additional features (storing the user's preferences in a cookie, for example) just as unobtrusively?

That is what aspect-oriented programming does for you. With the AOP framework you'll see shortly, you could have kept the original code and just added this in the application's startup logic:

```
Aop.around('getSuggestedTicket', cacheAspectFactory());
```

In this line of code, `cacheAspectFactory()` returns a completely reusable caching function that can intercept any call and, if its arguments have been seen before, return the same result.

Making Your Code More Reliable with AOP

It's easy to see how AOP produces more reliable code. First, it keeps your functions simple. They execute their Single Responsibility, and that is all. Simplicity begets reliability.

Second, it keeps your code DRY. The obvious point here is that multiple occurrences of the code represent multiple places that someone could later break, and multiple opportunities to get out of sync. But there's a more subtle point: You also don't want to repeat *the code that connects the new functionality (caching) to the old (getting a ticket).*

Consider all the logic in Listing 2-24 that was devoted to weaving the caching aspect into the code. Every time a developer follows this pattern, there is a chance he will make a mistake. Because of this, if you're serious about test-driven development, each time will require the full complement of unit tests. Those tests will look a lot like each other—more repetition!

> **NOTE** *It is just as important not to repeat the way a block of code connects to other code, as it is not to repeat the block itself.*

Third, it allows you to centralize the configuration of your application. If you create one function whose Single Responsibility is configuring your aspects, you have only one place to consult when you want an overview of your bells and whistles. More importantly, if you are hunting a bug and want to defoliate its habitat, you can easily turn off features such as caching. You can also turn *on* features such as argument checking. There may even be an aspect that you want to turn on and off according to an end-user's preferences.

Case Study: Building the Aop.js Module

Aspect-oriented programming consists of sticking functions together in new ways. What could be better-suited for such an enterprise than JavaScript? We would like to showcase a particularly elegant framework from Fredrik Appelberg and Dave Clayton, available for free at `https://github.com/davedx/aop`. Simply named `Aop.js`, it is a marvel of concision, compressed to an elegant minimum with every tool of the JavaScripter's art.

Take a few minutes to look over Listing 2-25. Don't worry if it's impenetrable at first. That is exactly our hope. You will use test-driven development (TDD) to make it all clear shortly.

LISTING 2-25: Aop.js

```
// Created by Fredrik Appelberg:
// http://fredrik.appelberg.me/2010/05/07/aop-js.html
// Modified to support prototypes by Dave Clayton
Aop = {
 // Apply around advice to all matching functions in the given namespaces
 around: function(pointcut, advice, namespaces) {
   // if no namespaces are supplied, use a trick to determine the global ns
   if (namespaces == undefined || namespaces.length == 0)
```

```
        namespaces = [ (function(){return this;}).call() ];
    // loop over all namespaces
    for(var i in namespaces) {
      var ns = namespaces[i];
      for(var member in ns) {
        if(typeof ns[member] == 'function' && member.match(pointcut)) {
          (function(fn, fnName, ns) {
              // replace the member fn slot with a wrapper which calls
              // the 'advice' Function
              ns[fnName] = function() {
                return advice.call(this, { fn: fn,
                                           fnName: fnName,
                                           arguments: arguments });
              };
          })(ns[member], member, ns);
        }
      }
    }
  },

  next: function(f) {
    return f.fn.apply(this, f.arguments);
  }
};

Aop.before = function(pointcut, advice, namespaces) {
  Aop.around(pointcut,
             function(f) {
               advice.apply(this, f.arguments);
               return Aop.next.call(this, f);
             },
             namespaces);
};

Aop.after = function(pointcut, advice, namespaces) {
  Aop.around(pointcut,
             function(f) {
               var ret = Aop.next.call(this, f);
               advice.apply(this, f.arguments);
               return ret;
             },
             namespaces);
};
```

Amazing, right? Also perhaps a little hard to digest all at once?

In the "Using a Dependency-Injection Framework" section of this chapter, you used TDD to build a reliable component from scratch. In this section, you will use TDD as an aid to understand existing code. In fact, when we discovered Aop.js, this is exactly what we did. We re-built most of it using TDD, gaining intimate knowledge of each line as we went.

One characteristic of TDD is that you don't code all the features of the application in one go. You add a test, code just enough to pass that test, possibly refactor, and repeat. Many developers wonder how such an incremental approach can possibly produce elegant code. We hope the following demonstration will put those fears to rest. Along the way, you'll encounter some features of JavaScript that make gems like Aop.js possible.

> **NOTE** *Test-driven development produces elegant code just as reliably as older methods.*

At its heart, AOP intercepts the execution of a function (the *target*), causing it to be preceded, followed, or surrounded by another function (the *advice*). You might concentrate on the "surround" case, for the others are just special cases of it. Following Fredrik's and Dave's lead, you will create a function, around, in an Aop object. The source is in the AOP directory of this chapter's download. See the remarks at the beginning of the chapter for details.

You could start with a bare version of this function, as you see in Listing 2-26.

LISTING 2-26: Empty Aop.around function (code filename: AOP\Aop_00.js)

```
Aop = {
  around: function(fnName, advice, fnObj) {
    // Initial version does nothing.
  }
};
```

Your first test, in Listing 2-27, is that Aop.around causes the original function to be replaced by the advice.

LISTING 2-27: Test that Aop.around causes the advice to execute (code filename: AOP\ Aop_01_tests.js)

```
describe('Aop', function() {
  describe('Aop.around(fnName, advice, targetObj)', function() {
    it('causes a call to the target function to execute the advice',function(){
      var targetObj = {
        targetFn: function () {
        }
      };
      var executedAdvice = false;
      var advice = function() {
        executedAdvice = true;
      };
      Aop.around('targetFn', advice, targetObj);
      targetObj.targetFn();
      expect(executedAdvice).toBe(true);
    });
  });
});
```

You created a target object, *targetObj*, that has a bare function, *targetFn*. You also have an *advice* function that just sets a flag, *executedAdvice*, when it executes. If you tie it all together with Aop.around, ('targetFn', advice, targetObj), you would expect that a call to the target will cause the advice to execute. Of course, this test fails (Figure 2-7) because Aop.around still does nothing.

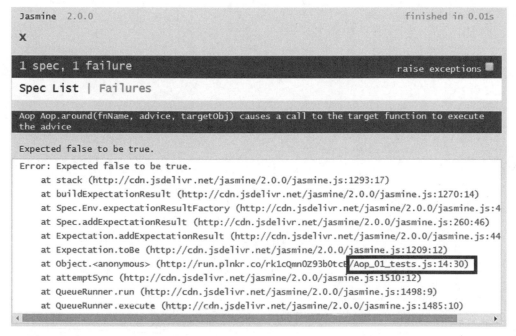

FIGURE 2-7

Next, you'd add just enough code to make it pass (Listing 2-28).

LISTING 2-28: Aop.around now executes the advice (code filename: AOP\Aop_01.js)

```
Aop = {
  around: function(fnName, advice, fnObj) {
    fnObj[fnName] = advice;
  }
};
```

Next, you want to allow your advice to wrap a call to the target. This means that you must pass some information about the target to the advice. You can do so by passing an object to the advice, in which you store the original target function. In the Listing 2-29 tests, this object is called *targetInfo* and the function is in the *fn* property.

LISTING 2-29: Testing an ability to pass information about the target to the aspect (code filename: AOP\Aop_02_tests.js)

```javascript
describe('Aop', function() {
  var targetObj,
      executionPoints;  // An array of execution events

  beforeEach(function() {
    targetObj = {
      targetFn: function() {
        executionPoints.push('targetFn');
      }
    };
    executionPoints = [];
  });

  describe('Aop.around(fnName, advice, targetObj)', function() {

    it('causes a call to the target function to execute the advice',function(){
      // . . . Discussed earlier . . .
    });

    it('allows the advice to wrap a call the target', function() {
      var wrappingAdvice = function(targetInfo) {
        executionPoints.push('wrappingAdvice - begin');
        targetInfo.fn();
        executionPoints.push('wrappingAdvice - end');
      };
      Aop.around('targetFn', wrappingAdvice, targetObj);
      targetObj.targetFn();
      expect(executionPoints).toEqual(
        ['wrappingAdvice - begin','targetFn','wrappingAdvice - end']);
    });
  });
});
```

You could make a new target object for the new test, edit-copying from the first, but it might occur to you that one target could work for both tests. As you saw earlier in this chapter, you can refactor the target object up to the scope of the outer describe, where it is available to all tests. This small exertion will be amply repaid in future tests.

Because your tests will modify the target, you would re-initialize the target in a beforeEach that gets executed ahead of each test, as you can see in Listing 2-29.

This fails because the current implementation of Aop.around makes no effort at all to supply an object with an fn property that holds the target function. So, you add the new feature shown in Listing 2-30.

LISTING 2-30: The aspect calls the target (code filename: AOP\Aop_02.js)

```javascript
Aop = {
  around: function(fnName, advice, fnObj) {
    var originalFn = fnObj[fnName];
```

```
    fnObj[fnName] = function () {
      var targetContext = {}; // We know this is wrong; return to it later.
      advice.call(targetContext, {fn:originalFn});
    };
  }
};
```

There are two things worth noting here. First, the `call` method. It is similar to `Invoke` in C# or Java. It calls the function (*advice* in this case) with the arguments given starting in the second parameter (just {fn: originalFn} here, but more could have been added). Its first parameter is the context in which the function should be called (its "*this*"). The context is important, but you have not yet written any test about it so you just use an empty object as a placeholder.

`Call` has a sister, `apply`, which expects the arguments to be in an array. If you want to write elegant JavaScript, you'll want to make `call` and `apply` second nature.

Second, notice how the original function is captured in a variable, *originalFn*. Its value is set when `Aop.around` is called. That's no surprise. The subtle marvel is that its value is still available to *fnObj[fnName]* after `Aop.around` has returned. (A C# or Java programmer might think that because *originalFn* is a local variable whose scope has exited, it, too, would have exited the stage.) This is an example of *closure*, another JavaScript feature to know and love if you want to follow in the footsteps of people like Fredrik Appelberg and Dave Clayton.

> **NOTE** *Plodding code, with a limited vocabulary of ideas, tends to be longer. Longer code presents a larger attack surface for errors. To write reliable, elegant code, get to know every corner of the language.*

The `Aop` object is beginning to take shape.

You might suspect that `Aop.around` can wrap a target in multiple layers, but in true TDD fashion you want to be sure, so you add the test in Listing 2-31. Rather than creating two aspects that are nearly identical, you create a factory to produce them. It's a relatively unimportant DRY moment, but these small points of beauty are what make a programmer's day worthwhile, right?

LISTING 2-31: Verifying that aspects can be in multiple layers (code filename: AOP\Aop_02_tests.js)

```
it('can chain, with the last one set up being executed around the others',
function() {
  var adviceFactory = function(adviceID) {
    return (function(targetInfo) {
      executionPoints.push('wrappingAdvice - begin ' + adviceID);
      targetInfo.fn();
      executionPoints.push('wrappingAdvice - end ' + adviceID);
    });
  };
  Aop.around('targetFn',adviceFactory('inner'), targetObj);
```

continues

LISTING 2-31 *(continued)*

```
        Aop.around('targetFn',adviceFactory('outer'), targetObj);
        targetObj.targetFn();
        expect(executionPoints).toEqual([
          'wrappingAdvice - begin outer',
          'wrappingAdvice - begin inner',
          'targetFn',
          'wrappingAdvice - end inner',
          'wrappingAdvice - end outer']);
      });
```

All the tests pass and you are ready for the next feature: passing arguments to the target. So far, the advice doesn't even know about the arguments. If it's going to pass them along, you must provide them. You can just add an *args* property to the *targetInfo* object that the advice gets. *TargetInfo* will now be this shape:

```
    { fn: targetFunction, args: argumentsToPassToTarget }
```

The earlier advices just called the target like this:

```
    targetInfo.fn();
```

but if you want to pass an array of arguments as if they were comma-separated on a call, you must use the `apply` function noted earlier:

```
    targetInfo.fn.apply(this, targetInfo.args);
```

These ideas appear in the new advice, *argPassingAdvice*, shown in Listing 2-32. The *targetObj* has also been enhanced to record the arguments it gets in the *argsToTaget* array. Programmers from other languages might be surprised that the *arguments* object provides the arguments passed to *targetObj* even though *targetObj* does not mention any arguments in its `function()` statement, but that's yet another example of the flexibility of JavaScript.

LISTING 2-32: Testing whether arguments can be passed to the target (code filename: AOP\
Aop_03_tests.js)

```
describe('Aop', function() {
  var argPassingAdvice, // An advice that passes arguments to the target
      argsToTarget;     // Arguments passed to targetObj.targetFn.
  // Other variables omitted for clarity.

  beforeEach(function() {
    targetObj = {
      targetFn: function() {
        executionPoints.push('targetFn');
        argsToTarget = Array.prototype.slice.call(arguments, 0);
      }
    };

    executionPoints = [];

    argPassingAdvice = function(targetInfo) {
```

```
      targetInfo.fn.apply(this, targetInfo.args);
    };

    argsToTarget = [];
  });

  describe('Aop.around(fnName, advice, targetObj)', function() {
    it('allows the advice to pass the normal arguments to the target',
    function() {
      Aop.around('targetFn', argPassingAdvice, targetObj);
      targetObj.targetFn('a', 'b');
      expect(argsToTarget).toEqual(['a','b']);
    });
  });

  });
```

When you run the test, it fails (Figure 2-8).

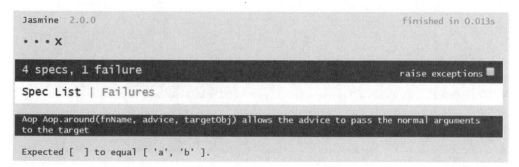

FIGURE 2-8

Each failure makes the test-driven developer happy because it means he gets to write more code. In this case, all you have to do is add *args: arguments* to the object passed to the advice (Listing 2-33).

LISTING 2-33: Passing arguments to the target (code filename: AOP\Aop_03.js)

```
Aop = {
  around: function(fnName, advice, fnObj) {
    var originalFn = fnObj[fnName];
    fnObj[fnName] = function () {
      var targetContext = {}; // Wrong; return to it later.
      advice.call(targetContext,{fn:originalFn, args:arguments});
    };
  }
};
```

Traditional developers may think in terms of tests that cover entire functions. You just saw an example of a test that covered one property, in one object, that was used in one line of code. Furthermore, that fraction of a fraction of a line of code was not even there before the test was written. This is test-driven development at its best. You are about to see another example.

You have just considered what goes into the target function; what about the return value that comes out of it? You want an advice to be able to pass that value back to the outside world if appropriate.

For that purpose, you add a `return` statement to your `targetObj.targetFn`. You can also make the `argPassingAdvice` return the value from its call to the target. None of the tests so far have counted on anything about return values, so they still pass, but what about the subject under test? Will it pass? Listing 2-34 shows a test that finds out. (Not shown: `targetObj.targetFn` has been changed to return a new variable, `targetFnReturn`.)

LISTING 2-34: Testing the return value (code filename: AOP\Aop_04_tests.js)

```
it("makes the target's return value available to the advice", function() {
  Aop.around('targetFn', argPassingAdvice, targetObj);
  var returnedValue = targetObj.targetFn();
  expect(returnedValue).toBe(targetFnReturn);
});
```

Another failure (Figure 2-9).

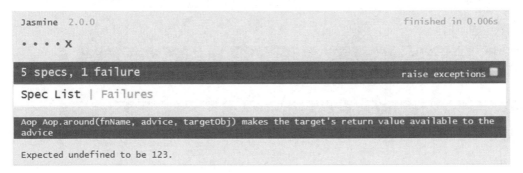

FIGURE 2-9

Because you have expected such a small increment of functionality, it is easy to add: just a `return` keyword in `Aop.around`, as in Listing 2-35.

LISTING 2-35: The aspect returns the value from its target (code filename: AOP\Aop_04.js)

```
Aop = {
  around: function(fnName, advice, fnObj) {
    var originalFn = fnObj[fnName];
    fnObj[fnName] = function () {
      var targetContext = {}; // Wrong; return to it later.
      return advice.call(targetContext, {fn:originalFn, args:arguments});
    };
  }
};
```

The target is now wrapped, it gets the expected arguments, and you can obtain its return value. There is only one more thing to consider. In JavaScript, it's all too easy to execute a function in a context it does not expect.

> **NOTE** *Because JavaScript functions can easily execute on objects that are not their original home, don't forget to test for proper context where appropriate.*

The tests in Listing 2-36 illustrate this idea.

LISTING 2-36: Testing that the target executes in the right context (code filename: AOP\ Aop_05_tests.js)

```javascript
it('executes the target function in the context of its object',function(){
  var Target = function() {
    var self = this;
    this.targetFn = function() {
      expect(this).toBe(self);
    };
  };
  var targetInstance = new Target();
  var spyOnInstance = spyOn(targetInstance,'targetFn').and.callThrough();
  Aop.around('targetFn',argPassingAdvice,targetInstance);
  targetInstance.targetFn();
  expect(spyOnInstance).toHaveBeenCalled();
});

it('executes the advice in the context of the target', function() {
  var advice = function() {
    expect(this).toBe(targetObj);
  };
  Aop.around('targetFn',advice,targetObj);
  targetObj.targetFn();
});
```

First, within the target function there is an expectation that *this* is the value that pertained when the Target was created with new. However, if the call were to fail completely, expect(*this*) .toBe(*self*) would never execute and the test would seem to pass. To guard against that, the test concludes with an expectation that the function was called.

The second test is similar, but without such caution. Jasmine reports an error. You can fix it by replacing the old *targetContext*, which you had set to an empty object, with *this* (Listing 2-37).

LISTING 2-37: Making the target execute in the right context (code filename: AOP\Aop_05.js)

```javascript
Aop = {
  around: function(fnName, advice, fnObj) {
    var originalFn = fnObj[fnName];
    fnObj[fnName] = function () {
      return advice.call(this, {fn:originalFn, args:arguments});
    };
  }
};
```

The tests pass.

There is one more detail to attend to. In Listing 2-32, the advice had to do this to call the next advice in the chain (or the decorated function, if there were no more advices):

```
return targetInfo.fn.apply(this, targetInfo.args);
```

This is less than ideal. Besides being a lot to type, it exposes the structure of *targetInfo* to consumers of Aop. Wouldn't it be better to encapsulate that in a function? Following Fredrik and Dave, you can make a helper function, Aop.next, which calls the next aspect or target in the chain.

The comments in Listing 2-38 show how each step of development could proceed. Listing 2-39 shows the final suite of tests.

LISTING 2-38: Adding Aop.next (code filename: AOP\Aop_06.js)

```
Aop = {
  around: function(fnName, advice, fnObj) {
    var originalFn = fnObj[fnName];
    fnObj[fnName] = function () {
      return advice.call(this, {fn:originalFn, args:arguments});
    };
  },

  next: function(targetInfo) {
  //This function was built up in these steps, test-by-test:
  //      targetInfo.fn();
  //      targetInfo.fn.apply({}, targetInfo.args);
  //return targetInfo.fn.apply({}, targetInfo.args);
    return targetInfo.fn.apply(this,targetInfo.args);
  }
};
```

LISTING 2-39: Testing Aop.next (code filename: AOP\Aop_06_tests.js)

```
Target = function() {
  var self = this;
  this.targetFn = function() {
    expect(this).toBe(self);
  };
};

/*** Previously discussed code omitted for clarity. ***/

describe('Aop.next(context,targetInfo)', function() {
  var advice = function(targetInfo) {
    return Aop.next.call(this,targetInfo);
  };
  var originalFn;
  beforeEach(function() {
```

```
        originalFn = targetObj.targetFn;
        Aop.around('targetFn',advice, targetObj);
    });
    it('calls the function in targetInfo.fn', function() {
        targetObj.targetFn();
        expect(executionPoints).toEqual(['targetFn']);
    });
    it('passes the arguments in targetInfo.args', function() {
        targetObj.targetFn('a','b');
        expect(argsToTarget).toEqual(['a','b']);
    });
    it("returns the value from targetInfo's function", function() {
        var ret = targetObj.targetFn();
        expect(ret).toEqual(targetFnReturn);
    });
    it('calls the target function in the given context', function() {
        var targetInstance = new Target();
        var spyOnInstance = spyOn(targetInstance,'targetFn').and.callThrough();
        Aop.around('targetFn',advice,targetInstance);
        targetInstance.targetFn();
        expect(spyOnInstance).toHaveBeenCalled();
    });
});
```

The tests pass and we now have a perfectly serviceable AOP component.

Referring back to Listing 2-25, you can probably envision the final step we could take toward Fredrik and Dave's Aop.js masterpiece—namely to allow one call to Aop.around to affect multiple functions. You may have noticed that the parameters to Aop.around in their version were named differently:

```
Aop.around(pointcut, advice, namespaces)
```

Where this chapter's Aop.js has *fnName*, they have *pointcut*. A *pointcut*, in AOP terms, specifies the points at which an aspect may cut in and do its thing. In Aop.js, it is a JavaScript regular expression, so the plain name of a function, as in this chapter, is a special case.

Also, where this chapter's Aop.js has *fnObj*, they have *namespaces*. In JavaScript, a namespace is just an object that contains other objects as properties. To avoid naming collisions, it is a good practice to put all of your application's code in a namespace. You can build hierarchies of namespaces like this:

```
var MyApp = {};

MyApp.Encryption = {};
MyApp.WebServices = {};
MyApp.UI = {};
```

and then you can put your functions in namespaces:

```
MyApp.WebServices.amazon = function () {
  // ...
  getIsbn: function(title, author, pubYear) {
      // ...
  }
};
```

The code developed so far in this chapter would only allow an aspect to be applied to one function, at the last level—for example, `MyApp.WebServices.amazon.getIsbn`. With the full `Aop.js`, we could apply it to every function that starts with "get" in multiple namespaces:

```
Aop.around(/^get/, advice, [ "MyApp.Encryption", "MyApp.WebServices" ]);
```

Even without this enhancement, you have built the heart of `Aop.js` with test-driven development. Incidentally, the final version available in this chapter's downloads, `Aop.js`, also has the `before` aspect and its tests. The test results in Figure 2-10 lay out all that `Aop.js` can do.

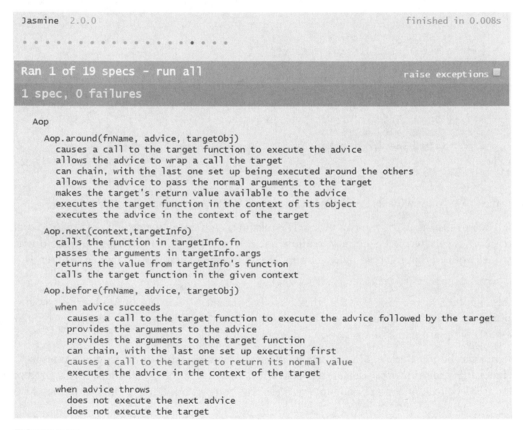

FIGURE 2-10

Other AOP Libraries

Although we like `Aop.js`, there are other choices such as AspectJS, AopJS jQuery plugin, and YUI's Do Class.

AspectJS

With a name like AspectJS, you know this one will rank high in the search listings. It is one of the early entries in the JavaScript AOP sweepstakes, and very full-featured. It has capabilities such as suspending and resuming aspects—features which would be easy enough to add to `Aop.js` if you need them, but which are already in AspectJS. The drawback is that AspectJS is much heavier as a result.

Another huge drawback is that AspectJS does not appear to have been updated since 2008 (`http://aspectjs.com/AJS_Release_History.htm`). JavaScript itself is evolving and you may feel it makes sense to use tools that are keeping up.

AopJS jQuery Plugin

Although the AopJS jQuery plugin is relatively new and does not yet have high stats on GitHub, you will probably run across it just because it's on the jQuery site (`http://plugins.jquery.com/aop`).

AopJS's author has taken the time to provide both jQuery- and AngularJS-friendly syntax options, as well as easy chaining of aspects, as in this example from the documentation.

```
var myProxy = AOP.aspect(myFunction)
                   .before(myAdvice1)
                   .afterReturning(myAdvice2)
                   .afterThrowing(myAdvice3);
```

The code does not have the concise elegance of `Aop.js`, but its capabilities are just a little more developed.

YUI's Do Class

The folks at Yahoo!'s YUI project really know what they're doing. One component of YUI is the `Do` class. It is very well documented at `http://yuilibrary.com/yui/docs/api/classes/Do.html`. `Y.Do` (Y is the namespace) is wonderful except for one thing: In August of 2014 Yahoo! announced that it was ceasing development of YUI.

Conclusion

Perhaps because AOP is so easy to implement in JavaScript, there aren't many toolkits for it. It's just not that big a problem. It seems that the heavyweight libraries have ceased development, leaving the minimalist alternatives that may never need updating.

In that world, it's hard not to be drawn to Fredrik Appelberg and Dave Clayton's `Aop.js`. Any module that does so much with only 50 lines of code including blanks and comments deserves to be not only adopted but loved.

For the remainder of this book, when we need AOP, we will use `Aop.js`.

USING A CODE-CHECKING TOOL

Code-checking tools perform static analysis, whereby they inspect the syntax and structure of source code without executing it. The purpose of the inspection is to find and report likely incorrect language usage that may lead to errors when the code is executed. Some static analysis tools also report deviations from coding style rules, and useful metrics like computational complexity.

These types of tools are generally referred to as linters to reflect their relation to the C programming language static code analysis tool, `lint`, which was developed in the late 1970s.

Throughout this section, we'll refer to static analysis tools as linters, and the process of performing static analysis as linting.

Making Your Code More Reliable with Linting Tools

Linting serves an important purpose when programming in JavaScript. If you're a developer coming from a compiled language like C# or Java, you're accustomed to the compiler informing you of grievous syntax errors such as omitting a statement-terminating semicolon or forgetting a closing curly brace. As an interpreted language, JavaScript doesn't have a compiler that complains when you've made a mistake. You won't be aware of any syntax errors until the code is executed.

Since you have adopted TDD, you will have a test to exercise every bit of production code before you even write it, right? When practicing TDD, it may be enticing to skip the configuration and use of a linter because the unit tests guarantee that your code is functioning as it should.

Linters do not verify that code is correct. Your linter can't tell you if the function you've written will return the correct value. It can tell you, however, that you've written code within your function that has a questionable format and may cause it to return an incorrect value.

Suppose you've been tasked with building an airline reservation system. The customer has requested that you implement functionality that will determine whether a particular passenger is eligible for a complimentary upgrade to a first class seat.

In order to be upgraded, a passenger needs to have flown a certain number of miles on the airline. For the purpose of this example, assume that a `passenger` object contains the passenger's first and last names, and an array integer trip lengths. Here's what a `passenger` would look like when created with the object-literal creation pattern:

```
var testPassenger = {
  firstName: "Seth",
  lastName: "Richards",
  tripMileages: [
    500,
    600,
    3400,
    2500
  ]
};
```

When calculating the miles a particular passenger has flown, you want to be able to reward members of the airline's frequent flier program. To do so, you'll provide a multiplier that will increase the mileage of each member's flight to reward the passenger for his or her loyalty.

As the first step, you might create a function that will scale trip mileage by a multiplier. In test-driven fashion, Listing 2-40 shows unit tests that verify that the function behaves as expected.

LISTING 2-40: Unit tests for calculateUpgradeMilages (code filename: Linting\Linting_01_tests.js)

```javascript
describe('calculateUpgradeMileages(tripMileages, memberMultiplier', function(){
  var testPassenger = null;

  beforeEach(function(){
    testPassenger = {
      firstName : 'Seth',
      lastName : 'Richards',
      tripMileages : [
        500,
        600,
        3400,
        2500
      ]
    };
  });

  it('returns original mileages when multiplier is 1.0', function(){
    expect(calculateUpgradeMileages(testPassenger.tripMileages, 1.0))
      .toEqual(testPassenger.tripMileages);
  });

  it('returns expected mileages when the memberMultiplier is 3.0', function(){
    var expectedResults = [], multiplier = 3.0;

    for(var i = 0; i<testPassenger.tripMileages.length; i++){
      expectedResults[i] = testPassenger.tripMileages[i] * multiplier;
    }

    expect(calculateUpgradeMileages(testPassenger.tripMileages, multiplier))
      .toEqual(expectedResults);
  });
});
```

Listing 2-41 shows an implementation of calculateUpgradeMileages that causes the unit tests to pass.

LISTING 2-41: Implementation of calculateUpgradeMileages (code filename: Linting\Linting_01.js)

```javascript
function calculateUpgradeMileages(tripMileages, memberMultiplier) {
  var upgradeMileage = [],
    i = 0;
  for (i = 0; i < tripMileages.length; i++) {
    var calcRewardsMiles = function(mileage) {
      return mileage * memberMultiplier;
    };
    upgradeMileage[i] = calcRewardsMiles(tripMileages[i]);
  }
  return upgradeMileage;
}
```

Finally, Figure 2-11 shows the Jasmine output of the unit tests.

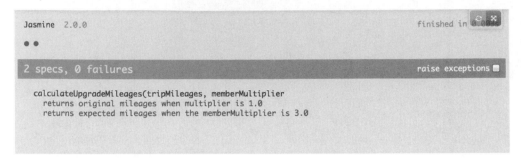

FIGURE 2-11

As you can see, the function returns the expected result and the tests pass. There is a potential problem in the code, however. Take a moment and see if you can identify the section of code in `calculateUpgradeMileages` that is troublesome. If it's not immediately apparent to you, fear not because you have your linting tool to help.

Introducing JSHint

JSHint is an open-source static analysis tool that describes itself in the following way:

> *JSHint is a community-driven tool to detect errors and potential problems in JavaScript code and to enforce your team's coding conventions.*

> `http://www.jshint.com/about`

JSHint is a fork of the JSLint project. JSLint was created and is maintained by Douglas Crockford. At the time they forked JSHint from JSLint, JSHint's creators felt that JSLint had become "too opinionated" and that a linting tool driven by the JavaScript community was needed.

Using JSHint

You can copy-and-paste your JavaScript code into the JSHint homepage at `http://www.jshint.com` and the linter will execute automatically. While perhaps convenient for identifying a problem in a piece of sample code for a blog post (or book), using this mechanism to execute the linter is not suitable for development of a JavaScript solution with even limited complexity.

Because the `calculateUpgradeMileages` function is a piece of sample code for a book, you can use the online tool at `http://www.jshint.com` to find the questionable construct in the function.

Figure 2-12 shows what JSHint says about `calculateUpgradeMileages`.

As you can see, JSHint provides the following warning:

```
Don't make functions within a loop.
```

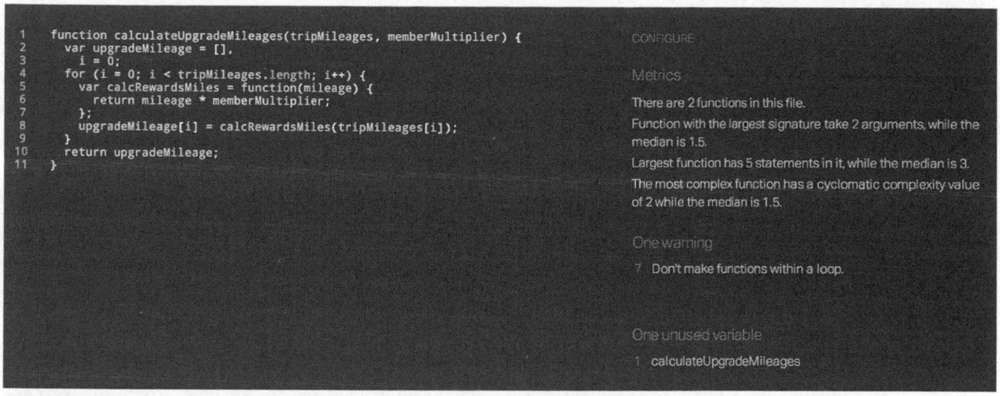

FIGURE 2-12

If you hadn't noticed it before, JSHint is helpfully pointing out that you've declared a function within the loop that iterates over the list of mileages. Your unit tests pass, so in this case creation of a function inside a loop doesn't result in a logic error. So what's the problem?

Remember that JSHint identifies questionable constructs in JavaScript code. We can certainly agree that whether the result is logically correct or not, re-declaring a function during each iteration of a loop is questionable. At a minimum, it's inefficient, and even though it didn't in this example, it's easy for the practice to result in incorrect and unreliable code.

> **NOTE** *See the JSHint documentation at* (`http://www.jshint.com/docs/options/#loopfunc`) *for the "Don't make functions in a loop" warning for an excellent example that leads to logically incorrect code.*

Assume for a moment that you have a very good reason for placing your function within the loop. Each time you execute JSHint on your code, which should be very often, it will present that warning. Do you have to somehow make note that you (and the rest of the developers on your team) can safely ignore that particular warning for that particular line?

Thankfully, the answer is no. JSHint provides the ability to "relax" its rules globally via configuration, or locally via specially formatted comments.

Listing 2-42 shows the function again, this time with a comment that tells JSHint that you're aware you're creating a function inside a loop, and you'd like to relax the `loopfunc` rule:

LISTING 2-42: Implementation of calculateUpgradeMileages, which disables loopfunc checking (code filename: Linting\Linting_02.js)

```
function calculateUpgradeMileages(tripMileages, memberMultiplier) {
  var upgradeMileage = [],
```

continues

LISTING 2-42 *(continued)*

```
      i = 0;
   for (i = 0; i < tripMileages.length; i++) {
     /*jshint loopfunc: true */
     var calcRewardsMiles = function(mileage) {
       return mileage * memberMultiplier;
     };
     /*jshint loopfunc: false */
     upgradeMileage[i] = calcRewardsMiles(tripMileages[i]);
   }
   return upgradeMileage;
 }
```

The comment /*jshint loopfunc: true */, which precedes creation of the function, tells JSHint to relax its loopfunc rule until it encounters another comment that tells it to stop relaxing the rule. The comment that causes the rule to no longer be relaxed, /*jshint loopfunc: false*/, appears right after the function declaration.

Providing the updated code that relaxes the loopfunc rule to the JSHint website yields the results shown in Figure 2-13.

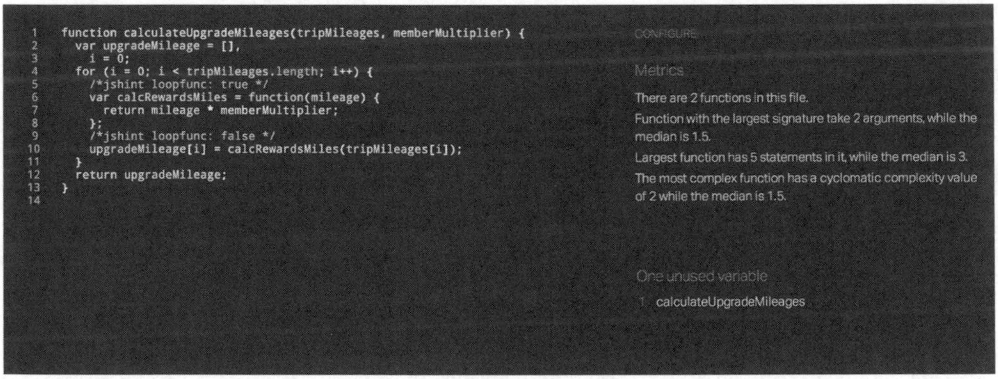

FIGURE 2-13

As you can see, JSHint makes note that you've relaxed the loopfunc rule and no longer warns about creation of a function within a loop.

In this example, you've disabled a single rule for the minimum number of lines necessary. It is possible to tell JSHint not to process any rules for a section of code. We recommend that this not be done unless absolutely necessary. If you'd suppressed the warning you were receiving by disabling all rules, it's easy to imagine how a colleague maintaining or extending your code at some point in the future could be deprived of helpful linting warnings.

> **NOTE** *The JSHint website provides full documentation for its multitude of configuration options at* http://www.jshint.com/docs/options.

If You Don't Run It, Bugs Will Come

Ideally, JSHint should be executed automatically any time you've made changes to your JavaScript code. Any manual mechanism could result in forgetting to run, or purposely not running, the linting tool. Linting is not something to be left to the end of a project, or even to the next build (your project has a repeatable, automated build process, right?). Your linter should provide continuous feedback as you're developing so that the code issues it identifies are addressed as early as possible.

JSHint is distributed in multiple ways, including an npm module for use with the server-side JavaScript engine node.js. There are also plugins to automatically execute JSHint natively or via node.js on your JavaScript files for many popular text editors and integrated development environments (IDEs), such as VIM, Emacs, Sublime Text, TextMate, and Visual Studio.

If your favorite editor or IDE doesn't have a JSHint plugin available, node.js task-execution packages such as Grunt and Gulp may be configured to watch for changes in your JavaScript files and automatically execute JSHint when a change is detected.

> ### TESTS ARE CODE, TOO
>
> It's important to note that JSHint should be executed against your unit tests as well as your application code. The linter is your first line of defense against potential errors in your unit tests that may lead to false results.

Alternatives to JSHint

JSHint is not the only JavaScript linting tool; it just happens to be the tool that provides the functionality that we require. Here are some alternatives to JSHint that you might want to consider if you're choosing a linting tool for your project.

JSLint

JSLint is a mature JavaScript linting tool that was created and is maintained by Douglas Crockford. Mr. Crockford is a key figure in the JavaScript community, known for both his work on JSLint and his work to popularize JSON.

JSLint is available as an npm module for node.js, as well as a JavaScript file for use in browser-like environments.

The JSLint homepage can be found at http://www.jslint.com.

ESLint

ESLint is a relatively new open-source linting tool created by Nicholas Zakas in 2013. Even though it is a young project, it is full-featured and very capable. A feature unique to ESLint is its modularity. You may define your own custom linting rules and load them into the linter at run time. This is very useful if you would like to enforce a coding standard unique to your organization.

ESLint is available as an npm module for node.js. The ESLint homepage can be found at http:// www.eslint.org.

Strict Mode

One more code-checking tool merits attention. Actually, it's not an external tool, but a JavaScript setting that was introduced with ECMAScript 5. If you include the following in a scope (either the global scope or a function), the JavaScript interpreter will process certain features differently.

```
'use strict';
```

With this directive in place, JavaScript will throw an error if you commit some common mistakes. These include using a variable without declaring it first, attempting to modify a read-only property, naming a variable with the reserved word arguments, and more.

When running on versions of JavaScript that do not support strict mode, the 'use strict' string will have no effect.

You will see an example of where strict mode can make a crucial difference in the "Default Binding and Strict Mode" section of Chapter 18. In the meantime, the listings in this book will use it just to get in the habit.

SUMMARY

In this chapter, we introduced some of our favorite techniques and tools for JavaScript development.

A unit-testing framework is absolutely essential for reliable software development. In this text, we will use Jasmine, which we have found easy to learn and very robust, but popular alternatives include QUnit and D.O.H.

As JavaScript applications become more complex, it becomes more important to keep their components clean and separate. Dependency injection is an important technique for doing just that. In this chapter, you worked through the test-driven development of a dependency-injection framework that will reappear in future chapters and may be useful in your own projects.

As another case study in TDD, you developed a toolkit for aspect-oriented programming. AOP allows you to enhance software components with common functionality such as caching, without changing those components at all. It's another way to simultaneously keep your code DRY, fulfill the Single Responsibility Principle, and adhere to the Open/Closed Principle.

Code-checking tools, known as linters, promote reliability at the micro level by alerting you to syntax mistakes or violations of standards. JSHint, JSLint, and ESLint are some of the most popular. Strict mode is another good way to avoid mistakes at the syntax level.

In the next chapter, you will explore the rich variety of ways in which JavaScript can construct objects. It sounds like a simple topic, but you will see that it is anything but.

3

Constructing Reliable Objects

WHAT'S IN THIS CHAPTER?

➤ Creating data as primitives, object literals, and modules

➤ Creating data with the new keyword

➤ Using methods of object creation to produce reliable objects

➤ Controlling inheritance using prototypal, classical, and functional patterns

➤ Using monkey-patching responsibly

WROX.COM CODE DOWNLOADS FOR THIS CHAPTER

The wrox.com code downloads for this chapter are found at www.wrox.com/go/ reliablejavascript on the Download Code tab.

Developers love dazzling effects in the user interface, elegant algorithms, and well-designed APIs, but often give little regard to the humble act of instantiating an object. JavaScript offers an unusually varied assortment of choices for doing just that. Some of them will make your code reliable, testable, and extensible; others represent the easy road to perdition.

This chapter surveys the most common ways to create an object, considering how well each one meets the SOLID and DRY criteria for reliability and testability introduced in Chapter 1.

Let's start with the most basic and build our way up.

USING PRIMITIVES

When we are hiring developers, we always ask candidates, "What are the primitive data types in JavaScript?" The most common answer is, "Just one: var." The next-most-common response is the opposite: to take a deep breath and rattle off enough types to fill a C# manual. Neither answer is correct.

JavaScript has exactly five primitive data types: String, Number, Boolean, Null, and Undefined. The language will coerce one type to another as needed, in famously surprising ways, but those five are it, at least in ECMAScript 5. (ECMAScript 6 adds the Symbol type. The `Object` type is not a primitive.)

A primitive has a value, but no properties, but the following code will run without error.

```
var str = "abcde";
console.log(str.length); // Output: 5
```

If *str* does not have a `length` property, how can this work? When the interpreter encounters `str.length`, it says, "Hmm . . . Looks like he's trying to work with an *object*. Let me make one for him." A `String` object is constructed from *str* and *its* `length` is reported. As quickly as the `String` was constructed, it is garbage-collected.

String, Boolean, and Number all have corresponding object wrappers, `String(value)`, `Boolean(value)` and `Number(value)`.

WETness (Write Everything Twice or We Enjoy Typing) can find its way into your code without your notice. Suppose you have a variable that represents the mass of an animal, in kilograms. You collect a value from the user and then do this:

```
if (inputMass < 0) {
  // Give an error that mass may not be negative
} else if (inputMass > 150000) {
  // Error: Even a blue whale is not that massive.
}
```

Then, in another part of your application, you do the same thing. Your code is no longer DRY, but what else could you do? You can't install range validation on a primitive. One way to solve this problem is to promote your datum from primitive to object. The object could have range validation and other features not available in primitives. We are not suggesting that every primitive should be an object, but it's something to consider on a case-by-case basis.

Another common problem is the repeated primitive. It's so much easier to type a value the second time than to put it in a variable and reference the variable everywhere. Turn away from the easy path! With rare exceptions, every constant that is referenced more than once should be put in a variable, and the variable referenced instead. Another approach is to inject it as a dependency. In addition to keeping your code DRY, either approach will make it easier to find all the places that use the value.

Table 3-1 summarizes how well primitives fare with SOLID and DRY principles.

TABLE 3-1: SOLID and DRY Summary for Primitives

PRINCIPLE	RESULT
Single Responsibility	You can't be more single-minded than a primitive!
Open/Closed	Open for extension? Not really. Closed for modification? Definitely. In fact, primitives are immutable
Liskov Substitution	Not applicable

Interface Segregation	Sorry; you can't implement an interface on a primitive, even though you might like to sometimes.
Dependency Inversion	Primitives have no dependencies.
Don't Repeat Yourself	Extreme temptation here!

USING OBJECT LITERALS

Next up the ladder from primitives are object literals—objects that are declared thus:

```
{ name: 'Koko', genus: 'gorilla', genius: 'sign language' }
```

It's helpful to distinguish between two ways of creating object literals. There are bare object literals:

```
var koko = { name: 'Koko', genus: 'gorilla', genius: 'sign language' };
```

and there are literals that are return values from functions:

```
var amazeTheWorld = function() {
  // . . .
  return { name: 'Koko', genus: 'gorilla', genius: 'sign language' };
}

var koko = amazeTheWorld();
```

The distinction is important because one is more DRY than the other. If you create multiple object literals that are supposed to have the same properties, you must repeat the property names. It's easy to get one wrong. Test-driven development can ensure that we return an object with the expected properties from a function, but there's no way to directly test a bare object literal that is buried in code.

Object literals may also have properties that are functions. Once again, if the literal is not created in a controlled manner, such as being returned from a function, there is no way to test these functions.

Unless an object literal is assigned to a variable (such as the Aop object you met in Chapter 2), it is problematic to address with aspect-oriented programming. An aspect needs a pointcut to which it applies (e.g, the name of a variable), but an object literal has no name. However, if an object literal is produced by a factory function, then that function could be wrapped in an "after" aspect that would tinker with the returned literal.

As for dependency injection, the opportunity simply does not arise in the case of bare object literals. A function that creates and returns a literal, however, may be perfectly available to the dependency-injection procedure that, as suggested in Chapter 2, should be in the startup code of the application.

A final weakness of bare object literals is that there is no validation in their construction. Formal constructors can do all sorts of validation on their arguments and guarantee a valid result. There are no such checks as you're slapping together a bare object literal.

For these reasons, we suggest that object literals not comprise important parts of the application, unless they are singletons or are created by well-tested code.

A good use of object literals is to pass a bundle of data from one place to another. For example, in *JavaScript: The Good Parts* (O'Reilly Media, 2008), Douglas Crockford suggests using an object literal rather than a long list of function arguments whose order might be difficult to get right. Furthermore, he points out, the absence of a property in the literal can be the signal to use a default value.

This can be very handy, but beware: You are putting a large testing burden on yourself if your function must be prepared for any combination of properties. You might consider using an object that has well-controlled and well-tested ways of construction, and maybe even an `isValid()` method.

Table 3-2 summarizes the SOLID and DRY aspects of object literals.

TABLE 3-2: SOLID and DRY Summary for Object Literals

PRINCIPLE	RESULT
Single Responsibility	In practice, bare object literals tend to be small enough that they don't get into trouble on this score. Larger ones that comprise the APIs of modules (see the next section) bear whatever responsibilities the module takes on.
Open/Closed	The ethos of object literals seems to invite unmanaged extensions. Beware!
Liskov Substitution	Not applicable
Interface Segregation	See the Module Pattern in the next section and monkey-patching in the final section of this chapter.
Dependency Inversion	Bare object literals fail here because they have no constructor in which to inject dependencies.
Don't **R**epeat **Y**ourself	Unless they are singletons, bare object literals will cause WET code. A big warning here!

USING THE MODULE PATTERN

The Module Pattern is one of the most venerable in JavaScript. It employs a function whose main purpose is data-hiding, and which returns an object that comprises the module's API. Modules come in two flavors: those that you can construct at will by calling a function, and those that are based on a function that executes as soon as it is declared.

Creating Modules-at-Will

Listing 3-1 is an example of a module that you can create whenever you want. Just call the module's function and get your API back.

LISTING 3-1: An example of the module-at-will pattern

```
// A global object that serves as a namespace, collecting
// all the objects (modules) that are to be available
// throughout the application.
var MyApp = MyApp || {};

// A module under the application's namespace.
// The function depends on another function, animalMaker, which can
// be injected.
MyApp.wildlifePreserveSimulator = function(animalMaker) {
  // Private variables
  var animals = [];

  // Return the API
  return {
    addAnimal: function(species, sex) {
      animals.push(animalMaker.make(species,sex));
    },
    getAnimalCount: function() {
      return animals.length;
    }
  };
};
```

You would use the module like this:

```
var preserve = MyApp.wildlifePreserveSimulator(realAnimalMaker);
preserve.addAnimal(gorilla, female);
```

Although the module returns an object literal, dependencies such as *animalMaker* can be injected into the outer function and find their way down to the literal.

Because modules can be injected into other modules, they are easy to extend. You inject the old version into the new, which wraps, exposes, and extends it as required. If the open/closed principle from Chapter 1 appeals to you, modules are ideal.

Aspects (see Chapter 2) may be applied to the returned object by first installing an "after" advice on `MyApp.wildlifePreserveSimulator`. This advice will get hold of the returned literal and modify it with further aspects as required.

Creating Immediate-Execution Modules

Often, the outer function is executed as soon as it is declared, returning the API just as the module-at-will did. The returned API is assigned to a namespaced global variable, which then becomes the singleton instance of the module. Listing 3-2 modifies Listing 3-1 in that way.

LISTING 3-2: A singleton module

```
var MyApp = MyApp || {};

MyApp.WildlifePreserveSimulator = (function() {
```

continues

LISTING 3-2 *(continued)*

```
    var animals = [];

    return {
      addAnimal: function(animalMaker,species, sex) {
        animals.push(animalMaker.make(species,sex));
      },
      getAnimalCount: function() {
        return animals.length;
      }
    };
}()); // <-Immediate execution!
```

The singleton can be used in code like this:

```
MyApp.WildlifePreserveSimulator.addAnimal(realAnimalMaker, gorilla, female);
```

The outer function executes right where you see it, not when invoked by the application's startup code. For this reason, its dependencies cannot be injected into the outer function unless they happen to be available as the function (immediately) executes. This is a little inconvenient. If you want a singleton, a more dependency-injection-friendly approach is to code the module with the module-at-will pattern and let the dependency-injection framework furnish the same instance each time it is requested. This is how AngularJS provides "service" singletons, for example.

Creating Reliable Modules

Whether your module is the at-will or immediate type, there are a few principles you'll want to keep in mind.

First, remember the Single Responsibility principle: Each module should have just one job. This will keep your APIs small, cohesive and manageable.

Second, if your module creates objects for its own use, ask yourself whether those objects ought to be provided by dependency injection—either directly or by injecting a factory.

Finally, if your module extends the behavior of another object, be sure not to change what the behavior *means* (its semantics). This is the Liskov Substitution principle

Table 3-3 is the SOLID and DRY scorecard for the Module Pattern.

TABLE 3-3: SOLID and DRY Summary for Modules

PRINCIPLE	RESULT
Single Responsibility	Because they are friendly to dependency injection and aspect-oriented decoration, it is easy to keep modules to a single responsibility.
Open/Closed	Modules are open to extension by being injected into other modules. Modules can be kept closed for modification if you're disciplined.
Liskov Substitution	As long as you don't change the semantics of any dependencies, you'll be okay.
Interface Segregation	A module with a cohesive API is JavaScript's equivalent of a segregated interface.

| Dependency Inversion | Modules-at-will can be injected with dependencies very easily. Either type of module can be injected into others. |
| Don't Repeat Yourself | Done right, modules are a very good way to keep your code DRY. |

USING OBJECT PROTOTYPES AND PROTOTYPAL INHERITANCE

Each and every object in JavaScript, regardless of the mechanism used to create it, has a linked prototype object from which it inherits properties. In this section, you learn about object prototypes and the basics of prototypal inheritance.

The Default Object Prototype

Object literals, familiar from a previous section, are automatically linked to the built-in `Object.prototype` object. Consider the `chimp` object defined thus:

```
var chimp = {
  hasThumbs: true,
  swing: function(){
    return 'swinging through the tree tops';
  }
};
```

The `chimp` object doesn't define a `toString` function, but executing

```
chimp.toString();
```

does not result in an undefined function error. In fact, it outputs a string representation of the `chimp` object (`'[object Object]'`, which isn't very descriptive).

When `chimp.toString()` is invoked, JavaScript examines the `chimp` object and determines that it doesn't directly define a `toString` function property. Next, it looks at *chimp*'s prototype, `Object.prototype`, which *does* define a `toString` function property. The found function is then executed and its value returned.

> **NOTE** `Object.prototype` *defines many useful functions. A complete list is available at* `https://developer.mozilla.org/en-US/docs/Web/JavaScript/Reference/Global_Objects/Object/prototype`.

If `chimp` defines its own `toString` function:

```
var chimp = {
  hasThumbs: true,
  swing: function(){
    return 'swinging';
  },
  toString: function(){
    return 'I am the chimpanzee';
  }
};
```

then JavaScript will immediately find chimp's toString implementation and execute it, yielding 'I am the chimpanzee'; chimp's prototype will not be examined.

Prototypal Inheritance

Even though Object.prototype has some useful properties, the power of JavaScript's prototypal inheritance comes from being able to replace that default prototype with a custom one. Assume that in addition to the chimp object, you also would like to create a bonobo object. Because they're related in the animal kingdom, you know the chimp object and the bonobo object will have many common properties.

To reduce the repetition of properties between the objects, you can create an object, named ape, which holds these common properties. You can then create chimp and bonobo objects that are linked to ape; this makes ape a *shared prototype*.

ECMAScript 5 provides the Object.create method, which handles creation of a new object linked to a provided prototype. The following snippet illustrates the use of Object.create to construct chimp and bonobo objects that have ape as a shared prototype:

```
var ape = {
  hasThumbs : true,
  hasTail: false,
  swing : function(){
    return 'swinging';
  }
};

var chimp = Object.create(ape);

var bonobo = Object.create(ape);
bonobo.habitat = 'Central Africa';

console.log(bonobo.habitat);    // 'Central Africa' (from bonobo)
console.log(bonobo.hasTail);    // false (from ape prototype)

console.log(chimp.swing());     // 'swinging' (from ape prototype)
```

As you can see, both bonobo and chimp inherit properties from ape. You should also note that bonobo has had the habitat property added directly to it; this property is shared with neither ape nor chimp.

Because ape is a shared prototype, any change to it will be reflected in both chimp and bonobo:

```
ape.hasThumbs = false;
console.log(chimp.hasThumbs);    // false
console.log(bonobo.hasThumbs);   // false
```

Prototype Chains

You may use multiple levels of prototypes, called *prototype chains*, to create multiple levels of inheritance. For example, suppose that ape has a prototype of primate, and then ape is used as the prototype of chimp:

```
var primate = {
  stereoscopicVision: true
```

```
};

var ape = Object.create(primate);
ape.hasThumbs = true;
ape.hasTail = false;
ape.swing = function(){
  return "swinging";
};

var chimp = Object.create(ape);

console.log(chimp.hasTail);          // false (from ape prototype)
console.log(chimp.stereoscopicVision); // true (from primate prototype)
```

To access `chimp.stereoscopicVision`, when it's not found directly on the `chimp` object, the JavaScript interpreter must traverse `chimp`'s prototype chain to `ape`, and then finally to `primate` where the property is found. If a property is accessed that does not exist anywhere in an object's prototype chain, `undefined` is returned.

Traversing deep prototype chains can cause poor performance, so we recommend keeping them as shallow as possible.

CREATING OBJECTS WITH NEW

In this section, you learn about the `new` object creation pattern in JavaScript and examine some of the pattern's benefits and pitfalls. You also see how use of the pattern will help keep your code SOLID and DRY.

The new Object Creation Pattern

The `new` object creation pattern's syntax in JavaScript is similar to the syntax used by the same pattern in classical languages C#, C++, or Java.

> **NOTE** *We use the term "classical" in the sense that the languages make use of* classes, *constructs that allow for the definition of custom types. Classical does not imply age as it does when referring to ancient Greek or Latin (though C++ is older than one of the authors of this book!).*

Listing 3-3 shows the `Marsupial` function, and it also shows the creation of instances of a `Marsupial` object using the `new` object creation pattern.

LISTING 3-3: The Marsupial function and its use as a constructor function (code filename: New Pattern\newpattern_01.js)

```
function Marsupial(name, nocturnal){
  this.name = name;
  this.isNocturnal = nocturnal;
```

continues

LISTING 3-3 *(continued)*

```
  }

  var maverick = new Marsupial('Maverick', true);
  var slider = new Marsupial('Slider', false);

  console.log(maverick.isNocturnal);  // true
  console.log(maverick.name);         // "Maverick"

  console.log(slider.isNocturnal);    // false
  console.log(slider.name);           // "Slider"
```

Within the `Marsupial` function, the arguments provided are assigned to properties of the instance being created. The lines that follow the definition of the `Marsupial` function show that the two instances of `Marsupial` created, `maverick` and `slider`, do have unique properties.

Potential for Bad Things to Happen

You should notice that there's nothing provided by the language that indicates that the `Marsupial` function should be used as a *constructor function*, (a function that has been written for use with the `new` keyword). Nor does JavaScript provide built-in protection if constructor functions are not executed with the `new` keyword. For this reason, most developers distinguish constructor functions by using PascalCase.

The potential for "bad things" to happen because of the omission of the `new` keyword when invoking a constructor function led Douglas Crockford to recommend that constructor functions not be used. (See *JavaScript: The Good Parts* by Douglas Crockford, O'Reilly Media, 2008.)

We're not so quick to dismiss use of constructor functions because they do allow for shared initialization code, and it isn't difficult to ensure `new` is used when it is required.

Enforcing the Use of new

While JavaScript doesn't do anything to enforce the use of `new` with constructor functions, adding such enforcement is an easy exercise in leveraging the `instanceof` operator. Listing 3-4 shows how to rewrite the `Marsupial` constructor function from Listing 3-3 to ensure that the function is executed with the `new` keyword.

LISTING 3-4: Enforcing use of new with instanceof (code filename: New Pattern\ newpattern_02.js)

```
  function Marsupial(name, nocturnal){
    if(!(this instanceof Marsupial)){
      throw new Error("This object must be created with new");
    }
    this.name = name;
    this.isNocturnal = nocturnal;
  }

  var slider = Marsupial('Slider', true);
```

HOW DOES *INSTANCEOF* WORK?

Listings 3-4 and 3-5 rely on `this instanceof Marsupial` returning `false`. The JavaScript `instanceof` operator inspects the prototype chain of the left-side operand, seeking the prototype of the right-side operand. If the right-side operand's prototype is found, the left-side operand is considered to be an instance of the right-side operand.

When a constructor function is executed with the `new` keyword, JavaScript creates a new empty object, links the new object's prototype to the `prototype` property of the constructor function, and executes the constructor function with `this` being the new object.

When `new` is omitted, none of those automatic steps occur. The constructor function is not bound to a new object when executed; in Listings 3-4 and 3-5 it is bound to the global object. Additionally, the `prototype` assignment doesn't occur, and thus `instanceof` returns false.

Figure 3-1 shows the error that is output to the console when
`var slider = Marsupial('Slider', true)` is executed.

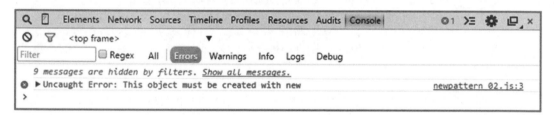

FIGURE 3-1

An alternative to throwing an error when `new` is not used is to automatically create an instance of an object using new and return that instead, as shown in Listing 3-5.

LISTING 3-5: Automatically create an instance with new (code filename: New Pattern\ newpattern_03.js)

```
function Marsupial(name, nocturnal){
  if(!(this instanceof Marsupial)){
    return new Marsupial(name, nocturnal);
  }
  this.name = name;
  this.isNocturnal = nocturnal;
}

var slider = Marsupial('Slider', true);

console.log(slider.name);  // 'Slider'
```

Listing 3-5 executes the `Marsupial` function without using `new`, but instead of throwing an error as in Listing 3-4, a `Marsupial` is created with the `new` keyword and returned. Using this mechanism, the programmer calling the function need not worry about whether Marsupial should be invoked with the new keyword; new is automatically used if it has been omitted.

On the surface, the automatic use of the new keyword seems helpful, but really all it does is allow the programmer to get away with mistakes. Consider the following:

```
var jester = Marsupial('Jester', false);
var merlin = new Marsupial('Merlin', false);
```

Both invocations of Marsupial produce an object as if they had been preceded by new even though only one of them is. If your team has adopted the convention of naming constructor functions with an uppercase first letter, the creation of the jester instance appears to be incorrect.

Consistency begets reliability, and as such we prefer the protection mechanism presented in Listing 3-4. Throwing an exception when new is omitted ensures that all Marsupial objects will be instantiated in the same way, contributing to a more consistent and reliable codebase. Additionally, when coupled with test-driven development, any exception generated via the omission of new will be identified immediately.

> **NOTE** *Automatic semicolon insertion, a JavaScript feature that also lets programmers get away with mistakes and allows for codebases to become inconsistent, is considered by Douglas Crockford to be one of the awful parts of JavaScript that shouldn't be relied upon* (JavaScript: The Good Parts *by Douglas Crockford, O'Reilly Media, 2008). Automatic* new *insertion, while perhaps not awful, should be avoided for the same reasons.*

The new object creation pattern also allows you to create function properties that are defined once and made available to all instances. Listing 3-6 shows how properties can be added to each instance of an object by defining them directly on the new object in the constructor function. The listing also illustrates that each object instance has its own copy of the function.

LISTING 3-6: Adding a function directly to the new object (code filename: New Pattern\ newpattern_04.js)

```
function Marsupial(name, nocturnal){
  if(!(this instanceof Marsupial)){
    throw new Error("This object must be created with new");
  }
  this.name = name;
  this.isNocturnal = nocturnal;

  // Each object instance gets its own copy of isAwake
  this.isAwake = function(isNight){
    return isNight === this.isNocturnal;
  }
}

var maverick = new Marsupial('Maverick', true);
```

```
var slider = new Marsupial('Slider', false);

var isNightTime = true;

console.log(maverick.isAwake(isNightTime));     // true
console.log(slider.isAwake(isNightTime));       // false

// each object has its own isAwake function
console.log(maverick.isAwake === slider.isAwake); // false
```

Function properties may also be added to the constructor function's `prototype`. Defining functions on the `prototype` of the constructor function has the added benefit of limiting the number of copies of the function to one, reducing the memory footprint, and increasing performance when creating a large number of object instances.

Listing 3-7 shows how to add a function property to the constructor function's `prototype`. The listing also illustrates that each object instance shares the implementation of the function.

LISTING 3-7: Adding a function to the constructor function's prototype (code filename: New Pattern\newpattern_05.js)

```
function Marsupial(name, nocturnal){
  if(!(this instanceof Marsupial)){
    throw new Error("This object must be created with new");
  }
  this.name = name;
  this.isNocturnal = nocturnal;
}
// Each object instance shares one copy of isAwake
Marsupial.prototype.isAwake = function(isNight){
  return isNight === this.isNocturnal;
}
var maverick = new Marsupial('Maverick', true);
var slider = new Marsupial('Slider', false);

var isNightTime = true;

console.log(maverick.isAwake(isNightTime));     // true
console.log(slider.isAwake(isNightTime));       // false

// the objects share a single instance of isAwake
console.log(maverick.isAwake === slider.isAwake); // true
```

To illustrate the performance gains that can be realized by utilizing the constructor function's prototype, we've created a sample on `http://jsperf.com` which pits the version of `Marsupial` that doesn't use the `prototype` against the version that does. You can run the comparison in your own browser by visiting `http://jsperf.com/performance-prototype-vs-non-prototype`, but to satisfy any immediate curiosity you have, Figure 3-2 shows the results of running the test in Chrome version 40 on OSX 10.10.

As Figure 3.2 shows, the version of `Marsupial` that uses the constructor's `prototype` to share a single copy of the `isAwake` function between all object instances is more than 90 percent faster than the version that creates a copy of the `isAwake` function for each object instance.

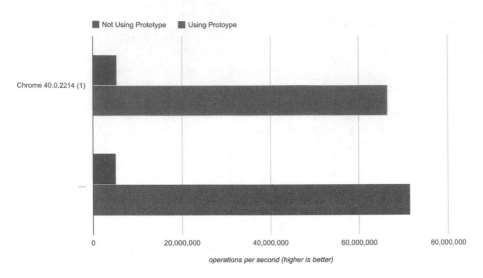

FIGURE 3-2

Table 3-4 summarizes how the new object creation pattern stacks up in terms of the SOLID and DRY principles.

TABLE 3.4: SOLID and DRY Summary for Objects Created with new

PRINCIPLE	RESULT
Single Responsibility	Certainly possible, but it's up to you to make sure that the objects you create are responsible for one thing, and one thing only. The ability to inject dependencies into constructor functions helps with this.
Open/Closed	Yes! The upcoming sections about inheritance illustrate how objects created with new may be extended.
Liskov Substitution	Yes, through judicious use of inheritance
Interface Segregation	Yes, again through use of inheritance and other code-sharing patterns
Dependency Inversion	A resounding yes. Dependencies may be injected into constructor functions with ease.
Don't **R**epeat **Y**ourself	The new object creation pattern results in very DRY code. Unfortunately, we haven't found a good way to use AOP with this pattern. This is a significant disappointment because AOP would be handy to encapsulate new enforcement. The reason AOP and new don't mix is that new creates an object that inherits from the prototype of the object being created. If that object has been wrapped with an aspect, then the aspect's prototype, not the object's, will be used. However, nothing prevents you from using AOP to decorate the functions of the new'd object's prototype.

USING CLASSICAL INHERITANCE

Because JavaScript doesn't have classes, it doesn't support classical inheritance like C# or C++. Its prototypal inheritance does allow for classical inheritance to be emulated, though. In this section, you see how to make JavaScript's prototypal inheritance behave somewhat like classical inheritance. Additionally, you are presented with both benefits and drawbacks of doing so.

Emulating Classical Inheritance

The basis of classical inheritance emulation in JavaScript is manipulation of a function's `prototype`. Let's assume that you would like to extend the behavior of the `Marsupial` function from the previous section to include properties specific to kangaroos, specifically a `hop` function.

To review, here's the `Marsupial` function, including `new` enforcement and the `isAwake` function we added to the `prototype` in Listing 3-7:

```
function Marsupial(name, nocturnal){
  if(!(this instanceof Marsupial)){
    throw new Error("This object must be created with new");
  }
  this.name = name;
  this.isNocturnal = nocturnal;
}
Marsupial.prototype.isAwake = function(isNight){
  return isNight === this.isNocturnal;
}
```

You could add `hop` to the `Marsupial` function's `prototype` (or directly to the object instance created by the function), but do you really want to? If you did, each and every object instance created by the `Marsupial` constructor function would have the `hop` function.

Because you only want kangaroos to be able to hop, changing `Marsupial` wouldn't get you to your goal. Changing `Marsupial` would also be a violation of the Open/Closed principle.

The best and most reliable solution is to extend `Marsupial` by creating a `Kangaroo` function that inherits from it. Listing 3-8 shows how to do this.

LISTING 3-8: Extending Marsupial using classical inheritance emulation (code filename: Classical\classical_01.js)

```
function Marsupial(name, nocturnal){
  if(!(this instanceof Marsupial)){
    throw new Error("This object must be created with new");
  }
  this.name = name;
  this.isNocturnal = nocturnal;
}
Marsupial.prototype.isAwake = function(isNight){
  return isNight == this.isNocturnal;
};

function Kangaroo(name){
```

continues

LISTING 3-8 *(continued)*

```
  if(!(this instanceof Kangaroo)){
    throw new Error("This object must be created with new");
  }
  this.name = name;
  this.isNocturnal = false;
}

Kangaroo.prototype = new Marsupial();
Kangaroo.prototype.hop = function(){
  return this.name + " just hopped!";
}
var jester = new Kangaroo('Jester');
console.log(jester.name);

var isNightTime = false;
console.log(jester.isAwake(isNightTime));  // true
console.log(jester.hop());                 // 'Jester just hopped!'

console.log(jester instanceof Kangaroo);   // true
console.log(jester instanceof Marsupial);  // true
```

You can see that the default `prototype` of the `Kangaroo` function has been replaced with a new instance of `Marsupial`, making `Marsupial` act almost like a class definition.

The Marsupial instance that is now the `prototype` of Kangaroo was extended by adding a `hop` function. Note that the `hop` function *wasn't* added within a `Marsupial` constructor function, nor was it added to the `Marsupial` constructor function's `prototype`; the `Marsupial` function has not been changed in any way. This implementation follows the Open/Closed principle exactly!

Repetition Killed the Kangaroo

Emulating classical inheritance, as shown in Listing 3-8, involves repetition of both code and memory use. Let's look once more at the assignment of the `Marsupial` instance to the `prototype` of the `Kangaroo` function:

```
Kangaroo.prototype = new Marsupial();
```

You may have noticed that no arguments were provided to the `Marsupial` constructor function. The arguments expected aren't known at the point in time that `Kangaroo`'s `prototype` is being set, and they won't be known until an instance of `Kangaroo` is created.

Because the arguments aren't known when the `prototype` is being configured, the assignment of properties done in the `Marsupial` function is repeated in the `Kangaroo` function:

```
function Marsupial(name, nocturnal){
  if(!(this instanceof Marsupial)){
    throw new Error("This object must be created with new");
  }
  this.name = name;
  this.isNocturnal = nocturnal;
}

function Kangaroo(name){
  if(!(this instanceof Kangaroo)){
```

```
    throw new Error("This object must be created with new");
  }

  // Repeated assignment of the name and isNocturnal properties!
  this.name = name;
  this.isNocturnal = false;
}
```

This obviously violates the DRY principle, and repetition can negatively impact the reliability of your code.

Additionally, the `name` and `isNocturnal` properties end up on both the prototype of `Kangaroo` (an instance of `Marsupial`) and on the instances of `Kangaroo` themselves. Because the `Marsupial` function was invoked without arguments, the values of the properties on `Kangaroo.prototype` are undefined. This is illustrated by inspecting an instance of `Kangaroo`, as shown in Figure 3-3.

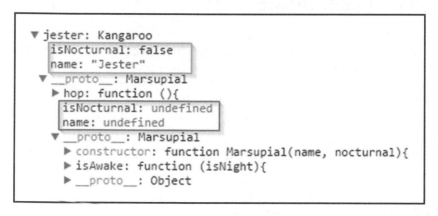

FIGURE 3-3

The first set of outlined properties are those belonging to the instance of `Kangaroo`, and the second set are those belonging to the instance of `Marsupial`, which is `Kangaroo`'s `prototype`.

Table 3-5 summarizes how well classical inheritance emulation satisfies the SOLID and DRY principles.

TABLE 3-5: SOLID and DRY Summary for Classical Inheritance Emulation

PRINCIPLE	RESULT
Single Responsibility	Classical inheritance emulation supports but doesn't enforce the Single Responsibility principle. Dependencies may be injected to help ensure your objects don't take on too many responsibilities. Use of the `new` keyword precludes use of aspect-oriented decoration of the constructor function itself.
Open/Closed	The pattern is all about the Open/Closed principle, as the code in Listing 3-8 highlights.
Liskov Substitution	The pattern fosters making extensions to dependencies rather than modifying them. As such, it helps you follow the Liskov Substitution principle.

continues

TABLE 3-5 *(continued)*

PRINCIPLE	RESULT
Interface Segregation	Not applicable
Dependency Inversion	Dependency inversion is possible via injection of dependencies into the inheriting object's constructor function.
Don't Repeat Yourself	Not so much. Initialization logic is repeated in the inheriting and inherited object creation functions. Prototype sharing does reduce the number of copies of a function, however.

USING FUNCTIONAL INHERITANCE

Functional inheritance provides the ability to hide data so that access to it can be controlled. In this section, you learn how functional inheritance eliminates the constructor repetition found in the emulation of classical inheritance. Also, you see how data can be made private, both to external consumers of an object and inheritors of an object. Whenever data are private rather than public, the surface area exposed to misuse and mistakes decreases and reliability increases.

The Module Pattern also nicely supports inheritance in a manner that eliminates the constructor logic duplication found when emulating classical inheritance. Once again, the goal is to create a `kangaroo` object that inherits from `marsupial` and adds the additional `hop` function. Listing 3-9 illustrates how to do this using the functional inheritance pattern and modules.

LISTING 3-9: The AnimalKingdom module with the marsupial and kangaroo functions (code filename: Functional\functional_01.js)

```
var AnimalKingdom = AnimalKingdom || {};

AnimalKingdom.marsupial = function(name, nocturnal){

    var instanceName = name,
        instanceIsNocturnal = nocturnal;

    return {
      getName: function(){
        return instanceName;
      },
      getIsNocturnal: function(){
        return instanceIsNocturnal;
      }
    }
}

AnimalKingdom.kangaroo = function(name){
    var baseMarsupial = AnimalKingdom.marsupial(name, false);

    baseMarsupial.hop = function(){
```

```
        return baseMarsupial.getName() + ' just hopped!';
    };

    return baseMarsupial;
}

var jester = AnimalKingdom.kangaroo('Jester');
console.log(jester.getName());          // 'Jester'
console.log(jester.getIsNocturnal());   // false
console.log(jester.hop());              // 'Jester just hopped!'
```

The baseMarsupial object created within and returned from AnimalKingdom.kangaroo is an instance of an object created with AnimalKingdom.marsupial. The AnimalKingdom.kangaroo function then extends the baseMarsupial instance to add the hop function. Once again, the hop functionality was added without making any modifications to AnimalKingdom.marsupial; there are no violations of the Open/Closed principle here.

A benefit that functional inheritance with modules provides over emulation of classical inheritance is that there's no need to repeat the AnimalKingdom.marsupial's creation logic in AnimalKingdom.kangaroo; AnimalKingdom.kangaroo uses AnimalKingdom.marsupial's creation function directly.

It doesn't get any more DRY than this.

Table 3-6 summarizes how well functional inheritance follows the SOLID and DRY principles.

TABLE 3-6: SOLID and DRY Summary for the Functional Inheritance Pattern

Principle	Result
Single Responsibility	Because functional inheritance uses the Module Pattern, it's also friendly to dependency injection and aspect-oriented decoration. You should have no problem limiting your inherited modules to a single responsibility.
Open/Closed	Functional inheritance gives you a perfect mechanism for extending—and thus avoiding modification of—your modules. See Listing 3-9 for a concrete example.
Liskov Substitution	Functional inheritance provides a way to extend modules without modifying them. As such, any inherited modules may be substituted for the modules they inherit from.
Interface Segregation	Again, functional inheritance is a variation on the Module Pattern. The cohesive APIs of your models are segregated interfaces.
Dependency Inversion	As long as the modules used in inheritance are modules-at-will, they can be injected with dependencies easily.
Don't Repeat Yourself	With proper design, functional inheritance with modules is a fantastic way produce DRY code.

MONKEY-PATCHING

What can possibly be good about a programming technique called monkey-patching? Done poorly, it is indeed as chaotic as it sounds. Done right, and dressed up with a name like Composing by Parts, it can become a respected tool.

Monkey-patching consists of tacking additional properties onto an object. JavaScript is perfectly happy to let you augment an object with a function from another object:

```
var human = {
  useSignLanguage: function() {
    return 'I am moving my hands. Can you understand me?';
  }
};

var koko = {};

koko.useSignLanguage = human.useSignLanguage;

// Outputs 'I am moving my hands. Can you understand me?'
console.log(koko.useSignLanguage());
```

The danger, of course, is that the function might expect things of its new home that aren't there. A more complete and robust version of the preceding code snippet is in Listing 3-10.

LISTING 3-10: Monkey-patching

```
var MyApp = MyApp || {};

MyApp.Hand = function() {
  this.dataAboutHand = {}; // etc.
};
MyApp.Hand.prototype.arrangeAndMove = function(sign) {
  this.dataAboutHand = 'new arrangement and movement per sign';
};

MyApp.Human = function(handFactory) {
  this.hands = [ handFactory(), handFactory() ];
};
MyApp.Human.prototype.useSignLanguage = function(message) {
  var sign = {};
  // Encode message into sign
  this.hands.forEach( function(hand) {
    hand.arrangeAndMove(sign);
  });
  return 'I am moving my hands. Can you understand me?';
};

MyApp.Gorilla = function(handFactory) {
    this.hands = [ handFactory(), handFactory() ];
};

MyApp.TeachSignLanguageToKoko = (function() {
  var handFactory = function() {
```

```
        return new MyApp.Hand();
    };
    // (Poor man's dependency injection.)
    var trainer = new MyApp.Human(handFactory);
    var koko = new MyApp.Gorilla(handFactory);

    koko.useSignLanguage = trainer.useSignLanguage;

    // Outputs 'I am moving my hands. Can you understand me?';
    console.log(koko.useSignLanguage('Hello!'));
}());
```

The monkey-patching takes place in this line toward the end:

```
koko.useSignLanguage = trainer.useSignLanguage;
```

The capability to use sign language is patched from the trainer to Koko. This only works because Koko happens to have hands—something the `Human.useSignLanguage` function requires to be part of its `this`. (that is, part of the object that `useSignLanguage` is "dotted with"). Although `useSignLanguage` originated in Human, calling it with `koko` before the dot (`koko.useSignLanguage`) causes Koko's hands to move, not the human's. Stated in more detail:

1. `koko.useSignLanguage('Hello!')` is called.

2. Because of the monkey patch, execution ends up in `MyApp.Human.prototype`
    `.useSignLanguage`.

3. That function accesses `this.hands`.

4. At that point, *this* is a `MyApp.Gorilla` object (*koko*) because that's the object on which `useSignLanguage` was called. Therefore, `MyApp.Gorilla` better have hands!

Because of possible (even future!) requirements that the borrowed function might have, the most reliable way to monkey-patch is to have the *donor object* manage the patch. It can ask the receiving object whether it meets the requirements.

```
MyApp.Human.prototype.endowSigning = function(receivingObject) {
    if (typeof receivingObject.getHandCount === 'function'
    && receivingObject.getHandCount() >= 2) {
      receivingObject.useSignLanguage = this.useSignLanguage;
    } else {
      throw new Error("Sorry. I can't endow you with signing abilities.");
    }
};
```

Of course, the receiving object must be prepared to answer the question:

```
MyApp.Gorilla.prototype.getHandCount = function() {
    return this.hands.length;
};
```

Finally, the human can endow the gorilla:

```
trainer.endowSigning(koko);
```

Using this technique, you can patch a whole cluster of functionality from one object to another. Classical programmers might think of this cluster as implementing an interface, but really it's more akin to multiple inheritance because it implements not only an interface but the code to go with it!

In Chapter 19, you will read much more about monkey patching, although under its other more respectable name, *method borrowing.*

Table 3-7 summarizes how well monkey-patching stacks up to the classic criteria for reliability and testability.

TABLE 3-7: SOLID and DRY Summary for Monkey-Patching

PRINCIPLE	RESULT
Single Responsibility	Although the donated cluster of functions comprises one responsibility, it might be argued that the donation adds a responsibility to the receiving object. However, this is only true in the same sense that an aspect adds a responsibility, which is to say it's not true at all.
Open/Closed	To the extent that monkey-patching is used responsibly, it does not violate the open/closed principle.
Liskov Substitution	As long as the donated functions have the same semantics in their new home as in the old, there's no problem here.
Interface Segregation	Upholding the Interface Segregation principle is what monkey-patching is all about!
Dependency Inversion	Dependencies may be injected into either the donating or receiving object as usual.
Don't **R**epeat **Y**ourself	In the hands of a creative but responsible developer, monkey-patching can be one more tool for maintaining DRY code.

SUMMARY

In this chapter, you saw several ways to create objects in JavaScript, and how well each way met the SOLID and DRY criteria from Chapter 1.

Primitives and object literals are simple to use, but tend to make your code repeat itself.

The Module Patterns is a definite step up. Not only does it encapsulate your data in ways that primitives and object literals do not, but it is more amenable to unit-testing and extension using aspect-oriented programming.

According to some members of the JavaScript community, the `new` object creation pattern should be avoided, but we're not so quick to dismiss it. Constructor functions, used by the pattern, allow for shared initialization code, and it isn't difficult to ensure `new` is used when it is required.

All JavaScript functions have a `prototype` property which may be used to efficiently share code and data between object instances. The prototype property also provides the mechanism by which JavaScript facilitates prototypical inheritance.

JavaScript's prototypical inheritance can be used to emulate classical inheritance, a concept you may be familiar with if you have experience in Java or C#. JavaScript also supports functional inheritance, which avoids some of the repetition that can occur with prototypical inheritance, and also supports data-hiding.

Finally, you saw how monkey-patching, used responsibly, can endow one object with capabilities from another.

The next chapter begins Part II of this book, which is devoted to using test-driven development to implement important programming patterns in JavaScript. The discussion kicks off with a review of the benefits of pattern-based code.

PART II
Testing Pattern-Based Code

Reviewing the Benefits of Patterns

WHAT'S IN THIS CHAPTER?

➤ Exploring how a simple pattern has brought us increasingly clear and reliable code

➤ Making your code simpler and clearer

➤ Looking ahead

CASE STUDY

World chess champion Magnus Carlsen was referring to chess, but he could have been talking about programming when he said: "[In] general good players use more long-term memory than short-term memory during a chess game. You use past experiences. It is the intuition that is largely based on the past experiences. So it is your experience that gives you a different impression of the new situations before you, and then you have to consider what impression you can use. *You must be able to continuously make up your mind about which past experience can be used.*" (`http://www.worldchesschampionship2013.com/2013/11/secret-of-magnus-carlsens-chess.html`)

Good chess players strike with flashes of tactical brilliance at the chessboard, and good programmers can spin beautiful algorithms at the keyboard, but the best ones *also* draw on patterns learned from experience and "continuously make up their minds about which can be used." A developer who draws on wisdom and experience from the past is likely to solve problems more economically and cleanly than one who must invent everything himself.

Patterns can range in scale from little idioms of the language (++*i*) up to the structure of the system itself (n-tier architecture). The pattern of looping through an array is an example of the tiny variety, but illustrates how patterns accumulate and improve through experience and how code becomes cleaner and more reliable through their use.

The first version of looping through an array is so old-fashioned that it is not even valid JavaScript (containing, as it does, a goto), but it is how programming was done before better patterns emerged.

```
ix=0;
the_test:
if (ix >= myArray.length) {
  goto the_end;
}
doSomething(myArray[ix]);
ix = ix+1;
goto the_test; // Pretend JavaScript has a goto statement.
the_end:
```

The goto statement led to code that was so hard to follow that its use became shunned. Shunning turned to banishment and now JavaScript doesn't even have a goto statement. A better pattern, the for loop, was incorporated into the language:

```
for (ix=0; ix<myArray.length; ++ix ) {
  doSomething(myArray[ix]);
}
```

The for version is better because it is more concise and clear. Isn't it easier to tell at a glance what the code is attempting to do? Doesn't there seem to be much less room for error than in the goto version?

Yet for was not the last word. The accumulation of experience and patterns was not complete. Looping through elements in an array is so common that the designers of ECMAScript 5 have provided an even more concise formulation:

```
myArray.forEach(doSomething);
```

This is even clearer because the entire for statement, with its initialization, test, and increment, has been replaced by the simple and obvious myArray.forEach.

Not only is it more clear, but it's more reliable. It is impossible to commit an off-by-one error in the condition because there is no condition. You can't reference the wrong element in the array because there are no subscripts.

Of course, myArray.forEach is only clear if you know what a forEach statement is and you are comfortable with callbacks. That brings us to the first main point of this chapter: how a broader vocabulary can help you produce more elegant code.

PRODUCING MORE ELEGANT CODE BY USING A BROADER VOCABULARY

It is a common misconception that code is simplest and easiest to understand when it employs only the most elementary concepts. On the contrary, an impoverished vocabulary results in longer, more tortuous programs.

Table 4-1 compares the `for` and `forEach` versions of the simple loop from the previous section.

TABLE 4-1: Comparing for and forEach

	FOR	FOREACH
Assignments	ix=0 ++ix	N/A
Property references	myArray.length	N/A
Array-element references	myArray[ix]	N/A
Conditional branching	ix<myArray.length	N/A
Function calls	doSomething(myArray[ix])	doSomething

Developers are so used to `for` loops that they may forget how much extra work is involved. The entire purpose of the code was to call `doSomething` on each element of the array, yet all those assignments, property references, and branching were dragged in. How can code ever be elegant in the midst of so much useless clutter?

That example was on a small scale, and the pattern has been codified in the language itself, but the same is true for patterns on a larger scale that are expressed in your own code or third-party libraries. For example:

➤ The Promise pattern (see Chapter 6) involves initiating an asynchronous action and providing callbacks for its success or failure. Once mastered, it leads to code that is more elegant, easier to understand, and far more reliable to code than an event-based alternative.

➤ Few developers without formal training will think to employ the Decorator pattern (see Chapter 12), but it can do a lot to uphold the Single Responsibility Principle (see Chapter 1) and bring the reliability that comes with it.

You can imagine how ugly, difficult, and inefficient your code would be if you were not acquainted with `for`, `forEach`, or the other looping constructs in the language. What a step up it would be to start programming with ordinary `for` statements! As the higher-level patterns in this book become part of your everyday vocabulary, your code will step up by an equal measure.

PRODUCING RELIABLE CODE WITH WELL-ENGINEERED, WELL-TESTED BUILDING BLOCKS

The seminal book *Design Patterns: Elements of Reusable Object-Oriented Software* by Erich Gamma, Richard Helm, Ralph Johnson, and John Vlissides (Addison-Wesley, 1994) has encouraged a generation of developers to construct reliable software by applying twenty-three patterns that have proven both useful and robust. As long as software is being written, those patterns will be employed.

However, song lyrics, when translated into a different language, often change their literal meaning in order to express the same emotion. If the beauty, rhythm, and rhyme are to be preserved, one must sing different words. The distinction made in *Design Patterns* between concrete and abstract classes has no literal translation to JavaScript, where everything is concrete and no classes exist. In the coming chapters, you will see how some of the classic patterns can find their expression in JavaScript.

You will also learn new patterns that are idiomatic to JavaScript and might not have such a prominent place in a classical language.

The patterns themselves are only half the story, however, and the second half at that. The first half is the testing story. (Remember: Test first!) Embarrassing experiences have taught all of us that we can mess up even the simplest pattern. The only way to verify that a pattern is correctly coded is to test it.

We have found that developers generally have a harder time knowing how to rigorously test code based on some of these patterns than learning how to code with the patterns themselves. Most of the rest of this book is therefore devoted to a test-first approach to learning various patterns, and an explication of how to proceed with a test-first approach to using them.

As you employ proven, elegant design patterns, and use best practices for testing your work, you will produce reliable code that gives you great satisfaction—both functionally and creatively. What more could a software developer want from his day job?

SUMMARY

In software development, there are small-scale patterns in the syntax and idioms of the language, and large-scale patterns for constructing entire systems. Like a top-notch chess player who can see familiar patterns in every new position, a good software developer has a broad vocabulary of patterns at his or her disposal. The developer can use these patterns as guides for thought and as well-tested building blocks to construct reliable systems.

The next chapter covers one of the most frequent patterns in JavaScript: the callback.

5

Ensuring Correct Use of the Callback Pattern

WHAT'S IN THIS CHAPTER?

➤ Creating and testing code that uses callback functions

➤ Creating and testing callback functions

➤ Identifying and addressing problems that are commonly encountered when implementing the Callback Pattern

WROX.COM CODE DOWNLOADS FOR THIS CHAPTER

The wrox.com code downloads for this chapter are found at www.wrox.com/go/ reliablejavascript on the Download Code tab. The code is in the Chapter 5 download and individually named according to the filenames noted throughout this chapter.

A *callback* is a function provided as an argument to a second function, which the second function will execute at some time in the future. That future time may be before the second function has exited, in which case the callback is considered *synchronous*. Alternatively, the future time may be after the second function has exited, in which case the callback is considered *asynchronous*. While all the examples in this chapter will use synchronous callbacks, the techniques (and potential problems) are also applicable to asynchronous callbacks. Chapter 6 will introduce promises, which are used exclusively with asynchronous callbacks.

The Callback Pattern is an important one to master when crafting reliable JavaScript because it is heavily used, both in the language proper and in many third-party libraries, such as JQuery.

The sections that follow illustrate how to create reliable callback functions when interacting with built-in JavaScript functions and third-party libraries. Creating code that uses the pattern will also be covered, as will testing code that makes use of the pattern. By the end of this chapter the Callback Pattern will be fully entrenched in your JavaScript vocabulary.

UNDERSTANDING THE PATTERN THROUGH UNIT TESTS

This section introduces you to the Callback Pattern via a series of unit tests. The unit tests will illustrate how to create callback functions, as well as how to write functions that accept callbacks. You may also get some ideas for how to develop code that uses callbacks in sound, test-driven fashion. Both this section and the next will expose common problems and mistakes that occur when implementing the Callback Pattern and ways to avoid and fix them.

Writing and Testing Code That Uses Callback Functions

In Chapter 2, you were asked to create a website for an upcoming JavaScript conference. Continuing with that example, your next task is to allow conference volunteers to check in attendees. The user interface will support selecting one or more attendees from a list, marking them as checked in, and registering the action in an external system. Implementing the check-in behavior behind the user interface is the `checkInService`, which is the module you will create.

Objects created by the `Conference.attendee` function are responsible for maintaining information about an attendee, including whether or not she has checked in. It will be up to the `checkInService` to manipulate those objects when attendees check in. `Conference.attendee` was written by your conscientious and capable colleague, Charlotte, and she has created a full unit test suite for it, so you may assume it functions reliably.

```
var Conference = Conference || {};
Conference.attendee = function(firstName, lastName){

  var checkedIn = false,
    first = firstName || 'None',
    last = lastName || 'None';

  return {
    getFullName: function(){
      return first + ' ' + last;
    },

    isCheckedIn: function(){
      return checkedIn;
    },

    checkIn: function(){
      checkedIn = true;
    }
  };
};
```

Based on the description of the task, you'll need to execute the `checkIn` function of one or more `attendee` objects.

It seems likely that you'll have to manipulate collections of attendees in other ways in the future, so it makes sense to create an `attendeeCollection` object that encapsulates a collection of `attendee` objects.

In order to check in each attendee, the `attendeeCollection` object will need to allow for an action to be performed on each of the attendees in the collection. You'll allow the action to be performed to be specified via a callback function.

The `attendeeCollection`, with the requisite `contains`, `add`, and `remove` functions, is defined in Listing 5-1. The `iterate` function has been stubbed out and is where your efforts will be focused.

LISTING 5-1: The initial implementation of the Conference.attendeeCollection module

```javascript
var Conference = Conference || {};
Conference.attendeeCollection = function(){
  var attendees = [];

  return {
    contains: function(attendee){
      return attendees.indexOf(attendee) > -1;
    },
    add: function(attendee){
      if (!this.contains(attendee)){
        attendees.push(attendee);
      }
    },
    remove: function(attendee){
      var index = attendees.indexOf(attendee);
      if (index > -1){
        attendees.splice(index, 1);
      }
    },

    iterate: function(callback){
      // execute callback for each attendee in attendees
    }
  };
};
```

Before you dive into implementing the `iterate` functionality, you need to write unit tests to verify its behavior. The unit tests for the `iterate` function are shown in Listing 5-2.

LISTING 5-2: Unit tests for the attendeeCollection.iterate function (code filename: Callbacks\attendeeCollection_tests.js)

```javascript
describe('Conference.attendeeCollection',function(){

  describe('contains(attendee)', function(){
    // contains tests
  });
  describe('add(attendee)', function(){
    // add tests
  });
  describe('remove(attendee)', function(){
    // remove tests
```

continues

LISTING 5-2 *(continued)*

```javascript
  });

  describe('iterate(callback)', function(){
    var collection, callbackSpy;

    // Helper functions
    function addAttendeesToCollection(attendeeArray){
      attendeeArray.forEach(function(attendee){
        collection.add(attendee);
      });
    }

    function verifyCallbackWasExecutedForEachAttendee(attendeeArray){
      // ensure that the spy was called once for each element
      expect(callbackSpy.calls.count()).toBe(attendeeArray.length);

      // ensure that the first argument provided to the spy
      // for each call is the corresponding attendee
      var allCalls = callbackSpy.calls.all();
      for(var i = 0; i < allCalls.length; i++){
        expect(allCalls[i].args[0]).toBe(attendeeArray[i]);
      }
    }

    beforeEach(function(){
      collection = Conference.attendeeCollection();
      callbackSpy = jasmine.createSpy();
    });

    it('does not execute the callback when the collection is empty', function(){
      collection.iterate(callbackSpy);
      expect(callbackSpy).not.toHaveBeenCalled();
    });

    it('executes the callback once for a single element collection', function(){
      var attendees = [
        Conference.attendee('Pete', 'Mitchell')
      ];
      addAttendeesToCollection(attendees);

      collection.iterate(callbackSpy);

      verifyCallbackWasExecutedForEachAttendee(attendees);
    });

    it('executes the callback once for each element in a collection', function(){
      var attendees = [
        Conference.attendee('Tom', 'Kazansky'),
        Conference.attendee('Charlotte', 'Blackwood'),
        Conference.attendee('Mike', 'Metcalf')
      ];
      addAttendeesToCollection(attendees);

      collection.iterate(callbackSpy);
```

```
            verifyCallbackWasExecutedForEachAttendee(attendees);
        });
    });
});
```

There's quite a bit of code to digest in Listing 5-2, but it isn't particularly complicated once you understand the primary goals of testing code that uses the Callback Pattern. The tests specific to callback functionality need to ensure that:

➤   The callback was executed the correct number of times.

➤   The callback was executed with the correct arguments each time.

The first step in achieving the testing goals is to create some sort of callback function that can keep a record of each time it is executed, including the arguments that were provided when it was executed. Jasmine spies, introduced in Chapter 2, provide this functionality (and more).

The tests for the `iterate` function in Listing 5-2 each use the `callbackSpy` Jasmine spy instance, which is initialized in the `beforeEach` block prior to the execution of each test via `callbackSpy = jasmine.createSpy();`.

> **NOTE** *A spy created with* `createSpy` *is a* bare spy. *Unlike spies created with a call to* `spyOn(someObject, 'someFunction')`, *bare spies don't require a pre-existing object and function to spy on.*
>
> *Bare spies have no functionality beyond "spy stuff" such as tracking invocations; you can't set them up to call through to the implementation of the spied on function (because there is none), nor can you configure them to call some other function when invoked.*
>
> *Even with these limitations, a bare spy is perfect to ensure that a callback function is executed appropriately.*

Each of the tests sets up the collection object, also created in the `beforeEach` block, to contain the number of `attendee` objects appropriate for the test.

The tests then execute `collection.iterate(callbackSpy);` which, once `iterate` is implemented, should cause `callbackSpy` to be executed once per attendee in the collection.

The helper function `verifyCallbackWasExecutedForEachAttendee` performs the heavy lifting in each test; it's responsible for ensuring that the goals for testing code using the Callback Pattern have been satisfied.

The `callbackSpy` automatically collects information about each time it is executed into an object that is added to its `calls` property. Comparing the number of times the spy was called—by counting the number of elements in the `calls` property—with the number of elements that were added to the collection with the statement

```
expect(callbackSpy.calls.count()).toBe(attendeeArray.length);
```

ensures `callbackSpy` was called a number of times equal to the number of `attendee` objects in the collection.

The rest of the `verifyCallbackWasExecutedForEachAttendee` is dedicated to verifying that each invocation of `callbackSpy` was provided with the correct argument, specifically the appropriate `attendee` in the collection.

```
var allCalls = callbackSpy.calls.all();
for(var i = 0; i < allCalls.length; i++){
  expect(allCalls[i].args[0]).toBe(attendeeArray[i]);
}
```

All of the calls recorded by `callbackSpy` are gathered and iterated through. Each of the `call` objects has an array property, `args`, which contains all of the arguments provided to that call. Comparing the first argument of each `call.args` with the corresponding `attendee` satisfies the second testing goal: that the callback is invoked with the correct arguments.

Now that you have tests in place that exercise the `iterate` function, it's time to implement it. You will recall from Chapter 4 that the `forEach` function is available as a property of JavaScript arrays, and it accepts a callback function that is executed once per element in the array, providing the element as the first argument to the callback.

The `forEach` function seems to be the perfect tool to implement the `iterate` function of the `attendeeCollection`. Listing 5-3 provides the fully implemented `attendeeCollection`.

LISTING 5-3: The full implementation of the attendeeCollection module (code filename: Callbacks\attendeeCollection.js)

```
var Conference = Conference || {};
Conference.attendeeCollection = function(){
  var attendees = [];

  return{
    contains: function(attendee){
      return attendees.indexOf(attendee) > -1;
    },
    add: function(attendee){
      if(!this.contains(attendee)){
        attendees.push(attendee);
      }
    },
    remove: function(attendee){
      var index = attendees.indexOf(attendee);
      if(index > -1){
        attendees.splice(index, 1);
      }
    },
    getCount: function(){
      return attendees.length;
    },

    iterate: function(callback){
```

```
            attendees.forEach(callback);
        }
    };
};
```

The implementation in Listing 5-3 causes all of the unit tests in Listing 5-2 to pass, as Figure 5-1 makes evident.

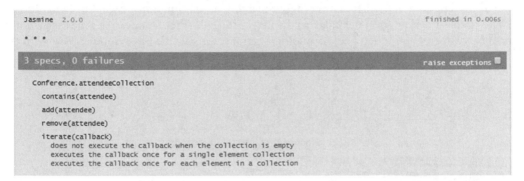

FIGURE 5-1

You now have a functional `attendeeCollection`, but you haven't completed the task that you were presented with at the beginning of this section. You still need to implement the code that checks in the attendees, and records the check-ins in an external system.

Writing and Testing Callback Functions

Now that you have `attendeeCollection`, implementing the additional required functionality is as simple as crafting a callback function that checks in an individual attendee. You could do this by defining an anonymous function that checks in an attendee and providing that anonymous function directly to the `attendeeCollection.iterate` function:

```
var attendees = Conference.attendeeCollection();

// Add the attendees that were selected in the UI

attendees.iterate(function(attendee){
  attendee.checkIn();
  // register check-in with external service
});
```

Even if you only have limited exposure to JavaScript, you've probably seen code that looks like the previous example many times. The capability to define a function and pass it immediately to another function as a callback is powerful feature of JavaScript, but its use can be a deviation from the path to reliability.

First, anonymous callback functions aren't unit-testable; there's no way to separate the callback from the function it's provided to. In the case of the example, the act of checking in an attendee has been coupled to the `attendeeCollection`. Therefore, to properly test that the attendees in the collection are checked in, you'd have to repeat the tests that you already created for the collection itself, except you'd test that the attendees were checked in and the check-ins recorded rather than the callback was executed. If testing even just a single anonymous function callback results in a WET test suite, imagine if multiple tasks were completed using anonymous functions: There would be a flood of repetition.

Second, and far less significant than the testing difficulty just mentioned, is that anonymous functions can make debugging more difficult. Because the anonymous function—by definition—doesn't have a name, there's nothing for a debugger to display in the call stack. Figure 5-2 is a screenshot of the Chrome Developer Tools when paused at a breakpoint set inside the anonymous function in the example.

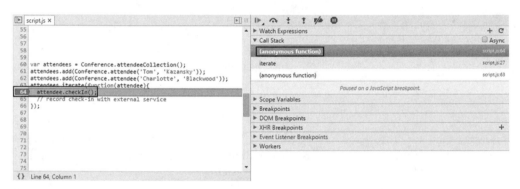

FIGURE 5-2

When waiting at the breakpoint, outlined on the left, Chrome displays `(anonymous function)` in the call stack, outlined on the right. When you don't have a function name to refer to, you don't have an inkling of the context in which the function is being executed. This complicates the debugging task.

This is made worse if you're debugging code reached through a series of anonymous callbacks. Each `(anonymous function)` entry in the call stack would represent a mystery you have to investigate in order to get a full picture of the context in which the code in question is being executed.

Thankfully, functions defined and provided directly as callbacks *can* be named. While this doesn't make them any more testable, it does make the debugging experience less challenging. This example is identical to the previous one except that it provides a name, `doCheckIn`, for the callback function:

```
var attendees = Conference.attendeeCollection();

// Add the attendees that were selected in the UI

attendees.iterate(function doCheckIn(attendee){
```

```
    attendee.checkIn();
    // record check-in with external service
});
```

Now the Chrome Developer Tools have something to list in the call stack, outlined in Figure 5-3, providing context to you (or some other developer) to make debugging a bit easier.

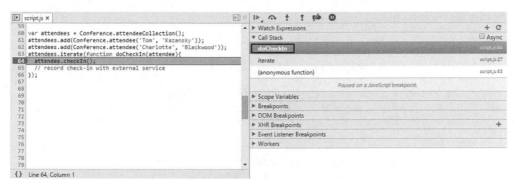

FIGURE 5-3

If anonymous (and named) functions defined and provided directly as callbacks lead to difficult-to-test code, what is a better—testable—way to implement the callback that checks in an attendee?

We suggest that checking in an attendee is a significant responsibility, one that should be encapsulated into its own module, called `checkInService`. Doing so provides a testable unit and also promotes code reuse by decoupling the act of checking in an attendee from the `attendeeCollection`.

> **NOTE** *Many people fear that test-driven development will lead to improvised, haphazard code. On the contrary, careful attention to the details of testing will improve the structure of your programs.*

Additionally, as the section "Using the Module Pattern" illustrated in Chapter 3, dependencies may be injected into `checkInService`. It's reasonable to consider registration of a check-in with an external system as a separate responsibility, so it is appropriate to inject an object that has the registration responsibility into `checkInService`. That object is an instance of `checkInRecorder`, a module you will develop later. (See Chapter 6.)

Listing 5-4 provides a test suite that exercises the basic functionality of the `checkInService` `.checkIn` function.

LISTING 5-4: Tests for the checkInService.checkIn(attendee) function (code filename: Callbacks\checkInService_tests.js)

```
describe('Conference.checkInService', function(){
  var checkInService,
      checkInRecorder,
      attendee;

  beforeEach(function(){
    checkInRecorder = Conference.checkInRecorder();
    spyOn(checkInRecorder, 'recordCheckIn');

    // Inject the checkInRecorder, with the spy configured on
    // its recordCheckIn function
    checkInService = Conference.checkInService(checkInRecorder);

    attendee = Conference.attendee('Sam', 'Wells');
  });

  describe('checkInService.checkIn(attendee)', function(){
    it('marks the attendee checked in', function(){
      checkInService.checkIn(attendee);
      expect(attendee.isCheckedIn()).toBe(true);
    });
    it('records the check-in', function(){
      checkInService.checkIn(attendee);
      expect(checkInRecorder.recordCheckIn).toHaveBeenCalledWith(attendee);
    });
  });
});
```

Extracting the check-in and check-in recording functionality into separate, decoupled modules yields unit tests for checkInService.checkIn that are succinct and simple.

The implementation of checkInService is equally simple and is shown in Listing 5-5.

LISTING 5-5: Implementation of the checkinService.checkIn(attendee) function (code filename: Callbacks\checkInService.js)

```
var Conference = Conference || {};

Conference.checkInService = function(checkInRecorder){
  // retain a reference to the injected checkInRecorder
  var recorder = checkInRecorder;

  return {
    checkIn: function(attendee){
      attendee.checkIn();
      recorder.recordCheckIn(attendee);
    }
  };
};
```

The entire test suite now passes, as shown in Figure 5-4.

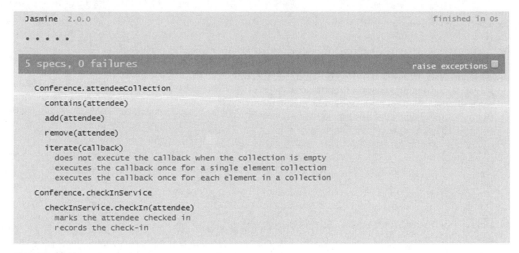

FIGURE 5-4

Finally, the following snippet shows how to tie together the three independent, tested, and reliable modules to complete the task of checking in a conference attendee using the Callback Pattern.

```
var checkInService = Conference.checkInService(Conference.checkInRecorder()),
    attendees = Conference.attendeeCollection();

// Add attendees selected in the UI to the attendee collection

attendees.iterate(checkInService.checkIn);
```

AVOIDING PROBLEMS

The preceding section illustrated how to use the Callback Pattern to create flexible, testable code. Along the way, you saw how anonymous callback functions can prevent your code from being decoupled, easy to test, and thus reliable.

Unfortunately, using anonymous callback functions isn't the only way to arrive at an unreliable implementation of the Callback Pattern. This section introduces two other situations that may lead to unreliable code: the presence of a "callback arrow" and unexpected values of *this* in callback functions. This section also covers ways to avoid such problems.

Flattening the Callback Arrow

The "callback arrow" is a specific, extreme case of the use of anonymous functions as callbacks. A cursory examination of Listing 5-6 makes it obvious how the callback arrow got its name.

LISTING 5-6: A callback arrow

```
CallbackArrow = CallbackArrow || {};

CallbackArrow.rootFunction = function(){
```

continues

LISTING 5-6 *(continued)*

```
    CallbackArrow.firstFunction(function(arg){
      // logic in the first callback
      CallbackArrow.secondFunction(function(arg){
        // logic in the second callback
        CallbackArrow.thirdFunction(function(arg){
          // logic in the third callback
          CallbackArrow.fourthFunction(function(arg){
            // Logic in the fourth callback
          });
        });
      });
    });
  };
  CallbackArrow.firstFunction = function(callback1){
    callback1(arg);
  };
  CallbackArrow.secondFunction = function(callback2){
    callback2(arg);
  };
  CallbackArrow.thirdFunction = function(callback3){
    callback3(arg);
  }
  CallbackArrow.fourthFunction = function(callback4){
    callback4(arg);
  };
```

The callbacks are nested one within the other, deeper and deeper, creating a whitespace arrow that points from the left margin to the right.

The code in Listing 5-6 is difficult to read, difficult to modify, and nearly impossible to unit test. It's a magnet for typos, mismatched curly braces, and logic errors that will fly toward each other as if in the Large Hadron Collider, exploding in a cascade of unreliability that will require a team of PhDs to sort out.

If you have code that looks like that in Listing 5-6, all is not lost. By extracting the anonymous functions into standalone, named functions, the situation becomes far less dire. Listing 5-7 shows one way the code could be refactored.

LISTING 5-7: Flattening the callback arrow

```
  CallbackArrow = CallbackArrow || {};

  CallbackArrow.rootFunction = function(){
    CallbackArrow.firstFunction(CallbackArrow.firstCallback);
  };
  CallbackArrow.firstFunction = function(callback1){
    callback1(arg);
  };
  CallbackArrow.secondFunction = function(callback2){
    callback2(arg);
  };
  CallbackArrow.thirdFunction = function(callback3){
```

```
    callback3(arg);
  };
  CallbackArrow.fourthFunction = function(callback4){
    callback4(arg);
  };
  CallbackArrow.firstCallback = function(){
    // logic in the first callback
    CallbackArrow.secondFunction(CallbackArrow.secondCallback);
  };
  CallbackArrow.secondCallback = function(){
    // logic in the second callback
    CallbackArrow.thirdFunction(CallbackArrow.thirdCallback);
  };
  CallbackArrow.thirdCallback = function(){
    // logic in the third callback
    CallBackArrow.fourthFunction(CallbackArrow.fourthCallback);
  };
  CallbackArrow.fourthCallback = function(){
    // logic in the fourth callback
  };
```

The outcome of executing `CallbackArrow.rootFunction` is the same in both Listing 5-6 and Listing 5-7; the code in the Listings is functionally equivalent. Though the sample code in Listing 5-6 appears tidy, production code that uses nested callbacks will include more logic that makes the visual arrow less apparent. You'll be happier with the flattened presentation than with code written in a manner similar to Listing 5-6.

An even greater benefit is that the code in Listing 5-7 is fully unit-testable; all of the functionality that was present in the nested, anonymous callback functions in Listing 5-6 has been extracted into function properties of `CallbackArrow` that may be individually unit-tested. What's more, because each of the callback functions is named, you won't be presented with `(anonymous function)` in the stack trace of your debugging tool.

Minding *this*

Special care must be used when referencing the *this* variable in your callback functions; its value may not be what you expect it to be.

Perhaps your next task for the JavaScript conference website is to write a module that counts the number of `attendee` objects in an `attendeeCollection` that have been checked in. Its structure will be similar to that of the `checkInService`; it will expose a function that may be provided to `attendeeCollection.iterate`. The unit tests for `checkedInAttendeeCounter` are presented in Listing 5-8.

LISTING 5-8: Unit tests for the Conference.checkedInAttendeeCounter module (code filename: Callbacks\checkedInAttendeeCounter_tests.js)

```
describe('Conference.checkedInAttendeeCounter', function(){
  var counter;

  beforeEach(function(){
    counter = Conference.checkedInAttendeeCounter();
```

continues

LISTING 5-8 *(continued)*

```
  });
  describe('increment()', function(){
    // increment tests
  });
  describe('getCount()', function(){
    // getCount tests
  });
  describe('countIfCheckedIn(attendee)', function(){
    var attendee;

    beforeEach(function(){
      attendee = Conference.attendee('Mike', 'Metcalf');
    });

    it('doesn\'t increment the count if the attendee isn\'t checked in',function(){
      counter.countIfCheckedIn(attendee);
      expect(counter.getCount()).toBe(0);
    });
    it('increments the count if the attendee is checked in', function(){
      attendee.checkIn();
      counter.countIfCheckedIn(attendee);
      expect(counter.getCount()).toBe(1);
    });
  });
});
```

The implementation of `Conference.checkedInAttendeeCounter` follows in Listing 5-9.

LISTING 5-9: Implementation of the Conference.checkedInAttendeeCounter module (code filename: Callbacks\checkedInAttendeeCounter.js)

```
var Conference = Conference || {};

Conference.checkedInAttendeeCounter = function(){
  var checkedInAttendees = 0;
  return{
    increment: function(){
      checkedInAttendees++;
    },
    getCount: function(){
      return checkedInAttendees;
    },
    countIfCheckedIn: function(attendee){
      if(attendee.isCheckedIn()){
        this.increment();
      }
    }
  };
};
```

The implementation contains no surprises and allows the unit tests to pass, as shown in Figure 5-5.

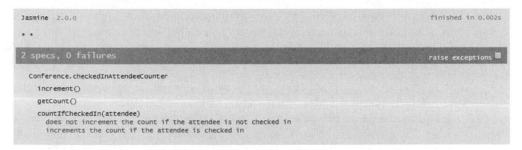

FIGURE 5-5

Notice, however, that `countIfCheckedIn` uses *this* to refer to the instance of `checkedInAttendeeCounter`. The unit tests indicate that all is well, but is it really? Can the `checkedInAttendeeCounter` be used with an instance of `attendeeCollection`? Executing the following code will provide the answer:

```
var checkInService = Conference.checkInService(Conference.checkInRecorder()),
    attendees = Conference.attendeeCollection();
    counter = Conference.checkedInAttendeeCounter();

// Add attendees selected in the UI to the attendee collection
attendees.add(Conference.attendee('Pete', 'Mitchell'));
attendees.add(Conference.attendee('Nick', 'Bradshaw'));

// check the attendees in
attendees.iterate(checkInService.checkIn);

// count the checked-in attendees
attendees.iterate(counter.countIfCheckedIn);

console.log(counter.getCount()); // 0 (!?!?)
```

Both of the attendees that were added should have been checked in, and they also should have been counted; our unit tests prove that all of the modules involved work as designed, but (at least) one of them doesn't work correctly. Otherwise, the count would be 2 and not 0. Figure 5-6 shows what is written to the console when the example is executed.

FIGURE 5-6

The error indicates that one of the functions within the `checkedInAttendeeCounter` is not defined. Further examination with the debugger shows that, when invoked by `attendeeCollection.iterator`, *this* in `checkedInAttendeeCounter` actually refers to the global `window` object and not the `checkedInAttendeeCounter` as desired.

The value of *this* is generally the object on which the function is called (most commonly the object that is "dotted with" the function). However, when you specify a callback function, you have no direct control over which object that will be. For this reason, many callback functions are designed to let you specify *this* explicitly.

The forEach function used by attendeeCollection.iterate allows *this* to be specified explicitly by providing a second argument: the object that *this* should refer to within the callback. Because you are the author of attendeeCollection.iterate, one solution to the problem would be to update attendeeColleciton.iterate to also accept the object that *this* should refer to as a second argument and pass it along to forEach. Doing so would allow *this* to be bound to the instance of checkedInAttendeeCounter that the countIfCheckedIn function expects.

Suppose, however, that attendeeCollection is part of a third-party library and you can't modify it. Is it possible to reliably reference the current object instance in your callbacks? Thankfully, the answer is yes.

First, you should create a unit test that recreates the scenario of checkedInAttendeeCounter .countIfCheckedIn being invoked with *this* referencing an object other than the checkedInAttendeeCounter instance, as demonstrated in Listing 5-10.

> **NOTE** *When you find a bug, it shows your test suite was not sufficient. Always write a failing test before fixing the bug.*

LISTING 5-10: Additional unit test to ensure "this" need not be bound to the instance of checkedInAttendeeCounter (code filename: Callbacks\checkedInAttendeeCounter_tests.js)

```
describe('Conference.checkedInAttendeeCounter', function(){
  var counter;

  // Existing tests omitted

  describe('countIfCheckedIn(attendee)', function(){
    var attendee;

    beforeEach(function(){
      attendee = Conference.attendee('Mike', 'Metcalf');
    });

    // Existing tests omitted

    it('doesn\'t need this to be the checkedInAttendeeCounter instance', function(){
      attendee.checkIn();
      // executes counter.countIfCheckedIn with this assigned to
      // an empty object
      counter.countIfCheckedIn.call({}, attendee);
      expect(counter.getCount()).toBe(1);
    });
  });
});
```

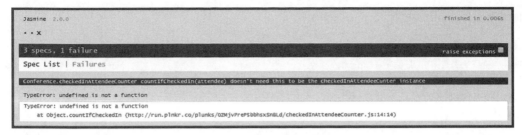

FIGURE 5-7

Figure 5-7 proves that the new unit test accurately recreates the scenario.

Modifying `Conference.checkedInAttendeeCounter` to retain a reference to itself via a variable named *self*, and referencing *self* rather than *this* in `countIfCheckedIn` ensures the `getCount` function is available. Listing 5-11 shows the new implementation of `Conference.checkedInAttendeeCounter`, and Figure 5-8 shows that this new implementation allows all the unit tests to pass.

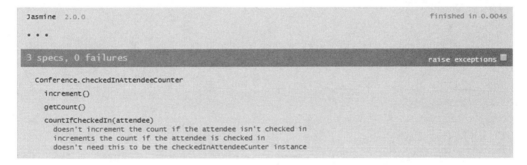

FIGURE 5-8

LISTING 5-11: Updated implementation of the Conference.checkedInAttendeeCounter module (code filename: Callbacks\checkedInAttendeeCounter.js)

```
var Conference = Conference || {};

Conference.checkedInAttendeeCounter = function(){
  var checkedInAttendees = 0,
      self = {
        increment: function(){
          checkedInAttendees += 1;
        },
        getCount: function(){
          return checkedInAttendees;
        },
        countIfCheckedIn: function(attendee){
          if(attendee.isCheckedIn()){
```

continues

LISTING 5-11 *(continued)*

```
                self.increment();
            }
        }
    };

    return self;
};
```

SUMMARY

In this chapter, you saw how to implement the Callback Pattern in a test-first fashion. You saw how to write tests for, and then implement, multiple callback functions, and learned how `this` isn't always what one might think. Also, you saw how anonymous callback functions are difficult to test, and that *nested* anonymous callbacks create a problematic—but fixable—callback arrow.

The next chapter introduces `Promises`, JavaScript objects that provide an alternative to callbacks when working with the results of asynchronous function calls, such as HTTP requests.

Ensuring Correct Use of the Promise Pattern

WROX.COM CODE DOWNLOADS FOR THIS CHAPTER

The wrox.com code downloads for this chapter are found at www.wrox.com/go/reliablejavascript on the Download Code tab. The code is in the Chapter 6 download and individually named according to the filenames noted throughout this chapter.

The last chapter illustrated how to code and test (or, more correctly, test and code) the Callback Pattern. In the main example, `checkInService.checkIn(attendee)` was used as a callback function in iteration through all attendees to check them into a JavaScript conference. This chapter will extend that feature, adding error handling and asynchronous processing.

Although this could be done with JavaScript events, ECMAScript 6 has introduced a better way: the `Promise` object. If you must support older browsers, polyfills are available.

UNDERSTANDING PROMISES THROUGH UNIT TESTS

A `Promise` is an object that encapsulates an asynchronous operation and what to do upon its eventual outcome. When the operation completes, a callback encapsulated in the `Promise` will be invoked. Actually, there can be two callbacks: one for success and one for failure. (The first callback does not have to represent success, but that's typical and it's a good place to start.)

Let's see how this works in practice.

Using a Promise

The example in Chapter 5 included an object called `checkInRecorder` with a `recordCheckIn` function. However, in the unit tests, a Jasmine spy took the place of `recordCheckIn`. The only expectation on the spy was that it was called. Consider the following from Listing 5-4 in Chapter 5:

```
expect(checkInRecorder.recordCheckIn).toHaveBeenCalledWith(attendee);
```

Such a minimal expectation was appropriate, for `checkInService`'s call to `checkInRecorder` was a simple fire-and-forget. Here is the relevant snippet from Listing 5-5 in Chapter 5:

```
Conference.checkInService = function(checkInRecorder){
  // retain a reference to the injected checkInRecorder
  var recorder = checkInRecorder;

  return {
    checkIn: function(attendee){
      attendee.checkIn();
      recorder.recordCheckIn(attendee);
    }
  };
};
```

What if you were to want more—maybe some error-handling, or maybe further processing upon success? You can imagine that a typical implementation of `checkInRecorder` would issue an `XMLHttpRequest` to cause the server to record the check-in. `CheckInRecorder` would listen for the `onreadystatechange` event associated with that request, take whatever action was appropriate for success or failure, and probably furnish an event to *its* caller (`checkInService`). Wiring that all up can be tedious and results in code that is a little helter-skelter. Wouldn't it be nice if you could do something like what's in Listing 6-1?

LISTING 6-1: checkInService.js (code filename: Promises\checkInService_01.js)

```
Conference.checkInService = function(checkInRecorder){
  'use strict';

  // retain a reference to the injected checkInRecorder
  var recorder = checkInRecorder;

  return {
    checkIn: function(attendee){
```

```
        attendee.checkIn();
        recorder.recordCheckIn(attendee).then(
          // Success
          attendee.setCheckInNumber,
          // Failure
          attendee.undoCheckIn);
      }
    };
  };
```

The idea, of course, is that recordCheckIn does its work asynchronously and *then* when it is done (note the call to then), either the success or failure callback is called. In this case, the callbacks are functions in the attendee object. You can guess what they do based on their names; the trivial details are in this chapter's downloads.

For all this to work, recordCheckIn must return an object with a then method, which takes two parameters: a function to call on success and one to call on failure. That happens to be the heart of a Promise.

Listing 6-2 expresses what is required, in the form of a unit test. It is a slight reworking of Listing 5-4, with the one additional test.

LISTING 6-2: Naïve unit test of checkInService.checkIn (code filename: Promises\checkInService_01_tests.js)

```
describe('Conference.checkInService', function(){
  'use strict';
  var checkInService,
      checkInRecorder,
      attendee;

  beforeEach(function(){
    checkInRecorder = Conference.checkInRecorder();
    checkInService = Conference.checkInService(checkInRecorder);
    attendee = Conference.attendee('Sam', 'Wells');
  });

  describe('checkInService.checkIn(attendee)', function(){

    describe('when checkInRecorder succeeds ', function() {
      var checkInNumber = 1234;
      beforeEach(function() {
        spyOn(checkInRecorder,'recordCheckIn').and.callFake(function() {
          return Promise.resolve(checkInNumber);
        });
      });

      // Same tests as in Chapter 5
      it('marks the attendee checked in', function() {
        checkInService.checkIn(attendee);
        expect(attendee.isCheckedIn()).toBe(true);
      });
```

continues

LISTING 6-2 *(continued)*

```
        it('records the check-in', function() {
          checkInService.checkIn(attendee);
          expect(checkInRecorder.recordCheckIn).toHaveBeenCalledWith(attendee);
        });

        // New test for Chapter 6
        it("sets the attendee's checkInNumber", function(done) {
          checkInService.checkIn(attendee);
          expect(attendee.getCheckInNumber()).toBe(checkInNumber);
        });
      });
    });
  });
```

The second `beforeEach` sets up a spy on `checkInRecorder.recordCheckIn` to make it return a `Promise`. In this case, it is a `Promise` that is *fulfilled*. Confusingly at first, the method that creates a fulfilled `Promise` is not `Promise.fulfill`, but `Promise.resolve`. You will see why later in this chapter.

Because the `Promise` is fulfilled (resolved), it causes the first callback of the `then` method to be called. The callback gets the result of the successful processing within the `Promise`— *checkInNumber* in this case. Creating an already fulfilled `Promise` is obviously a shortcut; you will see how to create more realistic `Promises` in the next section.

Now you would expect the following to happen:

1.   `checkInService.checkIn` is called in the unit test.

2.   That method entails a call to `recorder.recordCheckIn` (see Listing 6-1).

3.   The spy on `recordCheckIn` will cause it to return a resolved `Promise` with a value of `checkInNumber`.

4.   The success callback of `recordCheckIn(attendee).then` will be followed (see Listing 6-1 again).

5.   That success callback, `attendee.setCheckInNumber`, gets `checkInNumber` as a parameter.

6.   So, the expectation at the end of the unit test is met!

Every step of that sequence was true, but Figure 6-1 shows what happens.

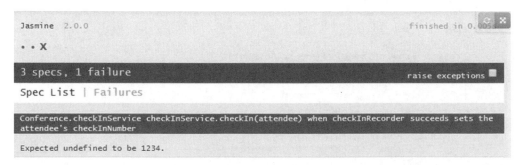

FIGURE 6-1

The error message indicates that at the time of the expectation, `checkInNumber` was not set. What could have gone wrong? It will become clear once you know two things:

➤ `Promises` are asynchronous.

➤ JavaScript is single-threaded, mimicking multi-threading with an event loop.

These facts imply that control does not flow into the success callback of the `Promise`'s `then` method until the next turn of JavaScript's event loop. (See *JavaScript is Single-Threaded* in Chapter 1.) The unit test does not give up its turn until it finishes—that is, until the expectation has already been stated. By the time the `Promise` is resolved, it is too late!

You can prove this by downloading the code for this chapter and setting some breakpoints. Running `checkInService_01.html` with breakpoints set in *checkInService_01.js* and `checkInService_01_tests.js`, you will see the code execute in this order:

1. The first line of the unit test:

   ```
   checkInService.checkIn(attendee);
   ```

2. The return of the `Promise` from the spy:

   ```
   Promise.resolve(checkInNumber);
   ```

3. The expectation on the second line of the unit test:

   ```
   expect(attendee.getCheckInNumber()).toBe(checkInNumber);
   ```

4. The success callback in `attendee.js` (too late!):

   ```
   sctCheckInNumber: function(number) {
   checkInNumber = number;
   }
   ```

So how can you ensure the reliability of `Promise`-based code through unit tests? The key is not to check the result of the code until the `Promise` has been "followed." This involves two things.

First, you would change `checkInService.checkIn` to return the value from the call to `then`. It happens that this is a `Promise`! Recall that `then` has two callbacks. You probably want to return a resolved `Promise` if you end up in the resolved/success callback, and a rejected `Promise` if you get to the rejected/failure callback. You could do this by making the `checkIn` function construct and return a `Promise` directly (you will see how to do that shortly), but after a little research, you learn that there is a shortcut, shown in Listing 6-3: You can make each callback return a `Promise`, and that `Promise` will become the resolved value of the `Promise` returned by `then`. In general, if a `then` callback returns a `Promise`-like object (basically one with a `then` function), that object flows out to be the resolved value of `then`. Otherwise, `then` wraps the return value of the callback in a resolved `Promise`, which it returns.

LISTING 6-3: Returning the result of then (code filename: Promises\checkInService.js)

```
var Conference = Conference || {};

Conference.checkInService = function(checkInRecorder) {
```

continues

LISTING 6-3 *(continued)*

```
'use strict';

// retain a reference to the injected checkInRecorder
var recorder = checkInRecorder;

return {
  checkIn: function(attendee){
    attendee.checkIn();
    return recorder.recordCheckIn(attendee).then(
      function onRecordCheckInSucceeded(checkInNumber) {
        attendee.setCheckInNumber(checkInNumber);
        return Promise.resolve(checkInNumber);
      },
      function onRecordCheckInFailed(reason) {
        attendee.undoCheckIn();
        return Promise.reject(reason);
      });
  }
};
};
```

Second, you cause the unit test not to issue its expectation until the `Promise` from `then` is *settled* (a term meaning either resolved or rejected). You do this by executing your expectation within a `then`, as in Listing 6-4.

LISTING 6-4: A better unit test of checkInService.checkIn (code filename: Promises\ checkInService_tests.js)

```
it("sets the attendee's checkInNumber", function(done) {
  checkInService.checkIn(attendee).then(
    function onPromiseResolved() {
      expect(attendee.getCheckInNumber()).toBe(checkInNumber);
      done();
    },
    function onPromiseRejected() {
      expect('This failure branch was executed').toBe(false);
      done();
    });
});
```

Because a `Promise` can be either resolved or rejected, it is a good idea to code both branches in your test. The rejection branch has an awkward-looking expectation:

```
expect('This failure branch was executed').toBe(false);
```

As of this writing, Jasmine does not have a better way to force a failure in asynchronous code. An enterprising person has added an explicit `fail` function to Jasmine (`https://github.com/pivotal/ jasmine/commit/ b1344d5c73c5e01a07e1ea435be3ed980f6db9de`), but it is not yet part of the official release. As silly looking as the expectation in the `onPromiseRejected` branch of the test is, it will display a perfectly informative error message in Jasmine's output.

You probably noticed something else: the calls to `done()` in both the resolve and reject branches. This is how Jasmine supports the testing of asynchronous code. You can see that `done` is the argument to the function on the first line of Listing 6-4. It is just the name you give to an argument and it could have been anything, but whatever you name it, you must call it when all of your asynchronous processing is complete. If you don't, Jasmine will issue a timeout failure.

If you omit the `done()` mechanism entirely (the parameter and both calls), Jasmine will let your test finish before the asynchronous work is complete. Your test will seem to pass, but only because neither the resolve nor reject branches will execute in time to affect the outcome! This means that if you were to remove all traces of `done` from Listing 6-4, the first expectation could be anything at all, and the test would pass! This highlights the importance of writing unit tests that fail before writing the code to make them succeed. There is also no harm in using your debugger to verify that your tests are executing as you expect.

> **NOTE** *Always use Jasmine's* `done()` *mechanism when testing asynchronous code.*

This snippet, also from `checkInService_tests.js` in this chapter's downloads, illustrates the testing of a failure branch.

```
describe('when checkInRecorder fails', function() {
  var recorderError = 'Check-in recording failed!';
  beforeEach(function() {
    spyOn(checkInRecorder,'recordCheckIn').and.returnValue(
      Promise.reject(new Error(recorderError)));
    spyOn(attendee,'undoCheckIn');
  });

  it("returns a Promise rejected with the expected reason", function(done){
    checkInService.checkIn(attendee).then(
      function promiseResolved() {
        expect('This success function to execute').toBe(false);
        done();
      },
      function promiseRejected(reason) {
        expect(reason.message).toBe(recorderError);
        done();
      });
  });
});
```

Constructing and Returning a Promise

The code so far spies on `checkInRecorder.recordCheckIn`, faking its return with a `Promise` `.resolve`. An actual `checkInRecorder` would make an HTTP request, probably through an `XMLHttpRequest` object. HTTP requests are one of the most common asynchronous operations you will use, and wrapping them in a `Promise` is very natural. (In fact, some forward-thinking architects have done exactly that. See, for example, the AngularJS `$http` object.)

It happens that your next job as you write the JavaScript conference's website is to implement the `checkInRecorder`. You are bursting with enthusiasm for `Promises` and eager to experiment with how a `Promise` can wrap an `XMLHttpRequest`, but you are also an experienced developer who knows the wisdom of proceeding in small steps. You decide to make sure you have a solid understanding of how to construct a `Promise` first, and add real HTTP later.

Drawing on the knowledge you already have, you craft the unit tests in Listing 6-5.

LISTING 6-5: Unit tests for checkInRecorder.recordCheckIn without HTTP (code filename: Promises\checkInRecorder_01_tests.js)

```javascript
describe('Conference.checkInRecorder', function() {
  'use strict';
  var attendee, checkInRecorder;
  beforeEach(function() {
    attendee = Conference.attendee('Tom','Jones');
    checkInRecorder = Conference.checkInRecorder();
  });

  describe('recordCheckIn(attendee)', function() {

    it('returns a Promise fulfilled with a checkInNumber ' +
        'if attendee is checked in', function(done) {
      attendee.checkIn();
      checkInRecorder.recordCheckIn(attendee).then(
        function promiseResolved(actualCheckInNumber) {
          expect(typeof actualCheckInNumber).toBe('number');
          done();
        },
        function promiseRejected() {
          expect('The promise was rejected').toBe(false);
          done();
        });
    });

    it('returns a Promise rejected with an Error ' +
        'if attendee is not checked in', function(done) {
      checkInRecorder.recordCheckIn(attendee).then(
        function promiseResolved() {
          expect('The promise was resolved').toBe(false);
          done();
        },
        function promiseRejected(reason) {
          expect(reason instanceof Error).toBe(true);
          expect(reason.message)
            .toBe(checkInRecorder.getMessages().mustBeCheckedIn)
          done();
        });
    });
  });
});
```

Now it is time to implement `checkInRecorder` to make the tests pass. Listing 6-6 is the result.

LISTING 6-6: Implementation of checkInRecorder without HTTP (code filename: Promises\
checkInRecorder_01.js)

```javascript
var Conference = Conference || {};

Conference.checkInRecorder = function() {
  'use strict';

  var messages = {
    mustBeCheckedIn: 'The attendee must be marked as checked in.'
  };

  return {
    getMessages: function() {
      return messages;
    },

    recordCheckIn: function(attendee) {
      return new Promise( function(resolve, reject) {
        if (attendee.isCheckedIn()) {
          resolve(4444); // For now, resolve with any number.
        } else {
          reject(new Error(messages.mustBeCheckedIn));
        }
      });
    }
  };
};
```

You have done a number of things right.

First, you have exposed the messages to your unit tests so you can verify the exact message in an expectation. More to the point of this chapter, you have constructed a Promise correctly:

➤ It is constructed with new.

➤ The argument to its constructor is a function that itself has two arguments. You may call them anything you wish, but resolve and reject convey their intent.

➤ To fulfill the Promise with a value, you call resolve with that value.

➤ To reject the Promise, you call reject with the reason. By convention, the reason is an Error object, giving you the benefit of a stack trace should you want one.

➤ You remembered to use done().

With this experience, you can imagine how you could have coded checkInService.checkIn with direct construction of the Promise rather than returning Promise.resolve and Promise.reject from the callbacks:

```javascript
checkIn: function(attendee){
    return new Promise( function checkInPromise(resolve, reject) {
      attendee.checkIn();
      recorder.recordCheckIn(attendee).then(
```

```
              function onRecordCheckInSucceeded(checkInNumber) {
                attendee.setCheckInNumber(checkInNumber);
                resolve(checkInNumber);
              },
              function onRecordCheckInFailed(reason) {
                attendee.undoCheckIn();
                reject(reason);
              });
          });
      }
```

Testing an XMLHttpRequest

With that preliminary implementation out of the way, you are ready to put a real XMLHttpRequest in recordCheckIn.

You search the web for a way to test XMLHttpRequest in Jasmine and soon come across jasmine-ajax on GitHub (https://github.com/pivotal/jasmine-ajax). After incorporating mock-ajax.js in your project as directed there, you elaborate on the earlier tests. Listing 6-7 shows the result, with new ideas highlighted. (The reason for the asterisked comments will be clear in a moment.)

> **LISTING 6-7:** Unit tests for checkInRecorder with HTTP (code filename: Promises\ checkInRecorder_tests.js)

```
describe('Conference.checkInRecorder', function() {
  'use strict';

  var attendee, checkInRecorder;
  beforeEach(function() {
    attendee = Conference.attendee('Tom','Jones');
    attendee.setId(777);
    checkInRecorder = Conference.checkInRecorder();

    // *** 1 ***
    // Install Jasmine's XMLHttpRequest-mocking library
    jasmine.Ajax.install();
  });

  afterEach(function() {
    // Let normal XMLHttpRequests take place when done.
    jasmine.Ajax.uninstall();
  });

  describe('recordCheckIn(attendee)', function() {

    it('returns a Promise fulfilled with a checkInNumber ' +
        'if attendee is checked in '+
        'and the HTTP request succeeds', function() { // *** 9 ***
      var expectedCheckInNumber = 1234,
          request;
      attendee.checkIn();

      // *** 2 ***
```

```
checkInRecorder.recordCheckIn(attendee).then(
  function promiseResolved(actualCheckInNumber) {
    // *** 8 ***
    expect(actualCheckInNumber).toBe(expectedCheckInNumber);
  },
  function promiseRejected() {
    expect('The promise was rejected').toBe(false);
  });

  // *** 4 ***
  request = jasmine.Ajax.requests.mostRecent();

  // *** 5 ***
  expect(request.url).toBe('/checkin/' + attendee.getId());

  // *** 6 ***
  request.response({
    "status": 200,
    "contentType": "text/plain",
    "responseText": expectedCheckInNumber
  });
});

it('returns a Promise rejected with the correct message ' +
  'if attendee is checked in '+
  'and the HTTP request fails', function() {
  var request;
  attendee.checkIn();
  checkInRecorder.recordCheckIn(attendee).then(
    function promiseResolved(actualCheckInNumber) {
      expect('The promise was resolved').toBe(false);
    },
    function promiseRejected(reason) {
      expect(reason instanceof Error).toBe(true);
      expect(reason.message)
        .toBe(checkInRecorder.getMessages().httpFailure);
    });
  request = jasmine.Ajax.requests.mostRecent();
  expect(request.url).toBe('/checkin/' + attendee.getId());
  request.response({
    "status": 404,
    "contentType": "text/plain",
    "responseText": "Some error message."
  });
});

it('returns a Promise rejected with an Error ' +
  'if attendee is not checked in', function(done) {
  checkInRecorder.recordCheckIn(attendee).then(
    function promiseResolved() {
      expect('The promise was resolved').toBe(false);
      done();
    },
    function promiseRejected(reason) {
      expect(reason instanceof Error).toBe(true);
      expect(reason.message)
```

continues

LISTING 6-7 *(continued)*

```
                .toBe(checkInRecorder.getMessages().mustBeCheckedIn);
            done();
          });
        });
      });
    });
```

Of course, you get failures all over the place until you put the XMLHttpRequest in checkInRecorder, as you see in Listing 6-8.

LISTING 6-8: Implementation of checkInRecorder with HTTP (code filename: Promises\ checkInRecorder.js)

```
var Conference = Conference || {};

Conference.checkInRecorder = function(){
  'use strict';

  var messages = {
    mustBeCheckedIn: 'The attendee must be marked as checked in.',
    httpFailure: 'The HTTP request failed.'
  };

  return {
    getMessages: function() {
      return messages;
    },

    recordCheckIn: function(attendee) {
      return new Promise( function(resolve, reject) {
        if (attendee.isCheckedIn()) {

          // *** 3 ***
          var xhr = new XMLHttpRequest();
          xhr.onreadystatechange=function onreadystatechange() {
            if (xhr.readyState==4) {
              if (xhr.status==200) {
                // *** 7 ***
                resolve(xhr.responseText);
              } else {
                reject(new Error(messages.httpFailure));
              }
            }
          };
          xhr.open("POST","/checkin/" + attendee.getId(),true);
          xhr.send();
        } else {
          reject(new Error(messages.mustBeCheckedIn));
        }
      });
    }
  };
};
```

Your colleague, Charlotte, rushes over when she hears your whoops and hollers as the unit tests pass. She wonders how you did it. You explain it to her, helpfully pointing to Listings 6-7 and 6-8. The asterisked numbers in the comments correspond to the steps of your explanation.

1. "Starting with Listing 6-7, I installed Jasmine's Ajax mocker in the `beforeEach` and removed it just to be safe in the `afterEach`," you tell Charlotte. "For the duration of each test, then, Jasmine will intercept all `XMLHttpRequests`, causing them to exhibit whatever behavior I specify.

2. "Taking the first test as an example, I executed `recordCheckIn` with expectations in the `then` method just as before. Neither branch of the `then` executes yet, again because the `Promise` is asynchronous and the test hasn't finished its turn on the event loop.

3. "However, moving to Listing 6-8, the function passed to the `Promise`'s constructor in `recordCheckIn` does execute, albeit with a **Fake**`XMLHttpRequest` thanks to Jasmine's mock.

4. "Back in Listing 6-7, after calling `recordCheckIn`, I obtain the request that was made through `FakeXMLHttpRequest` with a call to `jasmine.Ajax.requests.mostRecent()`.

5. "I can then verify that it was called with the correct URL.

6. "Now I trigger the response to the request by calling `request.response`.

7. "This causes the object literal given in the parameter to be received in `checkInRecorder` (see Listing 6-8), whose `Promise` is then resolved with the `responseText` I supplied in my test.

8. "That causes the `then` to be followed into the `promiseResolved` function of the unit test in Listing 6-7. The expectation is met and the test passes.

9. "In fact, because `request.response()` made the `Promise` resolve within the current turn of the event loop, the unit test is no longer strictly asynchronous, and Jasmine's `done()` mechanism is no longer required. "However," you add with a self-satisfied smile toward Charlotte, "it would have done no harm."

CHAINING PROMISES

Charlotte is a quick study and was able to grok the code at a glance while you were droning on. That gave her plenty of time to think about Listing 6-3, which was still displaying on your second monitor.

"With the code written this way," Charlotte continues, "you could chain one `then` after another, and each `then`'s resolve callback would only be executed on the success of the previous one. Something like this":

```
checkInService.checkIn(attendee)
  .then(
    function onCheckInResolved(checkInNumber) {
      // Print a badge and returns its number.
      return badgePrintingService.print(checkInNumber);
    });
  .then(
    function onBadgePrintResolved(badgeNumber) {
      return doorPrizeEnteringService.enter(attendee, badgeNumber);
    });
```

"I suppose you could do that," you reply. "However, you'd probably want a second (rejection) callback at each stage.

"Plus, the unit tests might require setting up multiple `XMLHttpRequest` objects. I see here [http://jasmine.github.io/2.0/ajax.html] that you can do that ahead of time with `jasmine.Ajax.stubRequest` instead of calling `request.response`."

"Sure, sure," Charlotte says, but she is already thinking about the potential for a mistake: "You know, if you forget the `return` keyword at any stage—let's say the one on the `badgePrintingService.print` line—you'll get (in this case) a `badgeNumber` of `undefined` in the next stage. I bet that's a pretty common mistake."

> **NOTE** *Be aware that if* `then`'s *executed callback doesn't return anything,* `then` *will return a Promise resolved with a value of* `undefined`.

Glad to be a step ahead of Charlotte for a change, you reply, "Yes. That's why I was sure to verify the actual `checkInNumber` in my tests."

"That's not quite the same thing," she answers, "but you were in the right frame of mind."

"I wonder," she continues, "what you would have done if there hadn't been a `jasmine.Ajax` library to use. [You try not to take this remark as meaning any offense.] For that matter, are there any general-purpose mocking libraries for `Promises`?"

The next day, she has the answer.

USING A PROMISE WRAPPER

"It turns out that manipulating `Promises` in unit tests is harder than you'd think," Charlotte says. "Your code was pretty simple [Why does she always say things like that?], but when you need to make a `Promise` resolve, you'll be stuck—I don't mean creating one in an already-resolved state; you've done that [See Listing 6-2]; I mean resolving or rejecting a `Promise` that already exists. If you look at the `Promise` API [https://developer.mozilla.org/en-US/docs/Web/JavaScript/Reference/Global_Objects/Promise], you'll see there's no way to do it!"

"I hadn't noticed that," you admit, "but now I see that the only methods on the `Promise` prototype are `then` and `catch`."

"Exactly," she continues. "But some very smart people [Again you try not to take offense.] have created wrappers, often called something like `Deferred`, that dependency-inject a `Promise`-like object, which can be a real `Promise` or, when unit-testing, a fake `Promise`.

"For example, with AngularJS [https://docs.angularjs.org/api/ng/service/$q] you would do this. [$q is Angular 1.3's implementation of a `Promise` library called Q [https://github.com/kriskowal/q.]"

```
var deferred = $q.defer();         // Create a "deferred" object
var promise = deferred.promise;    // It has a promise property...
deferred.resolve(1234);            // Resolves the promise with value 1234
```

"AngularJS 2.0 will revampt this somewhat," Charlotte concluded. (See Promises in Angular 2.0 at `https://docs.google.com/document/d/1ksBjyCgwuiEUGn9h2NYQGtmQkP5N9HbehMBgaxMtwfs/edit`.)

UNDERSTANDING STATES AND FATES

"When manipulating `Promises`, either real ones or fake ones through `Deferred`, you have to understand the difference between resolving a `Promise` and fulfilling it," Charlotte continues.

"The function for creating a fulfilled `Promise` was not called `Promise.fulfill` but `Promise.resolve`. That's because a `Promise` doesn't have to be resolved by fulfilling it with a value. It can be resolved to another `Promise`—which might already be rejected, or become rejected later! 'Resolved' just means that the fate of the Promise is sealed in one way or another: locked into a value or to the ultimate fate of another `Promise`.

"I found a web page on GitHub that explains it all very well, called States and Fates." (See `https://github.com/domenic/promises-unwrapping/blob/master/docs/states-and-fates.md`.)

"Basically, a `Promise` always has one of three *states*: fulfilled, rejected, or pending. They mean pretty much what you'd expect, although the technical definition has some fine shading.

"And there are two *fates*: resolved and unresolved. An unresolved `Promise` always has a pending state, but a resolved Promise might be in any of the three states, although fulfilled is the most typical.

"It is a little counter-intuitive that returning the `Promise` from a `then` whose rejection branch is followed could land you in the resolved branch of a unit test, but if that rejection callback returns a resolved `Promise`, or a bare value (which then converts to a resolved `Promise`), that is what will happen."

"As you said, that's probably a common mistake," you volunteer.

DISTINGUISHING STANDARD PROMISES FROM JQUERY PROMISES

"One more thing," Charlotte said. "It turns out that jQuery promises are not exactly `Promises` in the sense that we know. Kris Kowal, who wrote the Q library adapted by AngularJS, has a GitHub page that spells out the differences." (See `https://github.com/kriskowal/q/wiki/Coming-from-jQuery`.)

"Okay, then," you reply, hoping she'll stop.

SUMMARY

In this chapter, you learned how to construct and use `Promises`:

➤ A `Promise` encapsulates a future event and callbacks to execute upon success or failure of that event.

➤ The argument to its constructor is a function that wraps the asynchronous work. The function has two parameters: `resolve` and `reject`. Call one of them when you are ready to resolve or reject the `Promise`.

➤ The key method of a `Promise` object is `then`. It takes two parameters, each one a callback function.

➤ The first callback is followed when the `Promise` "resolves." It receives the resolved value as a parameter.

➤ The second callback executes when the `Promise` is "rejected." Its parameter is the reason for rejection. It is a good idea to make that an `Error` object, but a simple string works, too.

You also dealt with some of the pitfalls of testing `Promise`-based code, including:

➤ Because `Promises` are asynchronous, if you are not careful they will still be unresolved when the expectations of your test execute. This can cause your tests to pass when they shouldn't. Jasmine provides special support for testing asynchronous code in the form of the `done()` mechanism.

➤ When you unit-test code that uses `XMLHttpRequest`, you don't want to call the server, but you do want to simulate the asynchronous nature of HTTP. Jasmine provides an Ajax mocking library for this purpose.

➤ `Promises` are designed to be chained. Be sure your tests verify that execution flows into the expected `then` callback in all cases.

➤ `Promise` wrappers such as AngularJS's `$q` or Kris Kowal's `Q` are available to give you more control over the resolution and rejection of `Promises` in unit tests.

7

Ensuring Correct Use of Partial Function Application

WHAT'S IN THIS CHAPTER?

➤ Unit-testing a partial function application

➤ Adding a partial function application to an existing object with an aspect

➤ Distinguishing between a partial function application and currying

WROX.COM CODE DOWNLOADS FOR THIS CHAPTER

The wrox.com code downloads for this chapter are found at www.wrox.com/go/ reliablejavascript on the Download Code tab and in the Chapter 7 download.

Occasionally, you will use a function that has several arguments, but some of those arguments will always have the same values. Rather than supplying those values over and over again, it can be convenient to create a new function that wraps the original, supplying the constant arguments and exposing the rest. This technique is called *partial function application*.

Because you build on a known-good function, the new function is exceptionally easy to unit-test, making it a true friend on the road to reliable JavaScript.

UNIT-TESTING A PARTIAL FUNCTION APPLICATION

The upcoming JavaScript conference will be filled with thousands of hungry developers—not hungry for opportunities to program, which they all have in abundance, but hungry for food. Being a quirky lot, many of them have dietary restrictions: Some are vegan, while others eat only pizza. The conference will be jam-packed with events and it will be important to the attendees that they waste no time finding food. The next job for you and your colleague, Charlotte, is to help them.

Your role is to find a third-party web service that will locate nearby restaurants. Charlotte will program the UI using the service you find.

In no time at all, you locate third-party code with the API in Listing 7-1.

LISTING 7-1: Third-party API (code filename: PFA\ThirdPartyRestaurantApi.js)

```
var ThirdParty = ThirdParty || {};
ThirdParty.restaurantApi = function(){

  return {
    // Returns a Promise to return an array of restaurants serving the
    // specified cuisine within radiusMiles of the provided address
    getRestaurantsWithinRadius: function(address, radiusMiles, cuisine){
      // Promise resolves to an array of objects that look like:
      // {
      //   name: "Bill's Burgers",
      //   address: "123 Main St, AnyTown, 44444"
      // }
    }
  };
};
```

The API is great, but it's actually more than you need. For one thing, your *address* argument will never vary, always being equal to the conference's address. Second, the specs say that "nearby restaurants" will always mean those within 2 miles. That means the radiusMiles parameter will be constant as well.

To make Charlotte's job easier, you decide to extend the API with a function that does exactly what you need: getRestaurantsNearConference(cuisine).

"Extend the API. Hmm . . ." That phrase evokes memories of something you once read about aspect-oriented programming. You decide to use AOP to add the new function to the API returned by the restaurantApi function.

"The idea—the *only* idea," you tell yourself, "is that getRestaurantsNearConference(cuisine) should return whatever getRestaurantsWithinRadius(address, radius, cuisine) returns, with the fixed parameters of my address and radius. Because that is the *only* idea, my unit tests can be ridiculously simple."

You hack together the unit tests in Listing 7-2.

LISTING 7-2: Unit test for getRestaurantsNearConference (code filename: PFA/ThirdPartyRestaurantApiAspects_tests.js)

```
describe('ThirdParty.restaurantApi() aspects', function() {
  var api = ThirdParty.restaurantApi();

  describe('getRestaurantsNearConference(cuisine)', function() {
    var returnFromUnderlyingFunction = 'something',
        cuisine = 'Vegan';
```

```
    beforeEach(function() {
      spyOn(api, 'getRestaurantsWithinRadius')
        .and.returnValue(returnFromUnderlyingFunction);
    });

    it('calls getRestaurantsWithinRadius with the correct args', function() {
      api.getRestaurantsNearConference(cuisine);
      expect(api.getRestaurantsWithinRadius).toHaveBeenCalledWith(
        '415 Summer St, Boston, MA 02210',2.0,cuisine);
    });

    it('returns the value from getRestaurantsWithinRadius', function() {
      var ret = api.getRestaurantsNearConference(cuisine);
      expect(ret).toBe(returnFromUnderlyingFunction);
    });
  });
});
```

You note with satisfaction that your tests make no assumption about the type of data returned from the original function. As you saw in Chapter 6, unit-testing `Promise`-based code can be tricky. You didn't have to worry about that here.

In fact, because your spy has caused a particular object, and a strange one at that, to be returned from `getRestaurantsWithinRadius`, you can verify that this exact object is returned untouched. You don't want your aspect to return a value obtained through any other means because that would be outside the aspect's single responsibility. This is one of those happy times when a test that is easier to write is stronger as well.

You take a moment to savor the thought and then you are ready to work on the aspect itself.

CREATING AN ASPECT FOR PARTIAL FUNCTION APPLICATION

You want to add a function like this one to the API, wrapping the original function and applying fixed values for some of its parameters:

```
function getRestaurantsNearConference(cuisine) {
  return api.getRestaurantsWithinRadius(
    '415 Summer St, Boston, MA 02210', 2.0, cuisine);
}
```

After some review of Chapter 2, you code Listing 7-3.

LISTING 7-3: getRestaurantsNearConference (code filename: PFA/ThirdPartyRestaurantApiAspects.js)

```
// Add member getRestaurantsNearConference to ThirdParty.restaurantApi().

Aop.around(
  // Function whose return value should be modified.
```

continues

LISTING 7-3 *(continued)*

```
'restaurantApi',

// Function that modifies the return value
function addGetRestaurantsNearConference(targetInfo){

  // Original API returned from ThirdParty.restaurantApi().
  var api =  Aop.next.call(this,targetInfo);

  // Function that will be added to the API
  function getRestaurantsNearConference(cuisine) {
    return api.getRestaurantsWithinRadius(
      '415 Summer St, Boston, MA 02210', 2.0, cuisine);
  }

  // Add the function if it's not already there.
  api.getRestaurantsNearConference =
    api.getRestaurantsNearConference || getRestaurantsNearConference;

  // Return the revised API.
  return api;
},

// Namespace of the function whose return value should be modified
ThirdParty
);
```

In the unlikely event that the authors of the API ever add a `getRestaurantsNearConference` function of their own, the `||` trick in the assignment to `api.getRestaurantsNearConference` ensures yours will not replace it. By design, your unit tests will fail, notifying you of the change to the API.

But for now, the tests pass, as shown in Figure 7-1.

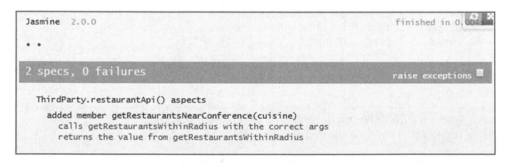

FIGURE 7-1

You check in the code and decide to treat yourself to some Internet surfing to learn more.

DISTINGUISHING BETWEEN PARTIAL FUNCTION APPLICATION AND CURRYING

You soon discover that there is a concept closely related to partial function application called *currying*. In fact, they are so closely related as to be often conflated.

Currying

Currying is the decomposition of a function that takes several arguments into several functions that take one argument each. The upshot is that instead of doing this:

```
getRestaurantsWithinRadius(address, radius, cuisine)
```

you can do this:

```
getRestaurantsCurried(address)(radius)(cuisine)
```

The first call, `getRestaurantsCurried(address)`, returns a function that takes a *radius* argument and returns yet another function, this time taking a *cuisine* argument. The deepest function in the nesting is finally equipped to yield the answer.

What prestidigitation makes this possible? The simplest, most concrete form is this:

```
function getRestaurantsCurried(address) {
  var self = this;
  return function(radius) {
    return function(cuisine) {
      return self.getRestaurantsWithinRadius(address, radius, cuisine);
    }
  }
}
```

More abstract forms abound on the Internet, but the foregoing conveys the spirit of currying best. (You will also notice that those abundant implementations of `curry` are invariably nothing more than a partial function application of one or more parameters—not magic wands that you can wave *one time* over *any function* to turn it into a sequence of functions, each returning a function, except for the last one, which is smart enough to know it can return the answer.)

Some programming languages make curried functions a way of life: In Haskell and ML, *all* functions take just one argument. Certain patterns and possibilities then emerge that are beyond the scope of this book, such as the study of lambda calculus (`http://plato.stanford.edu/entries/lambda-calculus/`).

Partial Function Application

Partial function application looks like currying at first glance, consisting as it does of turning a function that takes several arguments into one that takes fewer. In reality, it is almost the reverse, as the following implementation of `getRestaurantsNearConference` demonstrates. It builds *back up* from the curried parts created previously to a function that is functionally identical to the partial-function-application version from earlier in the chapter.

```
function getRestaurantsNearConference(cuisine) {
  return getRestaurantsCurried
    ('415 Summer St, Boston, MA 02210')(2.0)(cuisine);
}
```

SUMMARY

If you have code that calls a function with some arguments never varying, consider creating a new function that encapsulates the constancy. This is the technique of partial function application.

The unit tests of the new function become the correct and DRY place to verify that you are using the constants you expect. Happily, the unit tests don't have to (and should not) make any other assumptions about the original function, not even its return type.

Partial function application is often confused with currying. True currying does not apply any arguments, partially or otherwise. Rather, it breaks a multi-argument function down into a series of steps that each take a single argument. If you like the way partial function application helps you to avoid using arguments, you'll love the way *memoization* avoids executing the entire body of a function. That is the subject of the next chapter.

Ensuring Correct Use of the Memoization Pattern

WHAT'S IN THIS CHAPTER?

➤ Applying the Memoization Pattern to solve business problems

➤ Unit-testing implementations of the Memoization Pattern

➤ Unit-testing and generically implementing the Memoization Pattern as an aspect

WROX.COM CODE DOWNLOADS FOR THIS CHAPTER

The wrox.com code downloads for this chapter are found at www.wrox.com/go/reliablejavascript on the Download Code tab and in the Chapter 8 download.

The organizers of the JavaScript conference are pleased with the restaurant search functionality that you and Charlotte have baked into the website, except for one thing: It's costing them quite a bit of money. A third-party API retrieves the restaurants charges for each and every request made to it, and quite a bill was racked up just during development and testing.

The organizers have come to you and Charlotte to see if there's anything that can be done to reduce the damage to their credit card bill once the hungry conference attendees start using the feature.

"Many attendees will probably search for the same type of cuisine," posits Charlotte, "so we could save the results the first time any user searches for a cuisine, and return those results to the next user that searches for the same cuisine. It's unlikely that new restaurants will open up—or existing restaurants close down—during the conference, so the API will just return the same restaurants for each type of cuisine anyway."

While the solution sounds promising to the conference organizers, they're concerned that the work that's already been done with the third-party API will have to be thrown away.

"Not at all," you tell them. "We can create a façade, or wrapper, for the API that adds the ability to save and return previous search results. None of the existing code will have to change, or be discarded."

With the bottom line again looking safe and sound, the conference organizers direct you to get started on the façade without delay.

The pattern that Charlotte described, and that you have to implement, is the *Memoization Pattern*. Memoization saves the results of a function each time it is invoked, usually in a structure that is keyed by the arguments that were provided to the function. Then, when the function is invoked with arguments it has seen before, the saved value is looked up and returned immediately; the logic in the body of the function is not performed.

In cases where repeated calls are made to a function that performs a time- or resource-intensive calculation, the retrieval of the saved value will be significantly less costly than repeating the whole operation.

As far as patterns go, the Memoization Pattern is a simple one; it can be implemented in just a few lines of code. Its simplicity has lulled many developers into complacency: just a copy here and a paste there and voila, another memoized function . . . and duplicate code!

This chapter covers how to implement and test the Memoization Pattern. Also, you learn how the pattern can be applied using AOP, keeping your code DRY.

UNDERSTANDING THE PATTERN THROUGH UNIT TESTS

As Charlotte pointed out, it's unlikely that the set of restaurants serving a particular cuisine will change during the conference. It won't be a problem to retain the results of a request to the API in the browsers of the kiosks that will be deployed in the venue for the length of the browser session (likely the entire conference). As such, memoizing the results in a simple object is sufficient.

Because you're practicing test-first development, the first step in implementing the memoizedRestaurantApi façade is to put together some unit tests. To reduce the number of changes that Charlotte needs to make to the UI, you decide that the façade will expose the same function she's using in the aspect-enhanced third-party API, getRestaurantsNearConference.

Just as when you implemented the unit tests extending the third-party API to add the getRestaurantsNearConference method, you don't need to be concerned with the type of object that's actually returned by the API. Once again, you're able to avoid muddling up your unit tests with the details of testing asynchronous code that uses promises.

The unit tests for the memoizedRestaurantApi appear in Listing 8-1.

LISTING 8-1: Unit tests for memoizedRestaurantApi (code filename: Memoization\memoizedRestaurantApi_tests.js)

```
describe('memoizedRestaurantApi', function(){
  'use strict';

  var api,
      service,
```

```
      returnedFromService;

beforeEach(function(){
  api = ThirdParty.restaurantApi();
  service = Conference.memoizedRestaurantApi(api);
  returnedFromService = {};
});

describe('getRestaurantsNearConference(cuisine)', function(){

  it('invokes the api\'s getRestaurantsNearConference with the expected '+
  'argument', function(){
    var cuisine = "BBQ";
    spyOn(api, 'getRestaurantsNearConference');
    service.getRestaurantsNearConference(cuisine);

    var args = api.getRestaurantsNearConference.calls.argsFor(0);
    expect(args[0]).toEqual(cuisine);
  });

  it('returns the value returned by the 3rd-party API', function(){
    spyOn(api, 'getRestaurantsNearConference')
      .and.returnValue(returnedFromService);
    var value = service.getRestaurantsNearConference("Asian Fusion");
    expect(value).toBe(returnedFromService);
  });

  it('makes one api request when the same cuisine is requested ' +
  'multiple times', function(){
    var cuisine = "BBQ";

    spyOn(api, 'getRestaurantsNearConference')
      .and.returnValue(returnedFromService);

    var iterations = 5;
    for(var i = 0; i < iterations; i++){
      var value = service.getRestaurantsNearConference(cuisine);
    }

    expect(api.getRestaurantsNearConference.calls.count()).toBe(1);
  });

  it('resolves to the same value when same cuisine is requested' +
  'multiple times', function(){
    var cuisine = "American";

    spyOn(api, 'getRestaurantsNearConference')
      .and.returnValue(returnedFromService);

    var iterations = 5;
    for(var i = 0; i < iterations; i++){
      var value = service.getRestaurantsNearConference(cuisine);
```

continues

LISTING 8-1 *(continued)*

```
    expect(value).toBe(returnedFromService);
      }
    });
   });
  });
```

The tests validate the basic functionality added by memoization:

➤ That the third-party API is only queried once when multiple requests are made to the `getRestaurantsNearConference` function for the same cuisine

➤ That subsequent calls to `getRestaurantsNearConference` return the same restaurants that were returned by the third-party API

Satisfied that your tests dictate the correct functionality, you create the implementation in Listing 8-2.

LISTING 8-2: The implementation of memoizedRestaurantApi (code filename: Memoization\memoizedRestaurantApi.js)

```
var Conference = Conference || {};

Conference.memoizedRestaurantApi = function(thirdPartyApi){
  'use strict';

  var api = thirdPartyApi,
      cache = {};

  return {
    getRestaurantsNearConference: function(cuisine){
      if(cache.hasOwnProperty(cuisine)){
        return cache[cuisine];
      }

      var returnedPromise = api.getRestaurantsNearConference(cuisine);
      cache[cuisine] = returnedPromise;
      return returnedPromise;
    }
  };
};
```

As was noted early on in the chapter, implementing memoization didn't require a lot of effort (or code).

First, an empty cache object is initialized via `cache = {};` when the `memoizedRestaurantApi` is created.

When `getRestaurantsNearConference` is executed, rather than immediately making a request to the third-party API, the following is executed:

```
if(cache.hasOwnProperty(cuisine)){
  return cache[cuisine];
}
```

The code in the previous snippet queries the cache to see if it has a key that corresponds to the `cuisine` being sought. If so, the previously cached promise is immediately returned.

If the cache doesn't have an entry for `cuisine`, a request is made to the third-party API and the return promise is added to the cache via `cache[cuisine] = returnedPromise;` and then the promise is returned to the caller.

Figure 8-1 shows that the new implementation of `memoizedRestaurantApi` allows all the unit tests from Listing 8-1 to pass.

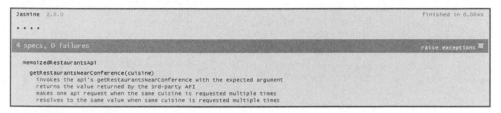

FIGURE 8-1

The problem at hand has been solved: The `getRestaurantsNearConference` function has had memoization applied, and the number of calls to the API has been reduced.

Charlotte, while appreciative that she can just drop in the `memoizedRestaurantApi` where she's used the third-party `restaurantApi`, has a suggestion for you.

"Couldn't you extend `restaurantApi` with an aspect that adds memoization, similar to the way you extended it to include `getRestaurantsNearConference`?"

"Of course," you reply, slightly red-faced. "That would eliminate the need for the `memoizedRestaurantApi`, and provide a general memoization aspect that we could apply elsewhere."

ADDING MEMOIZATION WITH AOP

Though it wasn't mentioned by name, we used the Memoization Pattern as an example in Chapter 2 when we discussed aspect-oriented programming as a tool that may be used to create reliable JavaScript. The example in Chapter 2 even involved caching the results of calls to a web service, just like the example presented in the last section.

Chapter 2 *didn't* delve into the details of creating the aspect that caches results from web service calls, so that's where this section will start. Next, this section covers application of the new aspect to the third-party `restauarantApi`.

Creating the Memoization Aspect

Your new goal is to extract the memoization code from `memoizedRestaurantApi` in Listing 8-2 into an aspect that can be applied to the `restaurantApi`, or any other code that could benefit from memoization.

As usual, the first step is to write unit tests that verify the aspect's functionality. A few of them have already been defined: They're the tests that were written in Listing 8-1 to validate the memoization functionality that was implemented in `memoizedRestuarantApi`. Listing 8-3 contains those tests, adapted to test the aspect, as well as a few additional tests to ensure that the aspect functions reliably.

The `returnValueCache` will be implemented as a module that defines a single function: `advice`. The `beforeEach` section of the unit tests decorate the test function with advice via the following statement:

```
Aop.around('testFunction', Aspects.returnValueCache().advice, testObject);
```

LISTING 8-3: Unit tests for the returnValueCache aspect (code filename: Memoization\returnValueCache_tests.js)

```
describe('returnValueCache', function(){
  'use strict';

  var testObject,
      testValue,
      args,
      spyReference,
      testFunctionExecutionCount;

  beforeEach(function(){
    // reset the execution count before each test
    testFunctionExecutionCount = 0;
    testValue = {};
    testObject = {
      testFunction:function(arg){
        return testValue;
      }
    };

    spyOn(testObject, 'testFunction').and.callThrough();

    // Hold on to a reference to the spy, since it won't be directly accessible
    // once the aspect has been applied to it.
    spyReference = testObject.testFunction;

    // Decorate the testObject.testFunction with the returnValueCache aspect
    Aop.around('testFunction', Aspects.returnValueCache().advice, testObject);

    args = [{key:"value"}, "someValue"];
  });

  describe('advice(targetInfo)', function(){
    it('returns the value returned by the decorated function on 1st execution',
    function(){
      var value = testObject.testFunction.apply(testObject, args);
      expect(value).toBe(testValue);
    });

    it('returns the value returned by the decorated function when executed ' +
    'multiple times', function(){
```

```
        var iterations = 3;

        for(var i = 0; i < iterations; i++){
          var value = testObject.testFunction.apply(testObject, args);
          expect(value).toBe(testValue);
        }
      });

      it('only executes the decorated function once when executed ' +
      'multiple times with the same key value', function(){
        var iterations = 3;

        for(var i = 0; i < iterations; i++){
          var value = testObject.testFunction.apply(testObject, args);
          expect(value).toBe(testValue);
        }
        expect(spyReference.calls.count()).toBe(1);
      });

      it('executes the decorated function once for each unique key value',
      function(){
          var keyValues = ["value1", "value2", "value3"];

          keyValues.forEach(function iterator(arg){
            var value = testObject.testFunction(arg);
          });

          // Execute each request again; results should be loaded
          // from cache, thus not executing the decorated function
          keyValues.forEach(function iterator(arg){
            var value = testObject.testFunction(arg);
          });

          // Decorated function should be executed only once per unique value
          expect(spyReference.calls.count()).toBe(keyValues.length);
      });

      // Additional tests that verify cache keys are calculated correctly, etc.
    });
  });
```

One of the more interesting aspects of the unit tests in Listing 8-3 is the mechanism used to keep track of the number of times the decorated function is executed. The natural choice is to create a spy on `testObject.testFunction`, and then apply the aspect to the spied-upon function. Everything works swimmingly until attempting to verify that the spy has been invoked.

Even though a spy was created on `testObject.testFunction`, decorating that function with an aspect essentially hides the spy. Because of this, an expectation such as the following:

```
expect(testObject.testFunction.calls.count()).toBe(1);
```

fails because `calls` is no longer a property of `testObject.testFunction`.

To work around this, a reference to the original spied-upon function is saved to `spyReference` *before* the aspect is applied to the function. This way, tests that depend upon knowing the number of times the decorated function is invoked may create expectations using `spyReference` like so:

```
expect(spyReference.calls.count()).toBe(1);
```

Implementing the aspect itself is trivial because you've already done it once in the `memoizedRestaurantApi`. The aspect is shown in Listing 8-4.

LISTING 8-4: Implementation of returnValueCache (code filename: Memoization\returnValueCache.js)

```javascript
var Aspects = Aspects || {};

Aspects.returnValueCache = function(){
'use strict';

  var cache = {};

  return {
    advice: function(targetInfo){

      // use the arguments provided to the function as the cache key
      // (convert to a string so that string comparison, rather than
      // object reference comparison, can be used)
      var cacheKey = JSON.stringify(targetInfo.args);

      if(cache.hasOwnProperty(cacheKey)){
        return cache[cacheKey];
      }

      // retrieve and execute the decorated function, storing its
      // return value in the cache
      var returnValue = Aop.next(targetInfo);
      cache[cacheKey] = returnValue;
      return returnValue;
    }
  };
};
```

Figure 8-2 shows the all-green unit tests for the `returnValueCache` aspect.

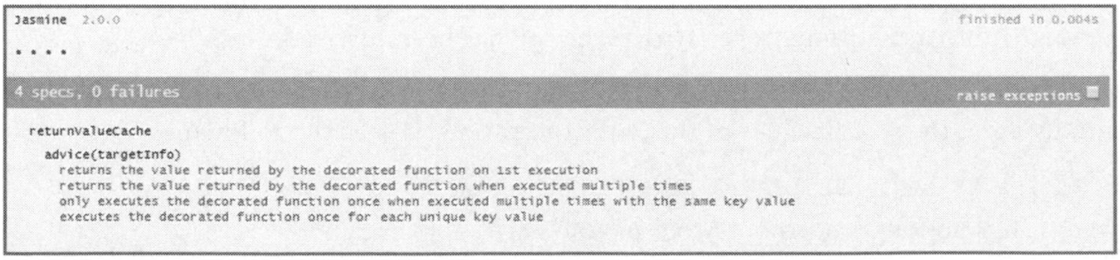

```
Jasmine  2.0.0                                                    finished in 0.004s

. . . .

4 specs, 0 failures                                              raise exceptions ▢

  returnValueCache
    advice(targetInfo)
      returns the value returned by the decorated function on 1st execution
      returns the value returned by the decorated function when executed multiple times
      only executes the decorated function once when executed multiple times with the same key value
      executes the decorated function once for each unique key value
```

FIGURE 8-2

Applying the returnValueCache Aspect to restaurantApi

The final step is to decorate the appropriate method of restaurantApi with the returnValueCache aspect. Decorating getRestaurantsNearConference would certainly cause the requests that Charlotte is making from the UI to be memoized, but a more general solution would be to apply the returnValueCache aspect directly to the restaurantApi function presented back in Listing 7-1, getRestaurantsWithinRadius. Doing this will cause getRestaurantsNearConference to be memoized, and will also automatically cause any other functions that make use of getRestaurantsWithinRadius to benefit from memoization as well.

Listing 8-5 presents ThirdPartyRestaurantApiAspects.js, originally presented in Listing 7-3, modified here to also memoize the getRestaurantsWithinRadius function.

LISTING 8-5: Decorating getRestaurantsWithinRadius with returnValueCache aspect (code filename: Memoization\ThirdPartyRestaurantApiAspects.js)

```
// Apply memoization to getRestaurantsWithinRadius

Aop.around(
  // Function whose return value should be modified.
  'restaurantApi',

  // Function that modifies the return value
  function addMemoizationToGetRestaurantsWithinRadius(targetInfo){

    // Original API returned from ThirdParty.restaurantApi().
    var api = Aop.next.call(this, targetInfo);

    // decorate the getRestaurantsWithinRadius function to add
    // memoization to it
    Aop.around('getRestaurantsWithinRadius',
      Aspects.returnValueCache().advice, api);

    // Return the revised API.
    return api;
  },

  // Namespace of the function whose return value should be modified
  ThirdParty
);

// Add member getRestaurantsNearConference to ThirdParty.restaurantApi().

Aop.around(
  // Function whose return value should be modified.
  'restaurantApi',

  // Function that modifies the return value
  function addGetRestaurantsNearConference(targetInfo){

    // Original API returned from ThirdParty.restaurantApi().
```

continues

LISTING 8-5 *(continued)*

```
        var api = Aop.next.call(this, targetInfo);

        // Function to add to the API
        function getRestaurantsNearConference(cuisine) {
          return api.getRestaurantsWithinRadius(
            '415 Summer St, Boston, MA 02210', 2.0, cuisine);
        }

        // Add the function if it's not already there.
        api.getRestaurantsNearConference =
          api.getRestaurantsNearConference || getRestaurantsNearConference;

        // Return the revised API.
        return api;
      },

      // Namespace of the function whose return value should be modified
      ThirdParty
    );
```

SUMMARY

Faced with potentially enormous credit card bills, the JavaScript conference's organizers challenged you and Charlotte to reduce the costs incurred through the use of the third-party `restaurantApi`.

The first attempt, creating a façade implementing the Memoization Pattern wrapped around `restaurantApi`, was successful in reducing calls to the `restaurantApi` but was not reusable and was susceptible to copy-and-paste reuse.

Thankfully, Charlotte suggested that the problem could also be solved by decorating `restaurantApi` with a memoizing aspect. How right she was! Plus, the memoizing aspect that was created was generic and easily reusable.

When implementing the Memoization Pattern, the unit tests you write should cover the following concerns:

➤   The function or resource of which the return values are being memoized should only be accessed the first time the memoized function is called with a particular key.

➤   Subsequent calls to the memoized function with a particular key should return the same value as the first call.

The next chapter presents testing, implementation, and use of an oft-maligned but powerful pattern: the Singleton.

Ensuring Correct Implementation of the Singleton Pattern

WHAT'S IN THIS CHAPTER?

➤ Using object literals as singletons

➤ Implementing and unit-testing the Singleton Pattern with immediate-execution modules

➤ Using dependency injection to provide singleton objects to modules

WROX.COM CODE DOWNLOADS FOR THIS CHAPTER

The wrox.com code downloads for this chapter are found at www.wrox.com/go/ reliablejavascript on the Download Code tab. They are in the Chapter 9 download and individually named according to the filenames noted throughout this chapter.

The entirety of Chapter 3 is dedicated to creating object instances, and a good portion of it describes patterns for creating *multiple instances* of similar objects. The chapter also covers techniques for sharing behavior between object instances, such as prototypal inheritance and functional inheritance.

There are times, however, when it is unnecessary or even undesirable to create multiple instances of an object. The Singleton Pattern may be employed in these cases where one, and only one, instance of an object should ever exist.

This chapter will illustrate how object literals may be considered singleton objects. It will also revisit how to create singleton objects using the immediate-execution modules, introduced in Chapter 3.

If you have experience in a language that supports multi-threading, such as C# or Java, you may notice that there's a topic not covered in this chapter: thread safety. Because JavaScript is a single-threaded language, complications that arise when an object is accessed from multiple threads need not be considered when creating reliable JavaScript singletons.

UNDERSTANDING THE PATTERN THROUGH UNIT TESTS

In Chapter 8, the `restaurantApi.getRestaurantsWithinRadius` function was memoized in order to reduce the number of calls to the third-party API used by the JavaScript conference website. The memoization functionality was nicely encapsulated into an aspect that may be applied to any other function in the website.

What happens, however, if two instances of the `restaurantApi` are created and the `getRestaurantsWithinRadius` function of each object is called with the same arguments? Does the call to the second object use the results that were cached when the call to the first object's function was made?

In this example, and many other cases when memoization has been applied to a function, the *desired* answer to the second question is: "Yes, it makes use of the results cached by the call to the first object's function." The next question, of course, is: "Do functions decorated with the `returnValueCache` behave that way?"

Unfortunately, the answer is no. Instances of `returnValueCache` each have their own internal cache object. This means that when an instance of the *restaurantApi* is created and has its `getRestaurantsWithinRadius` function decorated with the `returnValueCache`, that instance of `restaurantApi` has access only to the results of previous calls to its own `getRestaurantsWithinRadius`. It will not benefit from values cached within other instances of `restaurantApi`.

It would be nice if instances of `returnValueCache` could share a single cache rather than each having its own. If the `returnValueCache` had this capability, instances of `restaurantApi` could share the saved results of all `getRestaurantsWithinRadius` calls, regardless of the `restaurantApi` instance that held the function that was called.

Dependency injection, covered in Chapter 2, is a great mechanism to facilitate sharing of cache objects between `returnValueCache` instances. Modifying the `returnValueCache` module's function to optionally accept a cache object instance will move the code in the direction desired.

Implementing a Singleton Shared Cache with an Object Literal

The object literal is the simplest implementation of the Singleton Pattern in JavaScript. Unlike the other object creation patterns, there's no function to call to create another one, nor may the new keyword be used to create more.

The current implementation of the `returnValueCache` already uses an object literal as a cache, so injecting an optional object literal as the shared cache is the easiest way to add the desired functionality.

The unit tests shown in Listing 9-1 build upon those from Listing 8-3 in Chapter 8. By making the injected cache object optional, the original tests don't require any modification (beyond updates to account for some test refactoring). By extension, any code that utilizes the `returnValueCache` in its current state—without being provided a shared cache—also doesn't require any change.

```javascript
describe('returnValueCache', function(){

  'use strict';
  var testObject,
      testValue,
      args,
      spyReference;

  // Helper function to create a test object.  Includes adding the spy to
  // testFunction, and storing a reference to the spy in the spyReference
  // property of the returned object.
  function createATestObject(){
    var obj = {
      testFunction : function(arg){
        return testValue;
      }
    };
    spyOn(obj, 'testFunction').and.callThrough();

    // Hold on to a reference to the spy, since it won't be directly accessible
    // once the aspect has been applied to it.
    obj.spyReference = obj.testFunction;

    return obj;
  }

  /*** beforeEach omitted ***/

  describe('advice(targetInfo)', function(){

  /*** existing tests omitted ***/

    it('may share an injected cache between instances', function(){
      var sharedCache = {},
          object1 = createATestObject(),
          object2 = createATestObject();

      Aop.around('testFunction',
        new Aspects.returnValueCache(sharedCache).advice,
        object1);

      Aop.around('testFunction',
        new Aspects.returnValueCache(sharedCache).advice,
        object2);

      object1.testFunction(args);

      // Call to object2's testFunction should make use of the cached result
      // of the call to object1's testFunction.
```

continues

LISTING 9-1 *(continued)*

```
        expect(object2.testFunction(args)).toBe(testValue);

        // Thus, object2's testFunction should not be executed
        expect(object2.spyReference.calls.count()).toBe(0);
      });
    });
  });
```

As mentioned, a minor refactor of the unit tests was made to reduce duplication: The utility method `createATestObject` was added to encapsulate—you guessed it—the creation of test objects.

Figure 9-1 shows that all the pre-existing tests pass, but the new test exercising the ability to share a cache fails.

Listing 9-2 illustrates the modified `returnValueCache` accepting an object literal, and Figure 9-2 shows the tests all pass.

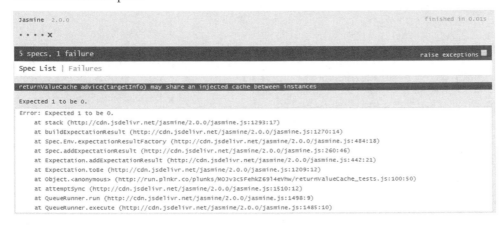

FIGURE 9-1

FIGURE 9-2

LISTING 9-2: Implementing a shared cache with an object literal (code filename: Singleton\
returnValueCache_01.js)

```
var Aspects = Aspects || {};

Aspects.returnValueCache = function(sharedCache){
```

```
    "use strict";

    // If a sharedCache is provided, use it.
    var cache = sharedCache || {};

    return {
      advice: function(targetInfo){

        // use the arguments provided to the function as the cache key
        // (convert to a string so that string comparison, rather than
        // object reference comparison, can be used)
        var cacheKey = JSON.stringify(targetInfo.args);

        if(cache.hasOwnProperty(cacheKey)){
          return cache[cacheKey];
        }

        // retrieve and execute the decorated function, storing its
        // return value in the cache
        var returnValue = Aop.next(targetInfo);
        cache[cacheKey] = returnValue;
        return returnValue;
      }
    };
  };
```

Now that the `returnValueCache` accepts a shared cache, all that's left is to slightly modify the application of the aspect to `restaurantApi.getRestaurantsWithinRadius`, as Listing 9-3 (adapted from Listing 8-5) illustrates.

LISTING 9-3: Applying returnValueCache using a shared object literal cache object (code filename: Singleton\applyAspect_01)

```
var Conference = Conference || {};
Conference.caches = Conference.caches || {};

// Create an object literal (singleton) to use as a cache
// for the restaurantApi.getRestaurantsWithinRadius function
Conference.caches.restaurantsWithinRadiusCache = {};

// Apply memoization to getRestaurantsWithinRadius

Aop.around(
  'restaurantApi',
  function addMemoizationToGetRestaurantsWithinRadius(targetInfo){

    // Original API returned from ThirdParty.restaurantApi().
    var api =  Aop.next.call(this, targetInfo);

    // decorate the getRestaurantsWithinRadius function to add
    // memoization (with a shared cache) to it
    Aop.around('getRestaurantsWithinRadius',
```

continues

LISTING 9-3 *(continued)*

```
            Aspects
            .returnValueCache(Conference.caches.restaurantsWithinRadiusCache).advice,
                api);

        // Return the revised API.
        return api;
    },
    ThirdParty
);
```

While the object literal is literally the simplest implementation of the Singleton Pattern, it lacks the ability to hide data and other desirable qualities that are provided by other object creation patterns, such as the Module Pattern.

Implementing a Singleton Shared Cache with a Module

In Listing 9-3, a shared cache was created within the `Conference.caches` namespace by declaring an object literal, `restaurantsWithinRadiusCache`. In many cases, an object literal—a key/value collection—is sufficient for use as a cache. There are cases, however, when a more capable cache is useful. It may be desirable to create a least recently used (LRU) cache that only stores a fixed number of values, replacing the oldest cached value with the newest. In other cases, it may be appropriate to only retain a value in the cache for a fixed period of time. Neither of these scenarios is easily implemented when an object literal is used as a cache.

Your ever-capable colleague, Charlotte, realized the usefulness of a more capable cache and provided `Conference.simpleCache`, a module that provides the functionality of the object literal-based cache, but via an API rather than direct property access. Charlotte's `Conference.simpleCache` is shown in Listing 9-4.

LISTING 9-4: The Conference.simpleCache module (code filename: Singleton\simpleCache.js)

```
var Conference = Conference || {};

Conference.simpleCache = function(){
    "use strict";

    var privateCache = {};

    function getCacheKey(key){
        return JSON.stringify(key);
    }

    return {

        // Returns true if key has an entry in the cache, false if
        // it does not.
        hasKey: function(key){
            return privateCache.hasOwnProperty(getCacheKey(key));
```

```
    },

    // Stores value in the cache associated with key
    setValue: function(key, value){
      privateCache[getCacheKey(key)] = value;
    },

    // Returns the cached value for key, or undefined
    // if a value for key has not been cached
    getValue: function(key){
      return privateCache[getCacheKey(key)];
    }
  };
};
```

Even though `Conference.simpleCache` does nothing more than provide an API for interacting with an object literal, Charlotte has created an interface that the `returnValueCache` may use to provide memoization functionality. In the future, new caching objects may be created that expose the same interface but exhibit different behavior, such as LRU or cache item timeout.

> **NOTE** *The* `simpleCache` *is not implemented as a singleton, nor is it intended to be. As provided by Charlotte,* `simpleCache` *has extracted functionality that was present in the* `returnValueCache` *into its own object. Using the Singleton Pattern to provide a single* `simpleCache` *object will be covered shortly.*

The `returnValueCache` does require a little bit of modification to use the `simpleCache`. Instead of creating an object literal if a shared cache is not provided, a new `simpleCache` will be created. Also, code in the advice will use the methods exposed by the `simpleCache` API rather than directly modifying properties of the cache object.

Only a small change is required in the unit tests from Listing 9-1 to account for the use of `simpleCache`. Listing 9-5 highlights the change.

LISTING 9-5: Unit tests for returnValueCache utilizing simpleCache (code filename: Singleton\returnValueCache_02_tests.js)

```
describe('returnValueSimpleCache', function(){

  /*** unmodified setup and utility function omitted ***/

  describe('advice(targetInfo)', function(){

    /*** unmodified tests omitted ***/

    it('may share an injected cache between instances', function(){
      // Create a simpleCache shared cache object
      var sharedCache = Conference.simpleCache(),
          object1 = createATestObject(),
```

continues

LISTING 9-5 *(continued)*

```
        object2 = createATestObject();

    Aop.around('testFunction',
      new Aspects.returnValueCache(sharedCache).advice,
      object1);

    Aop.around('testFunction',
      new Aspects.returnValueCache(sharedCache).advice,
      object2);

    object1.testFunction(args);

    // Call to object2's testFunction should make use of the cached result
    // of the call to object1's testFunction.
    expect(object2.testFunction(args)).toBe(testValue);

    // Thus, object2's testFunction should not be executed
    expect(object2.spyReference.calls.count()).toBe(0);
    });
  });
});
```

The updated version of `returnValueCache` can be found in the code sample file Singleton
\returnValueCache_02.js, and the passing test results are shown in Figure 9-3.

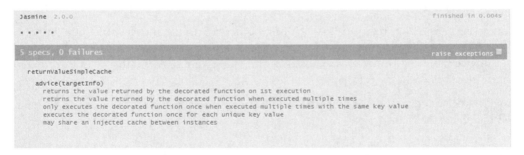

FIGURE 9-3

Now that `simpleCache` has been created and `returnValueCache` has been updated to use it, the
next step is to create the singleton cache object for use with the `restaurantApi`
`.getRestaurantsWithinRadius` function.

When the shared cache was an object literal, ensuring that only a single instance of the cache existed
was a simple matter because object literals *are* singletons. The scenario is a bit different now that a
module is being used as the cache: Each execution of the module function creates a new object instance.

To make sure that all instances of `restaurantApi` get the same instance of `simpleCache`, an implementation of the Singleton Pattern will be created in Listing 9-7 utilizing an immediate-execution
module that was introduced in Chapter 3. The `RestaurantsWithinRadiusCache` module will
expose a single function, `getInstance`, which will return the same instance of the `simpleCache`
each time it is called.

The single test in Listing 9-6 verifies the behavior of `getInstance`.

> **LISTING 9-6:** Unit test for RestaurantsWithinRadiusCache.getInstance (code filename: Singleton\restaurantsWithinRadiusCache_01_tests.js)

```
describe('Conference.caches.RestaurantsWithinRadiusCache', function(){
  'use strict';

  describe('getInstance', function(){
    it('always returns the same instance', function(){

      // ensure that .getInstance returns the same object
      // (.toBe uses reference equality)
      expect(Conference.caches.RestaurantsWithinRadiusCache.getInstance())
        .toBe(Conference.caches.RestaurantsWithinRadiusCache.getInstance());
    });
  });
});
```

And the implementation of `RestaurantsWithinRadiusCache` follows in Listing 9-7.

> **LISTING 9-7:** Implementation of RestaurantsWithinRadiusCache (code filename: Singleton\restaurantsWithinRadiusCache_01.js)

```
var Conference = Conference || {};
Conference.caches = Conference.caches || {};

// Create a simpleCache (singleton) to use as a cache
// for the restaurantApi.getRestaurantsWithinRadius function
Conference.caches.RestaurantsWithinRadiusCache = (function(){
  "use strict";

  var instance = null;

  return {
    getInstance: function(){
      if(!instance){
        instance = Conference.simpleCache();
      }
      return instance;
    }
  };
})();
```

In Listing 9-7, `RestaurantsWithinRadiusCache` is assigned the value returned from the immediately executed function, establishing it as a singleton object exposing the `getInstance` function. The first time `getInstance` is invoked, the hidden `instance` variable is populated with a `simpleCache`. Each additional call to `getInstance` returns that same `instance`.

> **NOTE** *An additional benefit of this implementation of the Singleton Pattern is that the* `instance` *object is instantiated lazily; it isn't created until the first time it's needed. This can be important if the creation of the* `instance` *object is costly in terms of time and/or memory.*

The passing unit test is shown in Figure 9-4.

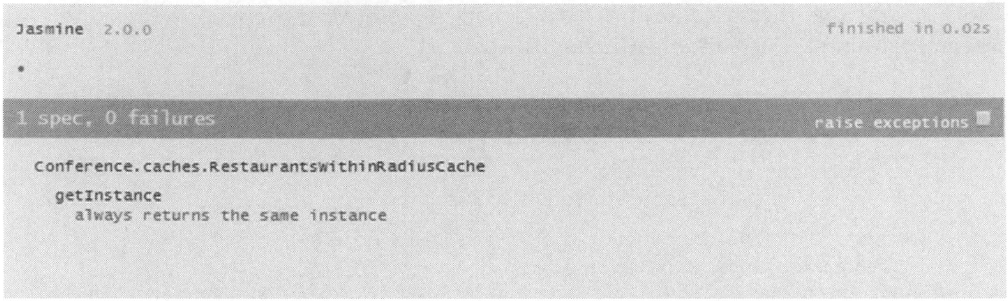

```
Jasmine  2.0.0                                                  finished in 0.02s

 •

 1 spec, 0 failures                                           raise exceptions ▪

   Conference.caches.RestaurantsWithinRadiusCache

     getInstance
       always returns the same instance
```

FIGURE 9-4

Last, but certainly not least, application of the `returnValueCache` aspect to the `restaurantApi.getRestaurantsWithinRadius` function must be updated to use the new `RestaurantsWithinRadiusCache` singleton. This is shown in Listing 9-8.

LISTING 9-8: Using RestaurantsWithinRadiusCache with the returnValueCache (code filename: Singleton\applyAspect_02.js)

```javascript
// Apply memoization to getRestaurantsWithinRadius

Aop.around(
  'restaurantApi',
  function addMemoizationToGetRestaurantsWithinRadius(targetInfo){

    // Original API returned from ThirdParty.restaurantApi().
    var api = Aop.next.call(this, targetInfo);

    // Retrieve the singleton cache instance
    var cache = Conference.caches.RestaurantsWithinRadiusCache.getInstance();

    // decorate the getRestaurantsWithinRadius function to add
    // memoization (with a shared cache) to it
    Aop.around('getRestaurantsWithinRadius',
      Aspects.returnValueCache(cache).advice, api);

    // Return the revised API.
    return api;
  },
  ThirdParty
);
```

SUMMARY

The Singleton Pattern is widely used in JavaScript. It's useful for creating namespaces so that the global namespace isn't polluted with your application's functions and variables. Additionally, it's fantastic for sharing data, like caches, between modules.

Implementations of the Singleton Pattern in JavaScript, such as object literals and immediate-execution modules, are easier to make reliable than in other languages because JavaScript is single-threaded. You need not worry about your singleton objects being accessed from multiple threads at the same time.

When implementing the Singleton Pattern, the primary concern that should be covered by unit tests is that only a single instance of the singleton object exists.

The next chapter covers the Factory Pattern, a technique for creating objects that provides additional abstraction and control over the object creational patterns that have already been discussed.

10

Ensuring Correct Implementation of the Factory Pattern

WHAT'S IN THIS CHAPTER?

➤   Unit-testing a factory

➤   Writing a reliable factory

WROX.COM CODE DOWNLOADS FOR THIS CHAPTER

The wrox.com code downloads for this chapter are found at www.wrox.com/go/
reliablejavascript on the Download Code tab. The files are in the Chapter 10 download
and are individually named according to the filenames noted throughout this chapter.

In JavaScript, a *factory* is simply a function whose purpose is to build and return an object.
Factories abound in JavaScript. The Object.create method introduced in ECMAScript 5 is a
factory built into the language. You have also met many factories in this book, although under
other names. For example, a *module* technically meets the definition in that its purpose is to
create and return an object, albeit with some data-hiding in the bargain.

Why would you want to use a factory to create an object instead of new or an ordinary function call? Broadly speaking, there are two reasons: increased control and increased abstraction. In this chapter, you will work with an example that illustrates both.

WRITING UNIT TESTS FOR A FACTORY

The JavaScript conference whose website you are developing will be packed with presentations. Your next job is to model these presentations for the site.

There are two kinds of presentations: regular presentations and presentations by vendors. The basic presentation has a title and an optional presenter. (Sometimes a presentation on a hot topic is created as a placeholder before a volunteer has been recruited.) The vendor presentation is the same, but also has a vendor name and, optionally, a product (Table 10-1).

TABLE 10-1: Presentation Types

	PRESENTATION	VENDORPRESENTATION
`title`	Required	Required
`presenter`	Optional	Optional
`vendor`		Required
`product`		Optional

Wanting to try your hand at prototypal inheritance with the `Object.create` method, you quickly code the classes shown in Listings 10-1 and 10-2. (Of course, you would code the unit tests first, as shown in this chapter's downloads.)

LISTING 10-1: Presentation (code filename: Factory\Presentation.js)

```
var Conference = Conference || {};
Conference.Presentation = function(title, presenter) {
  'use strict';  if (!(this instanceof Conference.Presentation)) {
    throw new Error(Conference.Presentation.messages.mustUseNew);
  }
  if (!title) {
    throw new Error(Conference.Presentation.messages.titleRequired);
  }
  this.title = title;
  this.presenter = presenter;
};

Conference.Presentation.messages = {
  mustUseNew: 'Presentation must be constructed with "new".',
  titleRequired: 'The title is required.'
};
```

LISTING 10-2: Vendor Presentation (code filename: Factory\VendorPresentation.js)

```
var Conference = Conference || {};
Conference.VendorPresentation = function(title, presenter,vendor,product) {
  'use strict';
  if (!(this instanceof Conference.VendorPresentation)) {
    throw new Error(
      Conference.VendorPresentation.messages.mustUseNew);
  }
  if (!vendor) {
    throw new Error(Conference.VendorPresentation.messages.vendorRequired);
```

```
    }
    Conference.Presentation.call(this,title,presenter);
    this.vendor = vendor;
    this.product = product;
};

Conference.VendorPresentation.prototype
    = Object.create(Conference.Presentation.prototype);

Conference.VendorPresentation.messages = {
    mustUseNew: 'VendorPresentation must be constructed with "new".',
    vendorRequired: 'The vendor is required.'
};
```

In Listing 10-2, prototypal inheritance is set up with this statement toward the end:

```
Conference.VendorPresentation.prototype
    = Object.create(Conference.Presentation.prototype);
```

The actual inheritance takes place with this nugget in the constructor:

```
Conference.Presentation.call(this,title,presenter);
```

The code works, but you notice how awkward it is to create a `VendorPresentation` that has no specific presenter. The presenter would have to be passed as an `undefined` parameter.

```
new VendorPresentation('The Title', undefined, 'The Vendor', 'The Product');
```

You would not be surprised if other optional properties were to creep into the specs later.

In addition, you anticipate other types of presentations: videos, seminars, and maybe more. Each will inherit from the `Presentation` object and each will have its own quirks of construction.

Finally, your ever-present colleague, Charlotte, plans to supply the data for your presentation objects in flattened form—just a one-level object literal. "Can't your code just figure out on its own what kind of presentation it is?" she asks impatiently.

Not wanting to disappoint Charlotte, you decide to create a `presentationFactory`. Its `create` method will indeed take a parameter that is just a bag of properties and figure out what to do.

Being nervous about the looseness of object literals, and following sound advice you heard somewhere to always code your negative tests first, you begin with the test in Listing 10-3.

LISTING 10-3: Negative test for presentationFactory (code filename: Factory\ presentationFactory_tests.js [excerpt])

```
describe('presentationFactory', function() {
    var factory = Conference.presentationFactory();

    describe('create(objectLiteral)',function() {
        it('throws if the parameter has unexpected properties', function() {
            var badProp = 'badProperty';
            function createWithUnexpectedProperties() {
```

continues

LISTING 10-3 *(continued)*

```
            var badParam = {};
            badParam[badProp] = 'unexpected!';
            factory.create(badParam);
        }
        expect(createWithUnexpectedProperties).toThrowError(
          Conference.presentationFactory.messages.unexpectedProperty + badProp);
      });
    });
  });
```

With that in place, you can quickly code Listing 10-4. This first step in `presentationFactory` verifies that the parameter has no unexpected properties.

LISTING 10-4: Checking the parameter in presentationFactory (code filename: presentationFactory.js [excerpt])

```
var Conference = Conference || {};
Conference.presentationFactory = function presentationFactory() {
  'use strict';
  return {
    // Create a Presentation or one of its descendants, depending
    // on the properties of the obj parameter.
    create: function(obj) {
      var baseProperties = ['title', 'presenter'],
          vendorProperties = ['vendor', 'product'],
          allProperties = baseProperties.concat(vendorProperties),
          p;
      for (p in obj) {
        if (allProperties.indexOf(p) <0){
          throw new Error(
            Conference.presentationFactory.messages.unexpectedProperty + p);
        }
      }
      // later: return a Presentation-derived object
    }
  };
};
Conference.presentationFactory.messages = {
  unexpectedProperty: 'The creation parameter had an unexpected property '
};
```

With the negative test and its corresponding code out of the way, it's time to say what the factory should actually do.

First, if the incoming parameter contains only the properties for a base `Presentation` object, then that's what the `create` method should return. It would be easy enough to code one unit test that uses such a parameter and verifies that a `Presentation` is returned, but that would leave two critical questions unanswered:

➤ How would you know that the correct parameters were passed to `Presentation`'s constructor?

➤ If they were passed to the constructor properly, how would you know that the object thus constructed was the one returned?

Paying attention to details such as these makes the difference between reliable JavaScript and JavaScript that merely hopes to be reliable. And it's really not that much trouble, as you can prove with Listing 10-5.

LISTING 10-5: Unit tests for creating a Presentation with the factory (code filename: presentationFactory_tests.js [excerpt])

```javascript
describe('presentationFactory', function() {
  'use strict';
  var factory = Conference.presentationFactory(),
      baseParameter = {
        title: 'How to Write Wonderful JavaScript',
        presenter: 'Rock Star'
      };

  describe('create(objectLiteral)',function() {
    /*** Previously discussed test omitted for clarity. ***/

    describe('with only base properties',function() {
      var fakePresentation = { title: 'How to Fake a Presentation' },
          spyOnConstructor,
          returnedPresentation;

      beforeEach(function() {
        spyOnConstructor = spyOn(Conference,'Presentation')
          .and.returnValue(fakePresentation);
        returnedPresentation = factory.create(baseParameter);
      });

      it("passes all values to Presentation's constructor", function() {
        expect(spyOnConstructor).toHaveBeenCalledWith(
          baseParameter.title, baseParameter.presenter);
      });

      it("calls the Presentation's constructor exactly once", function() {
        expect(spyOnConstructor.calls.count()).toBe(1);
      });

      it('returns the Presentation constructed', function() {
        expect(factory.create(baseParameter)).toBe(fakePresentation);
      });
    });
  });
```

The new tests are merely expectations on the effect of the `factory.create` in the `beforeEach`. The expectations are separated into their respective tests, but the `beforeEach` keeps the tests DRY.

Also notice that only a spy on `Presentation`'s constructor was called. The factory's responsibility is to call the correct constructor and return the result. It should not care about what the constructor does, and neither should the factory's unit tests.

That's all there is to testing the factory's ability to create base `Presentations`. The remaining portion of the unit tests (see Listing 10-6) pertains to creating `VendorPresentations`.

LISTING 10-6: Unit tests for creating a VendorPresentation with the factory (code filename: Factory\presentationFactory_tests.js [remainder])

```javascript
describe('with at least one VendorPresentation property', function() {
  var vendorParameter = {
      title: 'How to Write Wonderful JavaScript',
      presenter: 'Rock Star',
      vendor: 'JxTools',
      product: 'The JxToolkit'
    },
    fakeVendorPresentation = { title: vendorParameter.title },
    spyOnConstructor;

  beforeEach(function() {
    spyOnConstructor = spyOn(Conference,'VendorPresentation')
      .and.returnValue(fakeVendorPresentation);
  });

  it('attempts to create a VendorPresentation', function() {
    var expectedCallCount = 0;
    function createParam(propName) {
      var param = {},
          p;
      for (p in baseParameter) {
        param[p] = baseParameter[p];
      }
      param[propName] = vendorParameter[propName];
      return param;
    }
    // Create a parameter that has just each vendor property in turn
    ['vendor','product'].forEach(function(propName) {
      var param = createParam(propName);
      var presentation = factory.create(param);
      expect(spyOnConstructor.calls.count()).toBe(++expectedCallCount);
    });
  });

  it("passes all values to VendorPresentation's constructor",function() {
    factory.create(vendorParameter);
    expect(spyOnConstructor).toHaveBeenCalledWith(
      vendorParameter.title, vendorParameter.presenter,
      vendorParameter.vendor, vendorParameter.product);
  });

  it("calls the VendorPresentation's constructor exactly once", function() {
    factory.create(vendorParameter);
    expect(spyOnConstructor.calls.count()).toBe(1);
  });

  it('returns the VendorPresentation constructed', function() {
    expect(factory.create(vendorParameter)).toBe(fakeVendorPresentation);
  });
});
```

The last three tests are much like ones you saw for base `Presentations`, but the first test deserves a remark. It verifies that if you include *any* parameter from the ones that make it "look like" you want a `VendorPresentation`, then the factory will try to give you just that. It does this by looping through *all* the possible vendor-related parameters and creating a parameter for the factory that is a base parameter plus just the vendor property:

```
['vendor','product'].forEach(function(propName) {
```

A lazier but much less reliable test would be to try just one vendor-related parameter. Why not test them all while you're at it?

If you have been reading exceptionally closely, you might now wonder why this test does not consider the `Error` that will be thrown when the parameter to the `VendorPresentation` constructor has a *product* but no *vendor*. The answer is that the constructor is not actually executed! The spy is not set up with `.and.callThrough()`, so the constructor's code is never reached. All this test cares about is that an attempt is made to construct a `VendorPresentation`. The unit tests of `VendorPresentation` consider the error conditions; the present test stays DRY by not considering them all over again. This is similar to what happened in Chapter 6 when testing `Promise`-based code: By keeping the tests on-topic, you make them more robust.

IMPLEMENTING THE FACTORY PATTERN

Satisfied that your tests do what they should and pleased that they do not do more, you are ready to code the factory itself. There is not much to add: just the highlighted portion of Listing 10-7.

LISTING 10-7: presentationFactory in full (code filename: Factory\presentationFactory.js)

```
var Conference = Conference || {};
Conference.presentationFactory = function presentationFactory() {
  'use strict';

  return {
    // Create a Presentation or one of its descendants, depending
    // on the properties of the obj parameter.
    create: function(obj) {
      var baseProperties = [ 'title', 'presenter'],
          vendorProperties = ['vendor', 'product'],
          allProperties = baseProperties.concat(vendorProperties),
          p,
          ix;
      for (p in obj) {
        if (allProperties.indexOf(p) <0){
          throw new Error(
            Conference.presentationFactory.messages.unexpectedProperty + p);
        }
      }
      for (ix=0; ix<vendorProperties.length; ++ix) {
        if (obj.hasOwnProperty(vendorProperties[ix])) {
          return new Conference.VendorPresentation(
```

continues

LISTING 10-7 *(continued)*

```
                obj.title, obj.presenter, obj.vendor,obj.product);
        }
      }
      return new Conference.Presentation(obj.title,obj.presenter);
    }
  };
};
Conference.presentationFactory.messages = {
  unexpectedProperty: 'The creation parameter had an unexpected property '
};
```

Happily, all of the unit tests pass the first time, as shown in Figure 10-1:

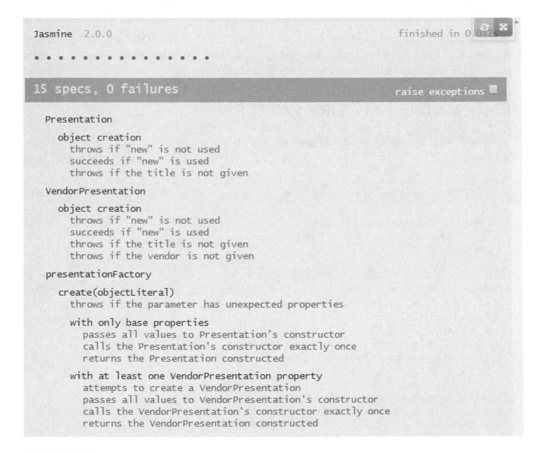

Jasmine 2.0.0   finished in 0.012s

• • • • • • • • • • • • • •

15 specs, 0 failures   raise exceptions ■

Presentation

  object creation
    throws if "new" is not used
    succeeds if "new" is used
    throws if the title is not given

VendorPresentation

  object creation
    throws if "new" is not used
    succeeds if "new" is used
    throws if the title is not given
    throws if the vendor is not given

presentationFactory

  create(objectLiteral)
    throws if the parameter has unexpected properties

  with only base properties
    passes all values to Presentation's constructor
    calls the Presentation's constructor exactly once
    returns the Presentation constructed

  with at least one VendorPresentation property
    attempts to create a VendorPresentation
    passes all values to VendorPresentation's constructor
    calls the VendorPresentation's constructor exactly once
    returns the VendorPresentation constructed

FIGURE 10-1

The factory neatly addresses your key concerns:

➤   The parameter to create, which can be an object literal, avoids the ugliness of undefined
    placeholder parameters.

➤ You can just toss whatever you have in the parameter, and the factory will figure out what you want.

➤ You are well-positioned to accommodate new types of presentations in the future.

➤ As an added bonus, the factory remembers for you that the objects must be created with new.

CONSIDERING OTHER FACTORY TYPES

Factories can be simpler or more complex than what you have seen here.

Sometimes, a factory creates only one type of object. For example, the object literals you saw in this chapter could have been produced by a presentationParameterFactory. As you read in Chapter 3, object literals have several disadvantages. A factory would address all of them.

The factory in this chapter had just one function: create. A variation is to have several create-type methods specialized for different purposes. JavaScript does not have the function overloading of languages such as C# or Java, so the methods would have to have different names. Alternatively, as described following Listing 1-4 in Chapter 1, a single method could do different things according to what it finds in arguments.

A factory can be a convenient place to set up an environment that all of its products will need. Sometimes, the environment will differ for unit-testing, functional testing, and production. You can use dependency injection to employ the factory fitted to the situation.

Finally, a factory is a natural candidate for a singleton, so the varieties of singletons you encountered in the last chapter apply.

SUMMARY

In this chapter, you created a factory that could produce any of a family of related objects. Typically, a factory has a method named something like create that takes one or more parameters. The create method inspects these parameters and produces an object according to what it finds.

A factory gives increased control over the creation of objects and provides an extra layer of abstraction.

Thorough unit tests for a factory should cover these concerns:

➤ The create function will reject incorrect parameters.

➤ The correct, underlying object-creation function is called with the expected parameters.

➤ The object returned from that call is the one returned from create.

In the next chapter, you will read about the Sandbox Pattern, which provides an even more abstract way to instantiate objects.

11

Ensuring Correct Implementation and Use of the Sandbox Pattern

WHAT'S IN THIS CHAPTER?

➤ Using the Sandbox Pattern to create loosely coupled code

➤ Implementing the Sandbox Pattern using test-driven development

➤ Understanding how the Sandbox Pattern controls access to resources and functionality

➤ Writing and testing code that will be isolated within a sandbox

WROX.COM CODE DOWNLOADS FOR THIS CHAPTER

You can find the wrox.com code downloads for this chapter at www.wrox.com/go/ reliablejavascript on the Download Code tab. The files are in the Chapter 11 download and are individually named according to the filenames noted throughout this chapter.

In his book *JavaScript Patterns* (O'Reilly, 2010), Stoyan Stefanov presents the Sandbox Pattern as a solution to some of the drawbacks of the practice of namespacing in JavaScript. In particular, he states that the Sandbox Pattern alleviates the reliance on a single global variable for the application and reduces the proliferation of long, dotted names to type and resolve at run time. While the Sandbox Pattern certainly does both of those things, we're most interested in another characteristic he mentions: the creation of an environment for modules to "play" in without impacting other modules and their sandboxes.

This chapter will use test-driven development to create an implementation of the Sandbox Pattern similar to the pattern presented in Stefanov's book. The implementation will focus on creating an extendable sandbox, and also one that allows for loosely coupled and well-tested code to be written.

UNDERSTANDING THE PATTERN THROUGH UNIT TESTS

The JavaScript conference organizers are pleased with all of the functionality that you, Charlotte, and the rest of the team have added to the conference's website. Among other features, the conference volunteers have the ability to check-in attendees, and conference attendees (and volunteers) can search for restaurants near the conference venue.

One feature that the conference organizers wish they had, however, is a dashboard that could give them an overall picture of what's going on with the conference and the operation of the website.

"No problem," you say. "What sort of data would you like to see on the dashboard?" Immediately, you're inundated with answers:

➤   The total number of people that have registered for the conference

➤   The names of the people that have registered for the conference

➤   The number of attendees that have checked-in

➤   The names of attendees that have checked-in

➤   The count of calls to the third-party restaurant API

➤   The weather forecast at the local airport

and so on and so forth. You write furiously and capture all their input, and note that each of the organizers wants to see a different collection of data on his dashboard.

During a discussion about the design of the feature with Charlotte, you note: "The types of data the organizers want displayed are really diverse, and what's to keep them from wanting to show more as we add features to the website?"

"Nothing," Charlotte responds, "so we should take care and create a solution that is extensible. Also, she continues, the feature will be much more reliable if we can ensure each part of the dashboard that displays data—let's call them widgets—is properly decoupled, especially from other widgets."

"I understand that reducing coupling between components is generally a good idea, but why do you think it's such a high priority in this case?" you ask.

"Well, you noted that each of the organizers wants to see a different collection of widgets on his dashboard. That implies that we're going to need to allow widgets to be enabled and disabled. If Widget A is coupled to Widget B and the organizer chooses to disable Widget B, Widget A won't function properly," answers Charlotte. "If you consider all the different combinations of widgets that could be displayed at one time, one or two coupled widgets could lead to late nights of debugging."

"Great point," you concede, "but do you have any idea how we could keep the widgets decoupled?"

"Absolutely. We can isolate each one in its own sandbox," Charlotte responds confidently, "and provide the tools the widget needs, and *only* the tools the widget needs, via the sandbox."

Creating a Widget Sandbox

As Charlotte stated, the goal of the widget sandbox is to isolate each of the widgets to ensure that it can function on its own. The Sandbox Pattern will also allow a controlled set of dependencies to be provided to each widget, giving it the tools that it needs to do its job.

Instantiating a Widget Sandbox

The `WidgetSandbox` constructor function will be designed to be used with the `new` keyword. Also, it will expect to be called with at least one argument: the function to create the widget that will be isolated within the sandbox. The unit tests that verify this behavior are shown in Listing 11-1.

LISTING 11-1: Initial WidgetSandbox constructor function unit tests (code filename: Sandbox\WidgetSandbox_01_tests.js)

```
describe("Conference.WidgetSandbox", function(){
  'use strict';

  describe("Constructor function", function(){
    it("throws if it has not been invoked with the 'new' keyword", function(){
      expect(function shouldThrow(){
        var sandbox = Conference.WidgetSandbox();
      }).toThrowError(Conference.WidgetSandbox.messages.mustBeCalledWithNew);
    });

    it("throws if a widget function is not provided", function(){
      [null, undefined, 1, "SomeString", false]
      .forEach(function testInvalid(notAFcn){
        expect(function shouldThrow(){
          var sandbox = new Conference.WidgetSandbox(notAFcn);
        }).toThrowError(Conference.WidgetSandbox.messages.fcnMustBeProvided);
      });
    });

    it("invokes the widget function with the sandbox as an arg", function(){
      var moduleFcn = jasmine.createSpy();
      var sandbox = new Conference.WidgetSandbox(moduleFcn);
      expect(moduleFcn).toHaveBeenCalledWith(sandbox);
    });
  });
});
```

The first test, which ensures that the `WidgetSandbox` is executed using the `new` keyword, will be familiar from Chapter 3.

The second test verifies the expectation that the sandbox be provided with a function it may execute to create an instance of the widget to be isolated. Notice that the test provides `undefined` as an argument, simulating executing `WidgetSandbox` with no arguments. It also goes one step further by providing arguments that aren't functions. This will ensure that the code written to implement `WidgetSandbox` does more than just verify that any old argument has been provided; it must verify that the argument provided is a function in order for the test to pass.

The final test ensures that the widget's function is executed with the sandbox instance provided as an argument.

The initial implementation of `WidgetSandbox` in Listing 11-2 causes the unit tests to pass, as you can see in Figure 11-1.

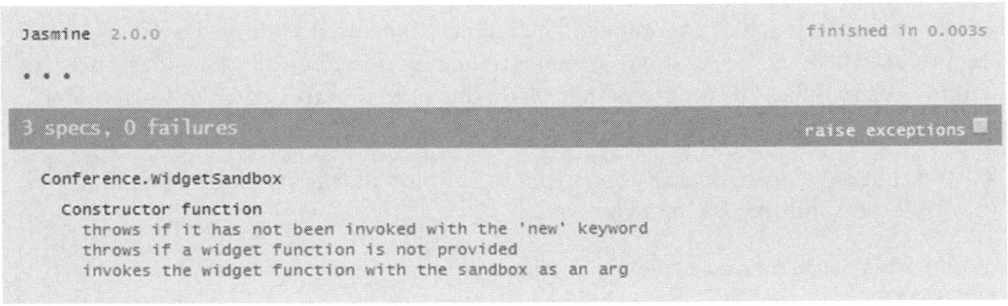

```
Jasmine  2.0.0                                          finished in 0.003s

• • •

3 specs, 0 failures                                     raise exceptions ▣

  Conference.WidgetSandbox

    Constructor function
      throws if it has not been invoked with the 'new' keyword
      throws if a widget function is not provided
      invokes the widget function with the sandbox as an arg
```

FIGURE 11-1

LISTING 11-2: Initial WidgetSandbox constructor function implementation (code filename: Sandbox\WidgetSandbox_01.js)

```javascript
var Conference = Conference || {};

Conference.WidgetSandbox = function(){
  'use strict';

  // Ensure that Conference.WidgetSandbox(...) has been invoked using the
  // new keyword
  if(!(this instanceof Conference.WidgetSandbox)){
    throw new Error(Conference.WidgetSandbox.messages.mustBeCalledWithNew);
  }

  var widgetFunction = arguments[0];

  if(typeof widgetFunction !== "function"){
    throw new Error(Conference.WidgetSandbox.messages.fcnMustBeProvided);
  }

  widgetFunction(this);
};

Conference.WidgetSandbox.messages = {
  mustBeCalledWithNew: "The WidgetSandbox function must be called with new",
  fcnMustBeProvided: "Widget function must be provided"
};
```

Providing Tools to the Widget via the Sandbox

While the `WidgetSandbox` is designed to isolate the dashboard widgets so they're loosely coupled, the widgets won't be very useful if they can't somehow interact with the DOM or retrieve information from web services. Like shovels and rakes that can be used in a physical sandbox, the `WidgetSandbox` should provide a set of tools that the widget can use to interact with its environment.

After conferring with Charlotte, you determine that you have an idea what some of the tools available to widgets should be, but not all. Rather than providing a fixed set of tools, you decide that it should be possible to extend the capabilities of the `WidgetSandbox` by adding new tools to it. Also, it should be possible to restrict what tools are available to each widget. If a widget doesn't need to interact with a web service, for example, it shouldn't have access to the tool that allows for AJAX communication.

Before beginning to implement the features that achieve these goals, some decisions need to be made:

1. Where will the tools be defined?

2. How will the tools be added to an instance of the `WidgetSandbox`?

3. How will the tools available to a widget be specified?

With Charlotte's input, you arrive at the following answers:

1. It makes sense to define the tools within the `Conference.WidgetTools` namespace.

2. Tools will be defined as modules, and a tool's module function will accept an instance of `WidgetSandbox`. The tool will add itself to the `WidgetSandbox` as a property in the following manner:

```
Conference.WidgetTools.toolA = function(sandbox){
  // Add toolA to sandbox
  sandbox.toolA = {
    function1: function(){
      // function1 implementation
    },
    function2: function(){
      // function2 implementation
    }
  };
};
```

3. The `WidgetSandbox` constructor will accept either:

   a. An array of the names of the tools that should be made available to the widget as its first argument, and the widget's function as its second argument—for example:

   ```
   var weatherSandbox = new Conference.WidgetSandbox(['toolA', 'toolB'],
     Conference.widgets.weatherWidget);
   ```

   b. Any number of individual tool name arguments, and the widget's function as its last argument—for example:

   ```
   var weatherSandbox = new Conference.WidgetSandbox('toolA', 'toolB',
     Conference.widgets.weatherWidget);
   ```

Even though it's last on the list of decisions, the specification of tools available to a widget will be where you start.

As the first step, you want to verify that the widget's function can be resolved when a list of tool names, either as an array or as individual arguments, is provided to the `WidgetSandbox` constructor function. Listing 11-3 provides tests that ensure this capability.

LISTING 11-3: WidgetSandbox constructor function with tool specification tests (code filename: Sandbox\WidgetSandbox_02_tests.js)

```javascript
describe("Conference.WidgetSandbox", function(){
  'use strict';

  describe("Constructor function", function(){

    it("throws if it has not been invoked with the 'new' keyword", function(){
      expect(function shouldThrow(){
        var sandbox = Conference.WidgetSandbox();
      }).toThrowError(Conference.WidgetSandbox.messages.mustBeCalledWithNew);
    });

    describe('new WidgetSandbox(toolsArray, widgetFcn)', function(){
      // Tests behavior when the list of tools is provided as an
      // array

      it("throws if a widget function is not provided", function(){
        [null, undefined, 1, "SomeString", false]
          .forEach(function testInvalid(val){
            expect(function shouldThrow(){
              var sandbox = new Conference.WidgetSandbox(['tool1', 'tool2'], val);
            }).toThrowError(Conference.WidgetSandbox.messages.fcnMustBeProvided);
          });
      });

      it("invokes the widget function with sandbox as an arg", function(){
        var widgetFcn = jasmine.createSpy();
        var sandbox = new Conference.WidgetSandbox(['tool1', 'tool2'],
          widgetFcn);
        expect(widgetFcn).toHaveBeenCalledWith(sandbox);
      });
    });

    describe("new WidgetSandbox('tool1',..., 'toolN', widgetFcn)", function(){
      // Tests behavior when the list of tools is provided as individual
      // arguments

      it("throws if a widget function is not provided", function(){
        [null, undefined, 1, "SomeString", false]
          .forEach(function testInvalid(val){
            expect(function shouldThrow(){
              var sandbox = new Conference.WidgetSandbox('tool1', 'tool2', val);
            }).toThrowError(Conference.WidgetSandbox.messages.fcnMustBeProvided);
          });
```

```
      });

      it("invokes the widget function with sandbox as an arg", function(){
        var widgetFcn = jasmine.createSpy();
        var sandbox = new Conference.WidgetSandbox('tool1', 'tool2', widgetFcn);
        expect(widgetFcn).toHaveBeenCalledWith(sandbox);
      });
    });
  });
});
```

Notice that in Listing 11-3 two `describe` blocks have been added: one that contains tests for when the `WidgetSandbox` constructor function is invoked with an array of tool names, and the other for when it is invoked with tool names as individual arguments. It's important that the constructor behave properly regardless of the mechanism used to provide the list of tool names. Figure 11-2 shows the failing unit tests.

FIGURE 11-2

In order to allow the failing tests to pass, the technique used to retrieve the widget function from the list of arguments must be adjusted. The current implementation assumes that the function will be passed as the first argument, which is no longer the case. Because of the decision you and Charlotte made, the widget function will always be the *last* argument provided to the `WidgetSandbox` constructor function.

Listing 11-4 shows the updated implementation of the `WidgetSandbox` that uses the correct argument as the widget function. Also, the `WidgetTools` namespace is initialized to a bare object.

LISTING 11-4: WidgetSandbox using the last argument as the widget function (code filename: Sandbox\WidgetSandbox_02.js)

```
var Conference = Conference || {};

Conference.WidgetSandbox = function(){
  'use strict';

  // Ensure that Conference.WidgetSandbox(...) has been invoked using the
  // new keyword
  if(!(this instanceof Conference.WidgetSandbox)){
    throw new Error(Conference.WidgetSandbox.messages.mustBeCalledWithNew);
  }

  var widgetFunction = arguments[arguments.length - 1];

  if(typeof widgetFunction !== "function"){
    throw new Error(Conference.WidgetSandbox.messages.fcnMustBeProvided);
  }

  var widget = widgetFunction(this);
};

// Create the empty tools namespace
Conference.WidgetTools = {};

Conference.WidgetSandbox.messages = {
  mustBeCalledWithNew: "The WidgetSandbox function must be called with new",
  fcnMustBeProvided: "Widget function must be provided"
};
```

All the unit tests now pass, as shown in Figure 11-3.

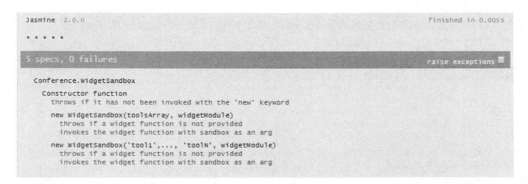

FIGURE 11-3

The next step in the process is to use the tool names provided to the WidgetSandbox constructor function to resolve the tool module functions and create instances of the tools. The case where the list of tool names is provided as an array is a bit simpler than the case where the tool names are provided as individual arguments, so you start there.

Based on the convention that you and Charlotte agreed on, each tool name provided should correspond to a property of `Conference.WidgetTools`. If a tool name is specified that does not have a corresponding property in that namespace, then a descriptive Error should be thrown. This will allow developers using the `WidgetSandbox` to quickly identify that they've asked for an unknown tool (or made a typo).

Assuming that a tool name corresponds to a valid tool, the tool's module function should be invoked with the instance of the `WidgetSandbox` as its only argument.

Listing 11-5 contains the unit tests for the described functionality.

LISTING 11-5: Unit tests for resolving tools whose names are specified in an array (code filename: Sandbox\WidgetSandbox_03_tests.js)

```
describe("Conference.WidgetSandbox", function(){
  'use strict';

  describe("Constructor function", function(){
    var widgetFcnSpy;

    beforeEach(function(){
      // Add test tools so the tests aren't dependent upon
      // the existence of actual tools
      Conference.WidgetTools.tool1 = function(sandbox){
        return {};
      };
      Conference.WidgetTools.tool2 = function(sandbox){
        return {};
      };

      // create a spy that may be used as the widget function
      widgetFcnSpy = jasmine.createSpy();
    });

    afterEach(function(){
      // remove the test tools
      delete Conference.WidgetTools.tool1;
      delete Conference.WidgetTools.tool2;
    });

    // *** Previously discussed tests omitted. ***

    describe('new WidgetSandbox(toolsArray, widgetFcn)', function(){
      // Tests behavior when the list of tools is provided as an
      // array

      // *** Previously discussed tests omitted. ***

      it("throws if an invalid tool is specified", function(){
        expect(function shouldThrow(){
          var badTool = 'badTool';
          var sandbox = new Conference.WidgetSandbox(['tool1', badTool],
            widgetFcnSpy);
        }).toThrowError(Conference.WidgetSandbox.messages.unknownTool+badTool);
```

continues

LISTING 11-5 *(continued)*

```javascript
        });

        it("invokes the tool module function with the sandbox", function(){
          spyOn(Conference.WidgetTools, 'tool1');
          spyOn(Conference.WidgetTools, 'tool2');

          var sandbox = new Conference.WidgetSandbox(['tool1', 'tool2'],
            widgetFcnSpy);

          expect(Conference.WidgetTools.tool1)
            .toHaveBeenCalledWith(sandbox);
          expect(Conference.WidgetTools.tool2)
            .toHaveBeenCalledWith(sandbox);
        });
      });

      describe("new WidgetSandbox('tool1',..., 'toolN', widgetFcn)", function(){
        // *** Previously discussed tests omitted. ***
      });
    });
  });
```

Now that the functionality to resolve tools by their names is being added, some tools need to be available in the agreed-upon namespace. The highlighted code in the `beforeEach` block creates `tool1` and `tool2`. Because `Conference.WidgetTools` is a singleton object, the test suite is a good citizen; it removes the test tools in an `afterEach` block. Doing so ensures that there are no side-effects caused by leaving the test tools in place. The new unit tests fail, as Figure 11-4 illustrates.

Listing 11-6 provides the updated `WidgetSandbox` which allows the new unit tests to pass.

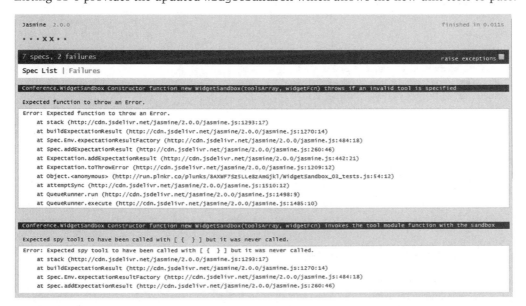

FIGURE 11-4

LISTING 11-6: WidgetSandbox constructor function that loads tools specified by an array of tool names (code filename: Sandbox\WidgetSandbox_03.js)

```javascript
var Conference = Conference || {};

Conference.WidgetSandbox = function(){
  'use strict';

  // Ensure that Conference.WidgetSandbox(...) has been invoked using the
  // new keyword
  if(!(this instanceof Conference.WidgetSandbox)){
    throw new Error(Conference.WidgetSandbox.messages.mustBeCalledWithNew);
  }

  var widgetFunction = arguments[arguments.length - 1],
      toolsToLoad = [];

  if(typeof widgetFunction !== "function"){
    throw new Error(Conference.WidgetSandbox.messages.fcnMustBeProvided);
  }

  if(arguments[0] instanceof Array){
    toolsToLoad = arguments[0];
  }

  toolsToLoad.forEach(function loadTool(toolName){
    if(!Conference.WidgetTools.hasOwnProperty(toolName)){
      throw new Error(Conference.WidgetSandbox.messages.unknownTool + toolName);
    }

    Conference.WidgetTools[toolName](this);
  }, this); // ensure 'this' refers to the sandbox instance within the callback

  var widget = widgetFunction(this);
};

// Create the empty tools namespace
Conference.WidgetTools = {};

Conference.WidgetSandbox.messages = {
  mustBeCalledWithNew: "The WidgetSandbox function must be called with new",
  fcnMustBeProvided: "Widget function must be provided",
  unknownTool: "Unknown tool requested: "
};
```

The code highlighted in Listing 11-6 adds the functionality described. If the first argument provided to the constructor function is an array, it is assigned to the local variable `toolsToLoad`. Each `toolName` in the `toolsToLoad` array is then checked for validity by ensuring that the `Conference.WidgetTools` namespace has a property with the specified name. Should an invalid `toolName` be encountered, an error is immediately thrown. Otherwise, the tool's module function is executed with the sandbox instance as an argument. As Figure 11-5 shows, all of the unit tests now pass.

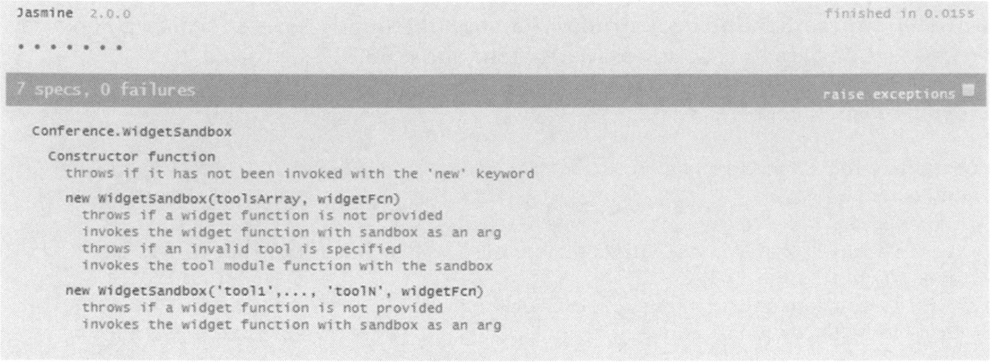

FIGURE 11-5

The final step in implementing the ability to specify the tools that should be available to the widget via the sandbox is to handle the case in which the list of tool names is provided as a series of individual arguments. The unit tests for this case mirror those that were just created for the array-of-tool-names case, and are shown in Listing 11-7. The fact that the unit tests currently fail is shown in Figure 11-6.

FIGURE 11-6

LISTING 11-7: Unit tests for resolving tools whose names are specified by a series of tool name arguments (code filename: Sandbox\WidgetSandbox_04_tests.js)

```
describe("Conference.WidgetSandbox", function(){
  'use strict';

  describe("Constructor function", function(){
```

```
    var widgetFcnSpy;

    // *** Previously discussed beforeEach & afterEach omitted. ***

    // *** Previously discussed tests omitted. ***

    describe('new WidgetSandbox(toolsArray, widgetFcn)', function(){
      // Tests behavior when the list of tools is provided as an
      // array

      // *** Previously discussed tests omitted. ***
    });

    describe("new WidgetSandbox('tool1',..., 'toolN', widgetFcn)", function(){
      // Tests behavior when the list of tools is provided as individual
      // arguments

      // *** Previously discussed tests omitted. ***

      it("throws if an invalid tool is specified", function(){
        var badTool = 'badTool';
        expect(function shouldThrow(){
          var sandbox = new Conference.WidgetSandbox('tool1', badTool,
            widgetFcnSpy);
        }).toThrowError(Conference.WidgetSandbox.messages.unknownTool+badTool);
      });

      it("invokes the tool module function with the sandbox", function(){
        spyOn(Conference.WidgetTools, 'tool1');
        spyOn(Conference.WidgetTools, 'tool2');
        var sandbox = new Conference.WidgetSandbox('tool1', 'tool2',
          widgetFcnSpy);
        expect(Conference.WidgetTools.tool1)
          .toHaveBeenCalledWith(sandbox);
        expect(Conference.WidgetTools.tool2)
          .toHaveBeenCalledWith(sandbox);
      });
    });
  });
});
});
```

Adding support for tool names provided as separate arguments requires a few changes to the WidgetSandbox constructor function. The updated code is shown in Listing 11-8.

LISTING 11-8: WidgetSandbox constructor function that loads tools specified by individual tool name arguments (code filename: Sandbox\WidgetSandbox_04.js)

```
var Conference = Conference || {};

Conference.WidgetSandbox = function(){
  'use strict';

  // Ensure that Conference.WidgetSandbox(...) has been invoked using the
  // new keyword
```

continues

LISTING 11-8 *(continued)*

```
  if(!(this instanceof Conference.WidgetSandbox)){
    throw new Error(Conference.WidgetSandbox.messages.mustBeCalledWithNew);
  }

  var widgetFunction,
      toolsToLoad = [],
      argsArray;

  // create a *real* array from arguments
  argsArray = Array.prototype.slice.call(arguments);

  // the widgetFunction will be the last element of the array; pop it off.
  widgetFunction = argsArray.pop();

  if(typeof widgetFunction !== "function"){
    throw new Error(Conference.WidgetSandbox.messages.fcnMustBeProvided);
  }

  toolsToLoad = (argsArray[0] instanceof Array)?
    argsArray[0] :
    argsArray;

  toolsToLoad.forEach(function loadTool(toolName){
    if(!Conference.WidgetTools.hasOwnProperty(toolName)){
      throw new Error(Conference.WidgetSandbox.messages.unknownTool + toolName);
    }

    Conference.WidgetTools[toolName](this);
  }, this); // ensure 'this' refers to the sandbox instance within the callback

  var widget = widgetFunction(this);
};

// *** Previously discussed code omitted ***
```

First, the array `argsArray` is created from the special `arguments` variable. Rather than populating the widget function variable `widgetFunction` by indexing into `arguments`, it is now populated by popping it off the end of `argsArray`.

> **NOTE** *The special variable* `arguments` *is available in every JavaScript function. It contains each of the arguments provided to the function, retrievable by index. Though it is array-like—its elements are available by index and it has a length property—it is not an* `Array`. *Luckily,* `Array.prototype.slice` *may be used to create an* `Array` *from most array-like objects. More details are available at* https://developer.mozilla.org/en-US/docs/Web/JavaScript/Reference/Global_Objects/Array/slice.

If `argsArray[0]` is an `Array` (indicating that the list of tool names has been provided as an `Array`), it is assigned to `toolsToLoad`. Otherwise, it is assumed that the tool names were provided as individual arguments. Because the widget function as been removed from `argsArray`, the only remaining elements are tool names. Thus, `toolsToLoad` is set to `argsArray`.

At this point, the `WidgetSandbox` has been implemented and is functioning correctly, as the unit test results in Figure 11-7 show.

```
Jasmine  2.0.0                                              finished in 0.019s

• • • • • • • • •

9 specs, 0 failures                                         raise exceptions ■

  Conference.WidgetSandbox

    Constructor function
      throws if it has not been invoked with the 'new' keyword

    new WidgetSandbox(toolsArray, widgetFcn)
      throws if a widget function is not provided
      invokes the widget function with sandbox as an arg
      throws if an invalid tool is specified
      invokes the tool module function with the sandbox

    new WidgetSandbox('tool1',..., 'toolN', widgetFcn)
      throws if a widget function is not provided
      invokes the widget function with sandbox as an arg
      throws if an invalid tool is specified
      invokes the tool module function with the sandbox
```

FIGURE 11-7

Creating and Testing Sandbox Tools

As it stands, the `WidgetSandbox` isn't real useful. While it isolates widget instances just fine, there are no tools that the widgets may use to do work.

You may recall that among the many items that the conference organizers want to be able to display on the dashboard are the names of the people that have registered for the conference. You volunteer to implement the tool that may be used to provide the registrant names to a widget.

An object responsible for managing attendee-registration tasks, `attendeeWebApi`, already exists. Among other methods, it provides `getAll()`, which returns a `Promise` that will resolve to an array of `attendee` objects. You decide that the tool you create, `attendeeNames`, will be a façade on `attendeeWebApi` that exposes the functionality required.

The unit tests for the `attendeeNames` tool follows in Listing 11-9.

LISTING 11-9: Unit tests for Conference.WidgetTools.attendeeNames (code filename: Sandbox\attendeeNames_tests.js)

```
describe("Conference.WidgetTools.attendeeNames", function(){
  'use strict';

  var attendeeWebApi,
```

continues

LISTING 11-9 *(continued)*

```
    sandbox;

beforeEach(function(){
  attendeeWebApi = Conference.attendeeWebApi();

  // the post method should NEVER be called.  Spy on it so that
  // it may be verified.
  spyOn(attendeeWebApi, 'post');

  // for the purpose of unit testing attendeeNames, sandbox
  // may be a bare object
  sandbox = {};
});

afterEach(function(){
  // After every test, make sure post was never called.
  expect(attendeeWebApi.post).not.toHaveBeenCalled();
});

it("adds itself to the provided sandbox object", function(){
  Conference.WidgetTools.attendeeNames(sandbox, attendeeWebApi);
  expect(sandbox.attendeeNames).not.toBeUndefined();
});

describe("attendeeNames.getAll()", function(){
  var attendees,
      attendeeNames;

  beforeEach(function(){
    Conference.WidgetTools.attendeeNames(sandbox, attendeeWebApi);

    // Populate an array of test attendees
    attendees = [
      Conference.attendee("Tom", "Kazansky"),
      Conference.attendee("Pete", "Mitchell"),
      Conference.attendee("Mary", "Metcalf")
    ];

    // Extract the names from the test attendees
    attendeeNames = [];
    attendees.forEach(function getNames(attendee){
      attendeeNames.push(attendee.getFullName());
    });
  });

  it("resolves to an empty array if there are no attendees", function(done){

    spyOn(attendeeWebApi, 'getAll').and.returnValue(
      new Promise( function(resolve, reject){
        resolve([]);
      })
    );

    sandbox.attendeeNames.getAll().then(function resolved(names){
```

```
      expect(names).toEqual([]);
      done();
    }, function rejected(reason){
      expect('Failed').toBe(false);
      done();
    });

  });

  it("resolves to the expected names if there are attendees", function(done){

    spyOn(attendeeWebApi, 'getAll').and.returnValue(
      new Promise( function(resolve, reject){
        resolve(attendees);
      })
    );

    sandbox.attendeeNames.getAll().then(function resolved(names){
      expect(names).toEqual(attendeeNames);
      done();
    }, function rejected(reason){
      expect('Failed').toBe(false);
      done();
    });

  });

  it("rejects with the underlying reason", function(done){
    var rejectionReason = "Reason for rejection";

    spyOn(attendeeWebApi, 'getAll').and.returnValue(
      new Promise( function(resolve, reject){
        reject(rejectionReason);
      })
    );

    sandbox.attendeeNames.getAll().then(function resolved(names){
      expect('Resolved').toBe(false);
      done();
    }, function rejected(reason){
      expect(reason).toBe(rejectionReason);
      done();
    });
  });
});
});
```

If you recall the details of unit-testing Promise-based code that were covered in Chapter 6, much of Listing 11-9 will be familiar. Like the functionality that's provided by the attendeeName tool, the tests are relatively simple. They verify that the Promise returned by attendeeWebApi.getAll() properly flows through the attendeeNames.getAll() method.

Also, the tests verify that the attendeeNames.getAll() method properly extracts and returns only the attendees' names, rather than the entirety of each attendee object. Aside from the fact that this is how you and Charlotte determined the attendeeNames tool should behave, why is this important? Suppose that the `attendee.undoCheckin()` method automatically persisted the state of the attendee's check-in directly to the server. If widgets were able to access this method, it would be possible for a widget developer to undo the check-in of an attendee even though it's not an action that the widget should be able to perform. By limiting the data returned, the `attendeeNames` tool doesn't give the widget developer the opportunity to make this mistake.

Another important validation, performed after each test, is that the `attendeeWebApi` `.post(attendee)` method is *never* called. One of the prime benefits of the Sandbox Pattern is that it provides a high level of control over the capabilities available to components that exist within the sandbox. In this case, it is not acceptable for a widget that uses the `attendeeNames` tool to execute the `post` method. Again, it's not an action a widget using the tool should ever be able to perform, so the `attendeeNames` tool doesn't expose it. The validation is put into place to help ensure that it doesn't become exposed and used in the future.

Listing 11-10 provides the implementation of the `attendeeNames` tool, and Figure 11-8 shows that the unit tests are passing.

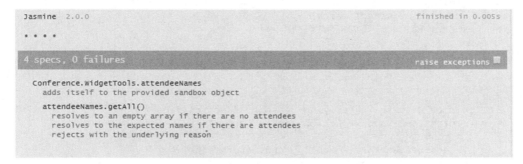

FIGURE 11-8

LISTING 11-10: Implementation of Conference.WidgetTools.attendeeNames (code filename: Sandbox\attendeeNames.js)

```
var Conference = Conference || {};
Conference.WidgetTools = Conference.WidgetTools || {};

Conference.WidgetTools.attendeeNames = function(sandbox,
  injectedAttendeeWebApi){
  'use strict';

  // Allow the attendeeWebApi to be optionally injected; useful for unit-testing
  var attendeeWebApi = injectedAttendeeWebApi || Conference.attendeeWebApi();

  sandbox.attendeeNames = {

    // Returns a promise that resolves to an array of attendee names
    getAll: function getAll(){
      return attendeeWebApi.getAll()
        .then(function extractNames(attendees){
```

```
      // extract and return only the full name of each attendee
      var names = [];
      attendees.forEach(function addName(attendee){
        names.push(attendee.getFullName());
      });
      return names;
    });
  }
 };
};
```

Creating Functions for Use with a Sandbox

Creating and testing modules designed to be isolated within a sandbox is relatively simple. The Sandbox Pattern dictates that isolated modules are only dependent upon an instance of the sandbox, and that the sandbox instance must be injected into the module. As discussed in Chapter 2, dependency injection increases the testability and reliability of your JavaScript code.

While you were working away on creating the `attendeeNames` tool, Charlotte was creating a `dom` tool that allows widgets to interact with the browser's Document Object Model (DOM).

> **NOTE** *A tool for interacting with the DOM? Why not just use jQuery? While it's tempting, remember that when correctly using the Sandbox Pattern, modules isolated by the sandbox should* only *interact with the sandbox. A sandbox can't prevent you from creating instances of objects that you shouldn't, or keep you accessing global objects, such as* `window` *or* `jQuery`. *Doing so violates the spirit of the pattern, however, and introduces dependencies where you're trying to avoid them.*

Between your `attendeeNames` tool and Charlotte's `dom` tool, you now have enough to create a widget for displaying attendee names. A portion of the unit tests for the widget is provided in Listing 11-11.

LISTING 11-11: Unit tests related to the attendeeNamesWidget's participation in the Sandbox Pattern (code filename: Sandbox\attendeeNamesWidget_tests.js)

```
describe("Conference.Widgets.attendeeNamesWidget(sandbox)", function(){
  'use strict';

  var sandbox;
  beforeEach(function(){
    sandbox = {};
  });

  it("throws if the dom tool isn't available", function(){
    expect(function shouldThrow(){
      Conference.Widgets.attendeeNamesWidget(sandbox);
    }).toThrowError(Conference.Widgets.messages.missingTool + 'dom');
```

continues

LISTING 11-11 *(continued)*

```
    });

    it("throws if the attendeeNames tool isn't available", function(){
      expect(function shouldThrow(){
        sandbox.dom = {};
        Conference.Widgets.attendeeNamesWidget(sandbox);
      }).toThrowError(Conference.Widgets.messages.missingTool + 'attendeeNames');
    });

    // Additional tests that ensure the attendeeNamesWidget functions as expected
  });
```

Only the unit tests that are specific to the widget's use with the sandbox object are provided; there's nothing particularly novel about testing the rest of the functionality of the widget. It is worth noting that it isn't necessary to use an instance of `WidgetSandbox` for testing. As far as the widget is concerned, the sandbox's only function is to provide tools; an object literal is sufficient to do this for testing purposes.

Listing 11-12 provides a skeletal implementation of the `attendeeNamesWidget`.

LISTING 11-12: Skeletal implementation of the attendeeNamesWidget (code filename: Sandbox\attendeeNamesWidget.js)

```
var Conference = Conference || {};
Conference.Widgets = Conference.Widgets || {};

Conference.Widgets.attendeeNamesWidget = function(sandbox){
  'use strict';

  // Fail immediately if the expected tools aren't available
  if(!sandbox.dom){
    throw new Error(Conference.Widgets.messages.missingTool + 'dom');
  }
  if(!sandbox.attendeeNames){
    throw new Error(Conference.Widgets.messages.missingTool + 'attendeeNames');
  }

  // retrieve attendeeNames and add them to the dashboard
  sandbox.attendeeNames.getAll().then(function resolved(names){
    // use sandbox.dom to display the list of names
  }, function rejected(reason){
    // use sandbox.dom to present an error message in the place
    // of the widget
  });
};

Conference.Widgets.messages = {
  missingTool: "Missing tool: "
};
```

Figure 11-9 shows that the unit tests for the widget are passing.

```
Jasmine  2.0.0                                         finished in 0.005s
 .  .

2 specs, 0 failures                                     raise exceptions ■

  Conference.widgets.attendeeNamesWidget(sandbox)
    throws if the dom tool isn't available
    throws if the attendeeNames tool isn't available
```

FIGURE 11-9

SUMMARY

This chapter presented the Sandbox Pattern as a mechanism to create loosely coupled modules with strictly controlled dependencies. Using test-driven development, you developed an implementation of the Sandbox Pattern (based on the pattern presented by Stoyan Stefanov in his book *JavaScript Patterns*).

The chapter covered the creation and testing of tools that add functionality to the sandbox. The chapter also described the benefit of using the tools as façades to restrict and control isolated modules' access to resources and functionality.

Additionally, the chapter demonstrated how to develop and unit-test a function for use within a sandbox.

To make your implementation of the Sandbox Pattern reliable, you should write unit tests to ensure that:

➤   A widget module function is provided to the sandbox's constructor function.

➤   Tools may be provided to the sandbox's constructor function either as an array or individual arguments.

➤   The tools specified for use in the sandbox are valid.

➤   The tools requested by a widget running within the sandbox are provided by the sandbox.

In Chapter 12, we discuss the Decorator Pattern, how it can be used to solve real-world problems, and how it can be implemented in a test-driven fashion.

12

Ensuring Correct Implementation of the Decorator Pattern

WHAT'S IN THIS CHAPTER?

> ➤ Using a decorator to neatly solve a real-world problem

> ➤ Using a "fake" to stand in for the decorated object during unit tests

> ➤ Using test-driven development to create a reliable decorator

WROX.COM CODE DOWNLOADS FOR THIS CHAPTER

You can find the wrox.com code downloads for this chapter at www.wrox.com/go/ reliablejavascript on the Download Code tab. The files are in the Chapter 12 download and are individually named according to the filenames noted throughout this chapter.

The Decorator Pattern is a way of augmenting the capabilities of an object without changing it. You have already met some examples in this book. The memoization aspect in Chapter 8 decorates the function to which it is attached, giving the function the added ability to return a result without doing much work, when it is called with parameters it has seen before. When you set up a Jasmine spy with .and.callThrough(), you are decorating the spied-on function, augmenting it with the ability to report how many times it was called, and so on.

In this chapter, you will take the decorating process further. Instead of decorating an isolated function, you will decorate an object that has multiple, coordinated functions. You will also get more practice with the Promise object you encountered in Chapter 6. Finally, this will be another in-depth case study of test-driven development.

The case study is inspired by something we encountered in real life, but it will make more sense if we cast it in the now-familiar terms of the JavaScript conference's website.

At the conference, attendees will be able to register in person. For the benefit of the in-person registrar, you have written a web page that lists the current attendees. If someone shows up who is not on the list, the press of a button invokes another page on which the registrar can key in a record for the newcomer.

People will be waiting in line, so response time is critical. That's why you decided on a fire-and-forget strategy. The New Attendee page issues an HTTP POST to the server and returns immediately to the Attendee List page without waiting for the POST to resolve its `Promise`. (See Chapter 6 for more on HTTP wrapped in `Promises`.) The Attendee List then does an HTTP GET for a fresh list, on which you expect to see the new registrant.

Except you don't!

A little debugging tells you that even though the POST was issued microseconds before the GET, the GET can return pre-POST data. Your research confirms that the HTTP specification does not guarantee that requests will be completely processed in the order received. Oops!

With response time being so important, you really don't want to hold your user hostage on the New Attendee page, not returning her to the Attendee List page until the POST completes. A POST failure will be extremely rare. It would be a shame to hobble the application because of such an unlikely event. Is there a better way?

Where there's a will, there's a way.

1. Before POSTing the new record, store it in an array of pending posts.

2. When the POST's `Promise` resolves (see Chapter 6), remove the record from the array.

3. In the meantime, append those pending records to GET's results (to the extent that the results do not already include them). This will let the Attendee List page show the POSTed record right away. The pending-post records will not yet have their attendee IDs, which are generated by the database. Those would be needed to carry out an update or delete, but in the meantime, at least you can list the names.

4. When the POST does return an attendee's ID, it should be plugged into any records that were appended to a GET in Step 3, enabling updates or deletes.

5. In the unlikely event that the POST fails, the application will display a message and remove the attendee from the Attendee List page, if the user is still there. In the meantime, the presence of what turns out to be a bogus entry on the list will have done no harm: Until that ID comes back (Step 4), your UI will not allow the record to be updated or deleted.

The preceding fives steps simplify a real production situation, which would also have to account for pending updates and pending deletes, but it will serve to illustrate the point.

You have an object, `attendeeWebApi`, which has methods `post(`*attendee*`)` and `getAll()`. They return `Promises` in the way that you saw in Listing 6-7 in Chapter 6, where an `XMLHttpRequest`'s success or failure caused a `Promise` to be resolved or rejected, and then the `Promise` was returned.

Implementation of the pending-post idea could get complicated, and will have nothing to do with the Single Responsibility of the `attendeeWebApi` object. Adhering faithfully to the Open/Closed Principle (see Chapter 2), you decide to leave `attendeeWebApi` alone but put the new functionality in an object that *wraps* attendeeWebApi. The wrapping object will have post and getAll methods that have the same parameters as the underlying ones, and the same semantics. The wrapper will take care of everything pertaining to the pending-POST list and delegate the real work to the wrapped attendeeWebApi. Your dependency-injection framework will cause the wrapper to be used everywhere instead of attendeeWebApi.

This is the Decorator Pattern, so you artfully name the outer object attendeeWebApiDecorator.

DEVELOPING A DECORATOR THE TEST-DRIVEN WAY

The first principle of unit-testing is to test the "unit" and no more. In the present case, you want to test attendeeWebApiDecorator but not the underlying attendeeWebApi. The next section describes the first step.

Writing a Fake for the Decorated Object

Usually, spies can stand in for an object that is not under test, but spies work most naturally on one function at a time. In this case, there are two functions that work together: The action of the post function should affect how getAll behaves. A small object that fakes this behavior will be more convenient than coordinated spies.

Listing 12-1 shows the result. The post method stores attendees in the attendees array, which acts as a pseudo-database. The getAll method returns them from there. To avoid doing the tests any unintentional favors, copies of the attendees are used rather than the original objects. (In real life, fresh attendee objects would be made from the database, and it's safest to duplicate this behavior.) A setTimeout mechanism is used to mimic the behavior of the real object.

LISTING 12-1: The fake attendeeWebApi (code filename: Decorator\fakeAttendeeWebApi.js)

```javascript
var Conference = Conference || {};

// A fake version of attendeeWebApi. It has the same methods as the real one,
// but is entirely client-side.
Conference.fakeAttendeeWebApi = function(){

  var attendees = []; // Fake database table.

  return {

    // Pretend to POST the attendee to the server.
    // Returns a Promise that resolves to a copy of the attendee
    // (to mimic getting a new version from the server), which
    // will at that point have a primary key (attendeeId) that was
    // assigned by the database.
    // If a test requires the Promise to reject, use a spy.
    post: function post(attendee) {
      return new Promise( function(resolve, reject) {
```

continues

LISTING 12-1 *(continued)*

```
          // setTimeout, even with a delay of only 5 milliseconds, causes
          // the resolution of the promise to be delayed to the next turn.
          setTimeout(function pretendPostingToServer() {
            var copyOfAttendee = attendee.copy();
            copyOfAttendee.setId(attendees.length+1);
            attendees.push(copyOfAttendee);
            resolve(copyOfAttendee);
          },5);
        });
      },

      // Return a Promise for all attendees. This Promise always resolves,
      // but in testing a spy can make it reject if necessary.
      getAll: function getAll() {
        return new Promise( function(resolve,reject) {
          // This setTimeout has a shorter delay than post's,
          // to imitate the conditions observed in real life.
          setTimeout(function pretendToGetAllFromServer() {
            var copies = [];
            attendees.forEach(function(a) {
              copies.push(a.copy());
            });
            resolve(copies);
          },1);
        });
      }
    };
  };
```

You are now ready to begin test-driven development, starting with error-handling. As previously mentioned, it is best to get the negative tests out of the way early. If you defer them to the end of development, you will be writing them when you're least interested in doing so, and it will be easy to do a less-than-adequate job. With a decorator, the negative tests have an additional advantage: They will often produce the shape of your finished product, as you will now see.

Writing Tests for Pass-Through of Errors

The `getAll()` method will ultimately delegate to the base `attendeeWebApi`'s `getAll()`. If the underlying method returns a rejected `Promise`, you want that rejection to flow up through the wrapper to the code that called it. After reviewing Chapter 6 on `Promises`, you code the test in Listing 12-2.

LISTING 12-2: Unit test for failure in getAll() (code filename: Decorator\attendeeWebApiDecorator_01_tests.js)

```
describe('attendeeWebApiDecorator', function() {
  'use strict';
  var decoratedWebApi,
      baseWebApi,
```

```
          underlyingFailure = 'Failure in underlying function';

      beforeEach(function() {
        baseWebApi = Conference.fakeAttendeeWebApi();
        decoratedWebApi = Conference.attendeeWebApiDecorator(baseWebApi);
      });

      describe('getAll()', function() {

        describe('on failure of underlying getAll', function() {

          it('returns the underlying rejected Promise', function(done) {
            spyOn(baseWebApi,'getAll').and.returnValue(
              new Promise( function(resolve,reject) {
                setTimeout(function() {
                  reject(underlyingFailure);
                },5);
              }));

            decoratedWebApi.getAll().then(
              function onSuccess() {
                expect('Underlying getAll succeeded').toBe(false);
                done();
              },
              function onFailure(reason) {
                expect(reason).toBe(underlyingFailure);
                done();
              });
          });
        });
      });
    });
```

As you read from the top of that listing, the decoratedWebApi is the subject under test. The baseWebApi is what the decorator wraps—a fakeAttendeeWebApi in this case. A beforeEach constructs them freshly for each test so there is no possibility of cross-test contamination.

This test is about failure so you code a spy on the fake's getAll that returns a rejected Promise. You want the spy to be as realistic as possible. Here, that means the Promise should not be rejected immediately, but asynchronously. You decide on a low-tech setTimeout to achieve this. If you were using one of the Deferred libraries mentioned at the end of Chapter 6, you could be more clever. The only disadvantage of setTimeout for the current case study is that you must be sure to make the timeout intervals longer for the posts than for the getAlls in order to simulate the real-life situation you're addressing. That sort of hidden dependency is a little ugly but it will do for the moment.

It is now time to create the subject under test.

Writing a Do-Nothing Decorator

Following the test-driven philosophy, you begin with the absolute minimum for your subject (see Listing 12-3).

LISTING 12-3: A do-nothing decorator

```
var Conference = Conference || {};
Conference.attendeeWebApiDecorator = function(baseWebApi){
  'use strict';

  return {

    post: function post(attendee) {
    },

    getAll: function getAll() {
    }
  };
};
```

Not surprisingly, this fails (see Figure 12-1).

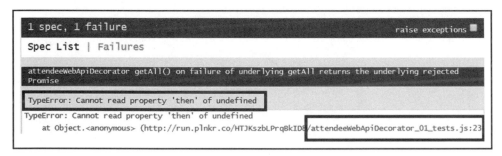

FIGURE 12-1

Because `getAll()` is empty, it returns `undefined`, which, of course, does not have a `then` method. The do-nothing decorator has served its purpose of sketching the overall shape, but now it's time to add some minimal functionality.

Adding Pass-Through Functionality to the Decorator

If the first step was to code a do-nothing decorator, the second step is to code one that has just a pass-through, as shown in Listing 12-4.

LISTING 12-4: Initial attendeeWebApiDecorator (code filename: Decorator\attendeeWebApiDecorator_01.js)

```
var Conference = Conference || {};
Conference.attendeeWebApiDecorator = function(baseWebApi){
  'use strict';

  return {

    post: function post(attendee) {
```

```
    },

  getAll: function getAll() {
    return baseWebApi.getAll();
  }
 };
};
```

Lo and behold, this makes the test pass (see Figure 12-2).

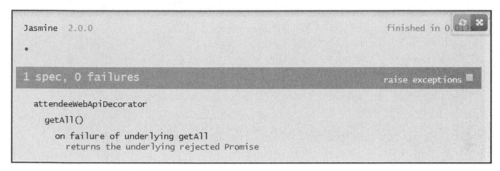

FIGURE 12-2

You do something similar for the post method and then turn your attention to another error condition: a post of a record that is already pending. You code the test in Listing 12-5. Recall from Chapter 6 that it is wise for a Promise to be rejected with an Error object, not just a bare message, and that a unit test should verify the exact message received so it knows that error was the expected one.

LISTING 12-5: Testing another error condition (code filename: Decorator\attendeeWebApiDecorator_02_tests.js [excerpt])

```
describe('when called for an attendee just posted', function() {
  it('returns a rejected promise',function(done) {
    decoratedWebApi.post(attendeeA);
    decoratedWebApi.post(attendeeA).then(
      function onSuccess() {
        expect('Post succeeded').toBe(false);
        done();
      },
      function onFailure(error) {
        expect(error instanceof Error).toBe(true);
        expect(error.message).toBe(
          decoratedWebApi.getMessages().postPending);
        done();
      });
  });
});
```

In order to make this test pass, the decorator must remember what it did in the first call to decoratedWebApi.post, and must expose its messages. Suddenly, the module grows to Listing 12-6.

LISTING 12-6: Detecting duplicate posts (code filename: Decorator\attendeeWebApiDecorator_02.js)

```javascript
var Conference = Conference || {};
Conference.attendeeWebApiDecorator = function(baseWebApi){
  'use strict';
  var self = this,

      // The records passed to the post function,
      // whose calls are not yet resolved.
      pendingPosts = [],

      messages = {
        postPending: 'It appears that a post is pending for this attendee'
      };

  // Return the element of 'posts' that is for the attendee,
  // or -1 if there is no such element.
  function indexOfPostForSameAttendee(posts,attendee) {
    var ix;
    for (ix=0; ix<posts.length; ++ix) {
      if (posts[ix].isSamePersonAs(attendee)) {
        return ix;
      }
    }
    return -1;
  }

  return {

    post: function post(attendee) {
      if (indexOfPostForSameAttendee(pendingPosts, attendee) >=0 ) {
        return Promise.reject(new Error(messages.postPending));
      }

      pendingPosts.push(attendee);

      return baseWebApi.post(attendee);
    },

    getAll: function getAll() {
      return baseWebApi.getAll();
    },

    getMessages: function getMessages() {
      return messages;
    }
  };
};
```

Things are starting to take shape, with the following new features added just to handle the error condition:

➤ The `pendingPosts` array stores the attendees passed to `post`.

➤ The `indexOfPostForSameAttendee` function can tell whether `pendingPosts` already has a given attendee. (It uses a new method in `Conference.attendee` called `isSamePersonAs`. See this chapter's downloads if you want the trivial details.)

➤ If the error condition is encountered, `post` returns a rejected `Promise`.

➤ The error message is exposed so the unit test can verify that it is getting the correct message.

The tests pass. With error pass-through working, maybe success pass-through is working as well? Could you be that lucky?

Verifying Pass-Through of Successes

In test-driven development, you're supposed to write code only to cause a failing test to pass. However, in the present case you have a hunch that the pass-through functionality you coded in order to make your negative tests pass will also cause simple positive tests to pass. You write the tests in Listing 12-7 to find out.

> **LISTING 12-7:** Tests to verify pass-through of successes (code filename: Decorator\attendeeWebApi_03_tests.js)

```
describe('attendeeWebApiDecorator', function() {
  'use strict';
  var decoratedWebApi,
      baseWebApi,
      attendeeA,
      attendeeB,
      underlyingFailure = 'Failure in underlying function';

  beforeEach(function() {
    baseWebApi = Conference.fakeAttendeeWebApi();
    decoratedWebApi = Conference.attendeeWebApiDecorator(baseWebApi);
    attendeeA = Conference.attendee('Mariano','Tezanos');
    attendeeB = Conference.attendee('Gregorio','Perez');
  });

  describe('post(attendee)', function() {

    describe('on success of the underlying post', function() {
      it('returns a Promise that resolves to an attendee with ID',
        function(done) {
          decoratedWebApi.post(attendeeA).then(
            function onSuccess(attendee) {
```

continues

LISTING 12-7 *(continued)*

```
        expect(attendee.getFullName()).toBe(attendeeA.getFullName());
        expect(attendee.getId()).not.toBeUndefined();
        done();
      },
      function onFailure() {
        expect('Failed').toBe(false);
        done();
      });
    });
  });

  // *** Previously discussed tests omitted. ***
  });

  describe('getAll()', function() {

    describe('on success of underlying getAll', function() {
      it('returns a Promise for all processed records, '
      +'if there are none pending',function(done) {
        spyOn(baseWebApi,'getAll').and.returnValue(
          new Promise( function(resolve,reject) {
            setTimeout(function() {
              resolve([attendeeA,attendeeB]);
            },1);
          }));
        decoratedWebApi.getAll().then(
          function onSuccess(attendees) {
            expect(attendees.length).toBe(2);
            done();
          },
          function onFailure() {
            expect('Failed in getAll').toBe(false);
            done();
          });
      });
    });

    // *** Previously discussed tests omitted. ***
    });
  });
```

The tests just verify that the decorated object behaves like the original. The post method returns a Promise that resolves to an attendee that now has an attendee ID. The getAll method returns the results from the decorated object's getAll.

The tests pass, but whenever you are writing tests *after* the code, it's a good idea to step through the new tests with a debugger and verify that all is going according to plan. You do, and it is.

You have now verified that the decorator follows the Liskov Substitution Principle, leaving intact the positive and negative semantics of the object it decorates (see Figure 12-3).

Now it's time to make the decorator do what it's here for.

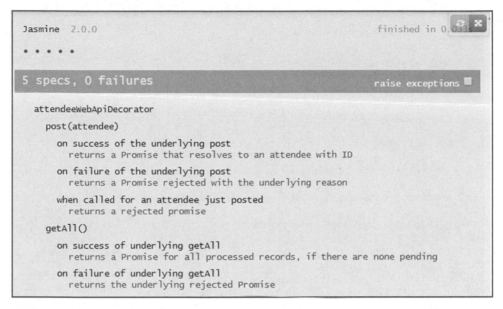

FIGURE 12-3

Adding the Decorator's Features

At its heart, the `attendeeWebApiDecorator` exists so the `getAll` function will return pending POSTs. That seems like a good place to start, so you code the unit test at the end of Listing 12-8.

LISTING 12-8: Test for getAll returning pending posts (code filename: Decorator\attendeeWebApiDecorator_04_tests.js)

```javascript
describe('attendeeWebApiDecorator', function() {
  'use strict';
  var decoratedWebApi,
      baseWebApi,
      attendeeA,
      attendeeB,
      underlyingFailure = 'Failure in underlying function';

  // Execute decoratedWebApi.getAll(), expecting it to return a resolved
  // Promise.
  // done       - The prevailing Jasmine done() function for async support.
  // expectation - A function that gives expectations on the returned
  //               attendees.
  function getAllWithSuccessExpectation(done,expectation) {
    decoratedWebApi.getAll().then(
      function onSuccess(attendees) {
        expectation(attendees);
        done();
```

continues

LISTING 12-8 *(continued)*

```
      },
      function onFailure() {
        expect('Failed in getAll').toBe(false);
        done();
      });
  }

  // *** Previously discussed code omitted. ***

  describe('getAll()', function() {

    describe('on success of underlying getAll', function() {

    // *** Previously discussed code omitted. ***

      it('returns a Promise for all processed records plus all pending ones',
      function(done) {
        decoratedWebApi.post(attendeeA).then(function() {
          decoratedWebApi.post(attendeeB); // Leave pending.
          getAllWithSuccessExpectation(done,function onSuccess(attendees) {
            expect(attendees.length).toBe(2);
            expect(attendees[0].getId()).not.toBeUndefined();
            expect(attendees[1].getId()).toBeUndefined();
          });
        });
      });
    });
  });

    // *** Previously discussed code omitted. ***
  });
});
```

In the test, you post `attendeeA` and then wait patiently for the post to resolve. After posting `attendeeB`, however, you do not wait but proceed immediately to `getAll()`. Where is `getAll()`? Because this is the second time you had to code the pattern of issuing a `getAll()` and testing its successful result, and because that's kind of a nuisance, you refactored the pattern to the function at the top of the listing, `getAllWithSuccessExpectation`.

Your expectation in the test is that `getAll()` returns both attendees—the first with an ID and the second without (because it's pending).

As expected, the test fails, with `getAll()` returning only one attendee (see Figure 12-4).

You fix this quickly by changing the `getAll` function in the decorator, as shown in Listing 12-9.

LISTING 12-9: getAll() adding the pending records (code filename:
Decorator\attendeeWebApiDecorator_04.js)

```
getAll: function getAll() {
  return baseWebApi.getAll().then(function(records) {
    pendingPosts.forEach(function(pending) {
```

```
      var ix = indexOfPostForSameAttendee(records,pending);
      if (ix<0) {
        records.push(pending);
      }
    });
    return records;
  });
},
```

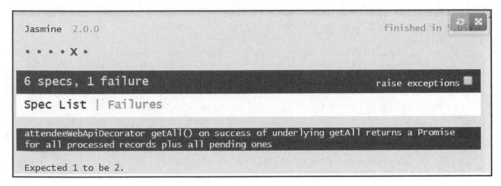

FIGURE 12-4

The decorator's `getAll` is now complete! It's time to test how `post` and `getAll` cooperate. The tests in Listing 12-10 express your intent.

LISTING 12-10: Testing cooperation between post and getAll (code filename: Decorator\attendeeWebApiDecorator_05_tests.js [excerpt])

```
describe('attendeeWebApiDecorator', function() {
    'use strict';

    describe('on success of the underlying post', function() {
        /*** Previously discussed test omitted. ***/

        it('causes an immediate getAll to include the record without ID',
        function(done) {
            decoratedWebApi.post(attendeeA);
            // Execute getAll without waiting for the post to resolve.
            getAllWithSuccessExpectation(done, function onSuccess(attendees) {
                expect(attendees.length).toBe(1);
                expect(attendees[0].getId()).toBeUndefined();
            });
        });
        it('causes a delayed getAll to include the record with ID',
        function(done) {
            decoratedWebApi.post(attendeeA).then(function() {
                // This time execute getAll after post resolves.
                getAllWithSuccessExpectation(done, function onSuccess(attendees) {
```

continues

LISTING 12-10 *(continued)*

```
            expect(attendees.length).toBe(1);
            expect(attendees[0].getId()).not.toBeUndefined();
          });
        });
      });
      it('fills in IDs of records already appended to getAll',function(done){
        var recordsFromGetAll, promiseFromPostA;
        // Issue the post and don't wait for it.
        promiseFromPostA = decoratedWebApi.post(attendeeA);
        // Immediately issue the getAll, and capture its results.
        decoratedWebApi.getAll().then(function onSuccess(attendees) {
          recordsFromGetAll = attendees;
          expect(recordsFromGetAll[0].getId()).toBeUndefined();
        });
        // Now wait for the post to finally resolve. (Remember that
        // its timeout is longer than getAll's.) When it does resolve,
        // We should see the attendeeId appear in the pending record that
        // getAll() obtained.
        promiseFromPostA.then(function() {
          expect(recordsFromGetAll[0].getId()).not.toBeUndefined();
          done();
        });
      });
    });
  });
});
```

The first test verifies that `getAll` is able to pick up pending records (those without attendee IDs). The second verifies that `getAll` will furnish records that have gotten their IDs, if they are available.

The final test verifies that if `getAll` returns a pending record, but the Promise corresponding to that record later resolves, then an ID will be injected into the record. You can use this as a signal to enable the update and delete functionality for this record on the Attendee List. The first two pass, but the third fails (see Figure 12-5).

The failure is in the final expectation of Listing 12-10. You can remedy it by adding the `then` block to the post in Listing 12-11.

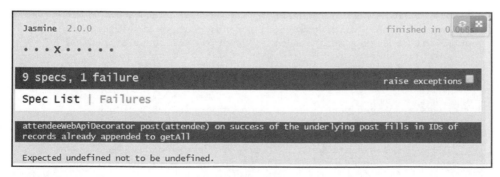

FIGURE 12-5

LISTING 12-11: The decorator's post function with backfilling of attendeeIds (code filename: Decorator\attendeeWebApiDecorator_05.js [excerpt])

```javascript
post: function post(attendee) {
  if (indexOfPostForSameAttendee(pendingPosts, attendee) >=0 ) {
    return Promise.reject(new Error(messages.postPending));
  }

  pendingPosts.push(attendee);

  return baseWebApi.post(attendee).then(
    function onPostSucceeded(attendeeWithId) {
      // When the post returns the attendee with an ID, put the ID in
      // the pending record because that record may have been added to
      // a getAll result and we want that result to benefit from the ID.
      var ix = pendingPosts.indexOf(attendee);
      if (ix >= 0) {
        pendingPosts[ix].setId(attendeeWithId.getId());
        pendingPosts.splice(ix, 1);
      }
      return attendeeWithId;
    });
},
```

The last thing to consider is what happens to getAll when the post fails. Before the post comes back, getAll should be none the wiser. Afterward, however, the failed record should not be included in getAll's results. Listing 12-12 shows these final tests.

LISTING 12-12: Final tests of post with getAll (code filename: attendeeWebApiDecorator_tests.js [excerpt])

```javascript
describe('on failure of the underlying post', function() {
  beforeEach(function() {
    // Cause the base's post to fail, but not until the next turn.
    spyOn(baseWebApi, 'post').and.returnValue(
      new Promise( function(resolve,reject) {
        setTimeout(function() {
          reject(underlyingFailure);
        },5);
      }));
  });

  /*** Previously discussed test omitted. ***/

  it('still allows an immediate getAll to include the record without an ID',
  function(done) {
    decoratedWebApi.post(attendeeA).catch(function() {
      // Without this catch, the rejection of the promise causes
      // an error to appear in the console.
    });
```

continues

LISTING 12-12 *(continued)*

```
    getAllWithSuccessExpectation(done, function onSuccess(attendees) {
      expect(attendees.length).toBe(1);
      expect(attendees[0].getId()).toBeUndefined();
    });
  });

  it('causes a delayed getAll to exclude the record',
  function(done) {
    decoratedWebApi.post(attendeeA).then(
      function onSuccessfulPost() {
        expect('Post succeeded').toBe(false);
        done();
      },
      function onRejectedPost() {
        getAllWithSuccessExpectation(done, function onSuccess(attendees) {
          expect(attendees.length).toBe(0);
        });
      });
  });
});
```

In the first test, a `getAll` that is processed before the failure is known should still return the pending (soon-to-fail) record. However, as the second test asserts, once the failure does become known, the record should not appear in `getAll`'s results. The first test happens to pass, but not the second (see Figure 12-6).

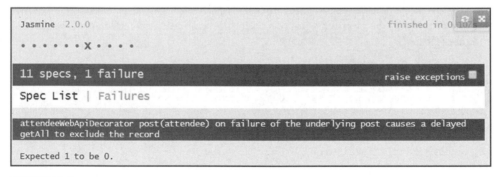

FIGURE 12-6

The problem is that `post` is not purging the pending records whose posts failed. That's easy to remedy with the bolded code in Listing 12-13.

LISTING 12-13: Final version of attendeeWebApiDecorator.post (code filename: Decorator\attendeeWebApiDecorator.js [excerpt])

```
post: function post(attendee) {
  if (indexOfPostForSameAttendee(pendingPosts, attendee) >=0 ) {
    return Promise.reject(new Error(messages.postPending));
```

```
            }

        pendingPosts.push(attendee);

        return baseWebApi.post(attendee).then(
            function onPostSucceeded(attendeeWithId) {
                // When the post returns the attendee with an ID, put the ID in
                // the pending record because that record may have been added to
                // a getAll result and we want that result to benefit from the ID.
                var ix = pendingPosts.indexOf(attendee);
                if (ix >= 0) {
                    pendingPosts[ix].setId(attendeeWithId.getId());
                    pendingPosts.splice(ix, 1);
                }
                return attendeeWithId;
            },
            function onPostFailed(reason) {
                var ix = pendingPosts.indexOf(attendee);
                if (ix >= 0) {
                    pendingPosts.splice(ix, 1);
                }
                return Promise.reject(reason);
            });
    },
```

The final test output in Figure 12-7 shows how far you've come.

```
Jasmine  2.0.0                                              finished in 0.0...

. . . . . . . . . . .

11 specs, 0 failures                                      raise exceptions ■

  attendeeWebApiDecorator

    post(attendee)

      on success of the underlying post
        returns a Promise that resolves to an attendee with ID
        causes an immediate getAll to include the record without ID
        causes a delayed getAll to include the record with ID
        fills in IDs of records already appended to getAll

      on failure of the underlying post
        returns a Promise rejected with the underlying reason
        still allows an immediate getAll to include the record without an ID
        causes a delayed getAll to exclude the record

      when called for an attendee just posted
        returns a rejected promise

    getAll()

      on success of underlying getAll
        returns a Promise for all processed records, if there are none pending
        returns a Promise for all processed records plus all pending ones

      on failure of underlying getAll
        returns the underlying rejected Promise
```

FIGURE 12-7

Generalizing the Decorator

The next logical step, which is beyond the scope of this chapter, would be to generalize the decorator. In a real-world application, there may be many objects that encapsulate related HTTP POSTs and GETs—not to mention PUTs and DELETEs. How might you generalize the decorator so you could use it in all cases? That is left as an exercise for you to do on your own. We mention it here to point out a final benefit of the Decorator Pattern: It can eliminate duplicate code.

SUMMARY

In this chapter, you used the Decorator Pattern to address a real-world limitation of an HTTP-based object, without modifying that object. The decorated object maintains focus on its Single Responsibility, while the decorator isolates the complicated new feature and, if generalized, can reduce code duplication.

You developed a decorator using a test-driven approach, with the following steps.

1. Code a fake for the decorated object (optional).

2. Write unit tests to verify that errors are passed up the call stack from the decorated object, through the decorator, and to the caller.

3. Write a do-nothing decorator and watch the tests fail.

4. Add pass-through functionality to the decorator so the tests pass.

5. Write tests to verify that the decorator will also pass signs of success to its caller.

6. Make those tests pass, if they do not already.

7. Add the decorator's special features, writing the unit tests first.

8. Consider generalizing the decorator.

The next chapter takes up another classic design element: the Strategy Pattern.

13

Ensuring Correct Implementation of the Strategy Pattern

WHAT'S IN THIS CHAPTER?

➤ Identifying opportunities to use the Strategy Pattern

➤ Implementing the Strategy Pattern using test-driven development

➤ Using the Factory Pattern to select strategies at run time

WROX.COM CODE DOWNLOADS FOR THIS CHAPTER

You can find the wrox.com code downloads for this chapter at www.wrox.com/go/ reliablejavascript on the Download Code tab. The files are in the Chapter 13 download and individually named according to the filenames noted throughout this chapter.

The Strategy Pattern is used to isolate multiple algorithms, or *strategies*, that perform a specific task into modules that may be swapped in and out at run time. This chapter uses test-driven development to show how, through the use of strategies, algorithms may be added or removed in a way that's independent from the client, or *context*, that uses them. The chapter will also describe how the Factory Pattern from Chapter 10 helps achieve this goal.

Additionally, the chapter will illustrate how programming to the interface of a strategy improves the testability, and thus reliability, of the code that consumes the strategy.

UNDERSTANDING THE PATTERN THROUGH UNIT TESTS

As an added convenience to attendees, the JavaScript conference organizers have negotiated discounted, fixed rates with three local cab companies for travel between the conference venue and the airport. The organizers are still trying to work out fixed rates with two limousine services for attendees that want to be transported in a bit more luxurious setting.

Even though deals with the limousine services are pending, the organizers would like to extend the conference website to add the ability to schedule transportation to the airport now, and add the ability to choose a limousine service once the deals have been made.

Because the conference is being held in a city in which the populace adopts technology early, each of the cab companies and limousine services offers a web service through which transportation may be scheduled. The conference's transportation-scheduling feature will have to make the appropriate request to the company that the attendee has chosen, and return the reservation confirmation number provided by the company. So they can track it on the conference website's dashboard, the conference organizers would also like to keep track of how many rides each of the companies provides.

Charlotte is assigned the task of creating the user interface that collects the following information from the attendee:

➤ Transport-company name

➤ Passenger name

➤ Departure time

She is also creating the auditing service that will be used to keep track of the rides each company gives. You're responsible for creating the module that will receive the data and schedule the reservation.

Implementing the transportScheduler Without the Strategy Pattern

You begin designing the `Conference.transportScheduler` module. It seems that it needs only a single method, `requestTransportation(transportDetails)`, which will make the correct request for the chosen transport-company, interpret and return the results, and make an audit entry if a ride is successfully scheduled.

The first cab company you choose to implement support for is RediCab. The unit tests you write look like this:

```
describe("Conference.transportScheduler", function(){
  'use strict';

  describe("requestTransport(transportDetails)", function(){
    describe("with RediCab", function(){
      it("makes the correct request to the RediCab web service", function(done){
        // test implementation
      });
      describe("when request successful", function(){
        it("records the ride with the audit service", function(done){
          // test implementation
        });
        it("resolves to the expected success value", function(done){
          // test implementation
```

```
        });
      });
      describe("when request unsuccessful", function(){
        it("does not record the ride with the audit service", function(done){
          // test implementation
        });
        it("returns the rejected promise", function(done){
          // test implementation
        });
      });
    });
  });
});
```

Let's skip the detail of making these tests pass one at a time; we've shown that process many times already (and we're going to refactor the code anyway). The implementation that makes the tests pass looks like this:

```
var Conference = Conference || {};

Conference.transportScheduler = function(transportAuditService, httpService){
  'use strict';

  return {
    requestTransport : function requestTransport(transportDetails){
      var rediCabRequest;

      switch(transportDetails.companyName){
        case "RediCab":
          rediCabRequest = {
            passenger: transportDetails.passengerName,
            pickUp: "Conference Center",
            pickUpTime: transportDetails.departureTime,
            dropOff: "Airport",
            rateCode: "JavaScriptConference"
          };
          httpService.post("http://redicab.com/schedulepickup", rediCabRequest)
            .then(function resolved(status){
              transportAuditService.recordRide(transportDetails.companyName);
              return status.confirmationNumber;
            });
          break;
      }
    }
  };
};
```

One aspect of the code that is immediately evident is that the requestTransport function has quite a few responsibilities. It needs to

➤ Determine the selected transportation company.

➤ Translate transportDetails into a structure that the transport company's web service expects.

➤ Make an HTTP request to the appropriate web service.

➤ Log successful requests to the audit service.

➤ Return the field from the HTTP response that represents the reservation's confirmation number.

You have a feeling that `transportScheduler` will just get bigger and more complex as additional cab companies (and eventually limousine services) are supported. You know that with increased complexity comes an increased potential for problems, reducing reliability. The thought of being responsible for an attendee missing a flight because the `transportScheduler` doesn't work properly prompts you to solicit feedback from Charlotte. She has a few suggestions for you.

"One thing you may consider is creating a separate module for each cab and limousine company, with the modules having a consistent interface," she suggests. "That way, the logic for scheduling a ride with each of the companies will be isolated into individually testable units."

"Also," she continues, "think about creating a factory function that knows how to create the appropriate transport company module. Doing so will eliminate the `switch` statement in `transportScheduler`. You can even inject the factory into `transportScheduler` so that `transportScheduler` is easier to test."

"Another benefit of isolating the functionality the way I've proposed," continues Charlotte, "is that the `transportScheduler` will no longer violate the open-closed principle the way it does now. It will be extendable by creating new transport company modules; it will not need to have its code changed at all in order to support new transport companies. The factory will be the only thing that needs to change when a new transport module is created."

Unsurprisingly, everything Charlotte suggests makes a lot of sense, and you set off to rewrite your code.

Implementing the transportScheduler Using the Strategy Pattern

Charlotte didn't come right out and say it, but each of the transport company modules she suggested creating represents a *strategy*. Each one encapsulates a company's scheduling algorithm, following a consistent interface. The interface is illustrated by the following code:

```
{
  schedulePickup : function schedulepickup(transportDetails){
    // Returns a Promise that resolves to a reservation confirmation
    // number.
  }
}
```

Because the interface will be implemented by each of the transport company modules, it's possible to code the `transportScheduler` against the interface rather than a concrete implementation. The `transportScheduler` provides the context in which the strategies are executed.

Also, Charlotte's suggestion of creating a factory to create the appropriate type of transport company module is a good one. As she suggested, and as illustrated in Chapter 10, the introduction of a factory will simplify the unit tests for `transportScheduler` because it can be injected, and thus mocked.

Following the principles of Chapter 10, you implement `Conference.transportCompanyFactory`, which follows in Listing 13-1.

LISTING 13-1: The implementation of transportCompanyFactory (code filename: Strategy\ transportCompanyFactory.js)

```
var Conference = Conference || {};
Conference.transportCompanyFactory = function(){
  'use strict';

  return {
    create: function create(transportDetails){
      // Use transportDetails to determine which
      // transport-company module should be created
      // and returned.
    }
  };
}
```

Creating transportScheduler Using Test-Driven Development

Now that you've decided on the interface that each of the transport company modules will expose and developed a factory that creates instances of transport-company modules, you're in a position to create the `transportScheduler`.

In contrast to the list of responsibilities that it had when the Strategy Pattern was not being used, the `transportScheduler` only needs to perform the following actions:

➤ Get a transport company module from the injected `transportCompanyFactory`.

➤ Invoke the transport company module's `schedulePickup` function.

➤ Log successful requests to the audit service.

The reduced list of responsibilities translates into a simplified suite of unit tests, the start of which follows in Listing 13-2.

LISTING 13-2: Unit tests for transportScheduler (code filename: Strategy\ transportScheduler_01_tests.js)

```
describe("Conference.transportScheduler", function(){
  'use strict';

  describe("module function", function(){
    // Simple tests to ensure that required dependencies have been provided

    it("throws if audit service argument is not provided", function(){
      expect(function shouldThrow(){
        var scheduler = Conference.transportScheduler(null, {});
      }).toThrowError(Conference.transportScheduler.messages.noAuditService);
```

continues

LISTING 13-2 *(continued)*

```
      });

      it("throws if company factory argument is not provided", function(){
        expect(function shouldThrow(){
          var scheduler = Conference.transportScheduler({}, null);
        }).toThrowError(Conference.transportScheduler.messages.noCompanyFactory);
      });
    });

  describe("scheduleTransportation(transportDetails)", function(){
    var scheduler,
      auditService,
      companyFactory,
      testDetails;

    beforeEach(function(){
      // Create instances of the dependencies to inject into the
      // transport scheduler instance; retain references so their
      // methods may be spied upon in tests.
      auditService = Conference.transportCompanyAuditService();
      companyFactory = Conference.transportCompanyFactory();

      // The instance of transportScheduler under test
      scheduler = Conference.transportScheduler(auditService, companyFactory);

      // Since companyFactory.create(transportDetails) will be
      // mocked in the tests, testDetails doesn't need to
      // be a real instance of a transportDetails object
      testDetails = {};
    });

    it("throws if transportDetails argument is not provided", function(){
      expect(function shouldThrow(){
        scheduler.scheduleTransportation();
      }).toThrowError(Conference.transportScheduler.messages.noDetails);
    });

    it("doesn't swallow exceptions thrown by company factory", function(){
      var companyFactoryError = "This was thrown by the company factory";
      spyOn(companyFactory, 'create').and.throwError(companyFactoryError);
      expect(function shouldThrow(){
        scheduler.scheduleTransportation(testDetails);
      }).toThrowError(companyFactoryError);
    });
  });
});
```

The tests in Listing 13-2 provide some basic coverage of negative cases that may occur as a result of incorrect use of the `transportScheduler`. The tests

```
it("throws if audit service argument is not provided", function(){/*test*/});
it("throws if company factory argument is not provided", function(){/*test*/});
```

ensure that the module-creation function throws when it's invoked without the arguments that it expects. The test

```
it("throws if transportDetails argument is not provided", function(){/*test*/});
```

performs a similar validation for the `scheduleTransportation(transportDetails)` function. Finally, the test

```
it("doesn't swallow exceptions thrown by company factory", function(){/*test*/});
```

ensures that the `scheduleTransportation(transportDetails)` function doesn't suppress any errors that are thrown by the injected transport company factory.

As there's no implementation for `transportScheduler`, the tests fail spectacularly. The code in Listing 13-3, however, allows them to pass. The passing tests are shown in Figure 13-1.

```
Jasmine  2.0.0                                                         finished in 0.008s

 • • • •

 4 specs, 0 failures                                               raise exceptions ■

  Conference.transportScheduler

   module function
     throws if audit service argument is not provided
     throws if company factory argument is not provided

   scheduleTransportation(transportDetails)
     throws if transportDetails argument is not provided
     doesn't swallow exceptions thrown by company factory
```

FIGURE 13-1

LISTING 13-3: Initial implementation of transportScheduler, which allows the negative tests to pass (code filename: Strategy\transportScheduler_01.js)

```javascript
var Conference = Conference || {};

Conference.transportScheduler = function(auditService, transportCompanyFactory){
  'use strict';

  if(!auditService){
    throw new Error(Conference.transportScheduler.messages.noAuditService);
  }
  if(!transportCompanyFactory){
    throw new Error(Conference.transportScheduler.messages.noCompanyFactory);
  }

  return {
    scheduleTransportation : function scheduleTransportation(transportDetails){
      if(!transportDetails){
        throw new Error(Conference.transportScheduler.messages.noDetails);
      }
      var company;

      company = transportCompanyFactory.create(transportDetails);
    }
  };
};
```

continues

LISTING 13-3 *(continued)*

```
  };

  Conference.transportScheduler.messages = {
    noAuditService: "An audit service instance must be provided.",
    noCompanyFactory: "A transport-company factory instance must be provided.",
    noDetails: "A transportDetails instance must be provided"
  };
```

Now that there's some confidence that the transportScheduler will report its misuse, the meat of its functionality can be implemented.

Recall that the interface each of the transport company modules will implement consists of a single function, schedulePickup(transportDetails), which returns a Promise that will resolve to the reservation's confirmation number. If the promise is resolved, the transportScheduler should record the successful reservation with the audit service.

With that in mind, Listing 13-4 provides the rest of the unit tests for the transportScheduler.

LISTING 13-4: Suite of tests for transportScheduler (code filename: Strategy\
transportScheduler_02_tests.js)

```
describe("Conference.transportScheduler", function(){
  'use strict';

  describe("module function", function(){
    // Simple tests to ensure that required dependencies have been provided

    /*** Previously discussed tests omitted ***/
  });

  describe("scheduleTransportation(transportDetails)", function(){
    var scheduler,
      auditService,
      companyFactory,
      testDetails,
      fakeCompany,
      confirmationNumber;

    beforeEach(function(){
      // Create instances of the dependencies to inject into the
      // transport scheduler instance; retain references so their
      // methods may be spied upon in tests.
      auditService = Conference.transportCompanyAuditService();
      companyFactory = Conference.transportCompanyFactory();

      // The instance of transportScheduler under test
      scheduler = Conference.transportScheduler(auditService, companyFactory);

      // Since companyFactory.create(transportDetails) will be
      // mocked in the tests, testDetails doesn't need to
```

```
      // be a real instance of a transportDetails object
      testDetails = {};

      confirmationNumber = "ABC-123-XYZ";

      // create a fake transport module that implements the schedulePickup
      // function.  By default, the returned Promise resolves to
      // confirmationNumber.  Spy on schedulePickup if a rejected promise
      // is needed.
      fakeCompany = {
        schedulePickup : function schedulePickup(transportDetails){
          return new Promise(function(resolve, reject){
            resolve(confirmationNumber);
          });
        }
      };
    });

  /*** Previously discussed tests omitted ***/

  it("retrieves the company module from the company factory", function(){
    spyOn(companyFactory, "create").and.returnValue(fakeCompany);

    scheduler.scheduleTransportation(testDetails);

    expect(companyFactory.create).toHaveBeenCalledWith(testDetails);
  });

  it("invokes the company's schedulePickup function", function(){
    spyOn(companyFactory, "create").and.returnValue(fakeCompany);

    // fakeCompany is configured to return a resolved promise; simply
    // call through
    spyOn(fakeCompany, "schedulePickup").and.callThrough();

    scheduler.scheduleTransportation(testDetails);

    expect(fakeCompany.schedulePickup).toHaveBeenCalledWith(testDetails);
  });

  describe("Successful scheduling", function(){
    beforeEach(function(){
      spyOn(companyFactory, "create").and.returnValue(fakeCompany);
    });

    it("resolves to the returned confirmation number", function(done){
      scheduler.scheduleTransportation(testDetails)
        .then(function resolved(confirmation){
          expect(confirmation).toEqual(confirmationNumber);
          done();
        }, function rejected(reason){
          expect("Should not have been rejected").toBe(false);
          done();
        });
```

continues

LISTING 13-4 *(continued)*

```javascript
    });

    it("logs with audit service", function(done){
      spyOn(auditService, "logReservation");

      scheduler.scheduleTransportation(testDetails)
        .then(function resolved(confirmation){
          expect(auditService.logReservation)
            .toHaveBeenCalledWith(testDetails, confirmationNumber);
          done();
        }, function rejected(reason){
          expect("Should not have been rejected").toBe(false);
          done();
        });
    });
  });

  describe("Unsuccessful scheduling", function(){
    var rejectionReason;

    beforeEach(function(){
      spyOn(companyFactory, "create").and.returnValue(fakeCompany);

      rejectionReason = "Was rejected";

      // Set up schedulePickup to return a rejected promise
      spyOn(fakeCompany, "schedulePickup")
        .and.returnValue(new Promise(function(resolve, reject){
          reject(rejectionReason);
        }));
    });

    it("allows the rejected Promise to flow to calling code", function(done){
      scheduler.scheduleTransportation(testDetails)
        .then(function resolved(confirmation){
          expect("Should not have been resolved").toBe(false);
          done();
        }, function rejected(reason){
          expect(reason).toEqual(rejectionReason);
          done();
        });
    });

    it("doesn't log anything with the audit service", function(done){
      spyOn(auditService, "logReservation");

      scheduler.scheduleTransportation(testDetails)
        .then(function resolved(confirmation){
          expect("Should not have been resolved").toBe(false);
          done();
        }, function rejected(reason){
          expect(auditService.logReservation).not.toHaveBeenCalled();
          done();
```

```
                });
              });
            });
          });
        });
```

The tests in Listing 13-4 verify that `transportScheduler` correctly coordinates interaction between the `transportCompanyFactory`, the transport company module instance returned by the factory, and the `transportCompanyAuditService`. The unit tests fail, as shown by Figure 13-2, because none of this coordination has been implemented.

FIGURE 13-2

Very little code is required to allow all of the unit tests to pass. The full implementation of `transportScheduler` appears in Listing 13-5.

LISTING 13-5: Full implementation of transportScheduler (code filename: Strategy\ transportScheduler_02.js)

```javascript
var Conference = Conference || {};

Conference.transportScheduler = function(auditService, transportCompanyFactory){
  'use strict';

  if(!auditService){
    throw new Error(Conference.transportScheduler.messages.noAuditService);
  }
  if(!transportCompanyFactory){
    throw new Error(Conference.transportScheduler.messages.noCompanyFactory);
  }

  return {
```

continues

LISTING 13-5 *(continued)*

```
        scheduleTransportation : function scheduleTransportation(transportDetails){
          if(!transportDetails){
            throw new Error(Conference.transportScheduler.messages.noDetails);
          }
          var company;

          company = transportCompanyFactory.create(transportDetails);

          return company.schedulePickup(transportDetails)
            .then(function successful(confirmation){
              auditService.logReservation(transportDetails, confirmation);
              return confirmation;
            });
        }
      };
    };

  Conference.transportScheduler.messages = {
    noAuditService: "An audit service instance must be provided.",
    noCompanyFactory: "A transport-company factory instance must be provided.",
    noDetails: "A transportDetails instance must be provided"
  };
```

Notice that neither the unit tests nor the implementation have a direct dependency upon a specific transport company module; they only depend on the simple interface that transport company modules will implement. Because of this, the different logic, or strategies, required to schedule transportation with each company may be isolated into individual modules. The `transportScheduler` doesn't need to have any idea which company module is in use.

All the unit tests from Listing 13-4 now pass, as shown in Figure 13-3.

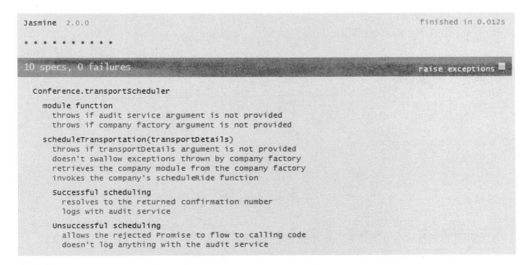

FIGURE 13-3

Creating a Strategy for Use with transportScheduler

One of the benefits of correct implementation of the Strategy Pattern is that strategies may be added or removed with very little code change. In fact, the `transportScheduler` will *never* have to change when a transport company is added or removed. Appropriately, only the module responsible for creating instances of transport company reservation strategies, the `transportCompanyFactory`, will have to change when a company is added or removed.

To complete the functionality that was originally implemented without using the Strategy Pattern, a company module for RediCab needs to be implemented. Because the interface that needs to be exposed by transport company modules is so simple and well defined, there's very little complexity in the module.

The unit tests for the module related to the implementation of the `schedulePickup(transportDetails)` strategy appear in Listing 13-6.

LISTING 13-6: Tests for the RediCab implementation of schedulePickup(transportDetails) (code filename: Strategy\redicabTransportCompany_tests.js)

```javascript
describe("redicabTransportCompany", function(){
  'use strict';

  var httpService,
      company,
      details,
      expectedData,
      testConfirmation;

  beforeEach(function(){
    httpService = Conference.httpService();

    company = Conference.redicabTransportCompany(httpService);

    details = {
      transportCompany: "RediCab",
      passengerName: "Pete Mitchell",
      departureTime: "7:30 PM"
    };

    // based on details, data posted should look like:
    expectedData = {
      passenger: details.passengerName,
      pickUp: "Conference Center",
      pickUpTime: details.departureTime,
      dropOff: "Airport",
      rateCode: "JavaScriptConference"
    };

    // An object similar to that returned by the RediCab api
    testConfirmation = {
      confirmationCode: "AAA-BBB-CCC",
      anticipatedCharge: 34.00
    };
```

continues

LISTING 13-6 *(continued)*

```
        });

    describe("schedulePickup(transportDetails)", function(){
        it("posts the expected data to the correct url", function(){

            spyOn(httpService, 'post')
              .and.callFake(function fake(url, data){
                expect(data).toEqual(expectedData);
                expect(url).toEqual(company.getSchedulePickupUrl());

                return new Promise(function(resolve, reject){
                  resolve(testConfirmation);
                });
              });

            company.schedulePickup(details);

        });

        it("resolves to the confirmation number", function(done){
            spyOn(httpService, 'post')
              .and.returnValue(new Promise(function(resolve, reject){
                  resolve(testConfirmation);
              })
              );

            company.schedulePickup(details).then(function resolved(confirmation){
              expect(confirmation).toEqual(testConfirmation.confirmationCode);
              done();
            }, function rejected(reason){
              expect("Should not have been rejected").toBe(false);
              done();
            });
        });
    });
});
```

And in Listing 13-7, the implementation of `redicabTransportCompany` allows the unit tests from Listing 13-6 to pass.

LISTING 13-7: Implementation of redicabTransportCompany (code filename: Strategy\redicabTransportCompany.js)

```
var Conference = Conference || {};
Conference.redicabTransportCompany = function(httpService){
  'use strict';

  var schedulePickupUrl = "http://redicab.com/schedulepickup";

  return{

    // schedules a pickup with RediCab.  Returns a promise
```

```
        // that resolves to the confirmation code returned by the
        // RediCab api.
        schedulePickup: function schedulePickup(transportDetails){
          var details = {
            passenger: transportDetails.passengerName,
            pickUp: "Conference Center",
            pickUpTime: transportDetails.departureTime,
            dropOff: "Airport",
            rateCode: "JavaScriptConference"
          };

          return httpService.post(schedulePickupUrl, details)
            .then(function resolve(confirmation){
              return confirmation.confirmationCode;
            });
        },

        // Returns the url that the pickup information should
        // be posted to
        getSchedulePickupUrl: function getSchedulePickupUrl(){
          return schedulePickupUrl;
        }
      };
    };
```

Notice that the implementation of `schedulePickup` is similar to the code that was originally written without the use of the Strategy Pattern. By using the Strategy Pattern, however, the code in `redicabTransportCompany` is solely concerned with the details of interacting with the RediCab API. The passing unit tests are shown in Figure 13-4.

FIGURE 13-4

Any number of additional transport company modules may be created in the same manner, none of which will require any change to the `transportScheduler` or any of the other transport-company modules.

SUMMARY

In this chapter, you saw how the Strategy Pattern can be used to isolate different algorithms for performing a task, in this case scheduling a ride with a transport company, and to allow the appropriate algorithm, or strategy, to be dynamically determined at run time. As additional transport company modules are added, the `transportCompanyFactory` may be extended to provide an instance of the appropriate module based on the type of transportation the user requires.

In addition, it described how the Factory Pattern from Chapter 10 can be used to create concrete instances of strategies. Doing so reduced testing complexity and ensured that the context in which the strategies were used didn't have to change when strategies were added or removed.

When creating strategy modules, it's important to write unit tests to verify that the implementations expose the correct interface. Chapter 16, "Conforming to Interfaces in an Interface-Free Language," contains additional information about ensuring that a JavaScript module conforms to an interface.

The next chapter covers the Proxy Pattern, a mechanism through which one object can manage access to another.

14

Ensuring Correct Implementation of the Proxy Pattern

WHAT'S IN THIS CHAPTER?

➤ Common uses of the Proxy Pattern

➤ Using a pre-fetching proxy to improve the responsiveness of a web page

➤ Using test-driven development to create a proxy

➤ Deducing the internal workings of a proxy without breaking data encapsulation

WROX.COM CODE DOWNLOADS FOR THIS CHAPTER

You can find the wrox.com code downloads for this chapter at www.wrox.com/go/ reliablejavascript on the Download Code tab. The files are in the Chapter 14 download and individually named according to the filenames noted throughout this chapter.

If you are an American, your entire life is literally governed by the Proxy Pattern. Although we live in a democracy, it is a *representative* democracy: We do not make laws directly but elect people who create laws on our behalf. We believe (rightly or wrongly) that our proxies in Congress and the White House can manage the lawmaking process better than we could. They have the time to become experts in national defense, healthcare, and other areas. We don't. If every little issue were decided by plebiscite, we would accomplish nothing else.

When the time comes to interpret those laws, we usually hire *another* proxy: an attorney who is an expert in the interpretation and navigation of the relevant laws.

In software design, it is sometimes useful to create a proxy object to manage access to an underlying object (called the *real subject*). It acts as an expert attorney, allowing its client code to use the real subject more effectively, or keeping its client out of trouble.

Common uses of the Proxy Pattern include:

➤ Pre-fetching data based on the client's usage patterns

➤ Making sure the client does not overwhelm the real subject with requests—for example, when the program should execute a relatively costly operation in response to mouse-movement or resize events. In theory, the operation should be done in response to every event, but in practice this makes the application perform poorly. A *debouncing* proxy can limit the responses to at most one every so many milliseconds.

➤ Preventing the client from accessing resources it should not

➤ Bundling n HTTP requests into one to avoid incurring the fixed costs for $n-1$ of the requests

In this chapter, you will work through the implementation of a pre-fetching proxy. The scenario is, of course, the JavaScript Conference's website.

After registering for the conference, an attendee will be able to see a list of other attendees. He or she can then click through any of them to see a complete profile. Because each profile can include one or more photos, you don't want to pull down all the profiles initially. However, you want response to be quick, so you have decided to pre-fetch the profiles most likely to be accessed from the currently showing page of the overall list.

You and colleague Charlotte discuss the concept.

"The hard part will be knowing which ones to pre-fetch," you observe.

Immediately Charlotte has an idea. "Some famous developers will attend. Probably their profiles will be the most popular."

You counter, "It will be too labor-intensive to sift through 10,000 attendees and mark the famous ones. And who's to say who's famous enough? There must be a better way."

"I know!" replies Charlotte. "The system can learn, over time, which ones are the most popular based on the number of click-throughs, and we can pre-fetch those."

"Great!" you agree. "Plus, we were planning to display thumbnail photos on the attendee list. Doubtless some of them will attract more clicks than others. With your idea, we will pre-fetch the most fetching ones."

Charlotte's eyes roll. "Whatever. Why don't you get to work on the client side? I'll modify the server code so it gives you the click-through count as part of each attendee's record."

DEVELOPING A PROXY THE TEST-DRIVEN WAY

Usually, unit tests should verify their subject's external behavior without regard to the subject's internals. A proxy presents a challenge because the internals are exactly what you *do* want to test. You want to know whether the proxy is properly managing the real subject.

In the present example, the external behavior of the proxy is to give you profiles as you ask for them. The internal behavior is whether, in addition, the proxy has prepared others for likely delivery.

There are two ways to test the internals. The less-preferable would be to allow the proxy to expose its list of pre-fetched profiles so your test could observe them directly. This has two obvious drawbacks. First, it breaks the proxy's data encapsulation, violating a fundamental principle of object-oriented design. Second, it increases the coupling of the proxy to the outside world by adding functions to its API. You always want to minimize coupling, not increase it.

Far better is to observe the effects of the proxy on the real subject and deduce the proxy's behavior from there.

The real subject of the pre-fetching proxy is the `attendeeProfileService` shown in Listing 14-1.

LISTING 14-1: The attendeeProfileService (code filename: Proxy\attendeeProfileService.js)

```
var Conference = Conference || {};
Conference.attendeeProfileService = function() {
  'use strict';
  var messages = {
    httpFailure: 'The HTTP request failed.'
  };
  return {
    // Return a Promise for the profile of an attendee
    getProfile: function(attendeeId) {
      return new Promise( function(resolve, reject) {
        var xhr = new XMLHttpRequest();
        xhr.onreadystatechange=function onreadystatechange() {
          if (xhr.readyState==4) {
            if (xhr.status==200) {
              resolve(xhr.responseText);
            } else {
              reject(new Error(messages.httpFailure));
            }
          }
        };
        xhr.open("GET","profile/" + attendeeId, true);
        xhr.send();
      });
    }
  };
};
```

The idea is exactly the same as the `checkInRecorder` you saw in Chapter 6. Although the `XMLHttpRequest` at the heart of `getProfile` will not return immediately, a `Promise` for its ultimate result *is* returned. When the `onreadystatechange` event finally fires, the `Promise` is either resolved or rejected, depending on the HTTP status code.

The proxy will be a function that takes the parameters shown in Listing 14-2.

LISTING 14-2: An empty proxy (code filename: Proxy\attendeeProfileProxy_01a.js)

```
var Conference = Conference || {};

// Manage access to the profiles of the attendees in an array (attendees),
// fetching them from an attendeeProfileService (profileService),
// and pre-fetching up to prefetchLimit most popular based on profileViews.
Conference.attendeeProfileProxy = function(
attendees, profileService, prefetchLimit) {

};
```

Note the second parameter, `attendeeProfileService`, which constitutes the real subject. It might seem natural for the proxy to instantiate its own subject, but furnishing it as a parameter allows you to use dependency injection. In unit-testing, you can inject an object on which you've installed a spy. If the architecture of the system were to require that no caller could possibly access the real subject directly, you would have to think of something more locked-down. One possibility would be to make the proxy into an aspect so that any call that looked like it was a call to the subject would flow through the proxy first.

When the proxy is created, it should pre-fetch up to the given `prefetchLimit`. That sounds simple enough, but there are a few boundary and error conditions to test. As usual, you want to start with those.

First, what if `prefetchLimit` is not a positive number? You could throw an error or simply not pre-fetch anything. You decide on the latter course and code the test in Listing 14-3.

LISTING 14-3: Testing a non-positive prefetchLimit (code filename: proxy\attendeeProfileProxy_01_tests.js)

```
describe('attendeeProfileProxy(attendees, profileService,prefetchLimit)',
function() {
  'use strict';
  var proxy = Conference.attendeeProfileProxy,
      profileService = Conference.attendeeProfileService(),
      attendees = [
        { attendeeId: 10, profileViews: "3" },
        { attendeeId: 11, profileViews: "0" },
        { attendeeId: 12 },
        { attendeeId: 13, profileViews: "3" },
        { attendeeId: 14, profileViews: "10"},
        { attendeeId: 15, profileViews: "2" },
        { attendeeId: 16, profileViews: "1" },
        ],
      spyOnProfileService;

  beforeEach(function() {
    spyOnProfileService = spyOn(profileService,'getProfile');
  });

  describe('initialization', function () {
```

```
        it('pre-fetches no profiles if prefetchLimit is not a positive number',
        function() {
          var notPositiveNumbers = [-1,0,undefined,'abc',function() {}];
          notPositiveNumbers.forEach(function(prefetchLimit) {
            proxy(attendees, profileService, prefetchLimit);
          });
          expect(spyOnProfileService.calls.count()).toBe(0);
        });
      });
    });
```

Stepping through from top to bottom, the first `var` just creates shorthand for `Conference` `.attendeeProfileProxy`.

On the next line, note the initialization of the profile service:

```
    profileService = Conference.attendeeProfileService()
```

This sort of non-trivial initialization is often an invitation to cross-test contamination: If one test changes the state of *profileService*, then it has polluted the starting condition for the next test. However, you know that your tests will not actually execute any code in *profileService*. Instead, they will get no farther than the spy that is set up in the `beforeEach`.

`attendeeProfileService` has just one function. If it were more complicated, you might consider writing a fake rather than using a spy.

The *attendees* initialized near the top are likely to be useful for many tests, so you put the variable in the outer scope. More will be said about the test data later.

Finally, you have the test itself, which is straightforward. The purpose of the test is to verify that no pre-fetching is done if the pre-fetch limit is not a positive number. You iterate through a variety of data that are not positive numbers, instantiating the proxy using each one. When all that is done, no profiles should have been pre-fetched.

> **NOTE** *You've decided to allow positive numbers that are not integers. If a number that is not quite an integer because of a rounding error shows up, why not let the proxy do its best?*

As with the Decorator Pattern, you can start with the do-nothing proxy from Listing 14-2. Because the test happens to verify that nothing is done, it passes (see Figure 14-1)!

A unit test that fails to fail makes you uncomfortable, as it should. Often, some snooping with the debugger can assure you that your test is sound, but this time there's no code to debug. You wisely decide to make the proxy pre-fetch one attendee, just so you can observe a failure. This little foray is shown in Listing 14-4.

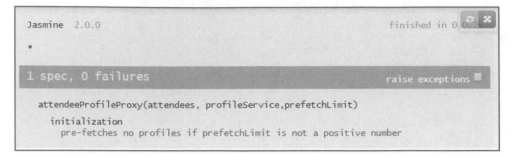

FIGURE 14-1

LISTING 14-4: Forcing the do-nothing test to fail (code filename:
Proxy\attendeeProfileProxy_01b.js)

```
var Conference = Conference || {};

// Manage access to the profiles of the attendees in an array (attendees),
// fetching them from an attendeeProfileService (profileService),
// and pre-fetching up to prefetchLimit most popular based on profileViews.
Conference.attendeeProfileProxy = function(
attendees, profileService, prefetchLimit) {
  'use strict';
  profileService.getProfile(attendees[0]);

};
```

Sure enough, Jasmine reports that the real subject's `getProfile` function has been called five
times—once for each member of the *notPositiveNumbers* array (see Figure 14-2).

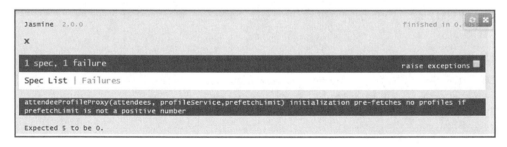

FIGURE 14-2

Satisfied that you have adequately tested the condition of *prefetchLimit* being too small, you consider what happens if it's too large. You add the test in Listing 14-5.

LISTING 14-5: Testing a prefetchLimit that is too large (code filename:
Proxy\attendeeProfileProxy_02_tests.js [excerpt])

```
    it('pre-fetches all the profiles if prefetchLimit exceeds ' +
    'the number of attendees', function() {
```

```
      proxy(attendees, profileService, attendees.length+1);
      expect(spyOnProfileService.calls.count()).toBe(attendees.length);
   });
```

You immediately learn that your do-nothing proxy needs to do more (see Figure 14-3).

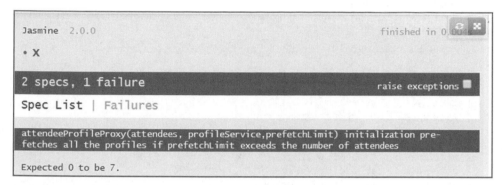

FIGURE 14-3

Listing 14-6 shows the easy remedy.

LISTING 14-6: Handling a prefetchLimit that is too large (code filename: Proxy\attendeeProfileProxy_02.js)

```
Conference.attendeeProfileProxy = function(
attendees, profileService, prefetchLimit) {
   'use strict';

   var ix,
       prefetched = {};

   function prefetch(attendeeId) {
     prefetched[attendeeId] = profileService.getProfile(attendeeId);
   }

   if (prefetchLimit > attendees.length) {
     prefetchLimit = attendees.length;
   }

   for (ix=0; ix<prefetchLimit; ++ix) {
     prefetch(attendees[ix].attendeeId);
   }
};
```

You are using an object, *prefetched*, as a dictionary. Its properties (the dictionary's keys) will be attendee IDs. The corresponding values will be the Promises for the pre-fetched profiles.

The function called prefetch is just a one-liner. That line could easily have been incorporated in the loop at the bottom. However, the function, sitting as it does at the top of the module and named as it is, serves to document exactly what it means to pre-fetch a profile.

Both tests now pass. With the boundary conditions tested, it's time to check out the core feature of the object, namely its ability to pre-fetch the most popular profiles. You add another test to the suite, which is now represented by Listing 14-7.

LISTING 14-7: Determining whether the proxy pre-fetches the most popular profiles (code filename: Proxy\attendeeProfileProxy_03_tests.js)

```javascript
describe('attendeeProfileProxy(attendees, profileService,prefetchLimit)',
function() {
  var proxy = Conference.attendeeProfileProxy,
      profileService = Conference.attendeeProfileService(),
      attendees = [
        { attendeeId: 10, profileViews: "3" },
        { attendeeId: 11, profileViews: "0" },
        { attendeeId: 12 },
        { attendeeId: 13, profileViews: "3" },
        { attendeeId: 14, profileViews: "10"},
        { attendeeId: 15, profileViews: "2" },
        { attendeeId: 16, profileViews: "1" },
        ],
      spyOnProfileService;

  beforeEach(function() {
    spyOnProfileService = spyOn(profileService,'getProfile');
  });

  describe('initialization', function () {

    // *** Previously discussed tests omitted. ***

    it("pre-fetches the 'prefetchLimit' most popular profiles", function() {
      var prefetchLimit = 3;
      proxy(attendees, profileService, prefetchLimit);
      expect(spyOnProfileService.calls.count()).toBe(prefetchLimit);
      expect(spyOnProfileService).toHaveBeenCalledWith(14);
      expect(spyOnProfileService).toHaveBeenCalledWith(10);
      expect(spyOnProfileService).toHaveBeenCalledWith(13);
    });
  });
});
```

As you saw in Chapter 2, Jasmine spies track their calls. That feature lets you determine the exact nature of each interaction with the proxy's real subject.

An easy mistake to make in unit-testing is to code your test just short of what it should be. If the test in Listing 14-7 were to contain only this line:

```javascript
expect(spyOnProfileService.calls.count()).toBe(prefetchLimit);
```

then you would know that three profiles had been pre-fetched, but you wouldn't know which ones. A more common error would be for the test to contain only these lines:

```javascript
expect(spyOnProfileService).toHaveBeenCalledWith(14);
```

```
expect(spyOnProfileService).toHaveBeenCalledWith(10);
expect(spyOnProfileService).toHaveBeenCalledWith(13);
```

In that case, you would not know whether *only* those three had been pre-fetched. So what happens when you run the test? Figure 14-4 is the result.

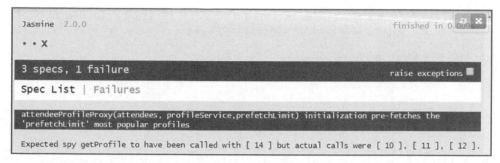

FIGURE 14-4

The first expectation, for the call count, was met, but the second, that attendee ID 14 was fetched, was not. Jasmine has very helpfully listed the attendee IDs that *were* fetched, and you can see that they were the first three in the test array. You are not surprised because you have made no attempt to pick the most popular.

You add sorting functionality to the proxy. While you're at it, you wrap both the sorting and the pre-fetching in an immediate-execution function to emphasize that this logic will execute only once, and to keep the new variable, `sortedAttendees`, from polluting the outer scope. You have even given a name, `prefetchAll`, to the immediate-execution function. This serves as documentation and a guidepost in any stack traces (see Listing 14-8).

LISTING 14-8: A first attempt at picking the most popular profiles (code filename: Proxy\attendeeProfileProxy_03a.js)

```
var Conference = Conference || {};

// Manage access to the profiles of the attendees in an array (attendees),
// fetching them from an attendeeProfileService (profileService),
// and pre-fetching up to prefetchLimit most popular based on profileViews.
Conference.attendeeProfileProxy = function(
attendees, profileService, prefetchLimit) {
  'use strict';
  var prefetched = {};

  function prefetch(attendeeId) {
    prefetched[attendeeId] = profileService.getProfile(attendeeId);
  }

  if (prefetchLimit > attendees.length) {
    prefetchLimit = attendees.length;
```

continues

LISTING 14-8 *(continued)*

```
    }

    (function prefetchAll() {
      var ix,
          sortedAttendees = attendees.slice().sort(function byViews(a,b) {
            return b.profileViews - a.profileViews;
          });
      for (ix=0; ix<prefetchLimit; ++ix) {
        prefetch(sortedAttendees[ix].attendeeId);
      }
    })();

  };
```

In the highlighted lines, `attendees.slice()` serves to make a copy of the *attendees* array so your sort operation will not affect the copy of the array that the proxy's caller is probably using for its own purposes.

The native JavaScript method `sort` takes a function that is supposed to return a positive value if the first parameter should sort after the second, a negative value for the opposite, or zero if they are equivalent for sorting purposes. For a descending sort, returning the second value minus the first usually does the trick, so that's what you have coded. How well does this work? See Figure 14-5.

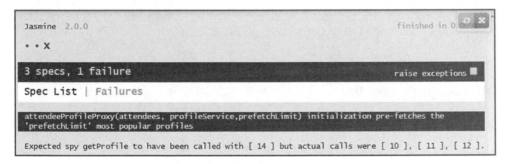

FIGURE 14-5

Yes. It's as if the sort never happened. Using a debugger, you can inspect exactly what's going on in the sort (see Figure 14-6).

The program is choking on the attendee whose `profileViews` property is missing. The difference between `b.profileViews` and `a.profileViews` is `NaN` (Not a Number).

When data come from a server, you cannot always count on every property being present. Most JSON serializers will allow default values not to be serialized, saving bandwidth. A `profileViews` value of zero could easily be deemed the default, causing a record to lack this property. You have wisely anticipated this in designing the `attendees` test array and now your foresight has paid off in the form of a failing test. (It's a good thing!)

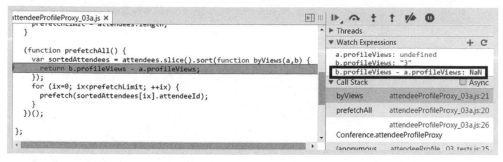

FIGURE 14.6

Speaking of the test data, another good thing about it is that the `profileViews` are quoted strings rather than bare numbers, just to make life a little harder for the tests. (Again, you never know what you'll get in serialized data.) More importantly, if the proxy sorts the strings *as strings*, the results will not be what you want because "10" will be considered less than "3." All too often, insufficient care is paid to the design of test data. Programmers use values that will allow tests to get away with too much. Let's face it: Writing test data is boring, but writing code is fun, so where is the care likely to be lavished? However, the test data are often as important as the test.

It takes only a little tweak to set things right (see Listing 14-9). Instead of `b.profileViews`, you code `(b.profileViews || 0)`, and the same for `a.profileViews`.

LISTING 14-9: Revised code for picking the most popular profiles (code filename: Proxy\attendeeProfileProxy_03b.js)

```
var Conference = Conference || {};

// Manage access to the profiles of the attendees in an array (attendees),
// fetching them from an attendeeProfileService (profileService),
// and pre-fetching up to prefetchLimit most popular based on profileViews.
Conference.attendeeProfileProxy = function(
attendees, profileService, prefetchLimit) {
  'use strict';

  var prefetched = {};

  function prefetch(attendeeId) {
    prefetched[attendeeId] = profileService.getProfile(attendeeId);
  }

  if (prefetchLimit > attendees.length) {
    prefetchLimit = attendees.length;
  }

  (function prefetchAll() {
```

continues

LISTING 14-9 *(continued)*

```
        var ix,
            sortedAttendees = attendees.slice().sort(function byViews(a,b) {
                return (b.profileViews || 0) - (a.profileViews || 0);
            });
        for (ix=0; ix<prefetchLimit; ++ix) {
            prefetch(sortedAttendees[ix].attendeeId);
        }
    })();

};
```

The tests pass (see Figure 14-7).

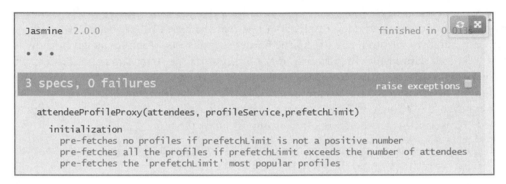

FIGURE 14-7

You now know that the proxy pre-fetches as expected, but does it deliver the pre-fetched profiles as it should?

Of course it doesn't! You haven't coded that part yet! Resisting the urge to produce useful code for the application, you code a test first (see Listing 14-10).

LISTING 14-10: Testing the return of a pre-fetched profile (code filename: Proxy\attendeeProfileProxy_04_tests.js)

```
describe('attendeeProfileProxy(attendees, profileService,prefetchLimit)',
function() {
    var proxy = Conference.attendeeProfileProxy,
        profileService = Conference.attendeeProfileService(),
        attendees = [
            { attendeeId: 10, profileViews: "3" },
            { attendeeId: 11, profileViews: "0" },
            { attendeeId: 12 },
            { attendeeId: 13, profileViews: "3" },
            { attendeeId: 14, profileViews: "10"},
```

```
                    { attendeeId: 15, profileViews: "2" },
                    { attendeeId: 16, profileViews: "1" },
                    ],
                spyOnProfileService;

            function makeServiceReturn(attendeeId) {
              return "Pretend this is the service's return value for attendeeId "
                    + attendeeId;
            }

            beforeEach(function() {
              spyOnProfileService = spyOn(profileService,'getProfile')
                .and.callFake(function(attendeeId) {
                  return makeServiceReturn(attendeeId);
                });
            });

            // *** Previously discussed tests omitted. ***

            describe('getProfile(attendeeId)', function() {
              var prefetchLimit = 3,
                  proxyInstance;

              beforeEach(function() {
                proxyInstance = proxy(attendees, profileService, prefetchLimit);
              });

              it('returns a pre-fetched profile when it is requested',function() {
                var attendeeId = 13,
                    profile = proxyInstance.getProfile(attendeeId);
                expect(profile).toBe(makeServiceReturn(attendeeId));
                expect(spyOnProfileService.calls.count()).toBe(prefetchLimit);
              });
            });
          });
```

Anticipating further tests, you have placed the *prefetchLimit* and *proxyInstance* variables in a scope that will be accessible to both the new test and future tests. The *proxyInstance* is initialized afresh for each test in a beforeEach.

In the test, you call getProfile on the proxy. You expect to get the return value from the underlying attendeeProfileService. But what is the strange makeServiceReturn call? Like the Decorator Pattern (see Chapter 12), the Proxy Pattern delegates the real work to its subject. It should not concern itself with one iota more of the subject's semantics than necessary. In the present case, the attendeeProfileProxy has no reason to care whether the underlying service is returning Promises, JSON objects, or anything else. Therefore, the tests need not *and should not* care, either. This is why the makeServiceReturn function, defined near the top of Listing 14-10, makes a return value that is intentionally silly. The spy on the profile service, initialized in the first beforeEach, has been modified to return the fake value.

In spite of doing all that work, you are delighted when the test fails (see Figure 14-8) because that means you get to write useful code.

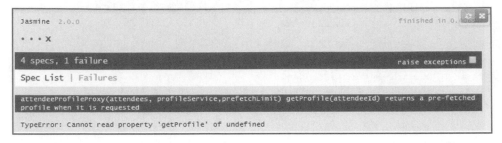

FIGURE 14-8

Jasmine is telling you that your test's call to `getProfile` took place on an object whose value is `undefined`, which would be `proxyInstance`. That's no surprise. Until now, `Conference.attendeeProfileProxy` has not returned any value! Your fix for that is in Listing 14-11, where the proxy returns an object literal that has a `getProfile` function.

LISTING 14-11: Verifying that the proxy returns an object which has a getProfile function (code filename: Proxy\attendeeProfileProxy_04.js)

```
var Conference = Conference || {};

// Manage access to the profiles of the attendees in an array (attendees),
// fetching them from an attendeeProfileService (profileService),
// and pre-fetching up to prefetchLimit most popular based on profileViews.
Conference.attendeeProfileProxy = function(
attendees, profileService, prefetchLimit) {
  'use strict';

  var prefetched = {};

  function prefetch(attendeeId) {
    prefetched[attendeeId] = profileService.getProfile(attendeeId);
  }

  if (prefetchLimit > attendees.length) {
    prefetchLimit = attendees.length;
  }

  (function prefetchAll() {
    var ix,
        sortedAttendees = attendees.slice().sort(function byViews(a,b) {
          return (b.profileViews || 0) - (a.profileViews || 0);
        });
    for (ix=0; ix<prefetchLimit; ++ix) {
      prefetch(sortedAttendees[ix].attendeeId);
    }
  })();

  return {
    getProfile: function getProfile(attendeeId) {
```

```
        return prefetched[attendeeId];
      }
    };
  };
```

Following sound test-driven methodology, your `getProfile` function does the bare minimum to fulfill your last test, returning the profile from the *prefetched* object. Once again, the proxy does not care whether that profile is actually a `Promise` for one or the profile itself. The proxy's Single Responsibility is to manage access to its real subject. It makes no claims about the subject's semantics. Figure 14-9 shows your success.

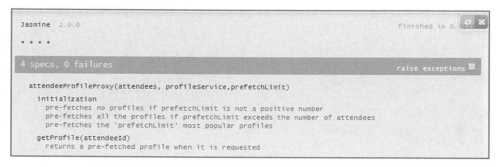

FIGURE 14-9

What about the case where the profile has *not* been pre-fetched? That's easy to test. Listing 14-12 shows the result.

LISTING 14-12: Testing the return of a profile that has not been pre-fetched (code filename: Proxy\attendeeProfileProxy_tests.js)

```
describe('attendeeProfileProxy(attendees, profileService,prefetchLimit)',
function() {
  var proxy = Conference.attendeeProfileProxy,
      profileService = Conference.attendeeProfileService(),
      attendees = [
        { attendeeId: 10, profileViews: "3" },
        { attendeeId: 11, profileViews: "0" },
        { attendeeId: 12 },
        { attendeeId: 13, profileViews: "3" },
        { attendeeId: 14, profileViews: "10"},
        { attendeeId: 15, profileViews: "2" },
        { attendeeId: 16, profileViews: "1" },
        ],
      spyOnProfileService;

  function makeServiceReturn(attendeeId) {
    return "Pretend this is the service's return value for attendeeId "
         + attendeeId;
```

continues

LISTING 14-12 *(continued)*

```
    }

    beforeEach(function() {
      spyOnProfileService = spyOn(profileService,'getProfile')
        .and.callFake(function(attendeeId) {
          return makeServiceReturn(attendeeId);
        });
    });

    // *** Previously discussed tests omitted. ***

    describe('getProfile(attendeeId)', function() {
      var prefetchLimit = 3,
          proxyInstance;

      beforeEach(function() {
        proxyInstance = proxy(attendees, profileService, prefetchLimit);
      });

      // *** Previously discussed test omitted. ***

      it('returns a non-pre-fetched profile when requested', function() {
        var attendeeId = 11,
            profile = proxyInstance.getProfile(attendeeId);
        expect(profile).toBe(makeServiceReturn(attendeeId));
        expect(spyOnProfileService.calls.count()).toBe(prefetchLimit+1);
      });
    });
  });
```

The new test calls `getProfile` on attendee 11, which will not have been pre-fetched because it is not one of the *prefetchLimit* most-viewed. The test expects the profile to be fetched, resulting in an additional call to the underlying service. The test fails on both counts (see Figure 14-10).

One last adjustment to the code (the last line of code in Listing 14-13) and all is well (see Figure 14-11).

LISTING 14-13: The completed attendeeProfileProxy (code filename: Proxy\attendeeProfileProxy.js)

```
var Conference = Conference || {};

// Manage access to the profiles of the attendees in an array (attendees),
// fetching them from an attendeeProfileService (profileService),
// and pre-fetching up to prefetchLimit most popular based on profileViews.
Conference.attendeeProfileProxy = function(
attendees, profileService, prefetchLimit) {
  'use strict';

  var prefetched = {};

  function prefetch(attendeeId) {
```

```
      prefetched[attendeeId] = profileService.getProfile(attendeeId);
    }

    if (prefetchLimit > attendees.length) {
      prefetchLimit = attendees.length;
    }

    (function prefetchAll() {
      var ix,
          sortedAttendees = attendees.slice().sort(function byViews(a,b) {
            return (b.profileViews || 0) - (a.profileViews || 0);
          });
      for (ix=0; ix<prefetchLimit; ++ix) {
        prefetch(sortedAttendees[ix].attendeeId);
      }
    })();

    return {
      getProfile: function getProfile(attendeeId) {
        return prefetched[attendeeId] || profileService.getProfile(attendeeId);
      }
    };
  };
```

FIGURE 14-10

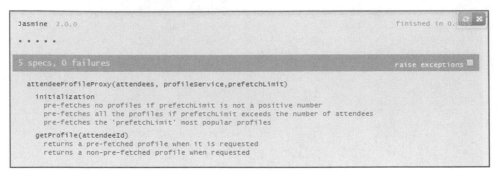

FIGURE 14-11

"I'm done," you tell Charlotte.

"You *think* you're done," she replies. "As long as we were going for efficiency, I decided not to send you the `profileViews` property if there weren't any."

"Been there; thought of that. Still done," you say with satisfaction.

SUMMARY

In this chapter, you worked through a case study of test-driven development of a proxy. Several principles became apparent:

➤ The Proxy Pattern consists of one object (the *proxy*) that manages interaction with another (the *real subject*).

➤ A proxy can help its consumers be more efficient in their use of the real subject, or keep them out of trouble.

➤ A proxy should be tested by observing its interaction with the real subject, rather than exposing the internals of the proxy. Jasmine's spies can be very helpful in this respect.

➤ To facilitate testing and dependency injection, pass the proxy's real subject as a parameter to the function that creates the proxy.

➤ If the real subject should never be exposed, you can implement the proxy as an aspect.

➤ Start your test-driven development with a do-nothing proxy.

➤ As always, test the error and boundary conditions first.

➤ Construct your test data with as much care as you construct the tests themselves.

In the next chapter, you'll have the pleasure of exploring one of JavaScript's most beloved idioms: chainable methods.

15

Ensuring Correct Implementation of Chainable Methods

WHAT'S IN THIS CHAPTER?

➤ Using chainable methods to create more elegant code

➤ Using test-driven development to implement chainable methods

➤ Writing DRY unit tests to verify that methods are chainable

➤ Showing how the `then` method of ECMAScript 6 promises enables chaining

WROX.COM CODE DOWNLOADS FOR THIS CHAPTER

The wrox.com code downloads for this chapter are found at `www.wrox.com/go/reliablejavascript` on the Download Code tab. The files are in the Chapter 15 download and individually named according to the filenames noted throughout this chapter.

Does the structure and syntax of the following JavaScript statement look familiar?

```
$;("#myDiv").text("JavaScript").removeClass("unreliable")
.addClass("reliable");
```

If you've done any client-side development since 2008 or so, chances are the answer is "Yes." The statement is written using jQuery, a popular client-side JavaScript framework that's used by over 52 million websites on the Internet according to `http://www.builtwith.com` in March 2015.

The jQuery code sample illustrates the use of *chainable methods*: functions constructed so they can be invoked one after another on the same object in a single statement.

You don't have to look far for other uses of chainable methods in JavaScript. You may have recognized that the `then` method of the `Promise` API used throughout the book is chainable.

> **NOTE** *The* then *method behaves a bit differently than the chainable methods that jQuery exposes, and that you'll create in this chapter:* then *doesn't always return the object on which it was invoked. The last section in this chapter explores this difference in depth.*

Exposing APIs that use chainable methods enables code that looks like this:

```
var obj = NS.createObj();
obj.setAttribute1("Attr1 Value");
obj.doThing1();
obj.doThing2();
```

to be transformed into this:

```
var obj = NS.createObj().setAttribute1("Attr1 Value").doThing1().doThing2();
```

The differences between the examples aren't major. The second example is a bit more succinct than the first: The `obj` variable is only referenced once, and three semicolons have been eliminated. We aren't perfect typists, so avoided keystrokes are avoided chances for typos.

The second example is also more expressive, and we feel that it's more elegant than the first. It's a single statement that has a sense of flow that the first example does not. Where the first example is blocky, the second reads from left to right, like an English sentence.

In this chapter you'll use test-driven development to create a module for the JavaScript conference website that exposes chainable methods as part of its API.

Many of the presenters speaking at the JavaScript conference have expressed interest in getting feedback about their presentations from attendees. The conference organizers have decided to extend the conference's website to provide a speaker evaluation page that attendees can access from their mobile devices or any of the kiosks around the conference venue.

The evaluation page will capture the:

- ➤ Presentation title
- ➤ Presenter's name
- ➤ Rating of value of the topics/concepts presented
- ➤ Rating of the presenter's speaking skills
- ➤ Likelihood that the attendee would attend another presentation by the speaker
- ➤ Comments the attendee would like to give to the speaker

The `presenterEvaluation` module, which will be developed in the next section, will be used to collate the information entered into the evaluation page. The evaluation data will then be persisted to the server for storage until the end of the conference, when it will be aggregated and provided to each of the presenters.

UNDERSTANDING THE PATTERN THROUGH UNIT TESTS

The responsibility of the `presenterEvaluation` module is a modest one: Its only job is to store the data that represents an attendee's rating of a presentation. It will expose a `set` method for each datum that it stores, and those `set` methods will be chainable.

In order for a method to be chainable, it must return the object on which it has been invoked. In JavaScript, the variable `this` refers to exactly that object. Thus, making a method chainable is as simple as having it return `this`.

> **NOTE** *A method becomes chainable when it returns* `this`.

The unit test that verifies the ability to chain additional function calls off of the `setPresenter` function follows in Listing 15-1.

LISTING 15-1: Ensuring setPresenter returns this (code filename: Chaining\presenterEvaluation_01_tests.js)

```
describe("Conference.presenterEvaluation", function(){
  'use strict';

  var evaluation;

  beforeEach(function(){
    evaluation = Conference.presenterEvaluation();
  });

  describe("setPresenter(presenterName)", function(){
    it("returns the instance on which it was invoked", function(){
      expect(evaluation.setPresenter("Presenter Name")).toBe(evaluation);
    };
  });
});
```

The unit test simply verifies that the value returned by the `setPresenter` function is the same as the object on which the `setPresenter` function was invoked.

The `presenterEvaluation` module with a `setPresenter` stub appears in Listing 15-2.

LISTING 15-2: The presenterEvaluation module with setPresenter stub (code filename: Chaining\presenterEvaluation_01.js)

```
var Conference = Conference || {};

Conference.presenterEvaluation = function(){
  'use strict';

  return{

    // Sets the name of the presenter this evaluation pertains to.  Returns
```

continues

LISTING 15-2 *(continued)*

```
        // the evaluation instance on which it was invoked, making it chainable.
        setPresenter: function setPresenter(presenterName){

        }

    };
};
```

Unsurprisingly, the unit test fails, as you can see in Figure 15-1.

FIGURE 15-1

Making the test pass is a simple affair; you simply need to add a single line. Listing 15-3 illustrates this.

LISTING 15-3: The presenterEvaluationModule with a chainable setPresenter function (code filename: Chaining\presenterEvaluation_02.js)

```
var Conference = Conference || {};

Conference.presenterEvaluation = function(){
    'use strict';

    return{

        // Sets the name of the presenter this evaluation pertains to.  Returns
        // the evaluation instance on which it was invoked, making it chainable.
        setPresenter: function setPresenter(presenterName){
            return this;
        }

    };
};
```

Figure 15-2 shows that the unit test now passes.

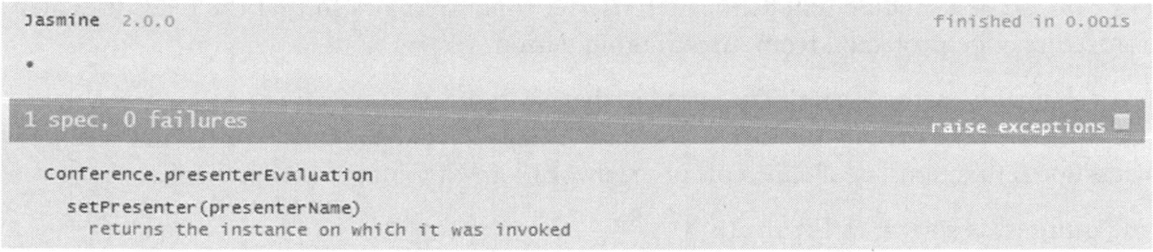

```
Jasmine  2.0.0                                                    finished in 0.001s

  .

  1 spec, 0 failures                                              raise exceptions ■

    Conference.presenterEvaluation
      setPresenter(presenterName)
        returns the instance on which it was invoked
```

FIGURE 15-2

The humble little `return this;` statement in Listing 15-3 is all that's required to make the `setPresenter` method chainable. As additional chainable methods are added to the `presenterEvaluation` module, such as `setPresentation`, they may be appended to the invocation of `setPresenter` like so:

```
var evaluation = Conference.presenterEvaluation()
  .setPresenter("Seth Richards")
  .setPresentation("Reliable JavaScript");
```

Chainable setter methods defined in this manner allow for succinct object creation and initialization.

A method that just returns the object on which it was invoked provides little value. To round out the functionality of the `setPresenter` method, you add a test that verifies that the instance has stored the presenter name properly, as demonstrated in Listing 15-4.

LISTING 15-4: Ensuring that the presenter name is stored (code filename: Chaining\presenterEvaluation_03_tests.js)

```
describe("Conference.presenterEvaluation", function(){
  'use strict';

  var evaluation;

  beforeEach(function(){
    evaluation = Conference.presenterEvaluation();
  });

  describe("setPresenter(presenterName)", function(){

    it("returns the instance on which it was invoked", function(){
      expect(evaluation.setPresenter("Presenter Name")).toBe(evaluation);
    });

    it("stores the presenter name", function(){
      var name = "Meg Ryan";
      evaluation.setPresenter(name);
      expect(evaluation.getPresenter()).toEqual(name);
    });

  });

});
```

The new test introduced in Listing 15-4 uses a function that hasn't been defined yet, `getPresenter`, to retrieve the name that has been stored in the `evaluation presenterEvaluation` instance. The `presenterEvaluation` module will define getter/setter function pairs so that the fields in which data are stored may be protected from direct manipulation.

An aspect of chainable methods that's illustrated in the new test is that they *don't have to be chained*. In the case of the new test, `evaluation.setPresenter(name)` is invoked and its return value is ignored. Also, no additional functions are chained off of the invocation. Chaining is an option, not a requirement.

The failing unit test is shown in Figure 15-3.

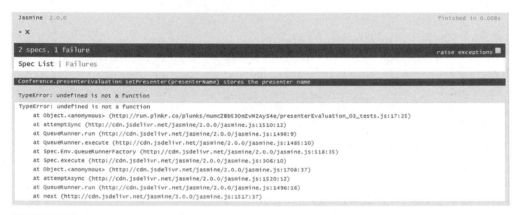

FIGURE 15-3

Listing 15-5 adds `getPresenter` to the `presenterEvaluation` module, and also completes the functionality of `setPresenter`.

LISTING 15-5: Fully implemented setPresenter and getPresenter (code filename: Chaining\presenterEvaluation_03.js)

```javascript
var Conference = Conference || {};

Conference.presenterEvaluation = function(){
  'use strict';

  var presenter = "";

  return {

    // Sets the name of the presenter this evaluation pertains to.  Returns
    // the evaluation instance on which it was invoked, making it chainable.
    setPresenter: function setPresenter(presenterName){
      presenter = presenterName;
      return this;
    },

    // returns the name of the presenter this evaluation pertains to
```

```
    getPresenter: function getPresenter(){
      return presenter;
    }
  };
};
```

As you can see in Figure 15-4, both of the unit tests now pass.

```
Jasmine  2.0.0                                                          finished in 0.001s

 . .

2 specs, 0 failures                                                    raise exceptions ▨

  Conference.presenterEvaluation

   setPresenter(presenterName)
     returns the instance on which it was invoked
     stores the presenter name
```

FIGURE 15-4

At this point, you've implemented one of the six chainable setter methods that the `presenterEvaluation` module needs to have in order to store each piece of data about an evaluation. While details such as data verification and validation will differ from one setter function to another, each of the functions will need to return `this`. As such, each function should have a test that verifies that `this` is properly returned.

Writing an individual test for each would involve a fair amount of repetition. One way to DRY out the tests is to introduce a single test that validates that all of chainable methods return `this`. Such a test appears in Listing 15-6.

LISTING 15-6: A single test that verifies all the setters are chainable (code filename: Chaining\presenterEvaluation_04_tests.js)

```
describe("Conference.presenterEvaluation", function(){
  'use strict';

  var evaluation;

  beforeEach(function(){
    evaluation = Conference.presenterEvaluation();
  });

  describe("exposes chainable setter functions", function(){
      it("that return the instance on which the setter was invoked", function(){

        // Create an array that contains a valid invocation (passes data
        // validation, etc.) of each of the functions that should be
        // chainable.
        var validCalls = [
          function(ev){ return ev.setPresenter("presenter name"); },
          function(ev){ return ev.setPresentation("presentation name"); }
          ];

        // Ensure that each of the functions in validCalls returns
```

continues

LISTING 15-6 *(continued)*

```
          // evaluation, making it chainable.
          validCalls.forEach(function ensureReturnsThis(fcn){
            expect(fcn(evaluation)).toBe(evaluation);
          });

        });
      });

      describe("setPresenter(presenterName)", function(){

        it("stores the presenter name", function(){
          var name = "Meg Ryan";
          evaluation.setPresenter(name);
          expect(evaluation.getPresenter()).toEqual(name);
        });

      });

    });
```

The new test builds an array of functions, `validCalls`. Each function in `validCalls` calls one of the setter functions exposed by `presenterEvaluation` and returns the value that the setter returns. The test then invokes each of the functions in `validCalls` and ensures that the value returned is the object on which the function was invoked, `evaluation`.

As each setter method that should support chaining is added to `presenterEvaluation`, a corresponding entry will be added to `validCalls` to validate the capability.

Notice that the original test that verified `setPresenter`'s ability to be chained has been removed. The new test provides that verification. Also notice an entry for a function that has not yet been defined, `setPresentation`, has been added to the `validCalls` array.

The new test fails, as shown in Figure 15-5, because `setPresentation` has not yet been implemented.

FIGURE 15-5

Listing 15-7 provides an updated implementation of `presenterEvaluation` that has the minimum implementation of `setPresentation` that allows the unit tests from Listing 15-6 to pass.

LISTING 15-7: Minimum implementation making setPresentation chainable (code filename: Chaining\presenterEvaluation_04.js)

```javascript
var Conference = Conference || {};

Conference.presenterEvaluation = function(){
  'use strict';

  var presenter = "";

  return{

    // Sets the name of the presenter this evaluation pertains to.  Returns
    // the evaluation instance on which it was invoked, making it chainable.
    setPresenter: function setPresenter(presenterName){
      presenter = presenterName;
      return this;
    },

    // returns the name of the presenter this evaluation pertains to
    getPresenter: function getPresenter(){
      return presenter;
    },

    // Sets the name of the presentation this evaluation pertains to.  Returns
    // the evaluation instance on which it was invoked, making it chainable.
    setPresentation: function setPresentation(presentationName){
      return this;
    }
  };
};
```

Again, the `return this;` statement in `setPresentation` is all that's required to make it chainable.

Now that `setPresentation` has been defined and is returning the object on which it was invoked, the new unit test passes. You can see this in Figure 15-6.

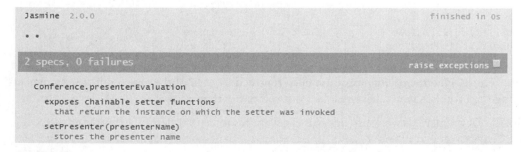

FIGURE 15-6

CHAINING THEN

Earlier in the chapter, we mentioned that a method becomes chainable when it returns `this`. When `this` is returned, multiple methods on the same object may be invoked. You leveraged this behavior when creating the `presenterEvaluation` module: Returning `this` allowed the chained methods to set properties on a single instance of the module.

We also mentioned that a `Promise`'s `then` method is chainable. The following sample from Chapter 6 shows the `checkInService.checkIn` method, which returns a `Promise`. The `Promise` that's returned is immediately chained with two `then` methods:

```
checkInService.checkIn(attendee)
  .then(
    function onCheckInResolved(checkInNumber) {
      // Prints a badge and returns its number.
      return badgePrintingService.print(checkInNumber);
    })
  .then(
    function onBadgePrintResolved(badgeNumber) {
      return doorPrizeEnteringService.enter(attendee, badgeNumber);
    });
```

Neither `onCheckInResolved` nor `onBadgePrintResolved` resolves to `this`, so presumably the `then` method is performing some action to ensure that additional `then` methods may be chained.

Perhaps the `then` method is manipulating the original `Promise` created and returned by `checkinService.checkIn`. That hypothesis can be tested by adjusting the sample slightly:

```
var originalPromise = checkInService.checkIn(attendee);

var firstThen = originalPromise.then(
  function onCheckInResolved(checkInNumber) {
    // Prints a badge and returns its number.
    return badgePrintingService.print(checkInNumber);
  });

var secondThen = firstThen.then(
  function onBadgePrintResolved(badgeNumber) {
    return doorPrizeEnteringService.enter(attendee, badgeNumber);
  });

console.log(firstThen instanceof Promise);    // true
console.log(secondThen instanceof Promise);   // true

console.log(firstThen === originalPromise);   // false
console.log(secondThen === firstThen);        // false
```

It's evident that while the `then` methods are returning `Promise` objects, they aren't returning the original promise. Had the original promise been returned by each of the `then` calls, the statements comparing the promises would have resulted in `true` rather than `false`.

The Mozilla Developer Network provides an excellent resource that describes Promises as specified by ECMAScript 6 at `https://developer.mozilla.org/en-US/docs/Web/JavaScript/Reference/Global_Objects/Promise`. The following excerpt from that page describes what the `then` method does behind the scenes.

*Appends fulfillment and rejection handlers to the promise, and **returns a new promise** resolving to the return value of the called handler.*

—Mozilla Developer Network (emphasis added)

The documentation confirms what the test demonstrated: The `then` function returns a new `Promise`; it does not return the original `Promise`. The `then` function does, however, add the fulfillment and rejection handlers to the original `Promise` so that they may be executed when the original `Promise` becomes resolved.

The implication is that methods don't need to return `this` in order to be chainable; they may also return a new object that's the same type as `this`.

> **NOTE** *A function that returns a new object with the same type as the object on which it was invoked is chainable.*

Returning a new instance to support chaining is appropriate for promises, but it would not be appropriate for the setter methods of the `presenterEvaluation` module. The intent of the setters is to mutate, or change, the values contained by the instance of `presenterEvaluation` on which they are invoked. A developer using the setters would likely be surprised if the setters each returned a new instance of `presenterEvaluation` rather than change the instance on which they were invoked.

SUMMARY

In this chapter, you saw how chainable methods can transform parts of your JavaScript code from blocky and repetitive to flowing and concise. You used test-driven development to implement two chainable functions.

To test chainability, it is often sufficient to simply ensure that a function returns `this`. As the `Promise then` function demonstrated, however, chainable functions don't always return `this`. On those occasions, it's necessary to test that the object returned has the correct type.

The next chapter is about interfaces—something JavaScript does not have. What is that chapter doing in this book? Read it and see.

PART III
Testing and Writing with Advanced JavaScript Features

16

Conforming to Interfaces in an Interface-Free Language

WHAT'S IN THIS CHAPTER?

➤ Understanding the benefits of interfaces in other languages

➤ Gaining the benefits of interfaces in JavaScript

➤ Simplifying consumption of an object with the Interface Segregation Principle

➤ Producing a registry in which you can define and enforce interfaces

WROX.COM CODE DOWNLOADS FOR THIS CHAPTER

The wrox.com code downloads for this chapter are found at www.wrox.com/go/ reliablejavascript on the Download Code tab. The files are in the Chapter 16 download and individually named according to the filenames noted throughout this chapter.

In a 2014 commercial for Google's business products (https://www.youtube.com/ watch?v=bA0Hmhnl1oE), a videoconference is just finishing:

> GOOGLER: So yeah, I think we're good. I think that about wraps it up. So ...
>
> *WOMAN #1: Great. I'll send a follow-up email.*
>
> GOOGLER: I don't ... There's nothing much to follow up on so I ...
>
> *WOMAN #2: Well, I think we should regroup.*
>
> GOOGLER: We just regrouped. This is the regrouping.
>
> *MAN #1: Cool. I'll ping you later.*
>
> GOOGLER: You're pinging me now. What do you want to ping about?
>
> *MAN #2: Next steps?*

GOOGLER: There are no next steps. We just solved them.

MAN #3: *Huh. All right ...*

A conversation between a JavaScript programmer and a C# or Java programmer could go much the same way. The JavaScripter throws some objects together and the C# or Java developer keeps insisting, "You can't do that! The program will fall apart without some interfaces to describe the objects." The JavaScript developer says, "No, there are no next steps. We just solved the problem."

Yet any JavaScripter who has worked on a team of more than one must admit that misunderstandings do occur. A member function that used to be called `makeAWidget` is renamed to `makeWidget`, breaking downstream code. An object literal's member variable is named in the singular, `objectID`, but someone puts an array of object IDs in it. (Hard to believe, but we have seen it happen.)

Strongly typed languages do their best to catch these misunderstandings at compile time, often by using interfaces. What is an interface, and why do programmers in these languages think they are worthwhile?

UNDERSTANDING THE BENEFITS OF INTERFACES

An interface describes a class, but has no executable code. Listing 16-1 shows an interface in C#.

LISTING 16-1: A C# interface

```
public interface IDoThings
{
    void ThingOne();
    int  ThingTwo();
}
```

With that interface defined, a class can inherit from it, thereby promising to implement it, as in Listing 16-2.

LISTING 16-2: A C# class implements the interface

```
public DoThings : IDoThings
{
    public void ThingOne()
    {
        // Function body
    }

    public int ThingTwo()
    {
        // Function body
    }
}
```

If the class fails to implement everything defined in the interface, the compiler will throw an error.

To a JavaScript programmer, this may seem like a lot of trouble. You're saying everything twice: once in the interface and again in the class. And so it is, but the trouble is not without repayment.

The surface benefit is that an interface makes clear what consumers of the class can expect, and what programmers of similar classes should implement.

Interfaces also act as a sort of double-entry accounting. If the implementation goes out of balance with the interface, the compiler will tell you about it.

On a deeper level, interfaces open a whole world of possibilities to the software engineer, enabling him to solve problems more elegantly. The Strategy Pattern you met in Chapter 13 is one example. When implemented in a strongly typed language, each algorithm implements a common interface. There is no need for a factory method to create the chosen algorithm; dependency-injection software can wire up the desired one through runtime configuration.

Every time you have coded a Jasmine spy in the unit tests throughout this book, you have used the interface philosophy, with the spy implementing the same interface as the real object. Of course, in JavaScript the interface is only implied, but in a strongly typed language it would be explicit and therefore more reliable.

Of the five pillars of SOLID software design you met in Chapter 1, three of them are interface-oriented. The Liskov Substitution Principle (the L in SOLID) states that all implementers of an interface should adhere to the same semantics. The Dependency Inversion Principle (the D) had consumers of a class "own" the interface from which the class inherited. The Interface Segregation Principle (the I) is the subject of the next section.

UNDERSTANDING THE INTERFACE SEGREGATION PRINCIPLE

As much as you may strive to make classes coherent and no larger than necessary, sometimes a consumer of a class needs only a fraction of its capabilities.

As an example, consider the attendee object from Chapter 6, reproduced here as Listing 16-3.

LISTING 16-3: attendee.js

```javascript
var Conference = Conference || {};
Conference.attendee = function(firstName, lastName){
  'use strict';

  var attendeeId,
    checkedIn = false,
    first = firstName || 'None',
    last = lastName || 'None',
    checkInNumber;

  return {
    setId: function(id) {
      attendeeId = id;
    },
```

continues

LISTING 16-3 *(continued)*

```
      getId: function() {
        return attendeeId;
      },

      getFullName: function(){
        return first + ' ' + last;
      },

      isCheckedIn: function(){
        return checkedIn;
      },

      checkIn: function(){
        checkedIn = true;
      },

      undoCheckIn: function() {
        checkedIn = false;
        checkInNumber = undefined;
      },

      setCheckInNumber: function(number) {
        checkInNumber = number;
      },

      getCheckInNumber: function() {
        return checkInNumber;
      }
    };
  };
```

If JavaScript had interfaces, `attendee` might implement two of them, which Listing 16-4 presents in pseudocode. One is designed for consumers who care only about an attendee's personal information, the other for consumers oriented toward managing the check-in process.

LISTING 16-4: Two possible interfaces in attendee.js

```
Interface attendeePersonalInfo:
    setId:              function(id)         returns undefined
    getId:              function()           returns a non-negative integer
    getFullName:        function()           returns a string

Interface attendeeCheckInManagement
    getId:              function()           returns a non-negative integer
    isCheckedIn:        function()           returns a boolean
    checkIn:            function()           returns undefined
    undoCheckIn:        function()           returns undefined
    setCheckInNumber:   function(number)     returns undefined
    getCheckInNumber:   function()           returns a non-negative integer
```

Now suppose several functions in other modules each take an `attendee` object as an argument. Suppose further that you wish to change `attendee`'s `getFullName` method. The functions in the other modules nicely show attendees as arguments (assuming the arguments were named helpfully), but you have no easy way to know which functions your change to `getFullName` will affect. Sure, you could do a text search for "getFullName" but then you'd also turn up like-named methods in other objects (maybe `presenter` or `sponsor`).

This is one problem that the Interface Segregation Principle is designed to solve. The consuming functions, instead of having arguments called `attendee`, could have `attendeePersonalInfo` or `attendeeCheckInManagement` arguments. Then, at a glance, you would know which functions your change might affect (again assuming the arguments are named in a non-deceptive manner).

Furthermore, if you needed to mock an argument for unit-testing, or inject another version of the object, you would be able to draw a tighter boundary around the `attendee`'s members that you actually need to mock or implement.

Finally, a developer who really only cares about the `attendeePersonalInfo` portion of an `attendee` only has to master that small API. A properly segregated interface will make his life easier.

These benefits are *enforced* in strongly typed languages, but they are certainly *available* in JavaScript if you're willing to program outside the box.

In the next section, you'll build a module by which you can define and enforce interfaces. The module is called `contractRegistry` because interfaces act as contracts between modules that define functionality and modules that consume it, and because in the next chapter you will use `contractRegistry`'s capabilities for purposes that are not, strictly speaking, interface-related.

USING TEST-DRIVEN DEVELOPMENT TO CREATE A CONTRACT REGISTRY

The contract registry as developed in this chapter will have the following capabilities, developed in this order:

1. Define a contract (interface).

2. Tell whether an object fulfills a contract.

3. Assert that an object fulfills a contract, throwing an `Error` if it does not.

4. Turn off all contract enforcement so your program can run faster in production.

5. Attach an aspect to enforce a contract on an object. (In concrete terms, this will mean adding an aspect to the function that creates the object, to inspect its return value.)

Figure 16-1 gives an advance peek at the passing unit tests you'll aim for.

Defining a Contract

A contract definition will consist of a name for the contract and a function that can evaluate an object and return `true` or `false` according to whether the object fulfills the contract. The `define` method, then, has this signature:

```
function define(contractName, evaluator)
```

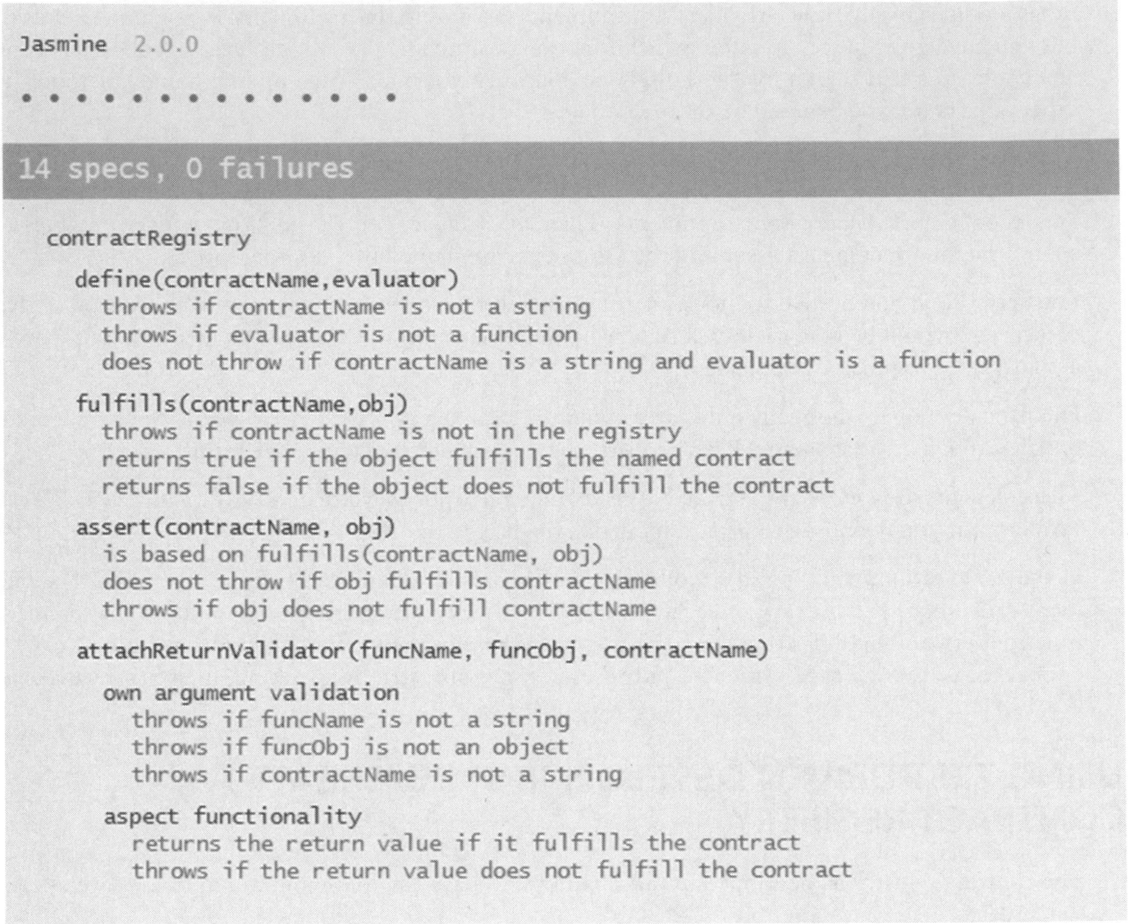

```
Jasmine  2.0.0

• • • • • • • • • • • • • • •

14 specs, 0 failures

  contractRegistry

    define(contractName,evaluator)
      throws if contractName is not a string
      throws if evaluator is not a function
      does not throw if contractName is a string and evaluator is a function

    fulfills(contractName,obj)
      throws if contractName is not in the registry
      returns true if the object fulfills the named contract
      returns false if the object does not fulfill the contract

    assert(contractName, obj)
      is based on fulfills(contractName, obj)
      does not throw if obj fulfills contractName
      throws if obj does not fulfill contractName

    attachReturnValidator(funcName, funcObj, contractName)

      own argument validation
        throws if funcName is not a string
        throws if funcObj is not an object
        throws if contractName is not a string

      aspect functionality
        returns the return value if it fulfills the contract
        throws if the return value does not fulfill the contract
```

FIGURE 16-1

Incidentally, having an evaluator *function* act as an "interface" is quite different from other languages' conception of interfaces as static *data*. This is not only necessary but welcome. It is necessary because JavaScript has no built-in way to evaluate conformance to an interface, and you must code it *somewhere*. It is welcome because a function can do much more than any data-oriented, interface-description language ever could. Plus, with a function riding along as a first-class object, it feels nice and JavaScripty, doesn't it?

With several chapters of test-driven development behind you, there is no need to belabor every step toward creating this method. Listing 16-5 shows its tests.

> **LISTING 16-5:** Unit tests for the define method (code filename: Interfaces\
> contractRegistry_01_tests.js)

```
describe('contractRegistry', function() {
  'use strict';
```

```
var registry;

beforeEach(function() {
  registry = ReliableJavaScript.contractRegistry();
});

describe('define(contractName,evaluator)', function() {

  it('throws if contractName is not a string',function() {
    expect(function() {
      registry.define(undefined,function() {});
    }).toThrow(new Error(registry.messages.nameMustBeString));
  });

  it('throws if evaluator is not a function', function() {
    expect(function() {
      registry.define('myContract','not a function');
    }).toThrow(new Error(registry.messages.evaluatorMustBeFunction));
  });

  it('does not throw if contractName is a string and evaluator is a function',
  function() {
    expect(function() {
      registry.define('myContract',function() {});
    }).not.toThrow();
  });
});
});
```

As usual, test-driven development begins with the error conditions. Beyond that, there's not much you can test when define is the only method in the object. You can't even test that it defines anything. However, until it does you won't get very far with the fulfills method (up next). Even so, you resist getting ahead of the tests and code only what's necessary to make the above tests pass. The result is Listing 16-6.

LISTING 16-6: Implementation of the define method (code filename: Interfaces\contractRegistry_01.js)

```
var ReliableJavaScript = ReliableJavaScript || {};
ReliableJavaScript.contractRegistry = function() {
  'use strict';

  return {
    define: function define(contractName, evaluator) {
      if (typeof contractName !== 'string') {
        throw new Error(this.messages.nameMustBeString);
      }
      if (typeof evaluator !== 'function') {
        throw new Error(this.messages.evaluatorMustBeFunction);
      }
    },

    messages: {
```

continues

LISTING 16-6 *(continued)*

```
            nameMustBeString: 'The contract name must be a string',
            evaluatorMustBeFunction: 'The evaluator must be a function',
        }
    };
};
```

The tests pass, as shown in Figure 16-2.

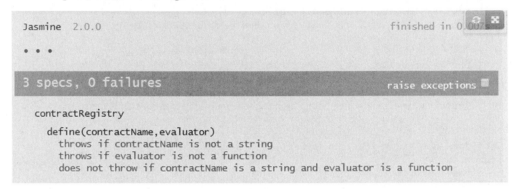

FIGURE 16-2

Determining Whether a Contract Is Fulfilled

The `fulfills` method will look like this:

```
function fulfills(contractName, obj)
```

It will return `true` if *obj* fulfills the named contract or `false` if it does not. Before you get to that, you first test the obvious error condition: that the named contract is not in the registry (see Listing 16-7).

LISTING 16-7: First test of the fulfills method (code filename: Interfaces\contractRegistry_02_tests.js [excerpt])

```
describe('fulfills(contractName,obj)', function() {

    it('throws if contractName is not in the registry',function() {
        function expectThrow(contractName) {
            expect(function() {
                registry.fulfills(contractName,{});
            }).toThrow(new Error(
                registry.getMessageForNameNotRegistered(contractName)));
        }
        [undefined,'abc'].forEach(expectThrow);
    });
});
```

In previous chapters, you saw how exposing an object's error messages allows unit tests to verify the exact errors. Sometimes, error messages include variable data. To keep the code DRY, the procedure for incorporating the variable data in a message is put in a function, `getMessageForNameNotRegistered`.

You can make the test pass (see Figure 16-3) with the code highlighted in Listing 16-8.

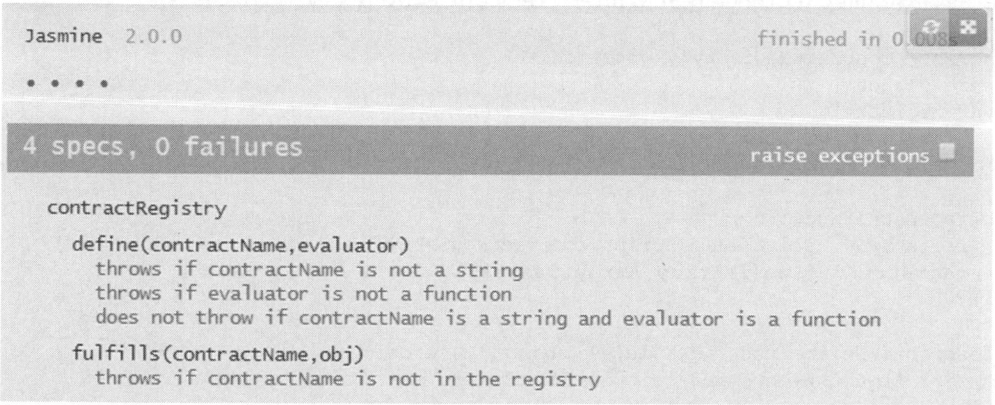

```
Jasmine  2.0.0                                        finished in 0.008s

• • • •

4 specs, 0 failures                                   raise exceptions ■

  contractRegistry
    define(contractName,evaluator)
      throws if contractName is not a string
      throws if evaluator is not a function
      does not throw if contractName is a string and evaluator is a function
    fulfills(contractName,obj)
      throws if contractName is not in the registry
```

FIGURE 16-3

LISTING 16-8: Make fulfills fail if contractName is not registered (code filename: Interfaces\
contractRegistry_02.js)

```javascript
var ReliableJavaScript = ReliableJavaScript || {};
ReliableJavaScript.contractRegistry = function() {
  'use strict';
  var registry = {};

  return {
    define: function define(contractName, evaluator) {
      // *** Omitted for clarity. ***
    },

    fulfills: function fulfills(contractName, obj) {
      if (!registry[contractName]) {
        throw new Error(this.getMessageForNameNotRegistered(contractName));
      }
    },

    messages: {
      nameMustBeString: 'The contract name must be a string',
      evaluatorMustBeFunction: 'The evaluator must be a function',
      nameMustBeRegistered: "The contract '_' is not in the registry",
    },

    getMessageForNameNotRegistered: function getMessageForNameNotRegistered(
    contractName) {
      return this.messages.nameMustBeRegistered.replace('_',contractName);
    },
  };
};
```

The new object at the top, *registry*, will hold the registrations, but so far define isn't putting anything there because no unit test has demanded it. This will finally catch up to you when you attempt to make the next tests (see Listing 16-9) pass.

LISTING 16-9: Tests that the fulfills method returns true or false depending on whether the contract is fulfilled (code filename: Interfaces\contractRegistry_03_tests.js)

```javascript
describe('contractRegistry', function() {
  'use strict';
  var registry,
      isArray = 'isArray',
      ary = [1,2,3];

  beforeEach(function() {
    registry = ReliableJavaScript.contractRegistry();
    registry.define(isArray,Array.isArray);
  });

  describe('define(contractName,evaluator)', function() {
    /*** Argument-checking omitted for clarity. ***/
  });

  describe('fulfills(contractName,obj)', function() {

    /*** Previously discussed test omitted. ***/


    it('returns true if the object fulfills the named contract',function() {
      expect(registry.fulfills(isArray,ary)).toBe(true);
    });
    it('returns false if the object does not fulfill the contract', function()
{
      expect(registry.fulfills(isArray,'not an array')).toBe(false);
    });
  });
});
```

The tests verify that `fulfills` returns `true` or `false` appropriately. They use a contract whose name is stored in the *isArray* variable. Near the top of the listing, note the following line:

```javascript
registry.define(isArray,Array.isArray);
```

It uses JavaScript's `Array.isArray` method as `isArray`'s contract-evaluator. Quick, lazy, and you know it works. Gotta love it, right?

The tests are in all kinds of hurt (see Figure 16-4) but are instantly set right (see Figure 16-5) when you add just one line to `define` and one to `fulfills`, to use the `registry` object installed earlier. The working code appears in Listing 16-10.

LISTING 16-10: Finishing the define method (code filename: Interfaces\contractRegistry_03.js)

```javascript
var ReliableJavaScript = ReliableJavaScript || {};
ReliableJavaScript.contractRegistry = function() {
  'use strict';
  var registry = {};

  return {
```

```
define: function define(contractName, evaluator) {
  // *** Argument checking omitted. ***
  registry[contractName] = evaluator;
},

fulfills: function fulfills(contractName, obj) {
  // *** Argument checking omitted. ***
  return registry[contractName](obj);
},

// *** snip ***
};
};
```

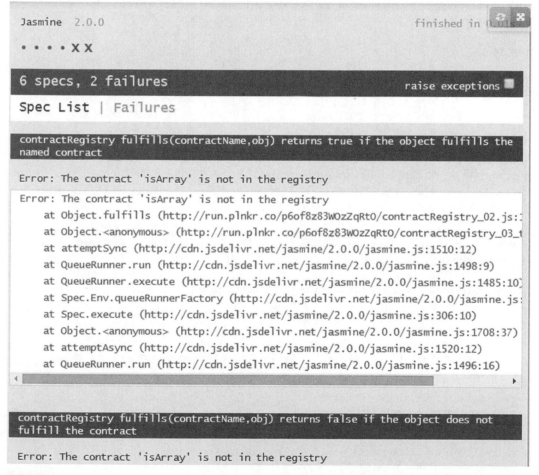

FIGURE 16-4

Steps 1 and 2 of the outline at the top of this section are now complete. Next, it will be useful to have a method that asserts that a contract is fulfilled, throwing an error if it is not.

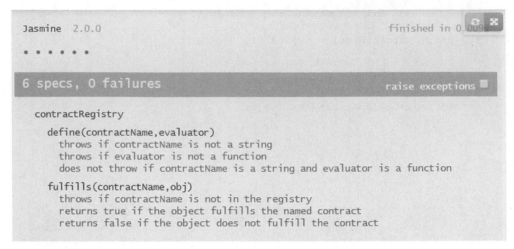

FIGURE 16-5

Asserting That a Contract Is Fulfilled

The assert method is similar to fulfills:

```
function assert(contractName, obj)
```

It should use the fulfills method to determine whether the contract is fulfilled, rather than duplicating the code. A test that ensures this also ensures that the argument-checking you have already put in fulfills will be carried into assert. That is the first test of Listing 16-11. The other two verify the core functionality of assert.

> **LISTING 16-11:** Testing the assert method (code filename: Interfaces\contractRegistry_04_tests.js [excerpt])

```javascript
describe('assert(contractName, obj)', function() {

  it('is based on fulfills(contractName, obj)', function() {
    spyOn(registry,'fulfills').and.callThrough();
    registry.assert(isArray,ary);
    expect(registry.fulfills).toHaveBeenCalledWith(isArray,ary);
  });

  it('does not throw if obj fulfills contractName', function() {
    registry.assert(isArray,ary);
  });

  it('throws if obj does not fulfill contractName', function() {
    var notAnArray = 'abc';
    expect(function() {
      registry.assert(isArray,notAnArray);
    }).toThrow(new Error(
      registry.getMessageForFailedContract(isArray,notAnArray)));
  });
});
```

Just a few lines make the tests pass, as shown in Listing 16-12.

LISTING 16-12: The assert method (code filename: Interfaces\contractRegistry_04.js)

```javascript
var ReliableJavaScript = ReliableJavaScript || {};
ReliableJavaScript.contractRegistry = function() {
  'use strict';
  var registry = {};

  return {
    // *** define and fulfill methods omitted ***

    assert: function assert(contractName,obj) {
      if (!this.fulfills(contractName,obj)) {
        throw new Error(this.getMessageForFailedContract(contractName,obj));
      }
    },

    messages: {
      // *** Other messages omitted ***
      failedContract: "The following does not fulfill contract '_': "
    },

    // *** snip ***

    getMessageForFailedContract: function getMessageForFailedContract(
    contractName, obj) {
      return this.messages.failedContract
          .replace('_',contractName)+ obj;
    }
  };
};
```

Bypassing Contract Enforcement

You might like the option to switch off all enforcement of contracts once your product has passed QA, particularly if your evaluator functions are time-consuming. (Keep in mind that you're free to make them much more elaborate than `Array.isArray`!)

The easiest, most efficient way to do this is to place an object's contracts in a separate `.js` file, and simply exclude that file from the production release. You will see an example of this in the next section.

With four of the requirements crossed off the list, only one remains.

Creating an Aspect to Enforce a Contract on a Returned (Created) Object

You could use what has been developed so far to enforce a contract on any object you create. For example, you could define and assert the two attendee-related contracts in the `attendee` module, as shown in Listing 16-13.

LISTING 16-13: Defining and asserting contracts on attendee (code filename: Interfaces\attendee_01.js)

```javascript
var Conference = Conference || {};
Conference.attendee = function(firstName, lastName, registry){
  'use strict';

  var // *** snip ***
    attendeePersonalInfo = 'Conference.attendee.personalInfo',
    attendeeCheckInManagement = 'Conference.attendee.checkInManagement';

  function fulfillsPersonalInfo(att) {
    return typeof att.setId === 'function' &&
           typeof att.getId === 'function' &&
           typeof att.getFullName === 'function';
  }

  function fulfillsCheckInManagement(att) {
    return typeof att.getId === 'function' &&
           typeof att.isCheckedIn === 'function' &&
           typeof att.checkIn === 'function' &&
           typeof att.undoCheckIn === 'function' &&
           typeof att.setCheckInNumber === 'function' &&
           typeof att.getCheckInNumber === 'function';
  }

  registry.define(attendeePersonalInfo, fulfillsPersonalInfo);
  registry.define(attendeeCheckInManagement, fulfillsCheckInManagement);

  var ret = {
    setId: function(id) {
      attendeeId = id;
    },
    getId: function() {
      return attendeeId;
    },

    // *** Other functions omitted for clarity. ***
  };

  registry.assert(attendeePersonalInfo, ret);
  registry.assert(attendeeCheckInManagement, ret);

  return ret;
};

// Sample usage
var registry = ReliableJavaScript.contractRegistry();
var a = Conference.attendee('Rock','Star', registry); // Does not throw.
```

That works, but it suffers from the drawback that the contract-enforcement is embedded in the object itself, somewhat violating the Single Responsibility Principle. Many developers would prefer an aspect-oriented solution.

The `attachReturnValidator` method that will be developed shortly attaches an aspect to a function that creates an object, where that object is supposed to conform to an interface. It looks like this:

```
function attachReturnValidator(funcName, funcObj, contractName)
```

With that function available, you can place the contract-related code outside of `attendee`. If you put such code in a separate file, then after QA is complete you can exclude the file from the shipped version, eliminating the overhead from the release.

Listing 16-14 shows how the `attendee` module from Listing 16-3, which has no injection or use of the registry, can be modified with an aspect thanks to `attachReturnValidator`. The modification is done through a separate file, `attendeeContracts.js`, which you would not include in the production release. It contains a function that creates the contracts for the two "interfaces" and then attaches aspects to `Conference.attendee` that ensure that any object it returns conforms to those interfaces.

LISTING 16-14: Using an aspect to assert a contract on attendee (code filename: Interfaces\attendeeContracts.js)

```javascript
var Conference = Conference || {};

// Call this function to install aspects that will verify that
// attendees created by Conference.attendee(firstName, lastName)
// are valid.
Conference.attendeeContracts = function attendeeContracts(registry) {
  'use strict';

  var attendeePersonalInfo = 'Conference.attendee.personalInfo',
      attendeeCheckInManagement = 'Conference.attendee.checkInManagement';

  function fulfillsPersonalInfo(att) {
    return typeof att.setId === 'function' &&
           typeof att.getId === 'function' &&
           typeof att.getFullName === 'function';
  }

  function fulfillsCheckInManagement(att) {
    return typeof att.getId === 'function' &&
           typeof att.isCheckedIn === 'function' &&
           typeof att.checkIn === 'function' &&
           typeof att.undoCheckIn === 'function' &&
           typeof att.setCheckInNumber === 'function' &&
           typeof att.getCheckInNumber === 'function';
  }

  registry.define(attendeePersonalInfo, fulfillsPersonalInfo);
  registry.define(attendeeCheckInManagement, fulfillsCheckInManagement);

  registry.attachReturnValidator('attendee',Conference,
                                 attendeePersonalInfo);
  registry.attachReturnValidator('attendee',Conference,
                                 attendeeCheckInManagement);
```

continues

LISTING 16-14 *(continued)*

```
};

// Sample usage:
// In application startup, instantiate a registry and attach aspects.
var registry = ReliableJavaScript.contractRegistry();
Conference.attendeeContracts(registry);
// Aspect installations for other modules would follow.

// Later, when an attendee is created, the aspects will ensure
// that it is valid.
var a = Conference.attendee('Rock','Star'); // Does not throw.
```

> **NOTE** *The sample code that invokes* attendeeContracts *at the bottom of Listing 16-14 is just to give you the general idea. A much cleaner procedure will be developed in Chapter 17.*

Now to develop the attachReturnValidator method.

The contractRegistry_tests.js download for this chapter contains the error-checking tests. Of more interest are the tests of the aspect functionality (see Listing 16-15).

LISTING 16-15: Tests of the return value-checking aspect (code filename: Interfaces\ contractRegistry_tests.js [excerpt])

```
describe('attachReturnValidator(funcName, funcObj, contractName)',
function() {
  var funcName = 'func',
      funcObj,
      returnValue = [1,2,3];

  beforeEach(function() {
    funcObj = {},
    funcObj[funcName] = function() {
      return returnValue;
    };
  });

  describe('aspect functionality', function() {

    it('returns the return value if it fulfills the contract',function() {
      registry.attachReturnValidator(funcName,funcObj,isArray);
      expect(funcObj[funcName]()).toEqual(returnValue);
    });

    it('throws if the return value does not fulfill the contract',
    function(){

      var isNumber = 'isNumber';
      registry.define(isNumber, function isNumber(ret) {
        return typeof ret === 'number';
```

```
      });
      registry.attachReturnValidator(funcName, funcObj, isNumber);
      expect(function() {
        funcObj[funcName]();
      }).toThrow(new Error(
          registry.getMessageForFailedContract(isNumber,returnValue)));
      });
    });
  });
```

The tests use an object, `funcObj`, and its member called `funcName`, which are set up in the `beforeEach`. The call `funcObj[funcName]()` returns an array (`returnValue`), so it conforms to the `Array.isArray` evaluator set up at the top of the test module, which you have already seen.

The first test is straightforward. After applying the aspect to the target function, it verifies that a call through the aspect to target returns the value unscathed.

In the second test, a different return validator is attached—one that expects the return value to be a number. When the return value turns out to be an array, the aspect should throw an error.

Skipping all the TDD steps with which you're now very familiar, Listing 16-16 shows the completed `attachReturnValidator` function. After some argument-checking, it uses the `Aop.around` method introduced in Chapter 2 to capture the target function's return value, assert that it fulfills the contract, and then return it.

LISTING 16-16: The attachReturnValidator method (code filename: Interfaces\contractRegistry.js [excerpt])

```
attachReturnValidator: function attachReturnValidator(
funcName, funcObj, contractName) {
  var self = this;
  if (typeof funcName !== 'string') {
    throw new Error(self.messages.funcNameMustBeString);
  }
  if (typeof funcObj !== 'object') {
    throw new Error(self.messages.funcObjMustBeObject);
  }
  if (typeof contractName !== 'string') {
    throw new Error(self.messages.nameMustBeString);
  }

  Aop.around(funcName,
    function(targetInfo) {
      var ret = Aop.next(targetInfo);
      self.assert(contractName,ret);
      return ret;
    }, funcObj);
}
```

The completed `contractRegistry` allows you to assert anything you wish about a newly created object, either as an aspect (refer to Listing 16-14) or in the object's code itself (refer to Listing 16-13).

If you prefer the aspect-oriented approach, you may wish to review the Module Pattern and Functional Inheritance in Chapter 3, as both of those object-creation patterns are aspect-friendly.

SUMMARY:

Interfaces, a staple of strongly typed languages, confer benefits that JavaScript programmers might secretly wish they could have. These include:

➤ Clarifying what consumers of a class can expect

➤ Detecting unwanted changes to a class's semantics

➤ Enabling elegant design patterns, which make your code more flexible and robust

The Interface Segregation Principle further simplifies the work of an object's consumers and helps the object's developers scope out ramifications of any changes.

In this chapter, you worked through the development of the `contractRegistry`, an object that can define and enforce interfaces JavaScript-style.

The next chapter takes this one step further, using the `contractRegistry` to validate arguments passed to a function. With both the inputs and the output guarded by contracts, you will have taken a significant step toward creating reliable JavaScript.

17

Ensuring Correct Argument Types

WHAT'S IN THIS CHAPTER?

➤ Augmenting Chapter 16's ContractRegistry to handle argument validation

➤ Packaging the new facility in an aspect

➤ Creating libraries of contracts, importing them into your application, and attaching them to your functions in aspects

➤ Comparing the ContractRegistry with TypeScript, a popular compile-time type-checker

WROX.COM CODE DOWNLOADS FOR THIS CHAPTER

You can find the wrox.com code downloads for this chapter at www.wrox.com/go/reliablejavascript on the Download Code tab. The files are in the Chapter 17 download and individually named according to the filenames noted throughout this chapter.

In strongly typed languages, you always know what you're going to get. If a function is declared with an integer parameter, you can be sure that an integer is exactly what will come across the call boundary. With this sort of rock-solid assurance, it is no wonder that mainframe banking systems, transportation systems, and especially defense systems are implemented in strongly typed languages such as Java, C#, COBOL, and Ada.

If Java is a banker and Ada a general, JavaScript is a scrappy entrepreneur, creatively making deals and attracting new customers. It is entirely fitting that JavaScript has become the language of the customer-facing portion of e-commerce, where agility, efficiency, and expressiveness are highly prized.

Sometimes an entrepreneur hits the big-time and decides to become a venture capitalist. In that world, being creative and having a sharp eye for opportunity are no longer enough. Increasingly, you rely on the numbers. Contracts replace handshakes. Discipline becomes the order of the day.

That is the station to which JavaScript has been promoted. Called on to manage larger and more-complex systems, it needs to acquire the discipline of a venture capitalist while maintaining the creativity of an entrepreneur: Seize the opportunities but manage the risks.

UNDERSTANDING THE OPPORTUNITIES AND RISKS POSED BY JAVASCRIPT'S TYPE-FREE PARAMETERS

Applications written in strongly typed languages devote a surprising portion of their code to managing those types. Classes are described with interfaces. Database tables are mapped to entity types. Services are guaranteed with data contracts. Data are conveyed from here to there with data-transfer objects. It all adds up to a lot of overhead.

JavaScript, with its nearly type-free semantics, presents a great opportunity for concision and elegance.

Unfortunately, while less code usually means less opportunity for error, in this case the code that is jettisoned is precisely the code that guarded against errors in the first place!

Of particular concern are functions' parameters and return values. These are the boundaries between one developer's code and another's. As such, they represent a particularly vulnerable site for misunderstandings and mistakes.

> **NOTE** *Parameters and return values are the boundaries between one developer's code and another's. That puts them at high risk for misunderstanding and mistakes.*

Like a good venture capitalist, you want to manage the risk. But how can you do this while maintaining JavaScript's entrepreneurial edge? You want the security of a contract but with minimal drag on the executing code.

EXTENDING THE CONTRACTREGISTRY TO CHECK ARGUMENTS

The last chapter was the beginning of just such an approach. You saw how to create a `ContractRegistry` that could validate a return value, ensuring it met whatever criteria you cared to specify. Now, you'll see how to check whether a function's incoming arguments meet expectations.

Chapter 16's `contractRegistry` used the module-at-will pattern from Chapter 3, which had the advantages of compactness and familiarity. In this chapter, the registry has been changed so its objects are created with the new keyword, and most of its methods are on the prototype rather than declared in the constructor. This lets you compare how the same idea is implemented in the module-at-will and 'new' paradigms. See, for example, the assert method and the messages object.

Scoping Out the Task

The ContractRegistry from the last chapter offered the following functions:

➤ define: Defines a contract by name

➤ fulfills: Tells whether an object fulfills a contract

➤ assert: Throws an error if an object does not fulfill a contract

➤ attachReturnValidator: Attaches an aspect that calls assert on a function's return value

To support argument-checking, you will add the following functions in this chapter:

➤ multipleFulfills: Like fulfills, but for multiple objects and multiple sets of contracts

➤ multipleAssert: Like assert, but for multiple objects and contracts

➤ attachArgumentsValidator: Attaches an aspect to a function to assert that incoming arguments meet expectations

Finally, one more function will prove convenient for installing libraries of contracts: defineMultiple iterates through an array of objects and defines a contract based on each one.

Determining Whether Every Variable in a Set Fulfills Its Contract

The multipleFulfills method will be the workhorse of the argument validator. It will have two parameters: a validator and the set of arguments to validate:

```
function multipleFulfills(validator, args)
```

The args parameter can be any array-like object. Typically, it will be the arguments to a function.

For flexibility and convenience, validator can be any of the following:

➤ A **string**, which will be interpreted as the name of a contract registered with define. In this case, the args parameter (the array as a whole) must fulfill the contract.

➤ An **array of strings**, in which case life gets a whole lot more complicated. Each string in the array is a comma-separated sequence of contract names. If the elements of args in the corresponding positions fulfill their contracts, multipleFulfills will return true. If not, multipleFulfills will try the next element in the validator array. If there are no more elements to try, false will be returned. In other words, the contracts are considered fulfilled if any element in the validator array contains a set of contracts that match the args.

➤ A **function**, which will be called with args and should return true or false. This is provided as a catch-all in case the string or string array is not sufficient.

To limit this chapter to a reasonable length, the error-checking that should comprise the first tests is relegated to this chapter's downloads. Listing 17-1 skips ahead to the simplest positive test, where validator is the actual validation function.

> **LISTING 17-1:** Testing multipleFulfills for a function validator (code filename: Parameters\ ContractRegistry_07_tests.js)

```javascript
describe('multipleFulfills(validator,args)', function() {

  describe('when validator is a function',function() {
    var args = ['a','b'];

    it('returns the result of the validator called on args', function() {
      function isLength2() {
        return arguments.length === 2;
      }
      function isLength3() {
        return arguments.length === 3;
      }
      expect(registry.multipleFulfills(isLength2,args)).toBe(true);
      expect(registry.multipleFulfills(isLength3,args)).toBe(false);
    });

    it('calls validator with the registry as the context',function() {
      function calledOnRegistry() {
        expect(this).toBe(registry);
      }
      registry.multipleFulfills(calledOnRegistry,args);
    });
  });
});
```

In the first test, both possible results from the validator, `true` and `false`, are tested. Either one alone would not have been sufficient. (How would you know that `true`, for example, had not been returned by coincidence?) Listing 17-2 will show an alternative technique.

As you will read in the next chapter, it is also important to verify the context of anything you do with `call` or `apply`. That is the subject of the second test. The implementation is simplicity itself.

> **LISTING 17-2:** Implementing multipleFulfills for a function validator (code filename: Parameters\ContractRegistry_07_tests.js)

```javascript
ReliableJavaScript.ContractRegistry.prototype.multipleFulfills =
function multipleFulfills(validator, args) {
  var self = this;

  // *** Argument validation omitted for clarity ***

  if (typeof validator === 'function' ) {
    return validator.apply(self,args);
  }
};
```

The next-most simple case is a validator that consists of a single string (a contract name). In the following test (Listing 17-3), note the funky *returnFromFulfills* variable. This trick is an alternative to checking both the `true` and `false` cases. The test only wants to verify that `multipleFulfills` returns *whatever* the underlying `fulfills` returns. Technically, it doesn't and shouldn't care about the type. It would be an understatement to say that it's unlikely that the particular value in *returnFromFulfills* would be returned by coincidence, so the one value is sufficient.

LISTING 17-3: Testing multipleFulfills for a string validator (code filename: Parameters\ContractRegistry_08_tests.js)

```javascript
describe('when validator is a string',function() {
  it('returns result of fulfills(validator,args)',
  function() {
    var validator='aContractName',
        args = ['a','b'],
        returnFromFulfills = 'this could be true or false';
    spyOn(registry,'fulfills').and.returnValue(returnFromFulfills);
    expect(registry.multipleFulfills(validator,args))
      .toBe(returnFromFulfills);
    expect(registry.fulfills).toHaveBeenCalledWith(validator,args);
  });
});
```

The implementation in Listing 17-4 is no more difficult than for the function-validator case.

LISTING 17-4: Implementing multipleFulfills for a string validator (code filename: Parameters\ContractRegsitry_08.js)

```javascript
ReliableJavaScript.ContractRegistry.prototype.multipleFulfills =
function multipleFulfills(validator, args) {
  var self = this;

  // *** Argument validation omitted for clarity ***

  if (typeof validator === 'string' ) {
    return self.fulfills(validator,args);
  }
  if (typeof validator === 'function' ) {
    return validator.apply(self,args);
  }
};
```

Now for the most complicated case, where the validator is an array of strings. Recall that each string will be a comma-separated sequence of contract names that correspond positionally to the elements of the `args` parameter. If `args` fulfills the comma-separated contracts in any `element`, `args`'s contract is considered fulfilled overall.

With a test-driven approach, you would start with the simplest case: an empty array. Although this is a simple case, the desired behavior is far from clear. Should `multipleFulfills` return `true` on the premise of no harm, no foul? Or should it return `false` because no set of contracts has been fulfilled? With a non–test-driven approach, this question probably would not even come up. You would code something that handled an array and, depending on your algorithm, the empty-array case would silently turn out one way or the other. Consumers of your `ContractRegistry`, lacking any unit tests to read, would be equally unlikely to consider this edge case. The odds of correct behavior would be 50-50.

Forced to make a choice, you decide to be generous and return `true` (see Listing 17-5).

LISTING 17-5: Testing multipleFulfills for a validator that is an empty array (code filename: Parameters\ContractRegistry_09_tests.js)

```
describe('when validator is an array',function() {
  it('returns true if the array is empty', function() {
    expect(registry.multipleFulfills([],[1,2,3]))
      .toBe(true);
  });
});
```

The implementation is even easier than what you've coded so far (see Listing 17-6).

LISTING 17-6: Implementing multipleFulfills for an empty-array validator array (code filename: Parameters\ContractRegistry_09.js)

```
ReliableJavaScript.ContractRegistry.prototype.multipleFulfills =
function multipleFulfills(validator, args) {
  var self = this;

  // *** Argument validation omitted for clarity ***

  if (typeof validator === 'string' ) {
    return self.fulfills(validator,args);
  }
  if (Array.isArray(validator)) {
    if (validator.length===0) {
      return true;
    }
  }
  if (typeof validator === 'function' ) {
    return validator.apply(self,args);
  }
};
```

Now it's time to get down to business with an array that has elements. There are many ways you could do this, but you decide that each element will have `name` and `evaluator` properties for the contract name and its evaluator.

The first test, again, should be the simple case of just one element in the array. It's a good thing the situation is simple because the test turns out to be a little involved (see Listing 17-7).

LISTING 17-7: Testing multipleFulfills for an array with one element (code filename: Parameters\ContractRegistry_10_tests.js)

```
describe('when validator is an array',function() {
  function passOrFail(contractName, arg) {
    return contractName==='passes';
  }
  it('returns true if the array is empty', function() {
    expect(registry.multipleFulfills([],[1,2,3]))
      .toBe(true);
  });

  it('returns true if validator is a single-element array whose ' +
    'contracts all pass', function() {
    var validator=['passes,passes,passes'],
        args = [1,2,3];
    spyOn(registry,'fulfills').and.callFake(passOrFail);
    expect(registry.multipleFulfills(validator,args)).toBe(true);
    expect(registry.fulfills).toHaveBeenCalledWith('passes',1);
    expect(registry.fulfills).toHaveBeenCalledWith('passes',2);
    expect(registry.fulfills).toHaveBeenCalledWith('passes',3);
  });

  it('returns false if validator is a single-element array that ' +
    'contains one failing contract', function() {
    var validator=['passes,fails,passes'],
        args = [1,2,3];
    spyOn(registry,'fulfills').and.callFake(passOrFail);
    expect(registry.multipleFulfills(validator,args)).toBe(false);
    expect(registry.fulfills).toHaveBeenCalledWith('passes',1);
    expect(registry.fulfills).toHaveBeenCalledWith('fails',2);
    // Only 2 calls necessary because should have settled on false
    // after the failure on the second argument
    expect(registry.fulfills.calls.count()).toBe(2);
  });

  it('evaluates no more contracts than necessary in a ' +
    ' single-element array', function() {
    var validator=['passes,fails,passes'],
        args = [1,2,3];
    spyOn(registry,'fulfills').and.callFake(passOrFail);
    expect(registry.multipleFulfills(validator,args)).toBe(false);
    // Only 2 calls necessary because should have settled on false
    // after the failure on the second argument
    expect(registry.fulfills.calls.count()).toBe(2);
  });
});
```

There are three new tests: the first with a validator array containing three contract elements that will all pass, the second with one element that fails, and a third to ensure that contract-evaluation stops once failure is known.

Implementation seems simple enough (see Listing 17-8). In fact, it's so simple that you decide to get a jump on what's coming up and code the loop through *all* elements.

> **LISTING 17-8:** Implementing multipleFulfills for a validator array that has one element (code filename: Parameters\ContractRegistry_10a.js)

```javascript
ReliableJavaScript.ContractRegistry.prototype.multipleFulfills =
function multipleFulfills(validator, args) {
  var self = this,
      index;

  // Evaluate one element in the validator array (only called when
  // validator is an array).
  function validateWithContractNameString(v) {
    var ix,
        contractNames = v.split(',');
    for (ix=0; ix<contractNames.length; ++ix) {
      if (!self.fulfills(contractNames[ix],args[ix])) {
        return false;
      }
    }
    return true;
  }

  // *** Argument validation omitted for clarity ***

  if (typeof validator === 'string' ) {
    return self.fulfills(validator,args);
  }
  if (Array.isArray(validator)) {
    for (index=0; index<validator.length; ++index) {
      if (validateWithContractNameString(validator[index])) {
        return true;
      }
    }
    return false;
  }
  if (typeof validator === 'function' ) {
    return validator.apply(self,args);
  }
};
```

Note the `validateWithContractNameString` function at the top of `multipleFulfills`. Its logic has been abstracted out of the loop to make the loop (bolded near the bottom) clearer.

Confident that the new code works (and it does), you run the tests and get an error! Without looking at Figure 17-1, can you guess what it is?

The error is in the "trivial" case of an empty array. This shows the importance of bothering with the so-called trivial test cases! It also shows what can happen when you code ahead of your tests: The looping logic, which was not necessary to make the test pass, was the tall grass in which the error hid.

Still, it's no big deal, and you can quickly correct it with the snippet in Listing 17-9. Chastened, you also remove the looping.

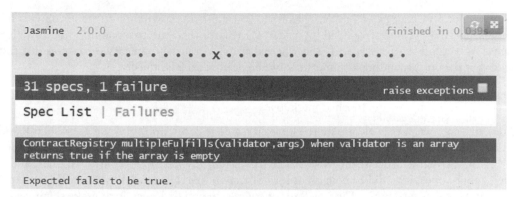

FIGURE 17-1

LISTING 17-9: Corrected implementation of multipleFulfills for a validator array that has one element (code filename: Parameters\ContractRegistry_10b.js)

```
if (Array.isArray(validator)) {
  return validator.length===0 ||
    validateWithContractNameString(validator[0]);
}
```

Now the tests pass (see Figure 17-2).

```
Jasmine  2.0.0                                          finished in 0.03

• • • • • • • • • • • • • • • • • • • • • • • • • • • • • • • •

31 specs, 0 failures                                    raise exceptions ■

  multipleFulfills(validator,args)

    argument validation
      throws if validator is not a string, array of strings, or function
      throws if args is not array-like

    when validator is a string
      returns result of fulfills(validator,args)

    when validator is an array
      returns true if the array is empty
      returns true if validator is a single-element array whose contracts all pass
      returns false if validator is a single-element array that contains one failing
      contract pass
      evaluates no more contracts than necessary in a single-element array

    when validator is a function
      returns the result of the validator called on args
      calls validator with the registry as the context
```

FIGURE 17-2

Suddenly aware of how edge cases can cause trouble, you think about what to do if the commas in the comma-separated list are surrounded by spaces. Or what if there are two commas in a row? It makes sense to trim off the extra spaces, and where there's no contract name (two commas in a row) you decide that the corresponding argument should be deemed to pass muster.

Does this make you realize anything else? Maybe something that is missing from ContractRegistry's supposedly finished methods?

A good test-driven developer is always on the lookout for edge cases, and thinking about blank and trimmed contract names might make you realize that the last chapter didn't consider them! (If you did think of that, congratulations!) Because multipleFulfills will trim its contract names, and not process empty ones, it would be consistent for define and fulfills to do something similar. You code some tests to verify this. The tests fail, of course, so you fix the code to make them pass. Because define and fulfills are the only functions with direct access to the private *registry* variable, that should do it. These changes are in the final downloads for this chapter.

> **NOTE** *A good test-driven developer is always on the lookout for edge cases. When he finds one, he considers whether it might be untested elsewhere.*

As you consider multipleFulfills, the highlighted lines in Listing 17-10 show what's needed. The download file ContractRegistry_11_tests.js has the new tests, which are not of interest here.

LISTING 17-10: Handling spaces and empty contract names in multipleFulfills (code filename: Parameters\ContractRegistry_11.js)

```
ReliableJavaScript.ContractRegistry.prototype.multipleFulfills =
function multipleFulfills(validator, args) {

  function validateWithContractNameString(v) {
    var ix,
        contractNames = v.split(/ *, */);
    for (ix=0; ix<contractNames.length; ++ix) {
      if (contractNames[ix].length===0) {
        continue;
      }
      if (!self.fulfills(contractNames[ix],args[ix])) {
        return false;
      }
    }
  }
  return true;
}
// *** The remainder of the function is unchanged. ***
```

Finally, you consider the case where there are more elements in the args array than comma-separated contracts. (There is no need to test the opposite case, where args is too short, because JavaScript will simply provide them as undefined when you access them.) This test, too, is the ContractRegistry_11_tests.js download. No new code was necessary to make it pass.

With all of that behind you, you are ready to handle the case of multiple validator strings. Recall that args should be said to fulfill its contractual obligations if even one of the validator strings represents a fulfilled set of contracts. You've already tested all the crazy conditions for individual contract strings, so you allow yourself to make this test simple (see Listing 17-11).

> **NOTE** *If you thoroughly test the single-element cases, you can often afford to test just the structure of the multiple-element scenarios.*

LISTING 17-11: Testing multiple contract strings in multipleFulfills (code filename: Parameters\ContractRegistry_12_tests.js)

```
it('allows args to fulfill any one of the elements in the array of ' +
'comma-separated strings of contract names', function() {
  var validator=[
        'passes,fails',
        'passes,passes',
        'fails,fails'
      ],
      args = [1,2];
  spyOn(registry,'fulfills').and.callFake(passOrFail);
  expect(registry.multipleFulfills(validator,args)).toBe(true);
  expect(registry.fulfills.calls.count()).toBe(4);
});
```

The implementation shows that you weren't too far off in the earlier looping (see Listing 17-12).

LISTING 17-12: Supporting multiple contract strings (code filename: Parameters\ContractRegistry_12.js)

```
ReliableJavaScript.ContractRegistry.prototype.multipleFulfills =
function multipleFulfills(validator, args) {

  // *** Other code is unchanged from previous listings ***

  if (typeof validator === 'string' ) {
    return self.fulfills(validator,args);
  }
  if (Array.isArray(validator)) {
    for (index=0; index<validator.length; ++index) {
      if (validateWithContractNameString(validator[index])) {
        return true;
      }
    }
    return validator.length===0;
  }
  if (typeof validator === 'function' ) {
    return validator.apply(self,args);
  }
};
```

All of the testing for `multipleFulfills` has laid a very solid foundation for `multipleAssert`, which is the next stage.

Asserting That Every Variable in a Set Fulfills Its Contract

Just as `assert` was nothing more than a test-and-throw wrapper for `fulfills`, `multipleAssert` is a test-and-throw wrapper for `multipleFulfills`. This makes the tests easy. Although the tests were developed one by one, and the code implemented accordingly, Listing 17-13 shows all of them together.

LISTING 17-13: Tests for multipleAssert (code filename: Parameters\ContractRegistry_13_tests.js)

```
describe('multipleAssert(validator,args)', function() {

  it('throws if multipleFulfills(validator,args) return false', function() {
    var validator='contractName',
        args = [123];
    spyOn(registry, 'multipleFulfills').and.returnValue(false);
    expect(function() {
      registry.multipleAssert(validator,args);
    }).toThrow(new Error(ContractRegistry.messages.argsFailedContract));
    expect(registry.multipleFulfills).toHaveBeenCalledWith(validator,args);
  });

  it('does not throw if multipleFulfills(validator,args) return true',
  function() {
    var validator='contractName',
        args = [123];
    spyOn(registry, 'multipleFulfills').and.returnValue(true);
    registry.multipleAssert(validator,args); // does not throw
    expect(registry.multipleFulfills).toHaveBeenCalledWith(validator,args);
  });

  it('returns the registry, enabling chaining', function() {
    expect(registry.multipleAssert(isArray, [])).toBe(registry);
  });
});
```

The first two tests, for the `false` and `true` cases respectively, spy on the underlying `multipleFulfills` and make it return the appropriate Boolean. The use of a spy isolates this test from any errors in `multipleFulfills`, but it then becomes important to verify that `multipleFulfills` is called with the correct arguments.

> **NOTE** *When using a spy to force a function to return a value, you should usually verify that the function is called with the correct arguments.*

The third test will be familiar from Chapter 15. It just verifies that `multipleAssert` is chainable. As you would expect, the implementation is a simple call to `multipleFulfills`, followed by `return this` (see Listing 17-14).

```
ReliableJavaScript.ContractRegistry.prototype.multipleAssert =
function multipleAssert(validator,args) {
  if (!this.multipleFulfills(validator,args)) {
    throw new Error(
      ReliableJavaScript.ContractRegistry.messages.argsFailedContract);
  }
  return this;
};
```

You now have everything necessary for checking the arguments passed to a function. In many situations, it will be most convenient to use an aspect for the task.

Packaging Argument-Checking in an Aspect

The next function in `ContractRegistry` is `attachArgumentsValidator`. It has this signature:

```
function attachArgumentsValidator(funcName, funcObj, validator)
```

The parameters `funcName` and `funcObj` are exactly as they were in `Aop.js`: the name of a function and the object or namespace in which it is defined. The `validator` parameter is the same as for `multipleAssert`.

Let's skip over the error-checking tests (which you *would* write first, of course!) and jump right to the tests of aspect functionality.

The arguments validator is a "before" aspect, but the return validator in Chapter 16 was an "after" aspect. That means you face different challenges in testing. Instead of testing that the underlying returned value flows properly through the aspect *to* the calling code, you will test that arguments make their way *from* the calling code to the aspect. To be thorough, you should also test that the underlying function's return value is returned unchanged. Those are the tests in Listing 17-15.

```
describe('attachArgumentsValidator(funcName, funcObj, validator)',
  function() {

    describe('aspect functionality', function() {
      var obj;
      beforeEach(function() {
        obj = {
          prop: 123,
          func: function func() {
            return arguments[0]+arguments[1];
          }
```

continues

LISTING 17-15 *(continued)*

```
        };
    });

    it('calls registry.multipleAssert(validator,arguments)', function() {
      function validator(args) {
        return this.prop === 123;
      }
      registry.attachArgumentsValidator('func',obj,validator);
      spyOn(registry,'multipleAssert').and.callFake(function(val,args) {
        expect(val).toBe(validator);
        expect(args.length).toBe(2);
        expect(args[0]).toBe('a');
        expect(args[1]).toBe('b');
      });
      obj.func('a','b');
      expect(registry.multipleAssert).toHaveBeenCalled();
    });

    it('allows the function to execute and return normally', function() {
      function validator(args) {
        return true;
      }
      registry.attachArgumentsValidator('func',obj,validator);
      spyOn(registry,'multipleAssert').and.returnValue(undefined);
      expect(obj.func('a','b')).toBe('ab');
    });
  });
});
```

And why not make `attachArgumentsValidator` chainable so you can do more things with the registry directly? That would be the test in Listing 17-16.

LISTING 17-16: Testing that attachArgumentsValidator is chainable (code filename: Parameters\ContractRegistry_14_tests.js)

```
it('returns the registry, enabling chaining', function() {
  expect(registry.attachArgumentsValidator(funcName,funcObj,contractNames))
    .toBe(registry);
});
```

The implementation (see Listing 17-17) is a simple call to `Aop.before`—the function you met in Chapter 2.

LISTING 17-17: Implementation of attachArgumentsValidator (code filename: Parameters\ContractRegistry_14.js)

```
ReliableJavaScript.ContractRegistry.prototype.attachArgumentsValidator =
function attachArgumentsValidator(funcName, funcObj, validator) {
```

```
    var self = this;

    // *** Argument validation omitted. ***

    Aop.before(funcName, function validateArguments() {
        self.multipleAssert(validator,arguments);
    }, funcObj );

    return this;
};
```

SUPPORTING CONTRACT LIBRARIES

You have the basic functions in `ContractRegistry`, and you have packaged both the return validator and the arguments validator as aspects. Now all you need are some contracts!

The downloads for this chapter include a module, `StandardContracts.js`, that offers contracts such as `'boolean'`, `'string'`, and `'nonNegativeInteger'`. The singleton function that contains these contracts returns them in an array:

```
return [
    { name: 'undefined',          evaluator: isUndefined },
    { name: 'boolean',            evaluator: isBoolean },
    { name: 'string',             evaluator: isString },
    { name: 'number',             evaluator: isNumber },
    { name: 'function',           evaluator: isFunction },
    { name: 'object',             evaluator: isObject },
    { name: 'array',              evaluator: isArray },
    { name: 'nonEmptyString',     evaluator: isNonEmptyString },
    { name: 'nonBlankString',     evaluator: isNonBlankString },
    { name: 'integer',            evaluator: isInteger },
    { name: 'nonNegativeInteger', evaluator: isNonNegativeInteger },
    { name: 'nonNegativeNumber',  evaluator: isNonNegativeNumber },
];
```

What's needed is a convenient way to add all those contracts to a `ContractRegistry`, and `ContractRegistry.defineMultiple` is designed for just that purpose:

```
function defineMultiple(contracts)
```

Its parameter is an array of objects that have `name` and `evaluator` properties, and it just adds them to the registry.

The tests and implementation are in this chapter's final-version downloads (`ContractRegistry.js` and `ContractRegistry_tests.js`). Of more interest is what you can do with the method. That is the subject of the next section.

PUTTING IT ALL TOGETHER

If you choose to use an aspect-oriented approach to code contracts, these could be the steps.

1. Pair each of your JavaScript modules with a module that defines its contracts. For example, `attendee.js` might have a companion `attendeeContracts.js`. By convention, this would expose two functions: `getContracts()` to return an array of the contracts that `attendee.js`

provides to other modules, and `attachValidators(registry)` to install the argument- and return-validating aspects developed above.

2.   Create a main `ContractRegistry` file for your application in which you

   ➤   Instantiate a `ContractRegistry` that you will use for your application.

   ➤   Use `ContractRegistry.defineMultiple` to add the standard contracts to that registry.

   ➤   Call `defineMultiple` with the `getContracts()` result for each module from Step 1.

   ➤   Call `attachValidators(registry)` for each of those modules to install validators that use your `ContractRegistry`.

3.   Include the code for the preceding steps during development and testing only. If you wish, you can omit the source files from the shipping version. Your contracts will thus incur no overhead at all.

Creating the Contracts Modules

You may recall the following two interfaces for `Conference.attendee` that were presented in pseudo-code in Listing 16-4:

```
Interface attendeePersonalInfo:
    setId:             function(id)        returns undefined
    getId:             function()          returns a non-negative integer
    getFullName:       function()          returns a string

Interface attendeeCheckInManagement
    getId:             function()          returns a non-negative integer
    isCheckedIn:       function()          returns a boolean
    checkIn:           function()          returns undefined
    undoCheckIn:       function()          returns undefined
    setCheckInNumber:  function(number)    returns undefined
    getCheckInNumber:  function()          returns a non-negative integer
```

Following Step 1 in the preceding list, the corresponding `attendeeContracts.js` would appear as you see in Listing 17-18.

LISTING 17-18: Contracts for attendee objects (code filename: Parameters\attendeeContracts.js)

```
var Conference = Conference || {};
Conference.attendeeContracts = function() {

  var personalInfo = 'Conference.attendee.personalInfo',
      checkInManagement = 'Conference.attendee.checkInManagement';

  return {
    getContracts: function getContracts() {

      function fulfillsPersonalInfo(att) {
        return typeof att.setId === 'function' &&
```

```
                typeof att.getId === 'function' &&
                typeof att.getFullName === 'function';
    }

    function fulfillsCheckInManagement(att) {
      return typeof att.getId === 'function' &&
             typeof att.isCheckedIn === 'function' &&
             typeof att.checkIn === 'function' &&
             typeof att.undoCheckIn === 'function' &&
             typeof att.setCheckInNumber === 'function' &&
             typeof att.getCheckInNumber === 'function';
    }
    return [
      { name: personalInfo,
        evaluator: fulfillsPersonalInfo },

      { name: checkInManagement,
        evaluator: fulfillsCheckInManagement },
    ];
  },

  attachValidators: function attachValidators(registry) {

    // Attach validators to Conference.attendee(firstName,lastName)
    var funcName = 'attendee';
    registry.attachArgumentsValidator(funcName, Conference,
        [ 'undefined',            // No names supplied (OK)
          'string',               // Just one name supplied
          'string,string']);      // Both names supplied.
    registry.attachReturnValidator(funcName,Conference,personalInfo);
    registry.attachReturnValidator(funcName,Conference,checkInManagement);

    // Use an aspect on the return value from
    // Conference.attendee(firstName,lastName).
    //  This return value happens to be an object literal.
    Aop.around(funcName,
      function attachAspectsToAttendeeObjectLiteral(targetInfo) {
        // Instance of an attendee returned from the attendee function.
        var instance = Aop.next(targetInfo);

        registry.attachArgumentsValidator(
                    'setId',instance, 'nonNegativeInteger');
        registry.attachReturnValidator(
                    'setId',instance, 'undefined');

        registry.attachReturnValidator(
                    'getId',instance, 'nonNegativeInteger');

        registry.attachReturnValidator(
                    'getFullName',instance, 'string');

        registry.attachReturnValidator(
                    'isCheckedIn',instance, 'boolean');

        registry.attachReturnValidator(
```

continues

```
                            'checkIn',instance, 'undefined');

            registry.attachReturnValidator(
                            'undoCheckIn',instance, 'undefined');

            registry.attachArgumentsValidator(
                            'setCheckInNumber',instance, 'nonNegativeInteger');
            registry.attachReturnValidator(
                            'setCheckInNumber',instance, 'undefined');

            registry.attachReturnValidator(
                            'getCheckInNumber',instance, 'nonNegativeInteger');

            return instance;
          }, Conference);
      }
    };
  };
```

That was a long listing, but you may be particularly interested in what happens in the
attachValidators function. The first part

```
attachValidators: function attachValidators(registry) {
    // Attach validators to Conference.attendee(firstName,lastName)
    var funcName = 'attendee';
    registry.attachArgumentsValidator(funcName, Conference,
        [ 'undefined',              // No names supplied (OK)
          'string',                 // Just one name supplied
          'string,string']);        // Both names supplied.
    registry.attachReturnValidator(funcName,Conference,personalInfo);
    registry.attachReturnValidator(funcName,Conference,checkInManagement);
```

is a straightforward application of the attachArgumentsValidator and attachReturnValidator
functions developed earlier.

The remainder shows how you can attach validators even to an object literal that is returned from a
function. The Aop.around call captures the object literal in the *instance* variable and then attaches
validators to it:

```
Aop.around(funcName,
    function attachAspectsToAttendeeObjectLiteral(targetInfo) {
      // Instance of an attendee returned from the attendee function.
      var instance = Aop.next(targetInfo);

      registry.attachArgumentsValidator(
                    'setId',instance, 'nonNegativeInteger');
      registry.attachReturnValidator(
                    'setId',instance, 'undefined');
```

Finally, the attachValidators function returns *instance*.

If Conference.attendee had been an object created with new, the code could have been simpler. The
attendee's functions (setId, getId, getFullName, and so on) would have been available directly.

Creating the Application's ContractRegistry

The next step is to create the application's `ContractRegistry` (see Listing 17-19).

LISTING 17-19: A sample main registry. (code filename: Parameters\
ConferenceContractRegistry.js)

```
var Conference = Conference || {};

// The Conference application's ContractRegistry, implemented as
// a singleton.
Conference.ConferenceContractRegistry = (function() {

  var registry = new ReliableJavaScript.ContractRegistry);

  var contractModules = [
      Conference.attendeeContracts(),
      // Add more modules here.
    ];

  registry.defineMultiple(ReliableJavaScript.StandardContracts);

  contractModules.forEach(function(m) {
    registry.defineMultiple(m.getContracts());
  });

  contractModules.forEach(function(m) {
    m.attachValidators(registry);
  });

  return registry;
}());
```

Bypassing Contracts for Production

To keep your production code lean and fast, you can remove all contract-related code by simply excluding the contract modules (Listing 17-18 was one example), the application's contract registry (Listing 17-19), and `ContractRegistry.js` itself from the distribution. That is the beauty of the aspect-oriented approach—the aspect-decorated code is unaware of the aspects, so you may remove them whenever it's appropriate.

COMPARING THE ASPECT-ORIENTED SOLUTION TO A STATIC SOLUTION

The `ContractRegistry` in this chapter and the previous one takes a dynamic, function-oriented approach to type validation. The open-source library TypeScript offers a static, declarative approach that makes JavaScript more like a compiled language, and you may wish to consider it as well.

Visit `http://www.typescriptlang.org` for all the particulars, but in broad outline it goes like this:

1. Instead of coding in JavaScript with `.js` files, you code in a superset of JavaScript, in `.ts` files. The extra language features include notations such as parameter types. Thus, `function(id)` becomes `function(id: number)`.

2. Many popular libraries have TypeScript type declarations provided in open-source projects.

3. Your build process includes a command to compile the `.ts` files to `.js`. Popular development environments such as Microsoft Visual Studio can make this transparent.

4. During the build process (not at run time), TypeScript does its best to identify type mismatches. As you would hope, the matching is done by "shape" of the object rather than exact type.

Considering the Advantages of TypeScript

TypeScript has several advantages:

➤ The syntax is fairly natural for programmers who are used to strongly typed languages.

➤ It can check variable usage in local variables, not just function arguments and return values.

➤ Less code is required than for the aspect-oriented approach. Just add `:number` after a parameter and you're done.

Considering the Advantages of Aspects

Although TypeScript has many devotees, there is a strong case to be made for the aspect-oriented approach as well:

➤ Aspects let you check much more than types. For example, you have seen how to require a non-negative integer rather than just a number.

➤ Because checking is done at run time rather than compile time, more information is available. Yet aspects are easy to remove if you don't want them to be part of the shipped version.

➤ There is no additional syntax to learn. You code in native JavaScript, not a superset.

➤ There is no compile-to-JavaScript step, so you continue to work with the code exactly as you created it.

You may discover that you have use for both. After all, C# and Java programmers use both a compiler (think TypeScript) and code contracts (think aspects).

SUMMARY

In this chapter, you rounded out the `ContractRegistry` from Chapter 16 with argument-checking. The exercise culminated in packaging the functionality in an aspect, `attachArgumentsValidator`.

A final step was to create modules for standard contracts and application-specific contracts. A `ContractRegistry` for the application was able to import all the contracts and add the appropriate aspects.

TypeScript presents a good alternative to aspects. TypeScript is coded in a superset of JavaScript that compiles down to JavaScript. You could say that TypeScript is to aspects as a compiler is to code contracts.

The next chapter dives deep into three powerful JavaScript functions: `call`, `apply,` and `bind`. Masterfully incorporating them in a program can make the difference between long, plodding, boring code and concise, elegant, awe-inspiring code.

18

Ensuring Correct Use of call, apply, and bind

WHAT'S IN THIS CHAPTER?

➤ Understanding how a function's call-site determines the value *this* will have within the function

➤ Using `call` and `apply` to explicitly specify the value this will have within a function

➤ Using polyfills to implement language features that aren't natively supported by a browser

➤ Using `bind` to permanently set the value of *this* in a function, regardless of its call-site details

WROX.COM CODE DOWNLOADS FOR THIS CHAPTER

You can find the wrox.com code downloads for this chapter at www.wrox.com/go/ reliablejavascript on the Download Code tab. The files are in the Chapter 18 download and individually named according to the filenames noted throughout this chapter.

Unlike classical languages such as C# and Java in which *this* always references the object that "contains" the function that's executing, the value of *this* in JavaScript varies based on how a function is executed. Undisciplined use of *this* has tripped up new and experienced JavaScript developers alike.

JavaScript follows a simple set of rules when determining what value *this* should be bound to. We'll review those rules in the next section to set the stage for the primary topic of this chapter: apply, call, and bind, the functions that JavaScript provides as part of Function.prototype, which allow programmers to explicitly control the value to which *this* is bound.

EXPLORING HOW THIS IS BOUND

In this section, we describe the four types of bindings that JavaScript uses to set the value of the *this* variable within a function:

➤ Default binding,

➤ implicit binding,

➤ new binding, and

➤ explicit binding

Default Binding

Before exploring the default *this* binding, here's a simple question: What do you think the last line in Listing 18-1 will write to the browser's console window?

LISTING 18-1: Default binding of this (code filename: CallApplyBind\defaultBinding_01.js)

```
function incrementValue(){
  this.val++;
};
// functions can have properties
incrementValue.val = 0;

incrementValue();
incrementValue();
incrementValue();

console.log("final value: " + incrementValue.val);  // ???
```

Because the incrementValue function was executed three times, it seems reasonable to expect that the last line in the Listing will output final value: 3. Figure 18-1 shows whether or not that's correct.

FIGURE 18-1

As the output that's outlined in Figure 18-1 shows, the final value of incrementValue.val isn't 3 as expected; it's 0.

The example illustrates the *default* binding behavior: A bare function call, that is one that is called directly and not via an object instance, has *this* bound to the global object. When JavaScript executes in the browser, that global object is window.

Notice that we specified that the object *this* is bound to depends on how the function is *called*, not how the function is *defined*. JavaScript uses the way in which a function is executed, the call site, to determine the proper *this* binding, not the function definition.

> **NOTE** *A function's call site determines the value to which* this *is bound within the function, not the function's definition.*

Given that the call site dictates the value *this* is bound to, how do you think the code in Listing 18-2 will behave?

LISTING 18-2: Default binding of this with a function reference (code filename: CallApplyBind\defaultBinding_02.js)

```
var obj = {
  val: 0,
  incrementValue: function incrementValue(){
    this.val++;
  }
}

// create a reference to the function defined in obj
var incrementRef = obj.incrementValue;

// execute the incrementValue function via the reference
incrementRef();
incrementRef();
incrementRef();

console.log("final value in object: " + obj.val);  // ???
```

Figure 18-2 shows the console output.

FIGURE 18-2

Once again, the intended target of the increment, in the case of Listing 18-2, obj.val, has not changed. Even though the incrementValue function is defined as part of obj, it is executed as a bare function call via the incrementRef reference. Again, the call site has determined that *this* should be bound to window.

Default Binding and strict Mode

You may be wondering: If obj.val isn't being incremented in the incrementValue function, what is? Because *this* is bound to the global object window, the statement this.val++ is equivalent to the statement `window.val++`. The listing doesn't initialize `window.val`, so `window.val` is automatically created and has its value set to `undefined`. `window.val` becomes `NaN` the first time the code tries to increment it—the result of trying to increment `undefined`—and remains `NaN` after each subsequent increment attempt.

Utilizing `strict` mode within the `incrementValue` function would have disallowed the automatic creation of the global variable `val` by binding *this* to `undefined`. When `strict` mode is in effect, an error is generated in cases when a global variable would otherwise have been automatically created. Listing 18-3 illustrates placing `incrementValue` into `strict` mode, and Figure 18-3 shows the resulting exception.

FIGURE 18-3

> **LISTING 18-3:** Default binding and strict mode (code filename: CallApplyBind\ defaultBinding_03.js)

```javascript
var obj = {
  val: 0,
  incrementValue: function incrementValue(){
    "use strict";
    // in strict mode, 'this' is bound to undefined rather than window
    // by default.
    this.val++;
  }
};

// create a reference to the function defined in obj
var incrementRef = obj.incrementValue;

// execute the incrementValue function via the reference
incrementRef();  // will generate an error
```

> **NOTE** *Use of* `strict` *mode turns likely logic problems into errors, shortening the debugging cycle and resulting in more reliable code.*

Implicit Binding

If you've programmed in a classical language such as C# or Java, implicit binding will probably feel natural to you. Implicit binding is, in effect, when a function is executed via a reference to an object.

When implicitly bound, the value of *this* is the object that "contains," or the context of, the function being executed. Listing 18-4, a minor variation of Listing 18-2, shows implicit binding at work.

LISTING 18-4: Implicit binding of this (code filename: CallApplyBind\implicitBinding_01.js)

```
var obj = {
  val: 0,
  incrementValue: function incrementValue(){
    this.val++;
  }
};

obj.incrementValue();
obj.incrementValue();
obj.incrementValue();

console.log("final value in object: " + obj.val);   // 3
```

Back in Listing 18-2, incrementValue is executed without a context via a variable that references it, incrementRef. In contrast, Listing 18-4 executes incrementValue via the obj object, thus providing obj as the context to which *this* is bound within the function. Because *this* is bound to obj, the statement

```
this.val++;
```

increments the val property of the obj object.

To really see that it's the call site rather than the declaration of a function that determines how *this* is bound, consider the code in Listing 18-5.

LISTING 18-5: Implicit binding of this with a global function definition (code filename: CallApplyBind\implicitBinding_02.js)

```
function valIncrementor(){
  this.val++;
}

var obj = {
  val: 0,
  incrementValue: valIncrementor
};

obj.incrementValue();
obj.incrementValue();
obj.incrementValue();

console.log("final value in object: " + obj.val);   // 3
```

In Listing 18-5, the function valIncrementor, which contains the this.val++ statement, is defined globally; its declaration is not contained within an object. When obj is defined, its incrementValue property is assigned to the valIncrementor function.

The globally defined valIncrementor function is then executed three times via incrementValue, the reference to it that's contained within the obj object. Even though valIncrementor is defined globally, it's called with `obj` as its context at the three call sites. Thus, `this` is bound to `obj`, and `obj.val` is incremented by the function.

new Binding

When constructor functions are executed, they aren't provided with a context object to which `this` can be bound. That means that within a constructor function, `this` is bound to the global object, right?

Thankfully, no, that's not the case. Chapter 3 illustrated the use of the `new` keyword to create object instances using constructors. Each of the examples using `new` employed `this` within the constructor function to manipulate the newly created object instance. We mentioned it then, and will reiterate now: When `new` is used with a constructor function, `this` is automatically bound to the new object.

The `this` binding behavior when the `new` keyword is used at a function call site allows the constructor function to set properties of the new object, as you can see in Listing 18-6.

LISTING 18-6: Binding of this within constructor functions (code filename: CallApplyBind\ newBinding_01.js)

```javascript
function Counter(){

    // When the constructor function is invoked with the new keyword,
    // 'this' is bound to the new object
    this.val = 0;
}
Counter.prototype.incrementValue = function(){
    // referencing 'this' within the function will still rely
    // upon implicit binding to ensure that 'this' references
    // the object instance when the function is invoked.
    this.val++;
};

var cnt = new Counter();
cnt.incrementValue();
cnt.incrementValue();
cnt.incrementValue();

console.log("final value in object: " + cnt.val);  // 3
```

It's worth noting that functions added to an object's prototype are still subject to call-site `this` binding rules. For instance, if `strict` mode is enabled and the `cnt` object's `incrementValue` function is invoked via a reference rather than via the `cnt` object, an error will occur, as Listing 18-7 and Figure 18-4 show.

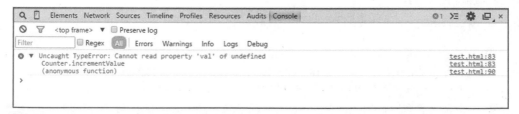

FIGURE 18-4

LISTING 18-7: Functions added to an object's prototype are subject to call-site binding rules (code filename: CallApplyBind\newBinding_02.js)

```
"use strict";

function Counter(){

    // When the constructor function is invoked with the new keyword,
    // 'this' is bound to the new object
    this.val = 0;
}
Counter.prototype.incrementValue = function(){
    // referencing 'this' within the function will still rely
    // upon implicit binding to ensure that 'this' references
    // the object instance when the function is invoked.
    this.val++;
};

var cnt = new Counter();
var incrementRef = cnt.incrementValue;

// Execute the function via a reference, triggering an error
incrementRef();
```

Explicit Binding

The final mechanism that JavaScript provides to bind the `this` variable is *explicit binding*. Explicit binding allows the caller of a function to specify the object to which `this` should be bound.

Explicit binding is performed via the `call`, `apply`, and `bind` methods that are part of the prototype of each and every JavaScript function. The next section explores `call`, `apply`, and `bind` with a focus on unit-testing code that utilizes those functions.

> **NOTE** *In JavaScript, functions are objects. As such, a function has a prototype that can—and does—contain other functions.*

CREATING AND TESTING CODE THAT USES CALL, APPLY, AND BIND

Based on the examples presented so far in this chapter, it may appear that JavaScript developers would benefit from avoiding the use of `this` altogether. After all, a programmer could induce a method that uses `this` to fail simply by executing the method via a reference rather than via the object on which it was defined.

Armed with the knowledge of how JavaScript determines the object `this` will be bound to, and the functions `call`, `apply`, and `bind`, which allow the programmer to specify the variable to which `this` should be bound, there's no reason the use of `this` should keep your JavaScript from being reliable. This section will present scenarios where `call`, `apply`, and `bind` are used and will highlight important aspects of testing code that uses those functions.

Using call and apply

We're grouping `call` and `apply` methods together because they do the same thing: Each immediately executes the function on which it's invoked with *this* bound to a provided context object.

Before exploring how to test code that uses `call` and `apply`, it's worthwhile to examine some simple examples of how the functions are used. Both `call` and `apply` accept a context object as their first argument. The context is what *this* will be bound to within the function. If the context is `undefined`, *this* will be bound to the global object (or set to `undefined` if `strict` mode is in effect).

The difference between the `call` and `apply` is that `call` is used when the number of parameters the function being invoked accepts is known; `call` allows the arguments to be passed individually. The `apply` method, on the other hand, allows the arguments to the function being invoked to be provided as an array rather than individually. This is useful when the number of arguments the function accepts is not known, or is variable.

Listing 18-8 illustrates simple uses of a function's `call` and `apply` methods.

LISTING 18-8: Using call and apply (code filename: CallApplyBind\callApply_01.js)

```javascript
var ReliableJavaScript = ReliableJavaScript || {};

ReliableJavaScript.addValues = function(value1, value2){
  // addValues accepts two arguments and expects
  // that 'this' has a method 'printResult'
  this.printResult(value1 + value2);
};

// Define an object that has a printResult function
var contextObject = {

  printResult: function printResult(toPrint){
    console.log("Result: " + toPrint);
  }

};

// Execute the addValues function using its call method.
// Provide contextObject as the object to which 'this' should be bound.
// Also, provide 2 and 3 as the values that addValues will add together

ReliableJavaScript.addValues.call(contextObject, 2, 3); // "Result: 5"

// Execute the addValues function using its apply method.
// Again, provide contextObject as the object to which 'this' should be bound.
// Also, provide an array containing the values 2 and 3 as the arguments that
// will be added together.
ReliableJavaScript.addValues.apply(contextObject, [2, 3]); // "Result: 5"
```

Use of `call` and `apply` within your code signifies that you're concerned about the value the *this* variable will have. As such, the value of *this* should be a primary concern of the unit tests that you write for code that uses `call` or `apply`.

In Chapter 5, the `attendeeCollection` module was created to manage collections of `attendee` objects. The `attendeeCollection` exposes the method `iterate`, which accepts a callback function that `iterate` invokes once for each `attendee` contained by the collection. The callback is executed once per `attendee` via the `Array.prototype.forEach` method. The portion of `attendeeCollection` pertinent to this discussion is repeated in Listing 18-9.

LISTING 18-9: The attendeeCollection module (excerpt) (code filename: CallApplyBind\ attendeeCollection.js)

```
var Conference = Conference || {};
Conference.attendeeCollection = function(){
  'use strict';

  var attendees = [];

  return{

    /* contains, add, remove and getCount omitted for brevity */

    iterate: function(callback){
      attendees.forEach(callback);
    }
  };
};
```

You may recall that the `checkedInAttendeeCounter` module (also created in Chapter 5) had an issue related to its use of *this* within the callback function provided to `iterate`, as you can see in the following example:

```
var checkInService = Conference.checkInService(Conference.checkInRecorder()),
    attendees = Conference.attendeeCollection(),
    counter = Conference.checkedInAttendeeCounter();

// Add attendees selected in the UI to the attendee collection
attendees.add(Conference.attendee('Pete', 'Mitchell'));
attendees.add(Conference.attendee('Nick', 'Bradshaw'));

// check the attendees in
attendees.iterate(checkInService.checkIn);

// count the checked-in attendees
attendees.iterate(counter.countIfCheckedIn);

console.log(counter.getCount()); // 0 (!?!?)
```

As mentioned earlier in this chapter, the fact that the `countIfCheckedIn` method is defined as part of the *counter* object does not necessarily mean that *this* will be bound to the `counter` object within `countIfCheckedIn`. In fact, because of the way the `attendeeCollection`'s `iterate` function is written, it is guaranteed that *this* will be bound to the global `window` object; the `countIfCheckedIn` method is invoked via the reference `callback` within `iterate`.

In Chapter 5, the *this* binding issue was addressed by retaining a reference to the instance of the `checkedInAttendeeCounter` in a variable named *self*, and using *self* in `countIfCheckedIn` rather than `this`. (See the section "Minding this" in Chapter 5 for a refresher.) Doing so ensured that `countIfCheckedIn` would work correctly even if `this` ended up not being bound to the `counter` object due to call site details.

Another solution would have been to leverage `Array.prototype.forEach`'s ability to accept a context object to be bound to `this` within the callback. That sounds strikingly familiar to how `call` and `apply` function, doesn't it? One might conclude that `Array.prototype.forEach` uses `call` under the covers.

Unfortunately for you and Charlotte, `Array.prototype.forEach` wasn't added to the language until ECMAScript 5. As such, it's a feature that Internet Explorer 8 doesn't support. According to NetMarketShare (`http://marketshare.hitslink.com`) Internet Explorer 8 was responsible for over 17 percent of web traffic in October 2014. With this number in mind, the organizers of the JavaScript conference want to ensure that the conference website supports Internet Explorer 8. Does this mean `forEach` can't be used? No, it doesn't.

Creating an Array.prototype.forEach Polyfill Using Test-Driven Development

Differences in browser support of ECMAScript features are regularly addressed using *polyfills*. A polyfill is a piece of code that implements a language feature that a developer expects to be implemented natively by the browser. A polyfill detects whether or not the language feature exists, and if the feature isn't present the polyfill plugs itself in the place of the feature. If a developer includes polyfills with her project, she is assured that the language feature the polyfill implements will be present even if the browser doesn't natively implement it.

Because Internet Explorer 8 doesn't support `Array.prototype.forEach`, and `Array.prototype.forEach` has already been used in the JavaScript conference website's code, a polyfill needs to be provided.

> **NOTE** *There are plenty of polyfills that exist for ECMAScript 5 features, including* `Array.prototype.forEach`. *While we don't advocate reinventing the wheel, implementing a polyfill for* `Array.prototype.forEach` *provides an excellent vehicle for creating and testing code that uses* `Function.prototype.call`.
>
> *Please note that because the focus of the polyfill implementation is the illustration of concepts rather than the actual replication of functionality, the polyfill that is created in this section should not be considered anything other than an incomplete sample; do not use it in real code!*

The first step in creating the polyfill for `Array.prototype.forEach` (even before writing unit tests) is to determine the interface and behavior of the feature as it's implemented in ECMAScript 5. The annotated ECMAScript 5 specification of `Array.prototype.forEach` is available at `http://es5` `.github.io/#x15.4.4.18`. Some of the key takeaways from that page are:

- ➤ The method signature is `Array.prototype.forEach(callbackFcn [, thisObj])`.
- ➤ The `thisObj` parameter is optional. If it is provided, it will be provided as the *this* object for each invocation of `callbackFcn`. If it is not provided, `undefined` will be provided to `callbackFcn` as the *this* object.

➤ The callback function `callbackFcn` will be executed once per element in the array, with the three arguments:

➤ The value of the element

➤ The index of the element

➤ The object being traversed

The annotated specification provides all the information needed to begin creating the unit test suite for the polyfill. As usual, tests for error conditions are written first and follow in Listing 18-10.

LISTING 18-10: Error condition unit tests for the Array.prototype.forEach polyfill (code filename: CallApplyBind\forEach_01_tests.js)

```
describe("arrayForEach(callbackFcn[, thisObj])", function(){

    var originalForEach;

    beforeEach(function(){
      // retain a reference to the original forEach implementation
      originalForEach = Array.prototype.forEach;

      // replace the original forEach implementation (if any) with the
      // polyfill being tested
      Array.prototype.forEach = Conference.polyfills.arrayForEach;
    });

    afterEach(function(){
      // restore the original forEach
      Array.prototype.forEach = originalForEach;
    });

    it("throws if callbackFcn is not a function", function(){

      var i,
      nonFunction = [
       undefined,
       "",
       {}
      ];

      // it's tempting to use Array.prototype.forEach here!
      for(i = 0; i < nonFunction.length; i++){
        expect(function(){
          [].forEach(nonFunction[i]);
        }).toThrowError(nonFunction[i] + " is not a function");
      }
    });
  });
```

Because `callbackFcn` must be provided and it must be executable, the first error condition test written is to ensure that the polyfill throws an exception if `callbackFcn` is not a function.

The steps taking place in the `beforeEach` and `afterEach` block are also worth examining. Because a polyfill is under development, it's appropriate to test it as it will be used in production: as part of `Array.prototype`. The environment in which the tests are executing may or may not already have an implementation of `Array.prototype.forEach`. In either case, the polyfill needs to be put in place, which is done via the following statement in the `beforeEach` block:

```
Array.prototype.forEach = Conference.polyfills.arrayForEach;
```

The original implementation (or lack thereof) is retained so that it can be restored after each test is executed.

With a stub implementation of `Conference.polyfills.arrayForEach`, the unit test in Listing 18-10 fails, as Figure 18-5 shows.

FIGURE 18-5

Satisfying the error condition test is a simple affair and is shown in Listing 18-11.

LISTING 18-11: Conference.polyfills.arrayForEach, which satisfies the error condition test (code filename: CallApplyBind\forEach_01.js)

```
var Conference = Conference || {};
Conference.polyfills = Conference.polyfills || {};

Conference.polyfills.arrayForEach = function(callbackFcn, thisObj){
  'use strict';

  if (typeof callbackFcn !== "function") {
```

```
            throw new Error(callbackFcn + ' is not a function');
        }
    };
```

Figure 18-6 proves that the check to ensure that `callbackFcn` is a function causes the unit test to pass.

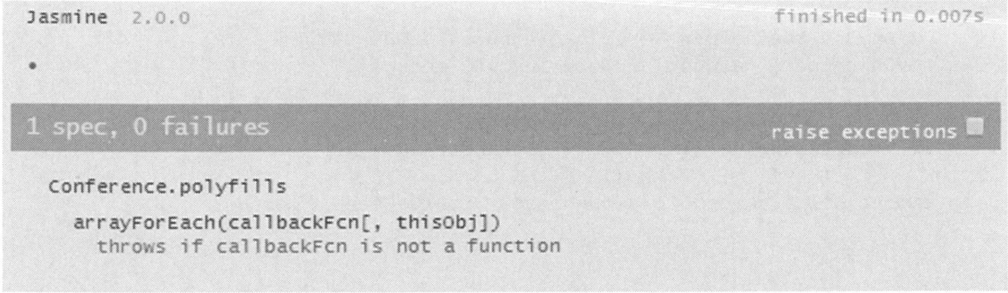

Jasmine 2.0.0   finished in 0.007s

1 spec, 0 failures   raise exceptions ◼

Conference.polyfills

  arrayForEach(callbackFcn[, thisObj])
    throws if callbackFcn is not a function

FIGURE 18-6

> **NOTE** *There are plenty of other error conditions that would be tested if the intent was to create a fully functional polyfill for* `Array.prototype.forEach`. *In the interest of getting to the meat of the example, use and testing of* `Function` `.prototype.call`, *we won't dawdle any longer.*

If the optional argument `thisObj` isn't provided, `undefined` should be used as the context object when `callbackFcn` is invoked. Recall that if `strict` mode is not in effect, when a function is provided `undefined` as a context, *this* binds to the global `window` object. Listing 18-12 contains a test to ensure that `callbackFcn` is executed as expected when `thisObj` is not provided.

LISTING 18-12: Testing that callbackFcn is executed with the correct context when thisObj is not provided (code filename: CallApplyBind\forEach_02_tests.js)

```
describe("Conference.polyfills", function(){
  'use strict';

  describe("arrayForEach(callbackFcn[, thisObj])", function(){

    /*** Previously discussed setup, cleanup and tests omitted ***/

    describe("without thisObj", function(){

      it("executes callbackFcn with an undefined context", function(){

        var helper = {
          // Callback that will be provided to .forEach
          expectThisToBeWindow : function(){
```

continues

LISTING 18-12 *(continued)*

```
        // verify that this has been bound to window
            expect(this).toBe(window);
          }
        };

        // spy on the helper so we can ensure it was called
        spyOn(helper, "expectThisToBeWindow").and.callThrough();

        // execute on a single element array
        [1].forEach(helper.expectThisToBeWindow);

        expect(helper.expectThisToBeWindow).toHaveBeenCalled();
      });
    });
  });
});
```

The test added in Listing 18-12 creates `helper`, an object that contains the function `expectThisToBeWindow`, which will be provided as the `callbackFcn` argument to `forEach`. Within `expectThisToBeWindow` exists an expectation that verifies that *this* has been bound to the `window` object. As mentioned previously, this is the expected behavior when a function has been executed in non-`strict` mode with `undefined` as the function's context. A spy is then set up on the callback so that the test can ensure that the callback was executed.

The main expectation of the test is the first one: `expect(this).toBe(window)`. However, if `arrayForEach` is so defective that execution never reaches that expectation, the test would pass when it should not. To guard against that possibility, the test spies on `helper.expectThisToBeWindow` and finishes with an expectation that it is called.

Figure 18-7 shows that the test does not pass with the polyfill in its current state. Note that the failure is generated because the callback was never invoked. Good thing that check was added!

FIGURE 18-7

Because the test only verifies a small aspect of the functionality of the polyfill (as it should), only a very small change is required to make the new test pass. The change is highlighted in Listing 18-13.

LISTING 18-13: Implementation of the polyfill that allows the test verifying that callbackFcn is bound to undefined to pass (code filename: CallApplyBind\forEach_2.js)

```javascript
var Conference = Conference || {};
Conference.polyfills = Conference.polyfills || {};

Conference.polyfills.arrayForEach = function(callbackFcn, thisObj){
  'use strict';

  var i;

  if (typeof callbackFcn !== "function") {
    throw new Error(callbackFcn + ' is not a function');
  }

  for(i = 0; i < this.length; i++){
    callbackFcn();
  }
};
```

Because the test only verifies the callback function's context is correct, simply executing the callback function via the reference `callbackFcn` is sufficient to allow the new test to pass. Figure 18-8 proves this.

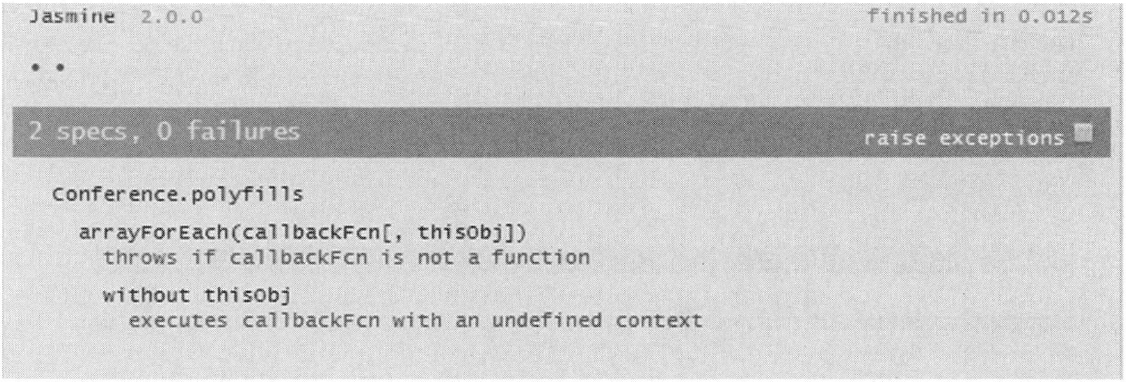

```
Jasmine  2.0.0                                              finished in 0.012s

• •

2 specs, 0 failures                                          raise exceptions ■

  Conference.polyfills

    arrayForEach(callbackFcn[, thisObj])
      throws if callbackFcn is not a function

    without thisObj
      executes callbackFcn with an undefined context
```

FIGURE 18-8

Next, a test needs to be written to ensure that the callback function has its context set to `thisObj` if `thisObj` is provided as an argument. Listing 18-14 provides the necessary test.

LISTING 18-14: Testing that callbackFcn has its context set to thisObj if thisObj is provided (code filename: CallApplyBind\forEach_03_tests.js)

```
describe("Conference.polyfills", function(){
  'use strict';

  describe("arrayForEach(callbackFcn[, thisObj])", function(){

    /*** Previously discussed setup, cleanup and tests omitted ***/

    describe("with thisObj", function(){

      it("executes callbackFcn with thisObj as its context", function(){
        var thisObj = {},
            helper = {
              expectThisToBeThisObj : function(){
                expect(this).toBe(thisObj);
              }
            };

        // spy on the helper so we can ensure it was called
        spyOn(helper, "expectThisToBeThisObj").and.callThrough();

        // execute on a single element array
        [1].forEach(helper.expectThisToBeThisObj, thisObj);

        expect(helper.expectThisToBeThisObj).toHaveBeenCalled();
      });
    });
  });
});
```

The test added to ensure thisObj is used as the context of callbackFcn when the thisObj has been provided is very similar to the test that verifies the context when thisObj has not been provided. The primary difference, highlighted in the listing, is that *this* is expected to be thisObj rather than window. Figure 18-9 illustrates that the new test fails.

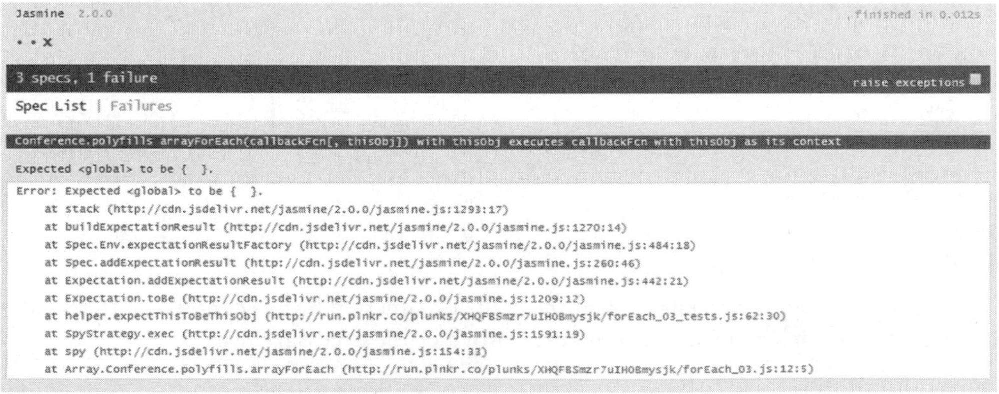

FIGURE 18-9

The situation is rectified by transforming the direct invocation `callbackFcn` into an invocation of `callbackFcn`'s `call` method. This transformation, and providing `thisObj` as the context for the call, is shown in Listing 18-15.

LISTING 18-15: Providing the correct context to callbackFcn with call (code filename: CallApplyBind\forEach_03.js)

```
var Conference = Conference || {};
Conference.polyfills = Conference.polyfills || {};

Conference.polyfills.arrayForEach = function(callbackFcn, thisObj){
  'use strict';

  var i;

  if (typeof callbackFcn !== "function") {
    throw new Error(callbackFcn + ' is not a function');
  }

  for(i = 0; i < this.length; i++){
    callbackFcn.call(thisObj);
  }
};
```

Notice that there's no verification that `thisObj` has been provided as an argument by the caller; it's just passed right along as the first argument to `callbackFcn`'s `call` method. Recall that when a function defines a parameter and the caller doesn't provide a corresponding argument, that parameter's value is `undefined` within the function. If `thisObj` isn't provided, `callbackFcn` should have its context set to `undefined` when it's invoked so no additional checks need to be put in place. Figure 18-10 shows that modification allows the new test, and the existing tests, to pass.

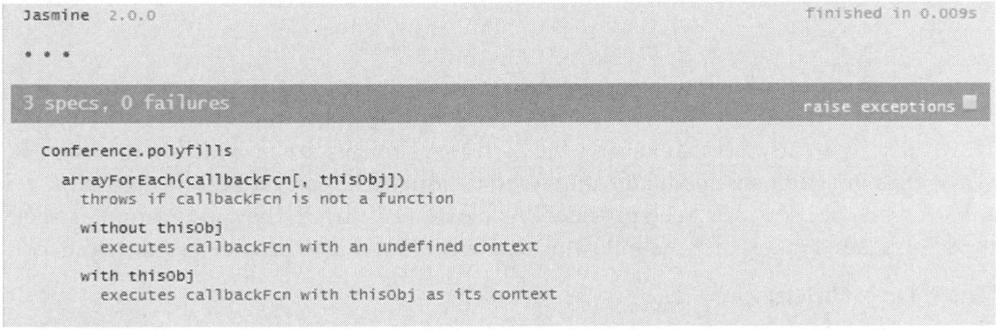

```
Jasmine 2.0.0                                              finished in 0.009s

• • •

3 specs, 0 failures                                        raise exceptions ■

  Conference.polyfills
    arrayForEach(callbackFcn[, thisObj])
      throws if callbackFcn is not a function
      without thisObj
        executes callbackFcn with an undefined context
      with thisObj
        executes callbackFcn with thisObj as its context
```

FIGURE 18-10

The final piece of the `forEach` polyfill to test—related to ensuring the correct use of `call`, at least—is that the callback is invoked with the correct arguments. The tests that verify the single-element array case are provided in Listing 18-16; those that test the multiple-element array case are left as an exercise for the reader.

LISTING 18-16: Tests that ensure callbackFcn is executed with the correct arguments (code filename: CallApplyBind\forEach_04_tests.js)

```
describe("Conference.polyfills", function(){
  'use strict';

  describe("arrayForEach(callbackFcn[, thisObj])", function(){

    /*** Previously discussed setup, cleanup and tests omitted ***/

    describe("without thisObj", function(){

      /*** Previously discussed tests omitted ***/

      it("executes callbackFcn with the expected arguments", function(){
        var testArray = [{}],
            callbackSpy = jasmine.createSpy();
        testArray.forEach(callbackSpy);
        expect(callbackSpy).toHaveBeenCalledWith(testArray[0], 0, testArray);
      });
    });

    describe("with thisObj", function(){

      /*** Previously discussed tests omitted ***/

      it("executes callbackFcn with the expected arguments", function(){
        var thisObj = {},
            testArray = [{}],
            callbackSpy = jasmine.createSpy();

        testArray.forEach(callbackSpy, thisObj);

        expect(callbackSpy).toHaveBeenCalledWith(testArray[0], 0, testArray);
      });
    });
  });
});
```

Listing 18-16 adds two tests: one that ensures the correct arguments are provided to the callback when `thisObj` has not been provided, and another that ensures the correct arguments are provided to the callback when `thisObj` has been provided. As mentioned earlier, the specification of `Array.prototype.forEach` dictates that the following arguments should be provided to the callback:

➤   The value of the element

➤   The index of the element

➤   The object being traversed

Both of the tests employ a bare jasmine spy to validate that the callback has been invoked with the correct parameters.

Listing 18-17 updates the implementation of the polyfill to provide the arguments, and Figure 18-11 shows that all of the unit tests pass.

```
Jasmine  2.0.0                                              finished in 0.012s

. . . . .

5 specs, 0 failures                                         raise exceptions ■

  Conference.polyfills
    arrayForEach(callbackFcn[, thisObj])
      throws if callbackFcn is not a function

    without thisObj
        executes callbackFcn with an undefined context
        executes callbackFcn with the expected arguments

    with thisObj
        executes callbackFcn with thisObj as its context
        executes callbackFcn with the expected arguments
```

FIGURE 18-11

LISTING 18-17: Providing the correct arguments to callbackFcn (code filename:
CallApplyBind\forEach_04.js)

```javascript
var Conference = Conference || {};
Conference.polyfills = Conference.polyfills || {};

Conference.polyfills.arrayForEach = function(callbackFcn, thisObj){
  'use strict';

  var i;

  if (typeof callbackFcn !== "function") {
    throw new Error(callbackFcn + ' is not a function');
  }

  for(i = 0; i < this.length; i++){
    callbackFcn.call(thisObj, this[i], i, this);
  }
};
```

Using bind

Where call and apply are used to invoke a function with *this* bound to a specific object, bind
returns a new function that *permanently* binds *this* to a specific object within the original function. The object bound to *this* within the original function may not be changed by executing the
function created by bind using the function's call or apply methods.

This behavior is useful when creating objects that contain *event handlers*, functions that respond to
external stimuli, such as browser DOM events.

When the browser executes an event handler in response to an event, such as a button click, it usually provides the DOM element that the event handler is bound to as the context of the event handler function. That means *this* is bound to the DOM element within the function handling the
event. If the event handler is contained within an object that needs to maintain state or communicate with other components, it may be desirable to guarantee that the event handler has *this* bound
to the object that contains it rather than the DOM element that the browser provides.

Suppose the JavaScript conference organizers have asked for the ability to see how many times visi-
tors leave the conference's website by clicking on a link to a conference sponsor's website. Charlotte

creates a module that's responsible for recording outgoing-link clicks in the website's database, `outgoingLinkClickRecorder`. You've been asked to create the module that's responsible for responding to the DOM click events and recording the clicks with the `outgoingLinkClickRecorder`. The module you create, the `outgoingLinkClickHandler`, should accept an injected instance of Charlotte's `outgoingLinkClickRecorder` and expose a single method: `handleClick`.

Because you know that the `handleClick` method is going to be executed in response to browser DOM events, you know that the browser will execute the method with the source DOM element as its context. Because you have to interact with the instance of `outgoingLinkClickRecorder` that's been injected into the `outgoingLinkClickHandler`, you'd really like to suppress the browser's behavior; you want *this* to be bound to the object that contains the `handleClick` method.

You have a hunch that `bind` can be used to attain this goal, but before you get too far ahead of yourself, you write a few unit tests to verify the behavior. The first of those tests appears in Listing 18-18.

LISTING 18-18: Test that ensures handleClick records a click when its containing object is provided as its context (code filename: CallApplyBind\outgoingLinkClickHander_tests_01.js)

```
describe("Conference.outgoingLinkClickHandler", function(){
  'use strict';

  var clickRecorder,
      clickHandler;

  beforeEach(function(){
    clickRecorder = Conference.outgoingLinkClickRecorder();
    spyOn(clickRecorder, "recordClick");

    clickHandler = Conference.outgoingLinkClickHandler(clickRecorder);
  });

  describe("handleClick()", function(){
    it("records a click if executed via the its containing object", function(){
      clickHandler.handleClick();
      expect(clickRecorder.recordClick).toHaveBeenCalled();
    });
  });

});
```

This first test simply ensures that `clickHandler.handleClick` properly records a click when *clickHandler*, the object containing the method, is provided as the method's context. A spy is set up on `clickRecorder.recordClick` in the `beforeEach` section so that the test can assert that `clickRecorder.recordClick` is executed.

With a stub implementation of `Conference.outgoingLinkClickHandler`, the unit tests from Listing 18-18 fail, as shown in Figure 18-12.

Listing 18-19 provides an implementation of `Conference.outgoingLinkClickHandler` that satisfies the unit tests.

FIGURE 18-12

LISTING 18-19: Implementation of outgoingLinkClickHandler that functions properly when executed via the object that contains it (code filename: CallApplyBind\outgoingLinkClickHandler_01.js)

```javascript
var Conference = Conference || {};

Conference.outgoingLinkClickHandler = function(clickRecorder){
  'use strict';

  return {

    // retain a reference to the injected clickRecorder
    linkClickRecorder: clickRecorder,

    // Constructs an object containing details of the click
    // and records the click with the clickRecorder
    handleClick: function handleClick (){
      // construct a linkDetails object
      var clickDetails = {};

      this.linkClickRecorder.recordClick(clickDetails);
    }
  };

};
```

The implementation of `outgoingLinkClickHandler` provided in Listing 18-19 assigns the injected `clickRecorder` object to the `linkClickRecorder` property of the new object instance. The `handleClick` method invokes `linkClickRecorder` via *this* to record the click details to the website's database. Figure 18-13 shows that the implementation allows the unit test to pass.

In order to ensure that the `handleClick` method behaves as expected when provided as an event handler that responds to a DOM event, you need to write some unit tests that invoke `handleClick` with an object other than its containing object as its context. Those tests follow in Listing 18-20.

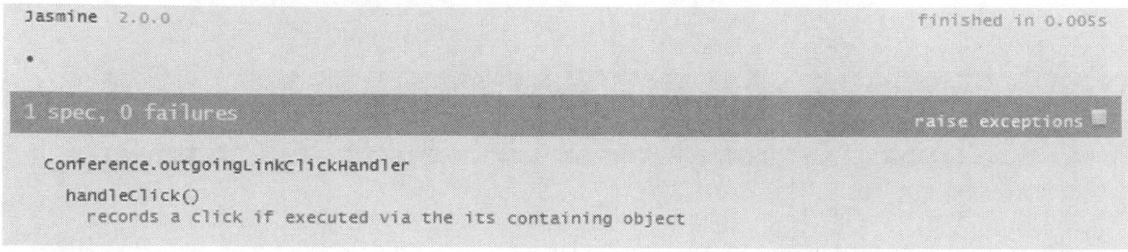

```
Jasmine  2.0.0                                        finished in 0.005s

  .

  1 spec, 0 failures                                 raise exceptions ▦

  Conference.outgoingLinkClickHandler
    handleClick()
      records a click if executed via the its containing object
```

FIGURE 18-13

LISTING 18-20: Tests that ensure handleClick records a click regardless of its context (code filename: CallApplyBind\outgoingLinkClickHandler_02_tests.js)

```javascript
describe("Conference.outgoingLinkClickHandler", function(){

  /*** Previously discussed setup omitted ***/

  describe("handleClick()", function(){

  /*** Previously discussed test omitted ***/

    it("records a click if provided undefined as its context", function(){
      clickHandler.handleClick.call(undefined);
      expect(clickRecorder.recordClick).toHaveBeenCalled();
    });

    it("records a click if provided a bare object as its context", function(){
      clickHandler.handleClick.call({});
      expect(clickRecorder.recordClick).toHaveBeenCalled();
    });
  });

});
```

The new tests verify the following:

➤ A click is recorded when `handleClick` is invoked with an undefined context.

➤ A click is recorded when `handleClick` is invoked with an object literal as its context.

Together, the original test and the two new tests ensure that the `handleClick` method functions properly regardless of the context provided to it. When these tests pass, you can be assured that `handleClick` will be able to handle click events with aplomb. The current implementation doesn't satisfy the new tests, as Figure 18-14 illustrates.

With `bind` in the back of your mind, you develop the implementation shown in Listing 18-21.

LISTING 18-21: Implementation of outgoingLinkClickHandler that employs bind (code filename: CallApplyBind\outgoingLinkClickHandler_02.js)

```javascript
var Conference = Conference || {};

Conference.outgoingLinkClickHandler = function(clickRecorder){
```

```
'use strict';

var handler = {

  // retain a reference to the injected clickRecorder
  linkClickRecorder: clickRecorder,

  // Constructs an object containing details of the click
  // and records the click with the clickRecorder
  handleClick: function handleClick(){
    // construct a linkDetails object
    var clickDetails = {};

    this.linkClickRecorder.recordClick(clickDetails);
  }
};

// replace handler.handleClick with a new copy of the function that
// is permanently bound to handler
handler.handleClick = handler.handleClick.bind(handler);

return handler;
};
```

FIGURE 18-14

Rather than directly returning a new instance as was done in the previous implementation, the new implementation of outgoingLinkClickHandler first assigns the new object to handler. Then the bind method of handler.handleClick is used to create a *new copy* of handler.handleClick that has this permanently bound to handler via:

```
handler.handleClick = handler.handleClick.bind(handler);
```

Finally, `handler` is returned to the caller. Figure 18-15 shows that the new implementation allows all of the unit tests to pass.

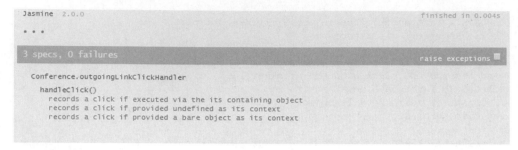

```
Jasmine  2.0.0                                            finished in 0.004s

• • •

3 specs, 0 failures                                      raise exceptions ■

Conference.outgoingLinkClickHandler
   handleClick()
      records a click if executed via the its containing object
      records a click if provided undefined as its context
      records a click if provided a bare object as its context
```

FIGURE 18-15

SUMMARY

This chapter covered a lot of ground. Before diving into the details of `call`, `apply`, and `bind`, we reviewed the types of bindings that JavaScript uses to set the value of *this* in a function:

➤ Default binding

➤ Implicit binding

➤ new binding

➤ Explicit binding

Also, the chapter described the call-site details that determine which of the bindings is used.

Next, we described the details of `call` and `apply`, which are used to explicitly set the value of *this* in a function. Along the way, we discussed the concept of polyfills and created a partial implementation of a polyfill for `Array.prototype.forEach` using test-driven development.

Finally, the chapter illustrated how to use `bind` to permanently bind *this* to a value within a function.

When you write a JavaScript function that uses *this*, you need to anticipate all the ways the function could be invoked. To ensure reliability, your unit test suite for the function that uses *this* should include tests that bind *this* to:

➤ null

➤ undefined

➤ an object other than the one on which the function is defined

Also, when writing a function that accepts a callback function as a parameter, it's common practice to accept another parameter that is the object to which *this* should be bound within the callback. The test suite for a function that accepts a callback and its *this* value should include tests to ensure that *this* is properly bound within the callback function.

The next chapter takes `call` and `apply` to the next level and demonstrates how they can be used to perform method borrowing.

19

Ensuring Correct Use of Method-Borrowing

WHAT'S IN THIS CHAPTER?

➤ Elegantly borrowing a function from another object

➤ Using an aspect or code contract to qualify the borrower

➤ Evaluating side effects on both borrower and donor

WROX.COM CODE DOWNLOADS FOR THIS CHAPTER

You can find the wrox.com code downloads for this chapter at www.wrox.com/go/
reliablejavascript on the Download Code tab. The files are in the Chapter 19 download
and are individually named according to the filenames noted throughout this chapter.

In the last chapter, we developed `Conference.polyfills.arrayForEach`, which you could use
to augment the capabilities of an old-style `Array` that lacked a `forEach` function of its own. The
focus was on developing `forEach` itself; the plugging-in to `Array` was trivial and carefree:

```
Array.prototype.forEach = Conference.polyfills.arrayForEach;
```

Carefree? *Really?*

One is reminded of the eager but untrained Luke Skywalker, who tells Jedi master Yoda, "I
am not afraid."

Yoda replies gravely, "You will be. You *will* be."

What's to be afraid of? Before you venture into the dangerous territory of method-borrowing,
you must be prepared to answer three questions.

➤ What does the method require of the borrowing object?

➤ What effect will executing the method have on the borrowing object?

➤ What might its execution do to the donor object?

Look again at `Conference.polyfills.arrayForEach` (with parameter-checking omitted). How would you answer those three questions?

```
Conference.polyfills.arrayForEach = function(callbackFcn, thisObj){
  var i;

  for(i = 0; i < this.length; i++){
    callbackFcn.call(thisObj, this[i], i, this);
  }
};
```

Fortunately, the answer to the second and third question is "No effect at all." Or rather, no effect except for side effects from the callback, but that is to be expected.

For the first question, however, the answer is less favorable. Can you see the hidden requirement on the borrower?

It turns out that the borrowing object should have a `length` property. (Without length, no error will be thrown, but if you expected `forEach` to iterate through just any object's properties, you would be disappointed.) Did you notice that none of our unit tests in Chapter 18 considered this?

In this chapter, we propose some techniques for asking these three questions in your code, ensuring that the responses are as you expect, and ensuring that they stay that way.

ENSURING THE BORROWING OBJECT IS SUITABLE

How can you determine whether the borrowing object meets the borrowed function's requirements? Certainly you must begin by inspecting the borrowed function. With luck, it is like all your functions: short, simple, and well-explored with clear unit tests.

Once you've gotten to know the function, you can add some comments and hope people read them:

```
// *** WARNING *** Only borrow this function if you have a length property!
Conference.polyfills.arrayForEach = function(callbackFcn, thisObj){
  // etc.
}
```

However, if you want to write reliable code, that's not very reliable. It's not even code!

Making the Borrowed Function Qualify the Borrower

The next step in sophistication is to make the borrowed function qualify the borrower. Of course you begin by writing a test (see Listing 19-1):

LISTING 19-1: Testing the qualification process (code filename: ForEach\forEach_01_tests.js)

```
describe('forEach(callbackFcn, thisObj)',function() {
  'use strict';
  it('throws if not called from an object with a numeric length property',
  function(){
    var ix,
        obj,
        withNoGoodLength = [
          { a: 1 }, {length: "not a number"},
```

```
          {length: Infinity}, {length: -1}, {length: 1.5 }
        ];

    function expectThrow(obj) {
      expect(function() {
        obj.forEach(function() {/* do nothing*/});
      }).toThrow();
    }

    for (ix=0; ix<withNoGoodLength.length; ++ix) {
      obj = withNoGoodLength[ix];

      // Borrow the polyfill.
      obj.forEach = Conference.polyfills.arrayForEach;
      // Expect it not to work.
      expectThrow(obj);
    }
  });
});
```

The test attempts to borrow `arrayForEach` into a variety of objects that don't have the requisite `length` property. Each one should throw.

The next step is to add the qualification logic (see Listing 19-2):

LISTING 19-2: Qualifying the caller (code filename: ForEach\forEach_01.js)

```
Conference.polyfills.arrayForEach = function(callbackFcn, thisObj){
  'use strict';
  var i;
  // Qualify whoever might borrow this function
  if (typeof(this) !== 'object' ||
  !(typeof this.length === 'number' && isFinite(this.length) &&
  Math.floor(this.length) === this.length && this.length>=0)) {
    throw new Error('The context for arrayForEach must be array-like.');
  }
  for(i = 0; i < this.length; i++){
    callbackFcn.call(thisObj, this[i], i, this);
  }
};
```

The test passes (see Figure 19-1) and you get a little dopamine rush.

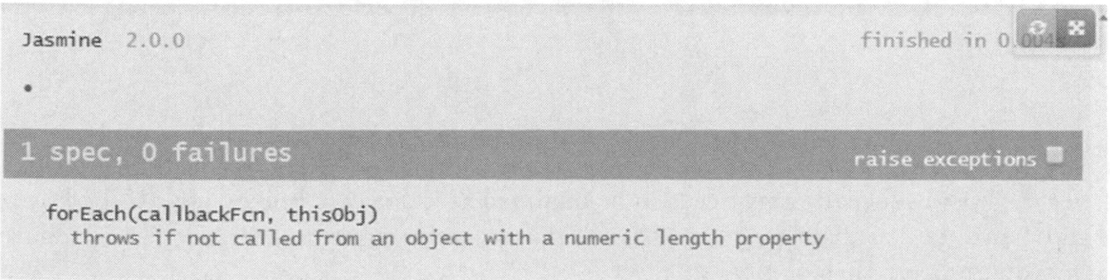

Jasmine 2.0.0 finished in 0.004s

1 spec, 0 failures raise exceptions ▣

forEach(callbackFcn, thisObj)
  throws if not called from an object with a numeric length property

FIGURE 19-1

As the dopamine ebbs, your mood cycles to mild depression as you contemplate the pollution of the code. You have doubled the length of `arrayForEach` without adding a lick of functionality. Furthermore, if another function were to need to verify the same thing (the presence of a `length` property), you'd have to repeat yourself. An aspect solves both of these problems.

Attaching an Aspect to the Borrowed Object

It is easy to package the new logic in an aspect. As a first step, you can use `Aop.before` (see Listing 19-3).

LISTING 19-3: Extracting the validation logic into an aspect (code filename: ForEach\ forEach_02.js)

```
var Conference = Conference || {};
Conference.polyfills = Conference.polyfills || {};
Conference.polyfills.arrayForEach = function(callbackFcn, thisObj){
  'use strict';
  var i;
  for(i = 0; i < this.length; i++){
    callbackFcn.call(thisObj, this[i], i, this);
  }
};

Aop.before('arrayForEach',function isObjectWithLength(obj){
  if (typeof(obj) !== 'object'
  !(typeof this.length === 'number' && isFinite(this.length) &&
  Math.floor(this.length) === this.length && this.length>=0)) {
    throw new Error('The context for forEach must be array-like.');
  }
},Conference.polyfills);
```

The aspect is attached after the function is defined, without cluttering it. It works the same: The unit test passes just as before (see Figure 19-2).

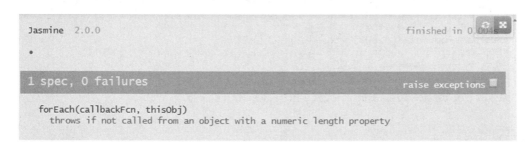

FIGURE 19-2

That's a little better, but it's not very efficient because the aspect will execute every time the function is called, yet the borrower really only needs to be qualified as it does the borrowing. (If the borrower has the `length` property at that time, you'd have to do something crazy in order for it not to have the `length` property from then on.)

But there is a more interesting problem with this approach. It requires the borrowing to take place *after* the aspect is applied. Otherwise, the borrower will get and hold a reference to the raw function, without the aspect. Listing 19-4 sets up a demonstration of the sequencing problem.

LISTING 19-4: A sequencing problem (code filename: Sequence\aspectSequenceProblem.js)

```javascript
//----------------------------------------------------------------
// Create the polyfill, then apply the aspect, then borrow it.
//----------------------------------------------------------------

Conference.polyfills.forEachWithEarlyAspect = function(callbackFcn, thisObj){
  var i;
  for(i = 0; i < this.length; i++){
    callbackFcn.call(thisObj, this[i], i, this);
  }
};
Aop.before('forEachWithEarlyAspect',function isObjectWithLength(obj){
  if (typeof(obj) !== 'object' ||
  !(typeof this.length === 'number' && isFinite(this.length) &&
  Math.floor(this.length) === this.length && this.length>=0)) {
    throw new Error('The context for forEach must be array-like.');
  }
},Conference.polyfills);

var objWithEarlyAspect = { /* no length property */ };
objWithEarlyAspect.forEach = Conference.polyfills.forEachWithEarlyAspect;

//----------------------------------------------------------------
// Create the polyfill, borrow it, then apply the aspect. (Wrong!)
//----------------------------------------------------------------

Conference.polyfills.forEachWithLateAspect = function(callbackFcn, thisObj){
  var i;
  for(i = 0; i < this.length; i++){
    callbackFcn.call(thisObj, this[i], i, this);
  }
};
var objWithLateAspect = { /* no length property */ };
objWithLateAspect.forEach = Conference.polyfills.forEachWithLateAspect;

// Applying the aspect too late!
Aop.before('forEachWithLateAspect',function isObjectWithLength(obj){
  if (typeof(obj) !== 'object'
  !(typeof this.length === 'number' && isFinite(this.length) &&
  Math.floor(this.length) === this.length && this.length>=0)) {
    throw new Error('The context for forEach must be array-like.');
  }
},Conference.polyfills);
```

The first half of the preceding code does things in the following order:

1. Define the polyfill.

2. Apply the aspect to qualify any borrower.

3.   Borrow the function.

The second half does things differently (and incorrectly):

1.   Define the polyfill.

2.   Borrow the function.

3.   Apply the aspect to qualify any borrower—too late!

Now you can run the same sort of test you saw earlier on each borrowing object, as shown in Listing 19-5.

LISTING 19-5: Testing the two sequences (code filename: Sequence\
aspectSequenceProblem_tests.js)

```
describe('aspect application', function() {
  'use strict';
  function doNothing() {
  }
  it('works when aspect applied before borrowing',
  function() {
    expect(function() {
      objWithEarlyAspect.forEach(doNothing);
    }).toThrow();
  });
  it('works when aspect applied after borrowing',
  function() {
    expect(function() {
      objWithLateAspect.forEach(doNothing);
    }).toThrow();
  });
});
```

The results (see Figure 19-3) show that if you apply the aspect after borrowing, it's too late.

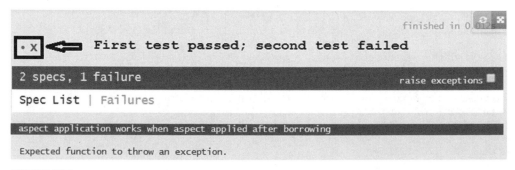

FIGURE 19-3

In our opinion, aspect-oriented programming is useful enough that one's programming technique should allow for it if at all possible.

It is also good technique to avoid what's called *temporal coupling*—the requirement to execute things in a certain order, especially if that order will not be obvious. As you saw in Chapter 17 (in the section "Putting It All Together"), applying all optional aspects in an application-configuration phase has the significant advantage that it's easy *not* to apply them. They're applied in one place, which can be skipped when you want streamlined code for production. The aspects as coded previously are optional but have a temporal coupling with the objects they modify. That prevents them from being part of the general configuration phase.

You've no doubt heard the aphorism, "Every software-design problem can be solved by adding a level of indirection." That is nowhere more true than in JavaScript. You can avoid the aspect-sequencing problem by borrowing not the function itself, but a wrapper function that in turn uses `apply` to execute the real function. This defers the method-binding until the method is actually executed—well after all aspects have been applied. Listing 19-6 shows how.

LISTING 19-6: Solving the sequencing problem with apply() (code filename: Sequence\borrowingWithApply.js [excerpt])

```
var objWithLateAspect = { /* no length property */ };
objWithLateAspect.forEach = function() {
  var args = Array.prototype.slice.call(arguments);
  return Conference.polyfills.forEachWithLateAspect.apply(this,args);
};
```

The direct way of borrowing:

```
objWithLateAspect.forEach = Conference.polyfills.forEachWithLateAspect;
```

has been replaced with functional indirection and an `apply`.

As you read in Chapter 18, the `apply` will execute `Conference.polyfills.forEachWithLateAspect)` but with the `this` supplied in the first argument, which, in this case, will be *objWithLateAspect*. The arguments to the function will be those supplied to the outer, anonymous function (the one assigned to *objWithLateAspect.forEach*.

With both borrowings done this way, both tests pass (see Figure 19-4).

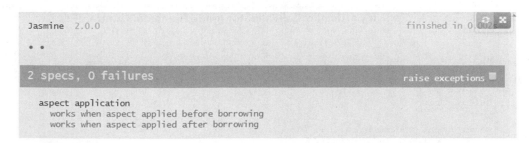

FIGURE 19-4

Although that solves the problem, it turns what used to be one very simple line of code:

```
objWithLateAspect.forEach = Conference.polyfills.forEachWithLateAspect;
```

into four complicated lines. Many developers would not count that as a win. But what if you could package the complication and forget about it?

Using a borrow() Method

Listing 19-7 shows one way to encapsulate the `apply` logic. It is a general-purpose utility function for borrowing.

LISTING 19-7: A general-purpose function-borrower (code filename: Utilities\utilities.js)

```
ReliableJavaScript.utilities.borrow =
function borrow(borrower, donor, funcName) {
  'use strict';
  borrower[funcName] = function() {
    var args = Array.prototype.slice.call(arguments);
    return donor[funcName].apply(this,args);
  };
};
```

Now a bare assignment like

```
borrower.func = donor.func;
```

becomes

```
ReliableJavaScript.utilities.borrow(borrower, donor, 'func');
```

which is just as simple in spite of having more characters. And of course, it is safer because it respects any aspects that have been applied to the borrowed function. That includes not only the aspect that qualifies the borrower, but the argument- and return-validators that you met in Chapters 16 and 17.

Adding an Object-Validator to the ContractRegistry

If you liked the `ContractRegistry` from those earlier chapters, why not enhance it with a way to attach this new type of aspect? In general terms, you need an aspect that validates the state of an object before a function call. Listing 19-8 shows this function, `ContractRegistry.attachPreCallValidator`. The new version of `ContractRegistry` and its unit tests are in the downloads for this chapter.

LISTING 19-8: ContractRegistry.attachPreCallValidator (code filename: ContractRegistry\ContractRegistry.js)

```
ReliableJavaScript.ContractRegistry.prototype.attachPreCallValidator =
function attachPreCallValidator(funcName, funcObj, contractName) {
  'use strict';
  var self = this;

  // *** Argument-checking omitted for clarity

  Aop.around(funcName,
```

```
        function validateObject(targetInfo) {
          self.assert(contractName,funcObj);
          return Aop.next.call(funcObj,targetInfo);
        }, funcObj);
    return this;
};
```

There remains the inefficiency mentioned earlier, that the borrowing object is vetted each time the function is called. However, because the validator is applied with the `ContractRegistry`, you can avoid it as described in "Bypassing Contracts for Production" in Chapter 17.

ANTICIPATING SIDE EFFECTS ON THE BORROWER

A borrowed function's requirement for certain properties and functions can make it a demanding guest, but its tendency to rearrange the furniture in its new home can make it downright impolite. Before the borrower allows the new function to move in, it should know what's in store.

Considering Side Effects from an Isolated Function

The simplest case is to borrow from a function that calls nothing else in its object. For example, take a look at the `OrderedObject` in Listing 19-9. Its prototype has a function, `forEachKey`, that is a riff on `arrayForEach`. It calls a function, *callbackFcn*, for each property that `Object.keys()` yields, in alphabetical order. To keep things simple, it does not have the option for *thisObj* that `arrayForEach` had, nor does the callback pass any arguments besides the property's name and value.

> **LISTING 19-9:** First version of OrderedObject (code filename: OrderedObject\
> OrderedObject_01.js)

```
var Conference = Conference || {};

Conference.OrderedObject = function() {
};

Conference.OrderedObject.prototype.forEachKey = function(callbackFcn) {
  'use strict';
  var ix,
      propName,
      orderedKeys = Object.keys(this).sort();

  for (ix=0; ix<orderedKeys.length; ++ix) {
    propName = orderedKeys[ix];
    callbackFcn.call(this,propName,this[propName]);
  }
};
```

Because `forEachKey` does not call any other function in `OrderedObject`, nor set any properties on *this*, you know it's not modifying `OrderedObject` at all. (Of course, the callback could do anything, but that is to be expected with a callback. We're talking about the `forEachKey` function itself.)

These two passing tests in Listing 19-10 show how `OrderedObject.forEachKey` can run on its own or as a borrowed function. Note, in the second test, how the borrowing can be done directly from the prototype, without having to create an instance of `OrderedObject`.

LISTING 19-10: Running OrderedObject.forEachKey in its original object or borrowed (code filename: OrderedObject\OrderedObject_01_tests.js)

```
describe('OrderedObject.forEachKey(callbackFcn)', function() {
  'use strict';
  var orderedObject,
      result;

  function processKey(key, value) {
    if (typeof value !== 'function' ) {
      result = result * 100 + value;
    }
  }

  beforeEach(function() {
    orderedObject = new Conference.OrderedObject();
    result = 0;
  });

  it('calls the callback for each key in the object, in order', function() {
    orderedObject.c = 11;
    orderedObject.a = 22;
    orderedObject.b = 33;
    orderedObject.forEachKey(processKey);
    expect(result).toBe(223311);
  });

  it('can be borrowed', function() {
    var borrower = { c:11, a:22, b:33 };
    ReliableJavaScript.utilities.borrow(
      borrower, Conference.OrderedObject.prototype, 'forEachKey');
    borrower.forEachKey(processKey);
    expect(result).toBe(223311);
  });
});
```

Considering Side Effects from a Function That Calls Other Functions

It's tempting to think that any function on the prototype is just as safe as `forEachKey` was. After all, prototype functions cannot access any private variables in the constructor, so they almost seem like stand-alone functions.

Not true. Consider the `OrderedObject` souped up with `trackedForEachKey` in Listing 19-11.

LISTING 19-11: trackedForEachKey (OrderedObject_02.js)

```javascript
Conference.OrderedObject = function() {
  'use strict';
  var self,
      propertyIterationCounts = {};

  this.incrementIterationCount = function incrementIterationCount(prop){
    if (!propertyIterationCounts[prop]) {
      propertyIterationCounts[prop] = 1;
    } else {
      ++propertyIterationCounts[prop];
    }
  };

  this.getIterationCount = function getIterationCount(prop) {
    return propertyIterationCounts[prop];
  };
};

Conference.OrderedObject.prototype.forEachKey = function(callbackFcn) {
  'use strict';
  var ix,
      propName,
      orderedKeys = Object.keys(this).sort();

  for (ix=0; ix<orderedKeys.length; ++ix) {
    propName = orderedKeys[ix];
    callbackFcn.call(this,propName,this[propName]);
  }
};

Conference.OrderedObject.prototype.trackedForEachKey = function(callbackFcn) {
  'use strict';
  var that = this;
  function callbackAndTrack(prop,value) {
    callbackFcn.call(that, prop, value);
    that.incrementIterationCount(prop);
  }

  this.forEachKey(callbackAndTrack);
};
```

Its (rather contrived) purpose is the same as forEachKey's but it keeps a record of how many times each property is visited.

The counts are kept in the private variable, *propertyIterationCounts*. As a private variable, it is declared in the constructor, not on the prototype. The constructor also establishes functions to increment and get the counts. Because those functions access the private variable, they, too, must be declared in the constructor and not on the prototype.

The trackedForEachKey function itself does not access private variables directly, which makes it reusable. As such, the prototype is the best place for it. It works by calling the earlier function, forEachKey, but with a callback that encapsulates the callback that was passed to it (*callbackFcn*) along with a call to incrementIterationCount.

The unit test in Listing 19-12 shows that it works.

LISTING 19-12: Test of ordinary call to trackedForEachKey (code filename: OrderedObject\ OrderedObject_02_tests.js)

```javascript
describe('OrderedObject', function() {
  'use strict';
  var orderedObject,
      result;

  function processKey(key, value) {
    if (typeof value !== 'function' ) {
      result = result * 100 + value;
    }
  }

  beforeEach(function() {
    orderedObject = new Conference.OrderedObject();
    result = 0;
  });

  // *** forEachKey tests omitted for clarity

  describe('trackedForEachKey(callbackFcn)', function() {

    beforeEach(function() {
      orderedObject.c = 11;
      orderedObject.a = 22;
      orderedObject.b = 33;
    });

    describe('in original object', function() {

      it('calls the callback for each key in the object, in order', function(){
        orderedObject.trackedForEachKey(processKey);
        expect(result).toBe(223311);
      });

      it('tracks how many times each property was visited', function() {
        var times = 2;
        for (var ix=0; ix<times; ++ix) {
          orderedObject.trackedForEachKey(processKey);
        }
        expect(orderedObject.getIterationCount('a')).toBe(times);
        expect(orderedObject.getIterationCount('b')).toBe(times);
        expect(orderedObject.getIterationCount('c')).toBe(times);
      });
    });

  });
});
```

And it does work (see Figure 19-5):

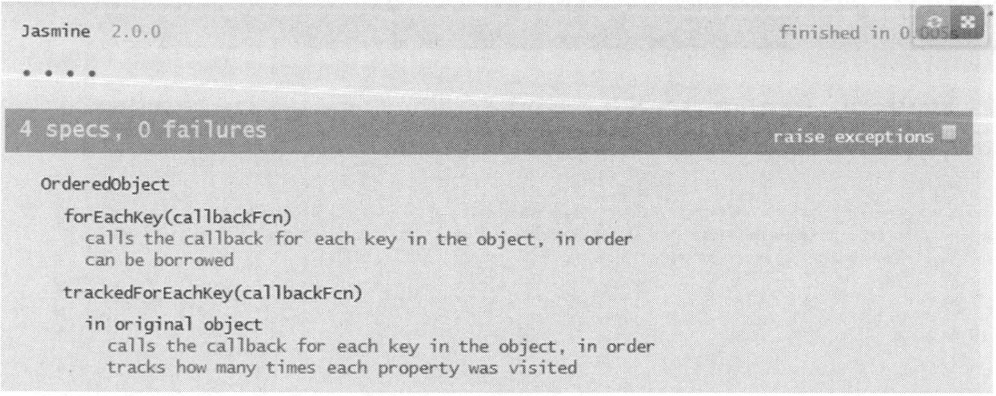

```
Jasmine  2.0.0                                    finished in 0.005

. . . .

4 specs, 0 failures                               raise exceptions ▪

  OrderedObject
    forEachKey(callbackFcn)
      calls the callback for each key in the object, in order
      can be borrowed
    trackedForEachKey(callbackFcn)

      in original object
        calls the callback for each key in the object, in order
        tracks how many times each property was visited
```

FIGURE 19-5

This function is safely on the prototype, and it works, but what do you think will happen if you borrow it as in Listing 19-13?

LISTING 19-13: Test of borrowing trackedForEachKey (code filename: OrderedObject\
OrderedObject_03_tests.js)

```javascript
describe('in borrowed object', function() {
  var borrower;
  beforeEach(function() {
    borrower = { c:11, a:22, b:33 };
    ReliableJavaScript.utilities.borrow(
      borrower, orderedObject, 'trackedForEachKey');
  });

  it('calls the callback for each key in the object, in order', function(){
    borrower.trackedForEachKey(processKey);
    expect(result).toBe(223311);
  });

  it('tracks how many times each property was visited', function() {
    var times = 2;
    for (var ix=0; ix<times; ++ix) {
      borrower.trackedForEachKey(processKey);
    }
    expect(borrower.getIterationCount('a')).toBe(times);
    expect(borrower.getIterationCount('b')).toBe(times);
    expect(borrower.getIterationCount('c')).toBe(times);
  });
});
```

The tests follow exactly the pattern of the earlier tests on `forEachKey`, where borrowing worked fine, but this time they fail (see Figure 19-6).

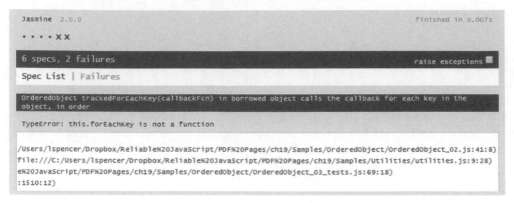

FIGURE 19-6

As you look at the following function again (from the end of Listing 19-11), you see that the failure is in the call on the last line. Although `trackedForEachKey` was borrowed, plain old `forEachKey`, on which it relies, was not.

```
Conference.OrderedObject.prototype.trackedForEachKey = function(callbackFcn) {
  var that = this;
  function callbackAndTrack(prop,value) {
    callbackFcn.call(that, prop, value);
    that.incrementIterationCount(prop);
  }

  this.forEachKey(callbackAndTrack);
};
```

Remember that when the borrower is the calling context, *this* refers to the borrower. That's why the borrower must have `forEachKey`. Even though it borrowed `trackedForEachKey` from the prototype, other functions on the prototype are not automatically available.

The borrower has two ways to supply `forEachKey`. First, if it happened to have one of its own, it would be addressed with *this* and get called with no effort. And this is the first side effect on the borrower: Its own functions can be called, whether that's planned or not.

> **NOTE** *Beware: A borrowed function can call its borrower's functions through* this.

The other way to supply `forEach` would be to borrow it, too. That would work, but that makes one *more* function whose side effects you must consider.

And you're not out of the woods yet. Did you notice the call to *that*.`incrementIterationCount`? (The variable *that* is required to save the outer *this*, which is the desired context for `incrementIterationCount`.) It is not on the prototype, so it does not even exist until there is a constructed `OrderedObject` to borrow it from.

The same goes for `getIterationCount`, which the borrower does not need in order to execute `trackedForEachKey` but will want eventually (!).

Again, the borrower could supply its own methods or create an `OrderedObject` and borrow from it. Listing 19-14 shows the latter approach.

LISTING 19-14: Borrowing from a concrete object (code filename: OrderedObject\ OrderedObject_04_tests.js)

```javascript
describe('OrderedObject', function() {
  'use strict';
  var orderedObject,
      result;

  function processKey(key, value) {
    if (typeof value !== 'function' ) {
      result = result * 100 + value;
    }
  }

  beforeEach(function() {
    orderedObject = new Conference.OrderedObject();
    result = 0;
  });

  // *** Earlier tests omitted.

  describe('trackedForEachKey(callbackFcn)', function() {

    beforeEach(function() {
      orderedObject.c = 11;
      orderedObject.a = 22;
      orderedObject.b = 33;
    });

    // *** Tests on original object omitted.

    describe('in borrowed object', function() {
      var borrower;
      beforeEach(function() {
        borrower = { c:11, a:22, b:33 };
        ReliableJavaScript.utilities.borrow(
          borrower, Conference.OrderedObject.prototype, 'trackedForEachKey');
        ReliableJavaScript.utilities.borrow(
          borrower, Conference.OrderedObject.prototype, 'forEachKey');
        ReliableJavaScript.utilities.borrow(
          borrower, orderedObject, 'incrementIterationCount');
        ReliableJavaScript.utilities.borrow(
          borrower, orderedObject, 'getIterationCount');

      });
      it('calls the callback for each key in the object, in order', function(){
        borrower.trackedForEachKey(processKey);
        expect(result).toBe(223311);
```

continues

LISTING 19-14 *(continued)*

```
      });

      it('tracks how many times each property was visited', function() {
        var times = 2;
        for (var ix=0; ix<times; ++ix) {
          borrower.trackedForEachKey(processKey);
        }
        expect(borrower.getIterationCount('a')).toBe(times);
        expect(borrower.getIterationCount('b')).toBe(times);
        expect(borrower.getIterationCount('c')).toBe(times);
      });
    });
  });
});
```

You can see that `incrementIterationCount` and `getIterationCount` were borrowed from the constructed object. Functions `trackedForEachKey` and `forEachKey` were still borrowed from the prototype but they, too, could have been borrowed from the *orderedObject* variable. Now everything works (see Figure 19-7).

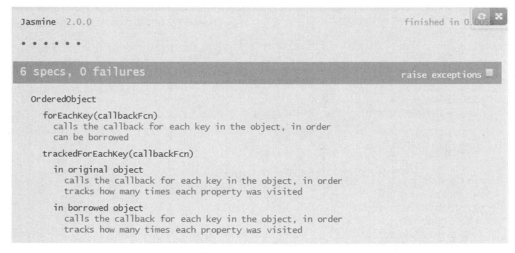

FIGURE 19-7

ANTICIPATING SIDE EFFECTS ON THE DONOR OBJECT

That last test verified that some counters in the donor object were incremented. Here again is the constructor from Listing 19-11, where you can see the affected variable: *propertyIterationCounts*.

```
Conference.OrderedObject = function() {
  var self,
      propertyIterationCounts = {};

  this.incrementIterationCount = function incrementIterationCount(prop){
    if (!propertyIterationCounts[prop]) {
      propertyIterationCounts[prop] = 1;
```

```
    } else {
      ++propertyIterationCounts[prop];
    }
  };

  this.getIterationCount = function getIterationCount(prop) {
    return propertyIterationCounts[prop];
  };
};
```

A carefree programmer might think that because he is transplanting a function from a donor object into a new object, the donor won't be affected when the new object calls the function. The preceding example shows how that belief is too optimistic. Even a function such as `trackedForEachKey`, which was on the prototype, can affect the variables of its donor object—and private ones at that.

> **NOTE** *Be aware that a borrowed function can still alter data in its old home.*

Believe it or not, things can get even more dicey. What if you borrow some of the functions on which the main borrowed function depends, but inadvertently supplied others of your own? One can envision using the `ContractRegistry` to allow the borrower to supply all the functions or none, but not just some. That is left as an exercise.

SUMMARY

In this chapter, you experienced the pleasures and pitfalls of borrowing functions. Although it's a mode of code reuse that is not as easy in many other languages, you must be careful of three things:

➤ The qualifications of the borrower

➤ Possible effects on the borrower

➤ Possible effects on the donor

Aspect-oriented programming can unobtrusively qualify the borrower. As for side effects, there is no substitute for careful analysis.

In Chapter 20, you will see another JavaScript method of code reuse: the mixin pattern.

20

Ensuring Correct Use of Mixins

WHAT'S IN THIS CHAPTER?

➤ Identifying situations in which using a mixin is appropriate

➤ Creating an extend function that safely "mixes" one object into another

➤ Creating and testing a mixin for use with an extend function

➤ Creating and testing a functional mixin

WROX.COM CODE DOWNLOADS FOR THIS CHAPTER

You can find the wrox.com code downloads for this chapter at www.wrox.com/go/ reliablejavascript on the Download Code tab. The files are in the Chapter 20 download and individually named according to the filenames noted throughout this chapter.

Mixins are a mechanism for code reuse in which the properties of one object, the *mixin*, are utilized by another, the *target*. This sounds similar to the topic covered in Chapter 19, method-borrowing, and it is. Both techniques may be used to share method implementations from one object to another, but there are a few key differences:

➤ The mixin object provides both data and methods to the target, whereas method-borrowing, as the name implies, limits the sharing to methods.

➤ The mixin object exists only to provide its properties to a target; it is not intended to function on its own.

➤ The mixin object's properties are added directly to the target object; the target object doesn't retain an explicit reference to the mixin.

Mixins are ideally suited for implementing functionality common to many object types, but not dependent upon the details of any of those types.

Suppose you'd like all of the objects in your system that are responsible for encapsulating data to expose an `asJSON()` convenience method that returns the contents of the object as a JSON string. Creating such a function is not complicated, as modern browsers provide the `JSON.stringify` method:

```
var dataObject1 = {
  propertyA: "a property",
  propertyB: "b property",

  asJSON: function asJSON(){
    return JSON.stringify(this);
  }
};

dataObject1.asJSON(); // '{ propertyA: "a property", propertyB: "b property" }';
```

While the function itself is simple, adding it to each of the individual data objects in a large system would lead to hundreds of lines of identical code. Not very DRY at all.

Let's continue the example and say that, against your better judgment, you've added the function to each of the data objects. What happens if a third-party JSON library that can generate a JSON string ten times faster than the browser's native method comes along and you want to update all of your data objects to employ the library? A lot of Find and Replace, that's what. There's a better way.

Because the `asJSON` method has no dependency upon the details of the object that contains it, it's a prime candidate for implementation as a mixin:

```
var asJSONMixin = {
  asJSON: function asJSON(){
    return JSON.stringify(this);
  }
};
```

This may be used to extend the data objects:

```
var dataObject1 = {
  propertyA: "a property",
  propertyB: "b property"
};

// Extend dataObject1 by adding the asJSONMixin to it (the details of the
// extend function will be covered later in the chapter)
extend(dataObject1, asJSONMixin);

// dataObject1 has the asJSON method, but didn't have to implement it itself
dataObject1.asJSON(); // '{ propertyA: "a property", propertyB: "b property" }';
```

By extending the data objects with a *traditional mixin*, one that has its properties copied into its target, which implements `asJSON` rather than implementing `asJSON` directly in each object, incorporation of the hypothetical JSON library is simple: Only the mixin needs to be updated.

In the coming sections, we show you how to create the `extend` function used in the sample and explain how our implementation of `extend` differs from those provided by libraries such as jQuery and underscore. We'll also show you how to create a traditional mixin using test-driven development. Finally, we explore functional mixins and how they differ, both positively and negatively, from traditional mixins.

CREATING AND USING MIXINS

This section revisits the `attendee` module that we used during the discussion of promises in Chapter 6. For reference, the `attendee` module is shown in Listing 20-1.

LISTING 20-1: The attendee module from Chapter 6 (code filename: Mixins\attendee_original.js)

```javascript
var Conference = Conference || {};
Conference.attendee = function(firstName, lastName){
  'use strict';

  var attendeeId,
    checkedIn = false,
    first = firstName || 'None',
    last = lastName || 'None',
    checkInNumber;

  return {
    setId: function(id) {
      attendeeId = id;
    },

    getId: function() {
      return attendeeId;
    },

    getFullName: function(){
      return first + ' ' + last;
    },

    isCheckedIn: function(){
      return checkedIn;
    },

    checkIn: function(){
      checkedIn = true;
    },

    undoCheckIn: function() {
      checkedIn = false;
      checkInNumber = undefined;
    },

    setCheckInNumber: function(number) {
      checkInNumber = number;
    },

    getCheckInNumber: function() {
      return checkInNumber;
    }
  };
};
```

Of the eight methods in the `attendee` module shown in Listing 20-1, two stand out as generic and may be useful for other objects. Can you identify them? If you found `getId()` and `setId(id)`, we're on the same page.

In Chapter 6, the `id`-related methods were added to `attendee` for the purpose of retaining an `attendee`'s unique identifier. The unique identifier may be used to store and retrieve the `attendee` via a web service. It's not beyond the realm of possibility that other entities used by the JavaScript conference's website will also have unique identifiers.

In other words, the concept of the unique identifier is not specific to `attendee`, nor is it dependent upon the details of the `attendee`. The implementation of the unique identifier is a great candidate for refactoring into a mixin. This section explores this refactoring.

Creating and Using a Traditional Mixin

As shown in the introductory example, traditional mixins rely upon a function to "mix" them into a target object. This function, which copies the mixin object's properties into the target, is traditionally called `mixin` or `extend`. We prefer `extend`, as it speaks to the action taking place: The target object is being *extended* by the mixin.

Creating the extend Function Using Test-Driven Development

As you might imagine, the `extend` function accepts two arguments:

➤ The object to extend, or `target`

➤ The object providing the extension, or *mixin*

As is our common practice, we'll start by ensuring that errors are thrown in exceptional cases. For the `extend` function, an error should be thrown if either the `target` or the `mixin` is not an object. The unit tests provided in Listing 20-2 ensure this functionality.

LISTING 20-2: Tests to ensure that extend throws if target or mixin is not an object (code filename: mixins\extend_01_tests.js)

```
describe("ReliableJavaScript.extend(target, mixin)", function(){
  'use strict';

  var notObjects = ["", null, undefined, 1];

  it("throws if the target argument is not an object", function(){
    notObjects.forEach(function(notObj){
      expect(function shouldThrow(){
        ReliableJavaScript.extend(notObj, {});
      }).toThrowError(ReliableJavaScript.extend.messages.targetNotObject);
    });
  });

  it("throws if the mixin argument is not an object", function(){
    notObjects.forEach(function(notObj){
      expect(function shouldThrow(){
```

```
              ReliableJavaScript.extend({}, notObj);
          }).toThrowError(ReliableJavaScript.extend.messages.mixinNotObject);
      });
  });
});
```

Each of the tests iterate through the `notObjects` array whose elements, you might have guessed, are not objects. The tests provide each element as `target` in the case of the first test, or `mixin` in the case of the second test, and ensure that the appropriate error is thrown. A stub implementation of `extend` doesn't satisfy these tests, as Figure 20-1 shows.

FIGURE 20-1

Listing 20-3 implements the verification that `target` and `mixin` are, in fact, objects. The expected messages are also added to the `messages` property of the `extend` function.

LISTING 20-3: Implementation of extend that verifies target and source are objects (code filename: Mixins\extend_01.js)

```
var ReliableJavaScript = ReliableJavaScript || {};

ReliableJavaScript.extend = function(target, mixin){
  'use strict';

  if(!target || typeof(target) !== "object"){
    throw new Error(ReliableJavaScript.extend.messages.targetNotObject);
```

continues

LISTING 20-3 *(continued)*

```
    }

    if(!mixin || typeof(mixin) !== "object"){
      throw new Error(ReliableJavaScript.extend.messages.mixinNotObject);
    }
  };
  ReliableJavaScript.extend.messages = {
    targetNotObject: "target is not an object",
    mixinNotObject: "mixin is not an object"
  };
```

The guard clauses highlighted in Listing 20-3 simply ensure that `target` and `mixin` are defined and are objects. Figure 20-2 shows that the clauses allow the unit tests to pass.

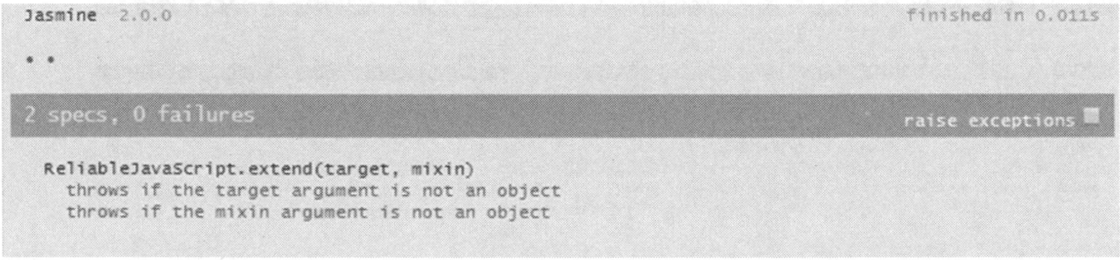

FIGURE 20-2

> **NOTE** *Chapter 17 presents an alternative mechanism for validating function arguments.*

The next step is to ensure that the `extend` method operates properly when the `mixin` argument is an empty object. When `mixin` is empty, `target` shouldn't be changed. Listing 20-4 provides the unit test to verify this functionality.

LISTING 20-4: Test to ensure that target isn't changed if mixin is a bare object (code filename: Mixins\extend_02_tests.js)

```
describe("ReliableJavaScript.extend(target, mixin)", function(){

  /*** Previously discussed tests omitted ***/

  it("doesn't alter target if mixin is a bare object", function(){
    var target = {
      property1: "a property",
      method1: function method1(){
        return "a method";
      }
    },
    method = target.method1;

    ReliableJavaScript.extend(target, {});

    // ensure that the target hasn't had any keys added or removed
```

```
      expect(Object.keys(target).sort()).toEqual(["method1", "property1"]);

      // ensure that the target's functionality hasn't been changed
      expect(target.property1).toEqual("a property");
      expect(target.method1).toEqual(method);
    });
  });
```

The test added in Listing 20-4 extends `target` with an empty object. It then verifies that no properties have been added to or removed from `target` by ensuring that `target`'s keys haven't changed. Finally, the test ensures that the functionality of `target`'s properties haven't changed.

Because the current implementation of `extend` does nothing more than ensure `target` and `mixin` are provided, the new test passes, as shown in Figure 20-3.

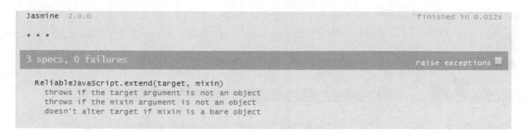

FIGURE 20-3

The next test verifies that the opposite situation, a bare `target` extended by a `mixin` with properties, functions correctly. Listing 20-5 presents the test for this.

LISTING 20-5: Test that ensures a bare target is properly extended (code filename: mixin\extend_03_tests.js)

```
describe("ReliableJavaScript.extend(target, mixin)", function(){

  /*** Previously discussed tests omitted ***/

  it("adds properties to a bare target", function(){
    var target = {},
        mixin = {
          property1: "first property",
          property2: "second property",
          method1: function method1(){
            return "first method";
          },
          method2: function method2(){
            return "second method";
          }
```

continues

LISTING 20-5 *(continued)*

```
        };

    ReliableJavaScript.extend(target, mixin);

    // Since target was initially bare, it should now be equivalent to mixin
    expect(target).toEqual(mixin);
    });
});
```

This test extends `target`, which is initialized as a bare object, with `mixin`, which contains multiple properties—both functions and data.

Because `target` was initially bare, the test can ensure that the properties of `mixin` were copied into `target` by ensuring that `target` and `mixin` are equivalent after the extension has occurred. The statement:

```
    expect(target).toEqual(mixin);
```

performs that test. This new test fails with the current implementation of `extend`, as Figure 20-4 shows.

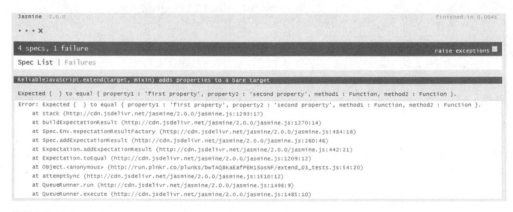

FIGURE 20-4

Listing 20-6 improves the implementation of `extend` to accommodate this new test.

LISTING 20-6: Making extend copy the properties of mixin to target (code filename: Mixin\ extend_03.js)

```
var ReliableJavaScript = ReliableJavaScript || {};
ReliableJavaScript.extend = function(target, mixin){
    'use strict';

    if(!target || typeof(target) !== "object"){
        throw new Error(ReliableJavaScript.extend.messages.targetNotObject);
    }

    if(!mixin || typeof(mixin) !== "object"){
        throw new Error(ReliableJavaScript.extend.messages.mixinNotObject);
```

```
        }

        for(var item in mixin){
          target[item] = mixin[item];
        }
    };
    ReliableJavaScript.extend.messages = {
      targetNotObject: "target is not an object",
      mixinNotObject: "mixin is not an object"
    };
```

The code added in Listing 20-6 is simple but powerful. It iterates through the properties of `mixin` and adds each property to `target`. The new implementation of `extend` satisfies all of the existing unit tests, as Figure 20-5 shows.

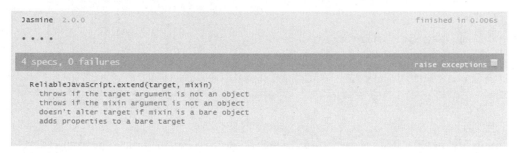

```
Jasmine  2.0.0                                                    finished in 0.006s

• • • •

4 specs, 0 failures                                                raise exceptions ■

ReliableJavaScript.extend(target, mixin)
   throws if the target argument is not an object
   throws if the mixin argument is not an object
   doesn't alter target if mixin is a bare object
   adds properties to a bare target
```

FIGURE 20-5

The `for` loop introduced to `extend` in Listing 20-6 copies the enumerable properties of `mixin` to `target`, including those properties that `mixin` may inherit through its prototype. While mixins provide a convenient mechanism to reuse code, their use can introduce complexity when you're attempting to determine the source of an object's behavior.

In order to reduce this complexity, we prefer to copy only the properties that the mixin directly defines. This eliminates the need to traverse a prototype chain when you're trying to find the source of a mixed-in property.

Listing 20-7 provides a test that ensures that properties that `mixin` inherits aren't copied to `target`.

LISTING 20-7: Test to ensure that mixin's inherited properties aren't copied into target (code filename: Mixin\extend_04_tests.js)

```
describe("ReliableJavaScript.extend(target, mixin)", function(){

  /*** Previously discussed tests omitted ***/

  it("doesn't add the mixin's inherited properties", function(){
```

continues

LISTING 20-7 *(continued)*

```
    var target = {},

        mixinBase = {
          baseProperty: "base property",
          baseMethod: function baseMethod(){
            return "this is the base method";
          }
        },

        // create the mixin object using mixinBase as its prototpe
        mixin = Object.create(mixinBase);

      mixin.mixinProperty = "mixin property",
      mixin.mixinMethod = function mixinMethod(){
        return "this is the mixin method";
      };

    ReliableJavaScript.extend(target, mixin);

    // Ensure that the target only contains the keys from the mixin object;
    // it should not contain any of the properties from mixinBase
    expect(Object.keys(target).sort()).toEqual(["mixinMethod", "mixinProperty"]);
  });
});
```

The test added in Listing 20-7 defines `mixinBase`, which is then used as the prototype of `mixin`. As such, `mixin` inherits the two properties defined by `mixinBase`, `baseProperty`, and `baseMethod`.

The test then defines two properties directly on `mixin`: `mixinProperty` and `mixinMethod`. The `extend` method is then used to extend `target` with `mixin`.

To ensure that the properties that `mixin` has inherited from `mixinBase` have not been copied to `target`, the expectation

```
expect(Object.keys(target).sort()).toEqual(["mixinMethod", "mixinProperty"]);
```

verifies that `target` has only the properties that were directly defined on `mixin`. Figure 20-6 shows that the new test fails, proving that the `extend` function doesn't yet have the desired behavior.

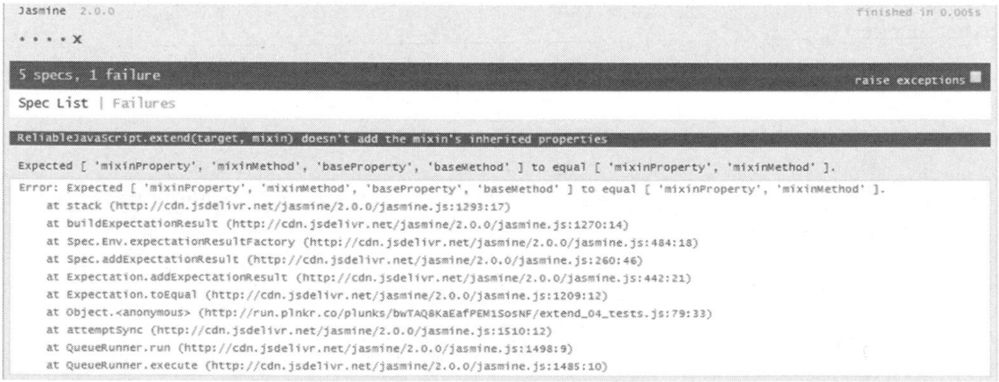

FIGURE 20-6

Listing 20-8 presents a modified `extend` function that only copies the properties directly defined on `mixin`.

LISTING 20-8: Implementation of extend that doesn't copy properties mixin has inherited (code filename: Mixin\extend_04.js)

```javascript
var ReliableJavaScript = ReliableJavaScript || {};
ReliableJavaScript.extend = function(target, mixin){
  'use strict';

  if(!target || typeof(target) !== "object"){
    throw new Error(ReliableJavaScript.extend.messages.targetNotObject);
  }

  if(!mixin || typeof(mixin) !== "object"){
    throw new Error(ReliableJavaScript.extend.messages.mixinNotObject);
  }

  for(var item in mixin){
    if(mixin.hasOwnProperty(item)){
      target[item] = mixin[item];
    }
  }
};
ReliableJavaScript.extend.messages = {
  targetNotObject: "target is not an object",
  mixinNotObject: "mixin is not an object"
};
```

Listing 20-8 simply introduces the condition that a property is only copied from `mixin` to `target` if the property is directly defined on `mixin`. Figure 20-7 shows that this added condition allows the unit test to pass.

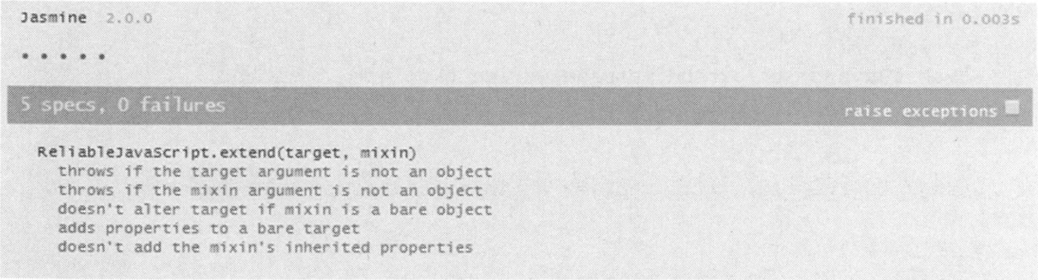

FIGURE 20-7

One aspect of `extend` that you may have noticed is that it blindly assigns the properties that it's mixing in to properties of `target`. If `target` happens to already have a property that `mixin` provides, `target`'s property will be overwritten with the one provided by `mixin`.

This is the behavior of the `extend` function provided by both the jQuery library (`http://api .jquery.com/jquery.extend/`) and the underscore library (`http://underscorejs.org/#extend`).

We don't believe this behavior promotes reliability. As an object can be extended by a mixin at any time in its lifespan, a mixin that changes an existing property of an object could have a negative impact on code that's not aware the mixin has been applied.

As such, the implementation of extend presented here will be altered so that an error is thrown if the application of mixin would overwrite an existing property of target. The tests in Listing 20-9 verify this behavior.

LISTING 20-9: Tests that ensure an error is thrown if a mixin will overwrite an existing property (code filename: Mixin\extend_05_tests.js)

```
describe("ReliableJavaScript.extend(target, mixin)", function(){

  /*** Previously discussed tests omitted ***/

  it("throws if the mixin will replace an 'own' property", function(){
    var target = {
          property1 : "property 1",

          // both target and mixin define method1
          method1 : function method1(){
            return "method 1";
          }
        },

        mixin = {
          property2 : "property 2",

          // both target and mixin define method1
          method1 : function method1(){
            return "mixin's method 1";
          }
        };
    expect(function(){
      ReliableJavaScript.extend(target, mixin);
    })
    .toThrowError(
      ReliableJavaScript.extend.messages.triedToReplace + "method1"
    );
  });

  it("throws if the mixin will replace an inherited property", function(){
    var
        targetBase = {
          baseProperty : "base property",
          baseMethod : function baseMethod(){
            return "baseMethod";
          }
        },
        target = Object.create(targetBase),
        mixin = {
          // target inherits baseProperty from targetBase
          baseProperty : "property 2",
          method2 : function method2(){
            return "mixin's method 2";
```

```
        }
      };

    expect(function(){
      ReliableJavaScript.extend(target, mixin);
    })
    .toThrowError(
      ReliableJavaScript.extend.messages.triedToReplace + "baseProperty"
    );
  });
});
```

The two tests in Listing 20-9 ensure that the `extend` function throws an appropriate error if `mixin` replaces an existing property of `target`. The first test ensures an error is thrown if the property replaced by `mixin` is defined directly on `target`. The second test ensures that an error is also thrown if the property replaced by `mixin` is inherited by `target`. Figure 20-8 shows that these tests fail with the current implementation of `extend`.

FIGURE 20-8

The updated implementation of `extend` that causes the appropriate errors to be thrown is provided in Listing 20-10.

LISTING 20-10: Implementation of extend that throws if mixin replaces an existing property of target (code filename: Mixin\extend_05.js)

```
var ReliableJavaScript = ReliableJavaScript || {};
ReliableJavaScript.extend = function(target, mixin){
```

continues

LISTING 20-10 *(continued)*

```
'use strict';

if(!target || typeof(target) != "object"){
  throw new Error(ReliableJavaScript.extend.messages.targetNotObject);
}

if(!mixin || typeof(mixin) != "object"){
  throw new Error(ReliableJavaScript.extend.messages.mixinNotObject);
}

for(var item in mixin){
  if(mixin.hasOwnProperty(item)){
    if(!(item in target)){
      target[item] = mixin[item];
    } else {
      throw new
        Error(ReliableJavaScript.extend.messages.triedToReplace + item);
    }
  }
}
};
ReliableJavaScript.extend.messages = {
  targetNotObject: "target is not an object",
  mixinNotObject: "mixin is not an object",
  triedToReplace: "mixin attempted to replace the existing property: "
};
```

The code highlighted in Listing 20-10 implements the necessary check to ensure that a `mixin` that defines a property that already exists on `target` causes an error to be thrown.

Checking for the presence of the property in `target` via

```
if(!(item in target))
```

does so without regard to whether the property is directly defined or inherited. This ensures that an exception will be thrown in either case. The passing unit tests in Figure 20-9 prove this to be true.

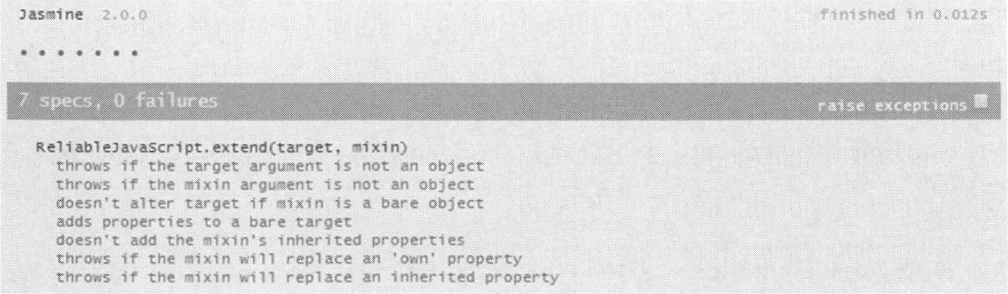

```
Jasmine  2.0.0                                              finished in 0.012s

· · · · · · ·

7 specs, 0 failures                                         raise exceptions ☐

ReliableJavaScript.extend(target, mixin)
  throws if the target argument is not an object
  throws if the mixin argument is not an object
  doesn't alter target if mixin is a bare object
  adds properties to a bare target
  doesn't add the mixin's inherited properties
  throws if the mixin will replace an 'own' property
  throws if the mixin will replace an inherited property
```

FIGURE 20-9

Creating a Traditional Mixin Using Test-Driven Development

With a fully implemented `extend` function, we can turn our attention to creating a traditional mixin that implements the unique identifier functionality that's used by the `attendee` module.

In order to provide all the functionality that the attendee module requires, the `idMixin` needs to provide both the property in which the identifier will be stored, along with the `getId` and `setId` methods. The first test, presented in Listing 20-11, ensures that `idMixin` provides those properties to the object it extends.

LISTING 20-11: Test to ensure that idMixin provides the appropriate properties (code filename: Mixin\idMixin_tests_01.js)

```
describe("Conference.mixins", function(){
  'use strict';

  var target,
      mixin;

  describe("idMixin()", function(){
    beforeEach(function(){
      target = {};
      mixin = Conference.mixins.idMixin();

      ReliableJavaScript.extend(target, mixin);
    });

    describe("when mixed in", function(){
      it("adds the expected properties to the target", function(){
        expect(Object.keys(target).sort()).toEqual(["getId", "id", "setId"]);
      });
    });
  });
});
```

The test suite starts with a `beforeEach` that initializes `target` to an empty object and `mixin` to an instance of the `idMixin`. The last step performed in the `beforeEach` is the extension of `target` by `mixin`.

The test simply ensures that `target` contains the properties `id`, `getId`, and `setId` after it has been extended. With only a stub implementation of `idMixin`, this test fails. Figure 20-10 shows the failure.

The test can be enticed to pass by returning an object with the requisite properties from the `idMixin` module. Listing 20-12 updates `idMixin` to do so, and Figure 20-11 shows that the update causes the unit test to pass.

> **LISTING 20-12:** Update idMixin to return an object with the expected properties (code filename: Mixin\idMixin_01.js)

```javascript
var Conference = Conference || {};
Conference.mixins = Conference.mixins || {};

Conference.mixins.idMixin = function(){
  'use strict';

  return {
    id: null,
    getId: null,
    setId: null
  };
};
```

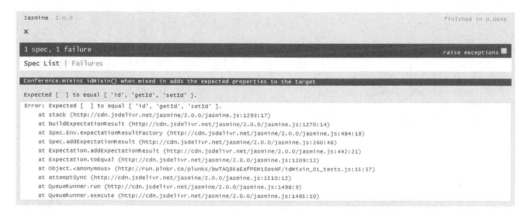

FIGURE 20-10

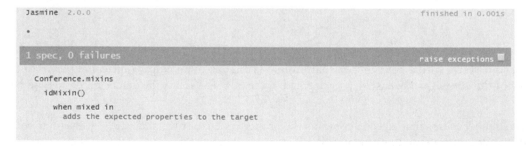

FIGURE 20-11

As implemented by the attendee module, the getId method returns undefined if it is called before an attendee's ID has been set. Once setId has been executed, subsequent execution of getId should return the value provided to setId. The tests in Listing 20-13 verify this functionality.

> **LISTING 20-13:** Tests that ensure correct functionality of getId and setId (code filename: Mixin\idMixin_02_tests.js)

```javascript
describe("Conference.mixins", function(){
```

```
'use strict';

var target,
    mixin;

describe("idMixin()", function(){

  /*** Previously discussed setup omitted ***/

  describe("when mixed in", function(){

    /*** Previously discussed test omitted ***/

    describe("getId() & setId(id)", function(){
      it("getId() returns undefined if setId(idValue) hasn't been called",
      function(){
        expect(target.getId()).toBe(undefined);
      });

      it("getId() returns the value set by setId(idValue)",
      function(){
        var id = "theId";
        target.setId(id);
        expect(target.getId()).toEqual(id);
      });
    });
  });
});
});
```

The first test in Listing 20-13 ensures that the value returned by getId is undefined if the ID hasn't been previously set via a call to setId. The second test in the listing verifies that getId returns the ID that was provided to setId. Figure 20-12 shows that these tests currently fail.

The implementation of idMixin that allows the test to pass is straightforward and appears in Listing 20-14.

LISTING 20-14: Full implementation of idMixin (code filename: Mixin\idMixin_02.js)

```
var Conference = Conference || {};
Conference.mixins = Conference.mixins || {};

Conference.mixins.idMixin = function(){
  'use strict';

  return {
    id: undefined,
    getId: function getId(){
      return this.id;
    },
    setId: function setId(idValue){
      this.id = idValue;
    }
  };
};
```

FIGURE 20-12

The updated implementation of `idMixin` initializes the `id` property to `undefined` and provides the appropriate implementations of `getId` and `setId`.

Recall that the `extend` function copies references to the properties of the mixin into properties of the target object. As such, when the methods provided to the target by the mixin are executed, *this* will be bound to the target object (as long as the methods are executed via the target object; see Chapter 18 for more details). The `idMixin` is guaranteed that the object containing the `getId` and `setId` methods will also contain the `id` property because the mixin itself provides it.

> **NOTE** *If a mixin depends on the target to provide a property, that mixin would need to ensure that the target contains the property in order to be completely reliable. We encountered this same problem in Chapter 19 when discussing method-borrowing.*
>
> *Mixins that depend upon only properties that they provide are simpler and more reliable than mixins that require their target to provide certain properties.*

The implementation of `idMixin` presented in Listing 20-14 allows all the unit tests to pass, as shown in Figure 20-13.

With the `idMixin` fully implemented, the final step is to integrate it into the `attendee` module. Listing 20-15 contains an excerpt from the original unit tests for the `attendee` module from Chapter 6.

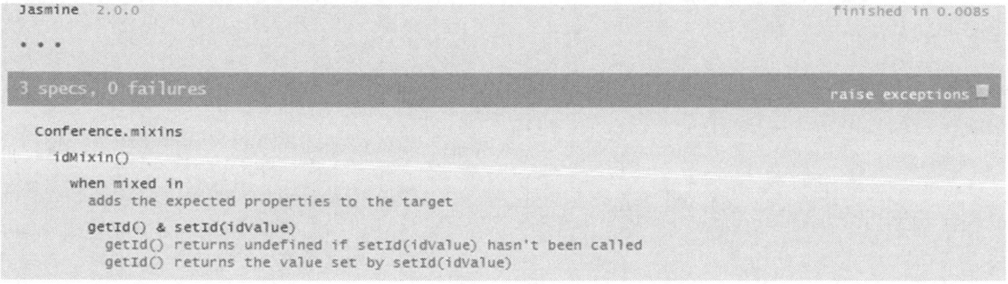

FIGURE 20-13

LISTING 20-15: Excerpt from the original unit tests for the attendee module (code filename: Mixin\attendee_tests.js)

```
describe('Conference.attendee', function() {
  'use strict';

  var attendee, firstName, lastName;

  beforeEach(function() {
    firstName = 'Tom';
    lastName = 'Jones';
    attendee = Conference.attendee(firstName, lastName);
  });

  it('sets and gets the primary key with setId(id) and getId()',function() {
    var id = 1234;
    attendee.setId(id);
    expect(attendee.getId()).toBe(id);
  });

  /*** Tests unrelated to getId/setId omitted ***/
});
```

As you can see, the test verifies that setId and getId function appropriately. Because the idMixin should now be used to provide the getId and setId methods, they're removed from the attendee implementation, as is the attendeeId variable used to store the ID. Unsurprisingly, doing so causes the unit test to fail, as shown in Figure 20-14.

Listing 20-16 shows how to incorporate the idMixin into the attendee module to provide the getId and setId functions.

LISTING 20-16: Extending attendee with idMixin (code filename: Mixin\attendee_idMixin.js)

```
var Conference = Conference || {};
Conference.attendee = function(firstName, lastName){
  'use strict';

  var checkedIn = false,
    first = firstName || 'None',
```

continues

LISTING 20-16 *(continued)*

```javascript
      last = lastName || 'None',
      checkInNumber,

      newAttendee = {
        getFullName: function(){
          return first + ' ' + last;
        },

        isCheckedIn: function(){
          return checkedIn;
        },

        checkIn: function(){
          checkedIn = true;
        },

        undoCheckIn: function() {
          checkedIn = false;
          checkInNumber = undefined;
        },

        setCheckInNumber: function(number) {
          checkInNumber = number;
        },

        getCheckInNumber: function() {
          return checkInNumber;
        }
      };

      // extend newAttendee with the idMixin
      ReliableJavaScript.extend(newAttendee, Conference.mixins.idMixin());

      // return the extended attendee
      return newAttendee;
  };
```

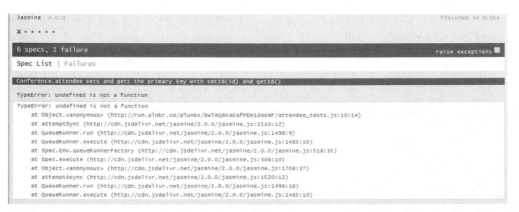

FIGURE 20-14

Rather than immediately returning an object, the `attendee` module now assigns the object containing the properties specific to an attendee into *newAttendee*. It then extends *newAttendee* with the object returned by `idMixin`, providing the `getId`/`setId` functionality that `attendee` previously defined itself. Finally, the extended *newAttendee* object is returned. Figure 20-15 shows that the attendee unit tests are once again passing.

```
Jasmine  2.0.0                                              finished in 0.003s

. . . . . .

6 specs, 0 failures                                         raise exceptions ■

  Conference.attendee
    sets and gets the primary key with setId(id) and getId()
    offers the full name with getFullName()
    is initially not checked in
    is checked in after a call to checkIn()
    is no longer checked in after undoCheckIn()
    sets the checkin number with setCheckInNumber() and gets it with getCheckInNumber()
```

FIGURE 20-15

There's one small, but significant, difference between `attendee`'s original implementation of `getId` and `setId` and the implementation of those methods as mixed in by the `idMixin` object. In the original implementation, the value provided to `setId` and returned from `getId` was captured in a variable that wasn't accessible to external code, `attendeeId`. (Listing 20-1 shows the original version of `attendee`.) By hiding the `attendeeId` variable, the `attendee` module could be certain that the variable could only be manipulated via the `setId` method.

The `idMixin`, however, adds `id` as a property of the object being extended, and the `getId` and `setId` methods manipulate that property. Because it's an exposed property of the object, `id` could be changed directly; using `setId` isn't required:

```
// Create an attendee that's extended by idMixin
var extendedAttendee = Conference.attendee();

extendedAttendee.setId(12);
console.log(extendedAttendee.getId());   // 12

extendedAttendee.id = -1;
console.log(extendedAttendee.getId());   // -1 (!!!)
```

While exposing properties on the extended object may be appropriate and acceptable in some cases, it's undesirable in this case. Does that mean the ID-related methods can't be added to `attendee` via a mixin? No, it doesn't.

Creating and Using a Functional Mixin

We were introduced to functional mixins by Angus Croll's blog post, "A fresh look at JavaScript Mixins" (`http://javascriptweblog.wordpress.com/2011/05/31/a-fresh-look-at-javascript-mixins/`). Functional mixins appeal to us for many reasons. Chief among their appealing aspects is the ability of functional mixins to hide data, something that we'd like for our mixin to implement unique identifier functionality.

In this section, we'll illustrate the creation of a functional mixin that provides `getId` and `setId` methods and stores the ID in a variable that's protected from external manipulation.

Unlike traditional mixins, functional mixins are designed to *add themselves* to the object they're extending; use of extend (or a similar method) is not required. One drawback to this, however, is that each functional mixin must verify that the object being extended doesn't already have a property it provides. Traditional mixins can rely on our implementation of the extend method's behavior of verifying that a mixin will not overwrite a property of the object being extended.

That knowledge in hand, the first tests that you need to write ensure that the functional mixin addId doesn't overwrite any existing properties, and that it throws errors instead. These tests appear in Listing 20-17.

LISTING 20-17: Tests that ensure addId throws errors rather than overwrite existing properties (code filename: Mixin\addId_01_tests.js)

```
describe("Conference.mixins", function(){
  'use strict';

  var target;

  describe("addId()", function(){
    beforeEach(function(){
      target = {};
    });

    it("throws if target.getId already exists", function(){
      target.getId = function getId(){ };
      expect(function shouldThrow(){
        Conference.mixins.addId.call(target);
      }).toThrowError(
        Conference.mixins.addId.messages.triedToReplace + "getId"
      );
    });

    it("throws if target.setId already exists", function(){
      target.setId = function setId(){ };
      expect(function shouldThrow(){
        Conference.mixins.addId.call(target);
      })
      .toThrowError(
        Conference.mixins.addId.messages.triedToReplace + "setId"
      );
    });
  });
});
```

The two tests are implemented as you might expect. The first attempts to extend a target that already implements getId, and the second attempts to extend a function that already implements setId. Both tests ensure that the correct error message is generated.

The mechanism used to extend *target* with the addId mixin should provide a hint about how addId will be implemented (or, if you've read Angus's blog post, you already know):

```
Conference.mixins.addId.call(target);
```

The tests execute `addId` via `call`, providing the object being extended as the context to use. The `call` method, described in detail in Chapter 18, binds `this` within the function to the context object provided, in this case `target`. The `addId` mixin will add itself to `target` by manipulating `this`.

With a stub implementation of `addId`, the unit tests fail, as Figure 20-16 shows.

FIGURE 20-16

Listing 20-18 provides an initial implementation of `addId` that performs the necessary property-checking.

LISTING 20-18: Initial implementation of addId that ensures existing properties aren't overwritten (code filename: Mixin\addId_01.js)

```
var Conference = Conference || {};
Conference.mixins = Conference.mixins || {};

Conference.mixins.addId = function(){
  'use strict';

  if('getId' in this){
    throw new Error(Conference.mixins.addId.messages.triedToReplace + "getId");
  }
  if('setId' in this){
```

continues

LISTING 20-18 *(continued)*

```
      throw new Error(Conference.mixins.addId.messages.triedToReplace + "setId");
    }
  };
Conference.mixins.addId.messages = {
  triedToReplace: "mixin attempted to replace the existing property: "
};
```

Since this has been bound to the object being extended, the addIn function simply needs to examine to properties of this to ensure existing properties won't be overwritten.

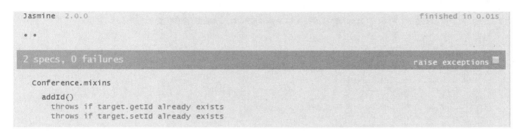

FIGURE 20-17

Figure 20-17 shows that the checks allow the unit tests to pass.

Finally, tests that verify the following need to be written:

➤ getId and setId are added to the object being extended.

➤ getId returns undefined if an ID hasn't been set.

➤ getId and setId work correctly together.

With the exception of the verification of properties, the tests are identical to those that were written for the traditional mixin. The tests are provided in Listing 20-19.

LISTING 20-19: Tests that verify that addId provides the appropriate functionality to the object being extended (code filename: Mixin\addId_02_tests.js)

```
describe("Conference.mixins", function(){
  'use strict';

  var target;

  describe("addId()", function(){
    beforeEach(function(){
      target = {};
    });

    /*** Previously discussed tests omitted ***/

    describe("when mixed in to a single object", function(){
```

```
      beforeEach(function(){
        // execute addId with this bound to target
        Conference.mixins.addId.call(target);
      });

      it("adds the expected properties to the target", function(){
        expect(Object.keys(target).sort()).toEqual(["getId", "setId"]);
      });

      describe("getId() & setId(idValue)", function(){
        it("getId() returns undefined if setId(idValue) hasn't been called",
        function(){
          expect(target.getId()).toBe(undefined);
        });

        it("getId() returns the value set by setId(idValue)",
        function(){
          var id = "theId";
          target.setId(id);
          expect(target.getId()).toEqual(id);
        });
      });
    });
  });
});
```

From the standpoint of verification of the functionality of setId and getId, the tests for the addId functional mixin are identical to those for the idMixin traditional mixin.

A difference in the tests is highlighted in Listing 20-20: The test that ensured the correct properties were added to the extended object for idMixin needed to verify that the id property was added to the extended object; the corresponding test for addId does not. The current implementation of addId doesn't satisfy the new unit tests, as Figure 20-18 shows.

Listing 20-20 provides the full implementation of the addId functional mixin.

LISTING 20-20: Full implementation of the addId functional mixin (code filename: Mixin\ addIn_02.js)

```
var Conference = Conference || {};
Conference.mixins = Conference.mixins || {};

Conference.mixins.addId = function(){
  'use strict';

  var id;

  if('getId' in this){
    throw new Error(Conference.mixins.addId.messages.triedToReplace + "getId");
  }
  if('setId' in this){
    throw new Error(Conference.mixins.addId.messages.triedToReplace + "setId");
```

continues

LISTING 20-20 *(continued)*

```
    }

    this.getId = function getId(){
      return id;
    };

    this.setId = function setId(idValue){
      id = idValue;
    };
  };
  Conference.mixins.addId.messages = {
    triedToReplace: "mixin attempted to replace the existing property: "
  };
```

FIGURE 20-18

The most notable aspects of final implementation of the addId functional mixin are:

➤ The functions getId and setId are added to the object being extended by augmenting *this*.

➤ The variable *id*, manipulated by getId and setId, is not externally accessible.

Figure 20-19 shows that all of the unit tests for addId now pass.

With a fully implemented addId functional mixin in hand, the final step is to integrate it into the attendee module. The first step is to remove the implementations of getId and setId, along with the variable used to store the ID, from attendee.

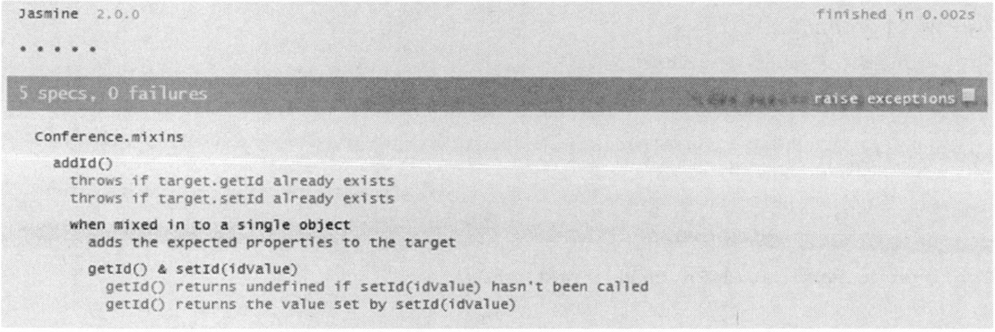

```
Jasmine  2.0.0                                                    finished in 0.002s

• • • • •

5 specs, 0 failures                                                  raise exceptions ▪

  Conference.mixins
    addId()
      throws if target.getId already exists
      throws if target.setId already exists
      when mixed in to a single object
        adds the expected properties to the target
      getId() & setId(idvalue)
        getId() returns undefined if setId(idvalue) hasn't been called
        getId() returns the value set by setId(idvalue)
```

FIGURE 20-19

This is the same first step that was performed when the idMixin traditional mixin was added to the attendee; you can refer to Figure 20-14 for proof that removal of the implementations of getId and setId causes an attendee unit test to fail.

Listing 20-21 shows how to extend attendee with the addId mixin.

LISTING 20-21: Extending attendee with the addId functional mixin (code filename: Mixin\attendee_addId.js)

```
var Conference = Conference || {};
Conference.attendee = function(firstName, lastName){
  'use strict';

  var checkedIn = false,
    first = firstName || 'None',
    last = lastName || 'None',
    checkInNumber,

    newAttendee = {
      getFullName: function(){
        return first + ' ' + last;
      },

      isCheckedIn: function(){
        return checkedIn;
      },

      checkIn: function(){
        checkedIn = true;
      },

      undoCheckIn: function() {
        checkedIn = false;
        checkInNumber = undefined;
      },

      setCheckInNumber: function(number) {
```

continues

LISTING 20-21 *(continued)*

```
        checkInNumber = number;
      },

      getCheckInNumber: function() {
        return checkInNumber;
      }
    };

  Conference.mixins.addId.call(newAttendee);

  return newAttendee;
};
```

Once again, the `attendee` module captures the object containing the properties specific to `attendee` into *newAttendee*. It then extends *newAttendee* by `calling addId` with *newAttendee* provided as the object to which *this* is bound. The `addId` functional mixin adds the `getId` and `setId` methods to *newAttendee*. Finally, the extended *newAttendee* is returned. Because it isn't added as a property of the extended object, the variable that is used to store the ID can only be changed via the `setId` method.

Figure 20-20 shows that the unit tests for attendee are all now passing.

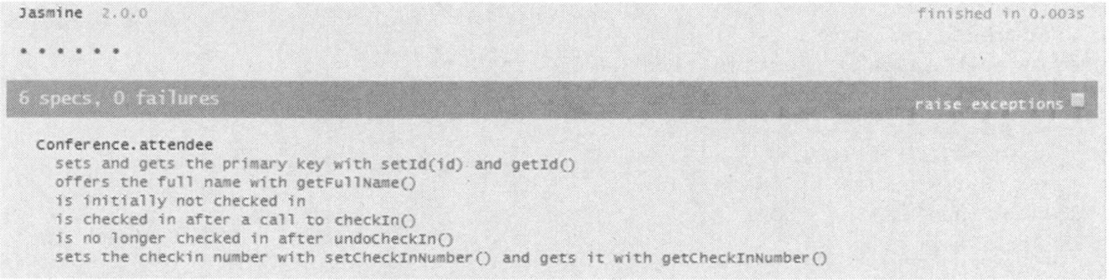

FIGURE 20-20

SUMMARY

This chapter explored how mixins may be used to DRY out your JavaScript by isolating common functionality, such as the maintenance of unique identifiers, into mixin objects.

Once appropriately isolated into a mixin, the functionality may be added to an object that requires it via a function that extends one object with another, in the case of a traditional mixin, or directly by the mixin itself, in the case of a functional mixin.

The chapter also discussed identifying functionality appropriate for isolation into a mixin, namely functionality that has no dependency upon the implementation of the objects into which it will be mixed. We also explained a potential pitfall of the `extend` methods provided by the jQuery and underscore libraries, the silent replacement of existing properties. We then avoided the pitfall in the version of `extend` that was implemented in this chapter.

Also, we demonstrated extension of an object via both a traditional mixin and a functional mixin by refactoring the `attendee` module.

When writing mixins, either traditional or functional, be sure to write unit tests to ensure:

➤ Properties on the target object aren't overwritten by the mixin.

➤ The target object provides the properties that the mixin depends on, if any.

➤ The expected properties are mixed-in.

➤ Functions that are mixed in behave correctly.

In the next chapter, we tackle the unique and challenging aspects of ensuring the reliability of complex mediator-based and observer-based program architectures.

21

Testing Advanced Program Architectures

WHAT'S IN THIS CHAPTER?

➤ Learning how the Observer Pattern leads to loosely coupled code

➤ Improving the reliability of the Observer Pattern with argument checking

➤ Coding a game using the Mediator Pattern

➤ Using the Interface Segregation Principle to simplify development with the Mediator Pattern

➤ Unit-testing a mediator and its colleagues

WROX.COM CODE DOWNLOADS FOR THIS CHAPTER

The wrox.com code downloads for this chapter are found at www.wrox.com/go/ reliablejavascript on the Download Code tab. The files are in the Chapter 21 download and individually named according to the filenames noted throughout this chapter.

Most programs you have written were probably written to achieve some goal. The architecture may have been the conventional, top-down variety that you learned along with object-oriented programming. The architectures you will consider in this chapter are different. They allow independent parts to interact in a decentralized manner. The overall goal happens as if by magic.

The patterns in question are known as the Observer and Mediator. They are similar in that they are decentralized, but the means of communication differ.

ENSURING RELIABLE USE OF THE OBSERVER PATTERN

If you've subscribed to daily newspaper delivery, you've participated in a real-life implementation of the Observer Pattern. By sending your subscription card to the newspaper publisher, you alerted the publisher that you would like to have the paper delivered to your home every day.

Once your address is on the publisher's list, there's nothing more that you need to do. When the paper is ready each day, the publisher dispatches a copy to your address and each of the other addresses in its list.

If you decide to discontinue daily delivery, all you must do is ask the publisher to remove your address from its list of addresses. The list of addresses the publisher maintains regularly grows and shrinks as new subscriptions are added and existing subscriptions are cancelled.

An important aspect of your relationship with the publisher is that all the newspaper publisher knows about you, or any of its other subscribers, is the address to which the paper should be delivered. The publisher doesn't know if your home is blue, if it's made of brick, or if it has three floors. The delivery of the newspaper doesn't rely on any of those aspects of your home. You can change your home's color or add a floor, and the paper will continue to show up.

If you describe the newspaper subscription example with the terminology of the intent of the pattern, as described by *Design Patterns*, you find the following:

➤ The newspaper publisher is the object with many dependencies.

➤ The newspaper subscribers are the dependencies.

➤ The release of the day's paper is the change in state.

➤ Delivery of the paper is the notification and update of the dependencies.

One of the goals of developers of reliable software is to minimize the number and scope of dependencies between objects. You may have noticed that intent of the pattern as described by *Design Patterns* uses a derivative of the word "dependency" not once, but thrice. Does that mean it should be avoided? Definitely not; it should be embraced. You can depend on it to help you write loosely coupled, reliable code.

In fact, one of the most appealing characteristics of the Observer Pattern is that the dependency between the *subject*, or object that changes state, and its *observers*, the dependents that are notified of the subject's state change, is well defined and narrow.

In this section, we show you how use of the Observer Pattern leads to loosely coupled code and also provide techniques for enhancing the reliability of implementations of the pattern.

Examining the Observer Pattern

The Observer Pattern is made up of two pieces:

➤ The object being observed (the subject)

➤ The objects observing the subject (the observers)

In order to support observation, the subject must provide:

➤ The capability for an observer to register itself so that it receives notifications

➤ The capability for an observer to unregister itself so that it stops receiving notifications

➤ The capability for the subject to send updates to its observers

Additionally, the observer must provide a method the subject can call to alert the observer to a change.

> **NOTE** *The subject and observers will usually provide other capabilities related to the business problem that they have been developed to address, but the capabilities listed are those that are required for them to participate in the Observer Pattern.*

Suppose that the organizers of the JavaScript conference have requested the capability to see information about attendee registrations. They'd like the capability to display the data in two ways:

➤ A counter that displays the total number of registrants

➤ A list of the names of the ten most recent registrants

As an additional wrinkle, the organizers would like the information to update in near real-time without requiring a browser refresh.

You decide that it would be appropriate to create two modules: one that displays the count and one that displays the names of the recent registrants. The module that displays the count could periodically poll the server to find out if there are any new registrants, and the module that displays the names could also periodically poll the server to find out if there are any new registrants.

"You could write a separate module that's responsible for polling for new registrants, and it can update the two modules responsible for displaying the information to the user," Charlotte suggests (can she read your mind?). "The polling module could allow the other modules to register for updates; it would be the subject in the Observer Pattern. The display modules would be the observers."

Charlotte's suggestion is appealing for many reasons. First, it nicely separates the concerns of retrieving updates from the server and displaying results to the user. Second, while there is a dependency between the display modules and the data retrieval module, it's very narrow; it's only the method on the observer that the subject will call to alert the observer to a change.

Your first task is to create the module that will act as the subject in this implementation of the Observer Pattern: the `recentRegistrationsService`. This module is responsible for periodically polling the server and retrieving the attendees that have registered since the last time it polled. Also, because it's participating in the Observer Pattern as a subject, the `recentRegistrationsService` must also provide the ability for observers to subscribe and unsubscribe, and the ability to notify each of the observers when a new attendee has registered.

The implementation of the `recentRegistrationsService` follows in Listing 21-1.

LISTING 21-1: The recentRegistrationsService (code filename: Observer\ recentRegistrationsServices.js)

```javascript
var Conference = Conference || {};

Conference.recentRegistrationsService = function(registrationsService){
    'use strict';

    var registeredObservers = [],
        service = {
            // Adds observer to the list of observers that will receive
            // notifications when a new attendee registers.
            addObserver: function addObserver(observer){
              return registeredObservers.push(observer);
            },

            // Removes observer from the list of observers, if it exists.
            removeObserver: function removeObserver(observer){
              var index = registeredObservers.indexOf(observer);
              if(index >= 0){
                registeredObservers.splice(index, 1);
              }
            },

            // Removes all observers,
            clearObservers: function clearObservers(){
              registeredObservers = [];
            },

            // Returns true if the provided observer is registered, false
            // otherwise.
            hasObserver: function hasObserver(observer){
              return registeredObservers.indexOf(observer) >= 0;
            },

            // Executes the update method provided by each of the registered
            // observers, providing the newly registered attendee, newAttendee, as
            // an argument.
            updateObservers: function updateObservers(newAttendee){
              registeredObservers.forEach(function executeObserver(observer){
                observer.update(newAttendee);
              });
            },

            // Causes the service to stop polling.  Once polling has been
            // stopped, it may not be restarted.
            stopPolling : function(){
              if(pollingProcess){
                clearInterval(pollingProcess);
                pollingProcess = false;
              }
            }
        },

        getNewAttendees = function getNewAttendees(){
```

```
        // calls the server and retrieves and returns a promise of an
        // array of the attendees that registered since the last time it
        // polled.
        return new Promise(function(resolve, reject){
        // Code to communicate with the server has been omitted.
          resolve([]);
        });
      },
      pollingProcess = setInterval(function pollForNewAttendees(){
        getNewAttendees().then(function processNewAttendees(newAttendees){
          newAttendees.forEach(function updateWithNewAttendee(newAttendee){
            service.updateObservers(newAttendee);
          });
        });
      }, 15000);

    return service;
  };
```

The `recentRegistrationsService` module provides the public methods shown in Table 21-1 that allow it to act as the subject in the Observer Pattern.

TABLE 21-1: Methods Allowing recentRegistrationsService as the Subject

METHOD	DESCRIPTION
addObserver(observer)	Adds observer to the list of observers that will receive an update each time an attendee registers
removeObserver(observer)	Removes observer from the list of observers so that it will no longer receive an update each time an attendee registers
updateObservers(newAttendee)	Executes each observer's update method, providing newAttendee as an argument

Along with the methods that are required to act as a subject, the `recentRegistrationsService` also provides some additional public methods, shown in Table 21-2, that aren't strictly required in order to participate in the Observer Pattern.

TABLE 21-2: Convenience Methods of recentRegistrationsService

METHOD	DESCRIPTION
clearObservers()	Removes all observers from the list of observers
hasObserver(observer)	Returns true if observer has been registered for updates from recentRegistrationsService, false otherwise
stopPolling()	Clears the interval set up to poll the server

In addition to exposing the public methods described in Tables 21-1 and 21-2, the `recentRegistrationsService` module has a private method, `getNewAttendees`, which is responsible for communicating with the server and retrieving the most recent registrants.

Just prior to returning the service instance, `service`, to the caller, the following is executed:

```
pollingProcess = setInterval(function pollForNewAttendees(){
  getNewAttendees().then(function processNewAttendees(newAttendees){
    newAttendees.forEach(function updateWithNewAttendee(newAttendee){
      service.updateObservers(newAttendee);
    });
  });
}, 15000);
```

The previous snippet of code sets up a recurring operation using `setInterval` to execute `getNewAttendees` every 15 seconds. The ID of the interval is retained in `pollingProcess` so that the polling may be canceled. The promise returned by `getNewAttendees` will resolve to an array with no elements if no attendees have registered in the last 15 seconds. Or, if registrations have occurred, the array will have one or more elements, each representing a newly registered attendee. For each new registration, `service`'s `update` method is executed with the new attendee provided as an argument.

> **NOTE** *While test-driven development was used to create the* `recentRegistrationsService`, *we're omitting the step-by-step description of doing so in the interest of brevity. The tests that led us to the implementation of* `recentRegistrationsService`, *shown in Listing 21-1, are available in* `Observer\recentRegistrationsService_initialTests.js`.

Figure 21-1 shows that the tests all pass.

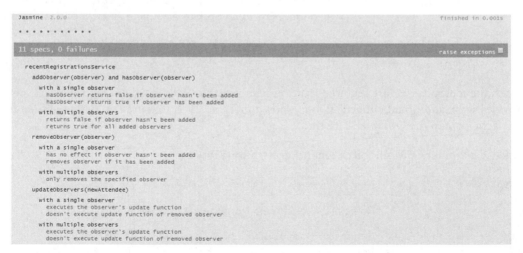

FIGURE 21-1

With a functional `recentRegistrationsService`, the subject in this implementation of the Observer Pattern, the next step is to create the modules that will display the total registration count and the most recent ten registrations. These act as the observers in this implementation of the Observer Pattern.

To reiterate, the only thing that an observer must provide to participate in the pattern is a function that the subject can execute when there's a change that the subject needs to notify the observer about. The `recentRegistrationsService` module expects that its observer will expose a function called `update` that accepts an `attendee` object. As such, the `totalAttendeeCount` and `mostRecentRegistrations` modules will each need to implement the `update` function.

> **NOTE** *Because* `totalAttendeeCount` *and* `mostRecentRegistrations` *will differ only in the details related to how they respond to updates from the* `recentRegistrationsService` *module, we're going to limit our examples to* `totalAttendeeCount`.

Listing 21-2 provides the unit tests for the functionality of the `totalAttendeeCount` module related to its role as an observer.

LISTING 21-2: Unit tests for the observer functionality of totalAttendeeCount
(code filename: Observer\totalAttendeeCount_initialTests.js)

```
describe("Conference.totalAttendeeCount", function(){
  'use strict';

  var recentRegistrations;

  beforeEach(function(){
    recentRegistrations = Conference.recentRegistrationsService();
    // we don't want the service polling; immediately stop it.
    recentRegistrations.stopPolling();
  });

  it("adds itself as an observer to the recentRegistrationsService", function(){
    spyOn(recentRegistrations, "addObserver");
    var countDisplay = Conference.totalAttendeeCount(0, recentRegistrations);
    expect(recentRegistrations.addObserver).toHaveBeenCalledWith(countDisplay);
  });

  describe("getCount()", function(){
    it("returns the initial count if update() has not been called", function(){
      var countDisplay = Conference.totalAttendeeCount(0, recentRegistrations);
      expect(countDisplay.getCount()).toEqual(0);
    });
  });

  describe("update(newAttendee)", function(){
    it("increments the count of attendees", function(){
      var initialCount = 0,
          countDisplay = Conference.totalAttendeeCount(initialCount,
            recentRegistrations);
      countDisplay.update(Conference.attendee("Tom", "Kasansky"));
```

continues

LISTING 21-2 *(continued)*

```
            expect(countDisplay.getCount()).toEqual(initialCount + 1);
        });
    });
});
```

The three tests in Listing 21-2 verify that

➤ The instance of `totalAttendeeCount` registers itself as an observer of the injected instance of `recentRegistrationsService`.

➤ The `getCount` method returns the initial count value provided to the module function.

➤ Executing the `update` method causes the value returned by `getCount` to be incremented by one.

It's important to ensure that the instance registers itself as an observer of `recentRegistrationsService` because that action is required in order for the module to provide any functionality. Also, if the `update` method doesn't increment the count of attendees, the conference organizers may mistakenly think that no one is registering for the conference.

Listing 21-3 provides an implementation of `totalAttendeeCount` that allows the unit tests to pass.

LISTING 21-3: Implementation of totalAttendeeCount that allows the observer-related unit tests to pass (code filename: Observer\totalAttendeeCount.js)

```
var Conference = Conference || {};

Conference.totalAttendeeCount = function(initialCount,
                                        recentRegistrationsService){
    'use strict';

    var currentCount = initialCount,
        registrations = recentRegistrationsService,
        render = function render(){
          // renders the current count in the DOM.
        };

    var module = {
        // Returns the total count of attendees that is displayed in the UI.
        getCount: function(){
          return currentCount;
        },

        // Increments the total count of attendees.
        update: function update(newAttendee){
          currentCount++;
          render();
        }
    };

    // Add module as an observer of the recentRegistrationsService
```

```
    registrations.addObserver(module);

    return module;
};
```

One thing that you should take away from Listing 21-3 is that there's very little code required to allow the `totalAttendeeCount` module to be an observer. The `totalAttendeeCount` module only needs to provide an `update` function that accepts an `attendee` and add itself as an observer of the `recentRegistrationsService` instance.

Figure 21-2 shows that the implementation of `totalAttendeeCount` in Listing 21-3 allows the unit tests from Listing 21-2 to pass.

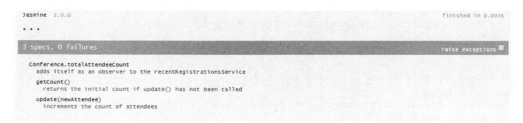

FIGURE 21-2

Now that both `recentRegistrationsService` and `totalAttendeeCount` have passing unit test suites, we've maxed out their reliability, right? Well no, not quite. The next section examines what more can be done to help make this implementation of the Observer Pattern defect resistant.

Enhancing the Reliability of the Observer Pattern

Consider the `addObserver` function from the `recentRegistrationsService`:

```
addObserver: function addObserver(observer){
    return registeredObservers.push(observer);
}
```

What happens if `observer` doesn't implement the update function that's required for it to participate in the Observer Pattern? It's happily added to the list of registered users, that's what. When it's time for `recentRegistrationsService` to update all of its observers, however, it will encounter the invalid observer and generate an `Error`. That doesn't sound very reliable, does it?

Adding insult to injury, debugging the problem is difficult because the error doesn't occur until the first update is attempted. It would be far more helpful if the error occurred when the invalid observer is added.

The problem could be alleviated by adding a check to `addObserver` that ensures `observer` has an `update` function. While that would address the issue, it isn't reusable; any other implementations of `addObserver` would need to perform the same check.

Instead, we'd rather leverage the `ContractRegistry` from Chapter 17 to apply the verification in a declarative manner. That way, any future objects that act as the subject of the Observer Pattern may utilize the verification as well.

Listing 21-4 shows a unit test that ensures an error is generated when callers provide an object that doesn't implement an `update` function as the `observer` argument to `addObserver`.

LISTING 21-4: Unit test for addObserver that verifies an error is generated if observer doesn't provide an update function (code filename: Observer\recentRegistrationsService_tests_01.js)

```javascript
describe("recentRegistrationsService", function(){
  'use strict';

  beforeEach(function(){
    service = Conference.recentRegistrationsService();
    service.stopPolling();
  });

  /*** Initial unit tests and setup omitted ***/

  describe("contract enforcement (may fail if ConferenceContractRegistry not " +
  "in use)", function(){

    it("requires observer to be provided to addObserver(observer)", function(){
      expect(function shouldThrow(){
        service.addObserver({});
      }).toThrow();
    });
  });

});
```

As you might have predicted, the test is extremely simple. It provides an object without an `update` function to `addObserver`, and ensures that an error is thrown. Figure 21-3 shows that, while simple, the test doesn't pass.

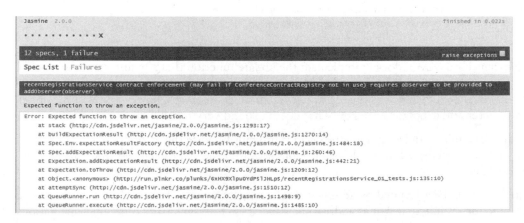

FIGURE 21-3

Implementing the check using the `ContractRegistry` and contract modules from Chapter 17 is almost as simple. First, a contract module that provides the evaluator function, `observerContracts`, must be created. It appears in Listing 21-5.

LISTING 21-5: Implementation of observerContracts (code filename: Observer\observerContracts.js)

```javascript
var Conference = Conference || {};

Conference.observerContracts = function observerContracts() {
  'use strict';

  return {
    getContracts: function getContracts() {
      function isObserver(thing) {
        return typeof thing.update === 'function';
      }

      return [
        { name: 'observer',
          evaluator: isObserver
        }
      ];
    },

    attachValidators: function attachValidators(registry) {
      // No validators
    }
  };
};
```

The `getContracts` function of the `observerContracts` module returns a single contract definition. The contract definition returned has a `name` of "observer" and an `evaluator` that ensures that `thing.update` is a function. The `observerContracts` module doesn't attach any validators of its own.

Along with `observerContracts`, a contract module that attaches an argument validator to the `addObserver` function of the `recentRegistrationsService` is required. That contract module, `recentRegistrationsServiceContracts`, appears in Listing 21-6.

LISTING 21-6: The recentRegistrationsServiceContracts contracts module (code filename: Observer\recentRegistrationsServiceContracts.js)

```javascript
var Conference = Conference || {};

Conference.recentRegistrationsServiceContracts =
function recentRegistrationsServiceContracts() {
```

continues

LISTING 21-6 *(continued)*

```
    'use strict';

    return {
      getContracts: function getContracts() {
        return [];
      },

      attachValidators: function attachValidators(registry) {
        Aop.around('recentRegistrationsService',
        function attachAspects(targetInfo) {
          var instance = Aop.next(targetInfo);

          registry.attachArgumentsValidator(
            'addObserver', instance, ['observer']);

          return instance;
        }, Conference);
      }
    };
};
```

The meat of Listing 21-6 appears in the attachValidators function. In attachValiadators, the "observer" validator defined in the observerContracts module is applied via aspect to the addObserver function of each recentRegistrationsService instance created.

The ConferenceContractRegistry, which appears in Listing 21-7, defines the contract from the observerContracts module and attaches the validator from the recentRegistrationsServiceContracts module.

LISTING 21-7: The ConferenceContractRegistry (code filename: Observer\ ConferenceContractRegistry.js)

```
var Conference = Conference || {};
// The Conference's ContractRegistry, implemented as a singleton.
Conference.ConferenceContractRegistry = (function() {
  'use strict';

  var registry = new ReliableJavaScript.ContractRegistry();

  var contractModules = [
      Conference.observerContracts(),
      Conference.recentRegistrationsServiceContracts()
      // Add more modules here.
    ];

  registry.defineMultiple(ReliableJavaScript.StandardContracts);

  contractModules.forEach(function(m) {
    registry.defineMultiple(m.getContracts());
  });

  contractModules.forEach(function(m) {
```

```
        m.attachValidators(registry);
    });

    return registry;
}());
```

The result is that the observer validator is applied to the `addObserver` function of the `recentRegistrationsService`, and the new unit test passes. Figure 21-4 shows that all of the `recentRegistrationsService` tests pass.

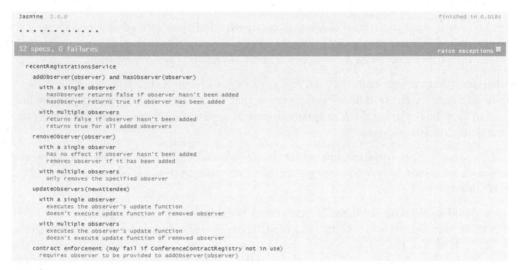

FIGURE 21-4

The end result is that, as long as the `ConferenceContractRegistry` is included on the conference's website (or along with the unit tests), you can be sure that an error will be generated whenever `addObserver` is invoked with an argument that cannot act as an observer.

In a manner similar to that which was used to ensure `addObserver` is invoked with a proper `observer` object, the `recentRegistrationsServiceContracts` module may be extended to validate that the argument provided to the `updateObservers` function satisfies the `Conference.attendee.personalInfo` contract that was created in Chapter 17. Likewise, the same may be done to ensure that the appropriate argument is provided to the `totalAttendeeCount` module's `update` function.

ENSURING RELIABLE USE OF THE MEDIATOR PATTERN

For over 50 years, the United States and Cuba had no official relationship. The longer the parties didn't talk, the less likely it seemed they ever would or could. Then, in 2014, Pope Francis wrote to Presidents Obama and Castro, appealing to them to "resolve humanitarian questions of common interest." Both countries responded—not to each other, mind you, because they still weren't talking, but to the Pope. After a few months, the leaders announced their intention to resume full diplomatic relations.

It wasn't the first time a mediator has played a key role in history, but that initial exchange exemplified the Mediator Pattern beautifully. The mediator initiates communication and gets the parties moving. They respond to him or her, and the mediator orchestrates the next step.

Examining the Mediator Pattern

In diplomacy, labor negotiations, and marriages, mediators are usually brought in to resolve trouble. In software design, the Mediator Pattern is a way to avoid it. While society works best when people talk freely with each other, a software system is the opposite: fewer lines of communication mean fewer ways to go wrong.

The pattern consists of several *colleagues*, which may perform different or similar tasks, and a single *mediator*, which orchestrates the overall effort. In its purest form, this orchestration consists only of managing the interactions between the colleagues and does not involve any business logic.

It just so happens that an opportunity to use this pattern has arisen during your work on the JavaScript conference's website. The organizers know that the caffeine-buzzed participants will want a way to keep busy during the few minutes between sessions. They have asked you to design and write a game for this purpose.

You decide to make it a two-person game rather than a solo exercise. After all, one reason people go to conferences is to network. Not having joysticks or other gaming devices, both players will be at the same keyboard.

The game will go like this. As in Figure 21-5, a matrix of nodes will be connected by paths. Several bots (the medium-sized dots) will wander the graph. There will also be two larger dots to represent the two players. It will be the players' task between them to encounter, and thereby knock off the board, every bot as quickly as possible. One player will use the keys 1, 2, 3 and 4 to navigate left, up, down and right, respectively. The other will use 6, 7, 8, and 9.

A game is a classic scenario for the Mediator Pattern. These are the colleagues and their responsibilities:

➤ `player`—Moves from its current node to a connected one, and informs the `mediator` that it has done so

➤ `bot`—Does the same as a `player`

➤ `gameLogic`—Contains the logic of the game, including determining when the game is over. It lays out the board in "normalized space" and puts players and bots on it. Normalized space is a square that is one unit across. It is up to the `svgDisplay` (described next) to present this in the browser.

➤ `svgDisplay`—Draws the game on an `svg` element. Receives instructions to do so from the `mediator`, but does not communicate anything back to the `mediator`.

And coordinating the actions of the colleagues is `mediator`, which

➤ Initializes the game by instantiating the `gameLogic` (with players and bots) and an `svgDisplay`.

➤ Hooks up the event listener for the keys.

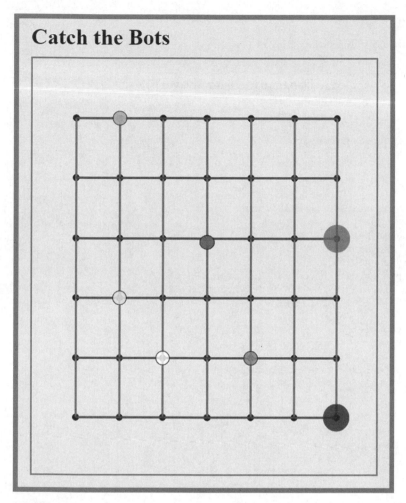

FIGURE 21-5

When a player or bot says it has moved, the mediator informs `gameLogic` and `svgDisplay`. When `gameLogic` says the game is over, the mediator unhooks the event listener.

Characteristic of the Mediator Pattern, when a `player` encounters a `bot`, it does not evict the `bot` on its own. Instead, it merely moves to the new node and informs the `mediator` that it has done so. The `mediator` passes this information to the `gameLogic`, which detects the collision and removes the `bot`. Yet even then, the `gameLogic` does not adjust the display; that's done through another message to `mediator`, which then tells `svgDisplay` to remove the `bot`.

Enhancing the Reliability of Mediator-Based Code

In this book, we have emphasized test-driven development, illustrating it with relatively small fragments of a hypothetical, larger system. For the current example, we offer the fully developed game in this chapter's downloads, but will touch on only the highlights of the development process.

Developing a Colleague

Listing 21-8 shows one of the colleagues: the player.

LISTING 21-8: The player object (code filename: Mediator\player.js)

```javascript
var Game = Game || {};

Game.player = function player(mediator) {
  'use strict';

  var me,
      node,
      id = (Game.player.nextId === undefined
        ? Game.player.nextId=0
        : ++Game.player.nextId),
      listenEvent = "keydown",
      elementWithKeydownAttached,
      // The first player gets keys 1-4 (keycodes 49-52)
      // The second player gets keys 6-9 (keycodes 54-58)
      keycodeForPath0 = id%2 ? 54 : 49;

  function handleKeydown(e) {
    var pathIx = e.keyCode - keycodeForPath0;

    if (pathIx>=0 && pathIx < Game.pathIndex.count) {
      me.move(pathIx);
    }
  }

  me = {
    getId: function() {
      return id;
    },

    setNode: function setNode(gameNode) {
      node = gameNode;
    },

    getNode: function getNode() {
      return node;
    },

    activate: function activate(elementForKeydown) {
      elementWithKeydownAttached = elementForKeydown;
      elementWithKeydownAttached.addEventListener(listenEvent,handleKeydown);
    },

    deactivate: function deactivate() {
      if (elementWithKeydownAttached) {
```

```
            elementWithKeydownAttached.removeEventListener(
                listenEvent,handleKeydown);
        }
    },

    // Attempt to move the player along the given path (designated
    // by a path index). Return true on success or false on failure.
    move: function move(pathIndex) {
        if (node.getConnectedNode(pathIndex)) {
            me.setNode(node.getConnectedNode(pathIndex));
            mediator.onPlayerMoved(me);
            return true;
        }
        return false;
    }
};

return me;
};
```

Typical of the Mediator Pattern, the `player` is instantiated with a `mediator` already in hand (third line of the listing). The `mediator` could be a complex object so this seems to introduce a broad coupling. However, you will soon see how the Interface Segregation Principle and judicious unit-testing mitigate this evil.

The simple `getId`, `getNode`, and `setNode` methods need no explanation (although if you haven't seen it before, you might be interested in the little trick of attaching a static variable, `nextId`, to the function when the variable is declared).

The `move` method is what the `mediator` will wire to a `keydown` event by calling the `activate` function. When `move` is invoked, it first checks that the requested movement is possible. If it is, it calls `setNode` with the new location and then informs the `mediator` that it should do whatever needs to be done when a player moves.

Testing a Colleague

Although the `player` object knows a little about the topography of the game (only what nodes are in the immediate vicinity), think of all the things it does *not* know. It doesn't know when the game is over, nor how many other `players` there are, nor anything about `bots`. It certainly doesn't know the game is displayed in SVG. All this ignorance is what makes `player` easy to test (see Listing 21-9).

LISTING 21-9: Testing the player object (code filename: Mediator\player_tests.js)

```
describe('player', function() {
    var player,
        fakeMediator;

    beforeEach(function() {
        fakeMediator = {
            onPlayerMoved: function() {}
```

continues

LISTING 21-9 *(continued)*

```
  };

  player = Game.player(fakeMediator);
});

describe('getId()', function() {
  it('returns a unique integer ID', function() {
    var player2 = Game.player(fakeMediator);
    expect(player2.getId()).not.toBe(player.getId());
  });
});

describe('setNode(gameNode)', function() {
  it('causes getNode() to return the node', function() {
    var node = Game.gameNode();
    player.setNode(node);
    expect(player.getNode()).toBe(node);
  });
});

describe('move(pathIndex)', function() {
  var originalNode, newNode;
  beforeEach(function() {
    originalNode = Game.gameNode();
    newNode = Game.gameNode();
    player.setNode(originalNode);
  });

  describe('if there is a path at that index', function() {
    var pathIndex = 2;
    beforeEach(function() {
      originalNode.connect(newNode, pathIndex);
    });

    it('moves the player to the new point', function() {
      player.move(pathIndex);
      expect(player.getNode()).toBe(newNode);
    });
    it('informs the mediator of the movement', function() {
      spyOn(fakeMediator,'onPlayerMoved');
      player.move(pathIndex);
      expect(fakeMediator.onPlayerMoved).toHaveBeenCalledWith(player);
    });
    it('returns true', function() {
      expect(player.move(pathIndex)).toBe(true);
    });
  });

  describe('if there is no path at that index', function() {
    it('keeps the player at the same node', function() {
      player.move(2);
```

```
        expect(player.getNode()).toBe(originalNode);
      });
      it('return false', function() {
        expect(player.move(2)).toBe(false);
      });
    });
  });
});
```

As usual, the output of successful unit tests do a great job of explaining in plain English what the object does (see Figure 21-6).

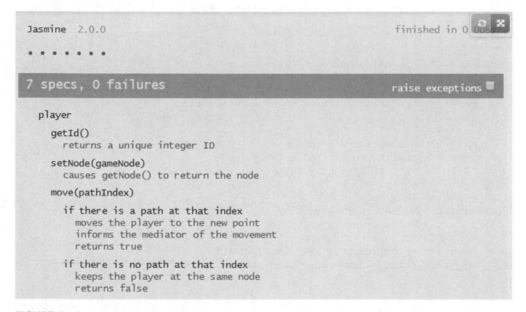

FIGURE 21-6

The overview is plain enough, but there are a few interesting things to notice about the tests.

First, at the very top of the listing, notice the *fakeMediator*.

```
fakeMediator = {
  onPlayerMoved: function() {}
};
```

A `mediator` of some sort is necessary to initialize the `player` (tenth line of the listing):

```
player = Game.player(fakeMediator);
```

However, if the unit tests completely cover `player`'s code (which they do), and they use a fake *that has only the functions needed for player*, the unit tests also verify that `player` only needs those functions. This allows you to segregate the mediator's interface, as you read in Chapter 16.

Segregating the Mediator's Interfaces

Where can you install and enforce a segregated interface? In the `ContractRegistry`, of course. This was also covered in Chapter 16, expanded in Chapter 17, and used a little in Chapter 19, but this game is the first full example of its pervasive use.

Listing 21-10 shows how the mediator's interfaces are established.

LISTING 21-10: The mediator's contracts (code filename: Mediator\mediatorContracts.js)

```javascript
var Game = Game || {};

Game.mediatorContracts = function mediatorContracts() {
  'use strict';

  return {
    getContracts: function getContracts() {
      function isMediatorForPlayer(thing) {
        return typeof thing === 'object' &&
               typeof thing.onPlayerMoved === 'function';
      }

      function isMediatorForBot(thing) {
        return typeof thing === 'object' &&
               typeof thing.onBotMoveStart === 'function';
      }

      function isMediatorForLogic(thing) {
        return isMediatorForPlayer(thing) &&
          isMediatorForBot(thing) &&
          typeof thing.onBotHit === 'function' &&
          typeof thing.endGame === 'function';
      }

      return [
        { name: 'mediatorForPlayer',
          evaluator: isMediatorForPlayer
        },
        { name: 'mediatorForBot',
          evaluator: isMediatorForBot
        },
        { name: 'mediatorForLogic',
          evaluator: isMediatorForLogic
        }
      ];
    },

    attachValidators: function attachValidators(registry) {

      registry.attachReturnValidator(
        'mediator', Game, 'mediatorForPlayer');
      registry.attachReturnValidator(
        'mediator', Game, 'mediatorForBot');
      registry.attachReturnValidator(
```

```
                    'mediator', Game, 'mediatorForLogic');
                }
            };
        };
```

You may recall the suggestion in the "Putting It All Together" section of Chapter 17 that you could use a module like the one above to supply contracts and validators. By convention, such a module would have `getContracts` and `attachValidators` methods. Then, a contract registry for the application would consume the methods from all such modules to assemble the contract registry. (In this chapter's downloads, `Mediator\GameContractRegistry.js` is that auto-assembling registry. You will see more of it shortly.)

The preceding `mediatorContracts.js` file has three contracts for the mediator: `mediatorForPlayer`, `mediatorForBot` and `mediatorForLogic`. The `mediatorForPlayer` interface requires only that the `thing` under consideration be an object and that it have an `onPlayerMoved` method.

Deciding Where to Put the Contracts

We have put the `mediatorForPlayer` contract in `mediatorContracts.js`, but you might feel that it belongs in `playerContracts.js`. The idea is not without merit. Suppose that the `mediator` and `player` modules are maintained by different people or even different teams. Now suppose that `mediator` changes in a way that requires a revision to the `mediatorForPlayer` contract. (This violates the Open/Closed Principle from Chapter 1, but sometimes life is not ideal.) Whoever makes the change might change the contract and think his job is done. The `player` object will verify that the incoming `mediator` fulfills the contract, but the contract no longer reflects `player`'s original expectations!

In contrast, suppose the `player` object (and its programmers) owned the `mediatorForPlayer` contract. That is, suppose the contract was in `playerContracts.js` instead of `mediatorContracts.js`. When `mediator`'s programmers make their change, they will not change the contract, which is outside of their domain. If the change breaks the contract, `player`'s unit tests will fail and `player`'s programmers will know they should adjust their code.

The idea that an interface is owned by the module that consumes it rather than by the module that fulfills it is part of some formulations of the Dependency Inversion Principle. The main disadvantage is that every module that consumes the interface must duplicate its description. That violates the DRY Principle.

So you have a choice. You can put contracts like `mediatorForPlayer` in `mediatorContracts.js` so `mediator`'s programmers know what might be a breaking change, or you can put them in the contract modules for the consuming objects so their unit tests will fail appropriately when `mediator` changes.

> **NOTE** *You can put the contracts intended for a module's consumers in that module's contracts module, or in the consumers' contract modules. The latter choice can lead to violations of the DRY Principle, but the former may be less effective at alerting you to errors. The assignment of responsibilities to your programmers may affect your choice.*

Wherever the contract resides, the next step is to put it to use.

Ensuring the Colleague Gets a Mediator with the Expected Interface

The `mediatorContracts.js` module created a `mediatorForPlayer` interface. Now `playerContracts.js` can ensure that whenever a `player` is created, it gets such a `mediator` (see Listing 21-11):

LISTING 21-11: The player's contracts (code filename: Mediator\playerContracts.js)

```javascript
Game.playerContracts = function playerContracts() {
  'use strict';

  return {
    getContracts: function getContracts() {
      function isPlayer(thing) {
        return typeof thing === 'object' &&
               typeof thing.getId === 'function' &&
               typeof thing.setNode === 'function' &&
               typeof thing.getNode === 'function' &&
               typeof thing.activate === 'function' &&
               typeof thing.deactivate === 'function';
      }

      return [
        { name: 'player',
          evaluator: isPlayer
        }
      ];
    },

    attachValidators: function attachValidators(registry) {
      registry.attachArgumentsValidator(
        'player', Game, ['mediatorForPlayer']);
      registry.attachReturnValidator(
        'player', Game, 'player');

      Aop.around('player', function attachAspectsToPlayer(targetInfo) {
        var instance = Aop.next(targetInfo);

        registry.attachReturnValidator(
          'getId', instance, 'nonNegativeInteger');

        registry.attachArgumentsValidator(
          'setNode', instance, ['gameNode']);

        registry.attachReturnValidator(
          'getNode', instance, 'gameNode');

        registry.attachArgumentsValidator(
          'move', instance, ['nonNegativeInteger']);
        registry.attachReturnValidator(
```

```
            'move',instance,'boolean');

          return instance;
        },Game);
      }
    };
  };
```

The first two lines of the `attachValidators` method cause the `mediatorForPlayer` contract to be checked against the argument to `Game.player`:

```
registry.attachArgumentsValidator(
  'player', Game, ['mediatorForPlayer']);
```

If something else is passed in, an exception is thrown. In return, `player` promises that it will return an object that meets the *'player'* contract:

```
registry.attachReturnValidator(
  'player', Game, 'player');
```

That contract is a promise to provide the methods you saw in `player`:

```
function isPlayer(thing) {
  return typeof thing === 'object' &&
         typeof thing.getId === 'function' &&
         typeof thing.setNode === 'function' &&
         typeof thing.getNode === 'function' &&
         typeof thing.activate === 'function' &&
         typeof thing.deactivate === 'function';
}
```

Importantly, it is not a guarantee of an actual player object (using `instanceof`, for example). Contracts that use characteristics instead of types keep your code in the JavaScript "duck-typing" idiom. In fact, you have already seen how this was useful when creating the `fakeMediator` in Listing 21-9.

Code contracts do add several layers of function-calling to each method they protect. Not only does that impede performance, but it can make debugging more complex. If you would like to remove code contracts for production or temporarily during debugging, it's as easy as removing this line from `index.html`:

```
<script src="GameContractRegistry.js"></script>
```

Without that line, the contract registry is never instantiated, much less populated, and contracts will have absolutely no footprint in your running code. (They don't run, but to keep them from *loading*, you can also remove the `<script>` tags for the contract modules, too.) For reference, Listing 21-12 is what you would be missing.

LISTING 21-12: The Game's Contract Registry (code filename: Mediator\
GameContractRegistry.js)

```
// The Game's ContractRegistry, implemented as a singleton.
Game.ConferenceContractRegistry = (function() {

  var registry = new ReliableJavaScript.ContractRegistry();

  var contractModules = [
      Game.normalPointContracts(),
      Game.gameNodeContracts(),
      Game.playerContracts(),
      Game.botContracts(),
      Game.gameLogicContracts(),
      Game.mediatorContracts(),
      // Add more modules here.
    ];

  registry.defineMultiple(ReliableJavaScript.StandardContracts);

  contractModules.forEach(function(m) {
    registry.defineMultiple(m.getContracts(registry));
  });

  contractModules.forEach(function(m) {
    m.attachValidators(registry);
  });

  return registry;
}());
```

The other colleagues in the game are similar in spirit. You can find their code and unit tests in this chapter's downloads, in the `Mediator` directory.

Developing a Mediator

The mediator is not a mastermind. Its role is just to get things started, make sure that every object knows what it needs to know until they decide to call it quits, and then close things down in an orderly way. Listing 21-13 shows the `mediator` for the game.

LISTING 21-13: The mediator (code filename: Mediator\mediator.js)

```
var Game = Game || {};

Game.mediator = function mediator() {
  'use strict';

  var logic,
      display,
      startTime,
      svgElement = document.getElementById('gameSvg');

  function moveBotStartInLogicAndOnDisplay(bot) {
```

```javascript
      logic.onBotMoveStart(bot);
      display.onBotMoveStart(bot);
    }

    var med = {

      startGame: function startGame() {
        logic.getPlayers().forEach(function(player){
          player.activate(document.getElementById('gameInput'));
        });
        startTime = new Date();
      },

      // Player calls this when he has moved.
      onPlayerMoved: function onPlayerMoved(player) {
        logic.onPlayerMoved(player);
        display.onPlayerMoved(player);
      },

      // Bot calls this function when it starts to move.
      onBotMoveStart: function onBotMoveStart(bot) {
        moveBotStartInLogicAndOnDisplay(bot);
      },

      // Bot calls this function when it has completed a move.
      onBotMoveEnd: function onBotMoveEnd(bot) {
        logic.onBotMoveEnd(bot);
      },

      // GameLogic calls this function when a bot is hit.
      onBotHit: function onBotHit(bot) {
        bot.setNode(undefined);
        moveBotStartInLogicAndOnDisplay(bot);
      },

      // GameLogic calls this function to end the game.
      endGame: function endGame() {
        var millisecondsToWin = new Date() - startTime;
        logic.getPlayers().forEach(function(player){
          player.deactivate();
        });
        // Use setTimeout to give the display a chance to remove the last bot
        // before we ask it to display the winning message.
        setTimeout(function() {
          display.endGame(millisecondsToWin);
        },500);
      }
    };

    logic = Game.gameLogic(med,6,7);
    display = Game.svgDisplay(med,svgElement,logic);

    return med;
};
```

When the `mediator` is instantiated, it creates the `gameLogic` and `svgDisplay` colleagues (at the end of the listing). The `gameLogic`, in turn, creates the `players` and the `bots`.

The mediator that other modules will see is in the *med* variable midway down the listing and returned at the end.

As you continue to look at the `player` colleague, you see that the flow of control goes like this:

1.   The `activate` method adds an event listener that will cause the appropriate `player`'s move method to be called when the right key is pressed.

2.   As you have seen, `player.move`, upon a successful transfer to a new node, calls `mediator.onPlayerMoved`.

3.   That method tells both the game logic and the display that the player has moved.

4.   Steps 2 and 3 continue until finally the `gameLogic` object detects that the game is over and calls `mediator.endGame`, which will unhook the event listener.

Testing the Mediator

The mediator's job involves lots of interaction with objects it's not supposed to know a great deal about, so you can guess that Jasmine spies will abound. Listing 21-14 shows some of the details.

LISTING 21-14: Testing the mediator (code filename: Mediator\mediator_tests.js)

```
describe('mediator', function() {
  'use strict';
  var gameNodes,
      numNodes = 10,
      fakeDisplay,
      fakeLogic,
      fakePlayer0, fakePlayer1, fakePlayers;
  beforeEach(function() {
    var nodeIx;
    gameNodes = [];
    for (nodeIx=0; nodeIx<numNodes; ++nodeIx) {
      gameNodes.push(Game.gameNode());
    }
    fakeDisplay = {
      onPlayerMoved: function(player) {},
      onBotMoveStart: function(bot) {},
      endGame: function() {},
    };
    fakePlayer0 = {
      activate: function() {},
      deactivate: function() {},
    };
    fakePlayer1 = {
      activate: function() {},
      deactivate: function() {},
    };
    fakePlayers = [ fakePlayer0, fakePlayer1 ];
```

```
    fakeLogic = {
      getPlayers: function() { return fakePlayers; },
      onPlayerMoved: function(player) {},
      onBotMoveStart: function(bot) {},
      onBotMoveEnd: function(bot) {},
      getNodes: function() { return gameNodes; },
      getBots: function() { return []; }
    };
    spyOn(Game,'svgDisplay').and.returnValue(fakeDisplay);
    spyOn(Game,'gameLogic').and.returnValue(fakeLogic);
    spyOn(fakeDisplay,'onPlayerMoved');
    spyOn(fakeDisplay,'endGame');
    spyOn(fakeLogic,'onPlayerMoved');
  });

  describe('startGame()', function() {
    it('activates both players', function() {
      var mediator = Game.mediator();
      spyOn(fakePlayer0,'activate');
      spyOn(fakePlayer1,'activate');
      mediator.startGame();
      expect(fakePlayer0.activate).toHaveBeenCalled();
      expect(fakePlayer1.activate).toHaveBeenCalled();
    });
  });

  describe('onPlayerMoved(player)', function() {
    var player;
    beforeEach(function() {
      var mediator = Game.mediator(),
          node = Game.gameNode();
      player = Game.player(mediator);
      player.setNode(node); // Pretend just moved here.
      mediator.onPlayerMoved(player);
    });
    it("informs the board of the player's new location", function() {
      expect(fakeLogic.onPlayerMoved).toHaveBeenCalledWith(player);
    });
    it("informs the display of the player's new location", function() {
      expect(fakeDisplay.onPlayerMoved).toHaveBeenCalledWith(player);
    });
  });

  /*** Remaining tests omitted. See this chapter's downloads. ***/
});
```

In the early part of the listing, fakes are set up for the display, the players, and the game logic. All the `mediator`'s tests care about is that these objects are called as expected, and spies are created for that purpose in the next part of the listing:

```
spyOn(Game,'svgDisplay').and.returnValue(fakeDisplay);
spyOn(Game,'gameLogic').and.returnValue(fakeLogic);
spyOn(fakeDisplay,'onPlayerMoved');
spyOn(fakeDisplay,'endGame');
spyOn(fakeLogic,'onPlayerMoved');
```

The first pair of spies intercept the creation of `svgDisplay` and `gameLogic`, causing the fakes to be returned. The remaining spies will detect when `onPlayerMoved` is called on those objects, and when the game ends. There is no `callThrough`, `callFake`, or `returnValue` on those spies because the only matter of interest is whether `mediator` has made the calls.

The tests of `onPlayerMoved` demonstrate how this plays out:

```
describe('onPlayerMoved(player)', function() {
  var player;
  beforeEach(function() {
    var mediator = Game.mediator(),
        node = Game.gameNode();
    player = Game.player(mediator);
    player.setNode(node); // Pretend just moved here.
    mediator.onPlayerMoved(player);
  });
  it("informs the board of the player's new location", function() {
    expect(fakeLogic.onPlayerMoved).toHaveBeenCalledWith(player);
  });
  it("informs the display of the player's new location", function() {
    expect(fakeDisplay.onPlayerMoved).toHaveBeenCalledWith(player);
  });
});
```

The expectations are simply that the spies were called with the correct parameters. This is typical when unit-testing a mediator. If the tests are more complicated than just verifying that the mediator makes the appropriate calls to the appropriate colleagues, your implementation of the Mediator Pattern may not be as pure as you might wish.

SUMMARY

The Observer and Mediator Patterns are closely related and their reliable development has much in common, including the following:

➤ When testing an observer (in the Observer Pattern) or a colleague (in the Mediator Pattern), you can use a fake of the subject/mediator.

➤ A mediator's interface can be broader than any one colleague needs. Consider segregating it. At a minimum, the fake in your unit tests will show what the segregated interface is.

➤ In both patterns, the handoffs are the critical piece. You can use code contracts to ensure that calls between subject/mediator and observer/colleague function as planned.

The next section of this book considers a few special or exotic subjects in testing.

PART IV
Special Subjects in Testing

22

Testing DOM Access

WHAT'S IN THIS CHAPTER?

➤ Writing UI unit tests in Jasmine

➤ Using jQuery to interact with the DOM in unit tests

➤ Ensuring UI events execute the correct event handlers

➤ Using a Profiler to identify opportunities for optimization

WROX.COM CODE DOWNLOADS FOR THIS CHAPTER

You can find the wrox.com code downloads for this chapter at www.wrox.com/go/reliablejavascript on the Download Code tab. The files are in the Chapter 22 download and are individually named according to the filenames noted throughout this chapter.

We've occupied many pages of this book describing how unit tests can help ensure the reliability of non-visual components of a web application, namely the JavaScript conference's website. There's no doubt that components of the website that don't have a user interface, such as the attendeeRegistrationService, should have associated unit test suites.

Users of the website, however, aren't aware that attendeeRegistrationService exists. Even though users interact with the service, they don't do so directly: They interact with it via the website's UI, presented via a web browser.

It's all well and good for an application to function correctly, but world-class software must please the end user. That means the user interface must function smoothly and quickly.

UNIT-TESTING UI

Unit tests for JavaScript that interacts with the browser's document object model, or DOM, are one way to ensure that a web application's UI functions properly. This section provides an example of what not to do when creating a UI, and addresses how the example can be refactored to be testable and reliable.

Examining Difficult-to-Test UI Code

Have you encountered—or created—an HTML file similar to that in Listing 22-1?

LISTING 22-1: HTML and JavaScript (code filename: DOMTesting\inline.html)

```html
<!DOCTYPE html>
<html>

  <head>
    <script type="text/javascript">
      var clickCount = 0,
          displayCount = function(){
            var countElement = document.getElementById("countDisplay");
            countElement.innerText = clickCount.toString();
          }
    </script>
  </head>

  <body>
    <button type="button" onclick="clickCount++; displayCount();">
      Increment
    </button>

    <span id="countDisplay">0</span>
  </body>

</html>
```

There's a `<script>` element inside the `<head>` tags, within which a variable, `clickCount`, and a function, `displayCount`, are defined.

The markup within the `<body>` tags defines a `<button>`, which, according to the value of the `onclick` attribute, increments `clickCount` and then executes `displayCount`. There's also a `<span>` with the ID `countDisplay`.

As you may have already determined, the code in Listing 22-1 simply tracks the number of times that the `<button>` is clicked and displays that click count alongside the `<button>`. Figure 22-1 shows how the markup renders when the page initially loads in the browser, and also how the page looks after the `<button>` has been clicked a few times.

As Figure 22-1 shows, the interaction with the button works as described: Each click increments the count that's displayed.

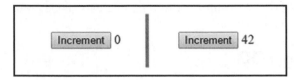

FIGURE 22-1

Even though the example functions as it should, Charlotte has a few suggestions.

First Charlotte points out that the HTML file doesn't exhibit separation of concerns: The JavaScript responsible for responding to click events and displaying the count is written directly in the HTML file with the markup that defines the UI. This severely limits reusability because JavaScript defined in an HTML page may only be used by that page. Charlotte suggests that extracting the JavaScript into its own file will allow the JavaScript code to be reusable and to improve its testability.

Also, Charlotte notes that the `clickCount` variable and `displayCount` function are defined in the global scope. Even though doing so causes no detrimental effects in this example, creating global variables is poor practice when writing reliable JavaScript. Encapsulating the variable and function into a module, and enabling `strict` mode, would ensure that the global scope isn't polluted.

Additionally, Charlotte points out that the `onclick` event handler contains multiple inline statements:

```
<button type="button" onclick="clickCount++; displayCount();">
   Increment
</button>
```

While including multiple statements in the event handler is perfectly valid, it's undesirable. A developer maintaining this code must inspect both the HTML and the JavaScript to get a complete picture of what happens when the button is clicked. Combining the statements into a single, descriptively named function such as `incrementAndDisplayClickCount` would make the code easier to understand. Encapsulating that new method *and* adding code that can set it as the button's click handler into a module would be even better. With a modular organization, it would be possible to understand the behavior being defined solely by examining the JavaScript. Creating a module containing the code would also improve its testability by allowing much of the logic to be tested without involving the UI at all.

Finally, the HTML elements and the JavaScript that interacts with them are tightly coupled. The coupling has multiple sources:

➤ The definition of the click event handler inline

➤ The hard-coded reference to the `id` of the `<span>` in which the count is displayed contained in the `displayCount` function: `var countElement = document.getElementById("countDisplay");`

As long as the click handler is defined inline and the reference to the display element is hard-coded, the only way to reuse the code in the example is to copy and paste it and update the handler and element reference in the new copy. Creating a configurable module to encapsulate the code would break the coupling, allowing the click-counting and display logic to be used with multiple HTML elements.

The next section will begin the process of transforming the difficult-to-test, single-use code presented in Listing 22-1 into a testable, reusable UI component.

Creating a UI Component Using TDD

As you've done many times before, you'll drive the development of the reusable UI component with unit tests. The Jasmine test framework supports UI unit tests without requiring any special setup or configuration when the tests are being executed within a browser, as the tests you'll write in this section will be.

> **NOTE** *Though the Jasmine framework itself doesn't require a browser DOM to run, this section is specifically about testing interaction with the DOM. As such, be aware that if you're adding UI tests to your own project and you're using a server-side test runner to execute the Jasmine tests, it may be necessary to configure the runner to execute the tests in a browser.*

Consider the actions that the event handler code performs when the `<button>` in Listing 22-1 is clicked:

1. The code increments a variable that contains the number of times the `<button>`has been clicked.

2. The code calls a function that updates the DOM.

Because manipulation of the UI is encapsulated into a function, you can create tests for the module that implements the enumerated behavior without yet being concerned with the DOM. The tests that ensure the click counting functionality works correctly follow in Listing 22-2.

LISTING 22-2: Initial tests for Conference.clickCountDisplay (code filename: DOMAccess\ clickCountDisplay_tests_01.js)

```
describe("Conference.clickCountDisplay", function(){
  'use strict';

  var display;

  beforeEach(function(){
    display = Conference.clickCountDisplay();
  });

  it("initializes the click count to 0", function(){
    expect(display.getClickCount()).toEqual(0);
  });

  describe("incrementCountAndUpdateDisplay()", function(){
```

```
    it("increments the click count", function(){
      var initialCount = display.getClickCount();
      display.incrementCountAndUpdateDisplay();
      expect(display.getClickCount()).toEqual(initialCount + 1);
    });

    it("executes the updateCountDisplay function", function(){
      spyOn(display, "updateCountDisplay");
      display.incrementCountAndUpdateDisplay();
      expect(display.updateCountDisplay).toHaveBeenCalled();
    });
  });
});
```

The tests in Listing 22-2 ensure that the new module's incrementCountAndUpdateDisplay function performs the same high-level actions that the inline click event handler from Listing 22-1 performed. Specifically, the tests verify that executing incrementCountAndUpdateDisplay causes the click count to be incremented and the function that updates the DOM to be executed. The tests also verify that the initial click count is 0.

Even though they're simple, these initial tests help define the API that the new module needs to expose. They also give you a protection against introducing defects while extending and refactoring the module's code. Figure 22-2 shows that the unit tests fail when the module's API methods aren't implemented.

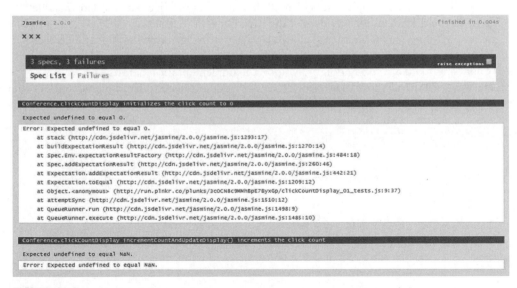

FIGURE 22-2

You fill in the module's API methods, yielding the code in Listing 22-3.

LISTING 22-3: Initial implementation of Conference.clickCountDisplay (code filename: DOMAccess\clickCountDisplay_01.js)

```javascript
var Conference = Conference || {};
Conference.clickCountDisplay = function(){
  'use strict';

  var clickCount = 0;

  return {
    getClickCount: function getClickCount(){
      return clickCount;
    },

    updateCountDisplay: function updateCountDisplay(){

    },

    incrementCountAndUpdateDisplay: function incrementCountAndUpdateDisplay(){
      clickCount++;
      this.updateCountDisplay();
    }
  };
};
```

The initial implementation of `Conference.clickCountDisplay` holds no surprises; it's as simple as the unit tests that drove its completion. The module function initializes the hidden variable `clickCount` to 0, and allows public retrieval of the variable via the function `getClickCount`. The function `incrementCountAndUpdateDisplay` does exactly what its name implies: It increments `clickCount` and invokes the `updateCountDisplay` method. Because the unit tests for `incrementCountAndUpdateDisplay` don't rely upon the implementation details of `updateCountDisplay`, the method `updateCountDisplay` doesn't need to be implemented in order for the unit tests in Listing 22-2 to pass, as Figure 22-3 shows.

FIGURE 22-3

Testing Code That Changes the DOM

Your initial foray into testing DOM interaction will be to design tests for the `updateCountDisplay` function. To test the `updateCountDisplay` function, you need to be able to add an element to the DOM that the function can manipulate from within a test. It's possible to add elements to the DOM using functions provided by the browser, but the ubiquitous jQuery library provides a browser-independent façade over browser-provided DOM interaction methods. Your tests for updateCountDisplay will use jQuery to provide an element for updateCountDisplay to update. Listing 22-4 shows the tests.

LISTING 22-4: Unit tests for updateCountDisplay (code filename: DOMAccess\ clickCountDisplay_02_tests.js)

```javascript
describe("Conference.clickCountDisplay", function(){
  'use strict';

  var display,
      displayElement;

  beforeEach(function(){
    // Create a jQuery element from a string that defines the DOM element
    displayElement = $("<span></span>");
    // and append it to the body
    $('body').append(displayElement);

    var options = {
      updateElement : displayElement
    };

    display = Conference.clickCountDisplay(options);
  });

  afterEach(function(){
    displayElement.remove();
  });

  /*** Code omitted for clarity ***/

  describe("incrementCountAndUpdateDisplay()", function(){

    /*** Code omitted for clarity ***/

    it("sets the text of the updateElement", function(){
      display.incrementCountAndUpdateDisplay();
      expect(displayElement).toHaveText(display.getClickCount());
      display.incrementCountAndUpdateDisplay();
      expect(displayElement).toHaveText(display.getClickCount());
    });
  });

  describe("updateCountDisplay()", function(){
    it("displays 0 if the count hasn't been incremented", function(){
      expect(displayElement).toHaveText("");
      display.updateCountDisplay();
      expect(displayElement).toHaveText("0");
    });
  });
});
```

Because `updateCountDisplay` changes the DOM based on the value of `clickCount`, and `clickCount` can only be changed via the `incrementCountAndUpdateDisplay` function, `updateCountDisplay` requires only a single unit test that ensures it behaves properly if it's invoked before `incrementCountAndUpdateDisplay` has been called. Additional testing of `updateCountDisplay` is performed indirectly via `incrementCountAndUpdateDisplay`.

We mentioned that tests for `updateCountDisplay` would need to be able to add an element to the DOM. The `beforeEach` section of the test suite was updated to add the necessary element:

```
// Create a jQuery element from a string that defines the DOM element
displayElement = $("<span></span>");
// and append it to the body
$('body').append(displayElement);
```

First, the `<span>` element that will display the count is created. Then, the `<span>` is appended to the `<body>` of the HTML page that the Jasmine tests are running in. The `<span>` element is also added to the new *options* variable that is provided to the module function:

```
var options = {
  updateElement : displayElement
};
display = Conference.clickCountDisplay(options);
```

The module will be able to access the `span` element via the `options.updateElement` property.

Listing 22-4 also introduced an `afterEach` to the test suite. The `afterEach` section performs only a single, but important, function: It removes the DOM element added in the `beforeEach`. Neglecting to remove the element would result in `<span>` elements accumulating on the page. Also, removing the element used in each test when the test completes reduces the likelihood that the order in which the tests are executed could change the outcome of the tests.

The single unit test for the `updateCountDisplay` function uses a matcher function you may not have seen before to ensure the expected value is displayed in the DOM: `toHaveText`. If you've reviewed the matcher functions that Jasmine provides, you'll recognize that `toHaveText` is not built-in to Jasmine. It's provided by the open-source library jasmine-jquery, which is maintained by Travis Jeffery. The library provides dozens of matchers that are especially useful when testing JavaScript that interacts with the DOM.

> **NOTE** *Jasmine-jquery has been provided with the downloads for this chapter, and it's also available on GitHub at* `https://github.com/velesin/jasmine-jquery`.

The test for `incrementCountAndUpdateDisplay` that was added to indirectly test the `updateCountDisplay` method also makes use of the `toHaveText` matcher. The test ensures that each time the `incrementCountAndUpdateDisplay` is called, the incremented `clickCount` value is displayed in the DOM.

Because you haven't implemented the `updateCountDisplay` function, the new tests fail, as Figure 22-4 shows.

The implementation that allows the new unit tests in Listing 22-4 to pass follows in Listing 22-5.

LISTING 22-5: Implementation of updateCountDisplay (code filename: DOMAccess\
clickCountDisplay_02.js)

```javascript
var Conference = Conference || {};
Conference.clickCountDisplay = function(options){
  'use strict';

  var clickCount = 0;

  // Production code would verify that
  // options is defined and that its properties
  // are of the expected type.

  return {

    updateCountDisplay: function updateCountDisplay(){
      options.updateElement.text(clickCount);
    }

    /*** Code omitted for clarity ***/
  };
};
```

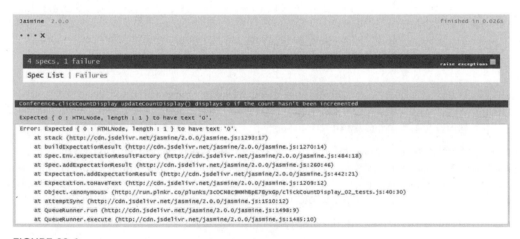

FIGURE 22-4

Listing 22-5 shows the updated module function that now accepts an options parameter. It also notes that verification of the options parameter has been consciously left out for this example.

Most importantly, Listing 22-5 provides an implementation of updateCountDisplay that uses the text method of the jQuery object provided via options.updateElement to set the DOM element's text property to the value of clickCount. With the addition of the implementation of updateCountDisplay, all of the unit tests pass once again, as Figure 22-5 shows.

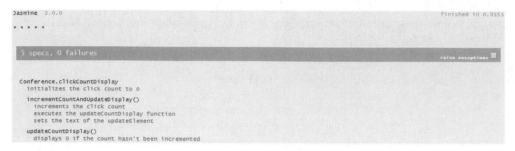

FIGURE 22-5

It's worth noting that at this point, a major portion of the `clickCountDisplay` module's functionality is fully implemented, yet you haven't had to make your tests click a DOM element. Because the actions performed when an element is clicked have been encapsulated into a function that may be unit-tested on its own, it's not necessary to perform a click. Instead, the function can be invoked directly, as you've done in the tests to this point. In the next section, you'll add tests for `clickCountDisplay` that click an element and ensure that `incrementCountAndUpdateDisplay` executes when the element is clicked.

Testing to Ensure Event Handlers Are Executed

If you recall the situation from Listing 22-1, the click event handler of the `<button>` was set directly in the markup:

```
<button type="button" onclick="clickCount++; displayCount();">
  Increment
</button>
```

You've already followed one of Charlotte's suggestions while implementing `clickCountDisplay`: You encapsulated the multiple statements originally defined inline in the click event handler into the `incrementCountAndUpdateDisplay` function.

Another one of Charlotte's suggestions was to give the module the capability to assign its `incrementCountAndUpdateDisplay` function as the target element's click handler so that the assignment doesn't need to occur in markup. Doing so, Charlotte suggested, would improve the reusability of the module. Her last suggestion worked out well, so you decide to follow this one as well.

In true test-driven fashion, you create the unit tests in Listing 22-6.

LISTING 22-6: Unit tests to ensure incrementCountAndUpdateDisplay is executed when the trigger element is clicked (code filename: DOMAccess\clickCountDisplay_03_tests.js)

```
describe("Conference.clickCountDisplay", function(){
  'use strict';

  var display,
      displayElement,
      clickElement;

  beforeEach(function(){
```

```
    // Create a jQuery element from a string that defines the DOM element
    displayElement = $("<span></span>");
    // and append it to the body
    $('body').append(displayElement);

    // Create the click element and append it to the body
    clickElement = $("<button></button>");
    $('body').append(clickElement);

    var options = {
      updateElement : displayElement,
      triggerElement : clickElement
    };

    display = Conference.clickCountDisplay(options);
  });

  afterEach(function(){
    displayElement.remove();
    clickElement.remove();
  });

  /*** Code omitted for clarity ***/

  it("executes incrementCountAndUpdateDisplay when the trigger " +
    "element is clicked", function(){
    spyOn(display, "incrementCountAndUpdateDisplay");
    clickElement.trigger('click');
    expect(display.incrementCountAndUpdateDisplay).toHaveBeenCalled();
  });

  /*** Code omitted for clarity ***/
});
```

Only one unit test? Really? Yes, really. By encapsulating the functionality as you have, you only need to ensure that clicking the specified trigger element executes the `incrementCountAndUpdateDisplay` function. The tests for `incrementCountAndUpdateDisplay` ensure that it, in turn, behaves as it should.

The changes to the test suite required to ensure the event handler is invoked begin in the `beforeEach` block. As you did when testing with the display element, you create an element that the test will "click" and append that element to the `body` of the HTML page the tests are executing in. That element is also provided to the `clickCountDisplay` module function via the `triggerElement` property of the *options* variable. The `afterEach` has a corresponding change to remove the element from the DOM when the test completes.

The new unit test spies on the `incrementCountAndUpdateDisplay` method of the *display* instance of the `clickCountDisplay` module. The test then uses the jQuery `trigger` method to trigger a click event on the element whose clicks are being counted. Finally, the test verifies that triggering the click event executed the `incrementCountAndUpdateDisplay` function. The new test fails, as Figure 22-6 illustrates.

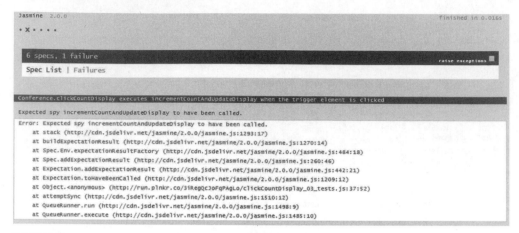

FIGURE 22-6

Listing 22-7 shows the updated implementation of the `clickCountDisplay` module.

LISTING 22-7: Implementation of clickCountDisplay that configures the click event handler
(code filename: DOMAccess\clickCountDisplay_03.js)

```javascript
var Conference = Conference || {};
Conference.clickCountDisplay = function(options){
  'use strict';

  var clickCount = 0;

  // Production code would verify that
  // options is defined and that its properties
  // are of the expected type.

  var clickCounter = {
    getClickCount: function getClickCount(){
      return clickCount;
    },

    updateCountDisplay: function updateCountDisplay(){
      options.updateElement.text(clickCount);
    },

    incrementCountAndUpdateDisplay: function incrementCountAndUpdateDisplay(){
      clickCount++;
      this.updateCountDisplay();
    }
  };

  options.triggerElement.on('click', function clickBinder(){
    clickCounter.incrementCountAndUpdateDisplay();
  });

  return clickCounter;
};
```

Instead of immediately returning the new instance created by `clickCountDisplay`, the module function assigns it to the `clickCounter` variable. Then the `clickBinder` function is registered as a handler of the `options.triggerElement`'s click event via the jQuery on function. The `clickBinder` function will invoke the `clickCounter.incrementCountAndUpdateDisplay` function when the `triggerElement` click event is triggered, causing the click count to be incremented and the display to be updated. Finally, `clickCounter` is returned to the caller. With that, the unit tests all pass, as shown in Figure 22-7, and the implementation of the `clickCountDisplay` module is complete.

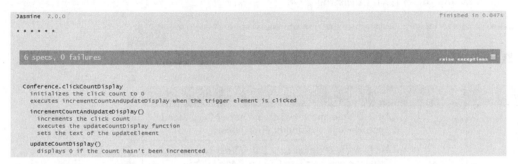

FIGURE 22-7

Keeping UI Tests from Being Brittle

The tests that you *didn't* write in the preceding section are just as important as the tests that you did write. When writing unit tests for the UI, it's tempting to test the appearance of the UI:

➤ Are the DOM elements in the right place?

➤ Are the DOM elements the correct size?

➤ Is the correct font being used?

➤ Is the background color correct?

And so on and so forth.

While it's possible to write unit tests for everything enumerated (and more), unit tests that verify visual appearance tend to be brittle. The UI of a web application is likely to change more often than any other aspect, quickly making any tests that validate appearance out-of-date.

Generally speaking, UI unit tests should be limited to functionality, such as:

➤ Is the correct handler executed when an element is clicked?

➤ Are elements of the UI that the user is not authorized to see hidden?

➤ Does a `<select>` contain the expected elements?

Tests of visual appearance should more often than not be left to manual testing or screenshot-based testing tools that can quickly determine deviations from the expected appearance.

OPTIMIZING YOUR CODE WITH A PROFILER

We've all done it: written code that is less than beautiful in order to achieve efficiency and the improved response time that goes with it. But was it worth it? How did we know? In this section, you will see how to use your browser's profiler to answer those questions.

Detecting Inefficiencies

The task before you is simple. You just need to create a web page that lists attendees at the JavaScript conference, and their interests. There are several thousand, so efficiency might be a concern.

Figure 22-8 shows what the page will look like. (The attendees will come from all over the world. That's why their names range from Hipapipige Baba to Zawet Zuziyukuku. Either that, or they are random.)

You quickly develop the HTML in Listing 22-8.

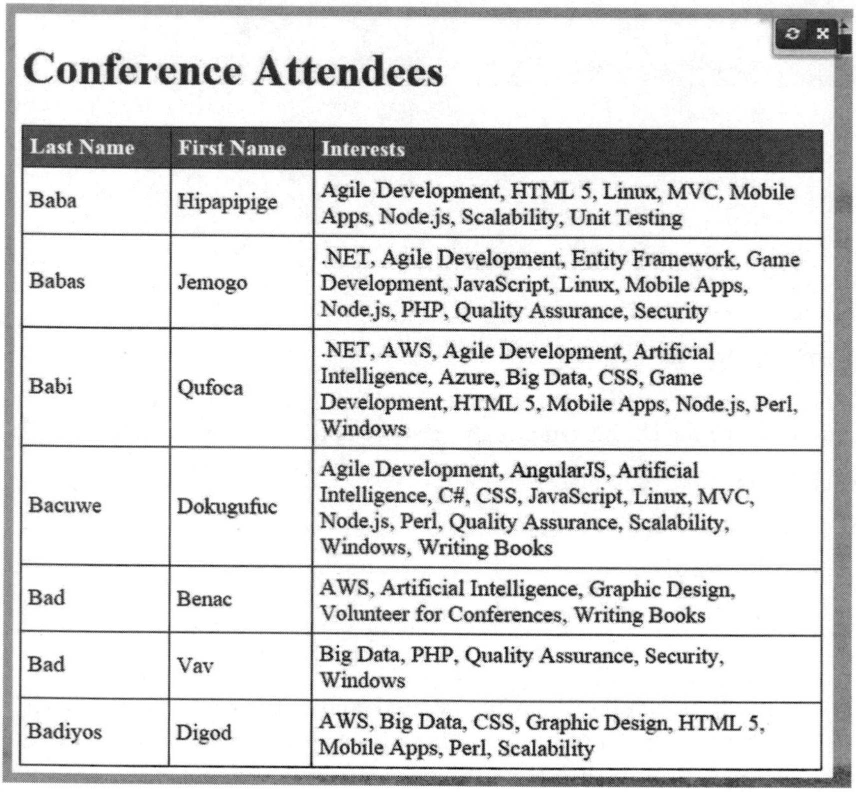

Conference Attendees

Last Name	First Name	Interests
Baba	Hipapipige	Agile Development, HTML 5, Linux, MVC, Mobile Apps, Node.js, Scalability, Unit Testing
Babas	Jemogo	.NET, Agile Development, Entity Framework, Game Development, JavaScript, Linux, Mobile Apps, Node.js, PHP, Quality Assurance, Security
Babi	Qufoca	.NET, AWS, Agile Development, Artificial Intelligence, Azure, Big Data, CSS, Game Development, HTML 5, Mobile Apps, Node.js, Perl, Windows
Bacuwe	Dokugufuc	Agile Development, AngularJS, Artificial Intelligence, C#, CSS, JavaScript, Linux, MVC, Node.js, Perl, Quality Assurance, Scalability, Windows, Writing Books
Bad	Benac	AWS, Artificial Intelligence, Graphic Design, Volunteer for Conferences, Writing Books
Bad	Vav	Big Data, PHP, Quality Assurance, Security, Windows
Badiyos	Digod	AWS, Big Data, CSS, Graphic Design, HTML 5, Mobile Apps, Perl, Scalability

FIGURE 22-8

LISTING 22-8: HTML to display attendees (code filename: Profiler\index.html)

```html
<!DOCTYPE html>
<html>
  <head>
    <link rel="stylesheet" href="style.css" />
    <script src="attendee.js"></script>
    <script src="attendeePage.js"></script>
  </head>

  <body>
    <h1>Conference Attendees</h1>
    <table id="attendeeTable">
      <tr>
```

```
        <th>Last Name</th>
        <th>First Name</th>
        <th>Interests</th>
      </tr>
      <!-- Rows will be added by the attendeePage.js script.-->
    </table>
  </body>
</html>
```

The `<body>` element has an `onload` attribute that invokes `Conference.attendeePage`
`.addAttendeesToPage()`, the function at the end of Listing 22-9.

LISTING 22-9: Proof-of-concept code to fill the list of attendees (code filename: Profiler\
attendeePage.js)

```javascript
var Conference = Conference || {};
Conference.attendeePage = (function attendeeList() {
  'use strict';
  var attendees = [];

  function fetchAttendees() {
    /*** Lines omitted for clarity. ***/

    for (ix=0; ix<5000; ++ix) {
      var firstName = randomName(),
          lastName = randomName(),
          interests = chooseInterests();
      attendees.push(Conference.attendee(firstName, lastName, interests));
    }
  }

  function byLastNameThenFirstName(a,b) {
      return a.getLastName().localeCompare( b.getLastName()) ||
             a.getFirstName().localeCompare(b.getFirstName());
  }

  function displayAttendee(attendee) {
    var table = document.getElementById('attendeeTable'),
        tr = document.createElement('tr'),
        tdLastName = document.createElement('td'),
        tdFirstName = document.createElement('td'),
        tdInterests = document.createElement('td'),
        isFirstInterest = true;
    tr.appendChild(tdLastName);
    tr.appendChild(tdFirstName);
    tr.appendChild(tdInterests);
    tdLastName.innerHTML = attendee.getLastName();
    tdFirstName.innerHTML = attendee.getFirstName();

    tdInterests.innerHTML = '';
    attendee.getInterests().forEach(function addInterest(interest) {
      if (!isFirstInterest) {
        tdInterests.innerHTML += ', ';
      } else {
```

continues

LISTING 22-9 *(continued)*

```
        isFirstInterest = false;
      }
      tdInterests.innerHTML += interest;
    });

    table.appendChild(tr);
  }

  return {
    addAttendeesToPage: function() {
      fetchAttendees();
      attendees.sort(byLastNameThenFirstName);
      attendees.forEach(displayAttendee);
    }
  };
}());
document.addEventListener('DOMContentLoaded',
          Conference.attendeePage.addAttendeesToPage);
```

A lot happens in the three lines of `addAttendeesToPage` (at the end of the listing). The attendees are fetched (okay, randomly generated), sorted, and then displayed.

You run the page and performance isn't too bad, but you will be handing your work off to Charlotte for final integration with the server so you don't want to embarrass yourself. Is there any way its performance could be improved?

You decide to break out Chrome's profiler and find out. (We are using Chrome because it is by far the most popular among developers. Internet Explorer offers a similar facility.)

To use the profiler, you follow these steps.

1. Launch the page. You can do this by downloading the Profiler directory in this chapter's downloads and then double-clicking on `index.html`.

2. Press F12 to open Chrome's developer panel. (F12 is also the magic button for Internet Explorer.)

3. Select the Profiles tab. One of the profiling options is Collect JavaScript CPU Profile. That is the one you want for this exercise. Make sure it is selected (see Figure 22-9).

4. Press either the Start button or the circular, gray button in the upper-left corner of the Profiles tab (see Figure 22-9 again).

5. Very quickly, press the refresh button on your browser.

6. When the page comes back, press either the circular button again (which will have been red during profiling) or the Start/Stop button again (whose text will have changed from Start to Stop during profiling).

7. A display like Figure 22-10 will appear. If necessary, select the "Tree (Top Down)" view.

There are three modes in which the data can be displayed. The Tree (Top Down) view is the most intuitive. This view lists the top-level functions and, for each one, how much time is spent in the function proper (the Self column) and how much time in the function plus all the functions it calls (the Total column).

The other choices are Heavy (Bottom Up) and Chart. You will see how to use those shortly.

In the Tree view of Figure 22-10, the list of functions happens to end with the only one you have any control over, namely `addAttendeesToPage`. You can focus on that one alone by clicking on the arrows to expand the call tree. The result is shown in Figure 22-11.

You are not concerned with optimizing the `fetchAttendees` function because it's only a fake, but it is interesting to note that it took only 1.75 percent of the time within the `addAttendees` function, in spite of all its random-number computations and string concatenations (refer back to Listing 22-9). Even sorting 5,000 attendees took only 11.57 percent of the time. By far the bulk of the time was spent in `displayAttendee` and the functions it called. This is typical of programs in the browser. Accessing the DOM is usually more costly in terms of CPU time than other operations.

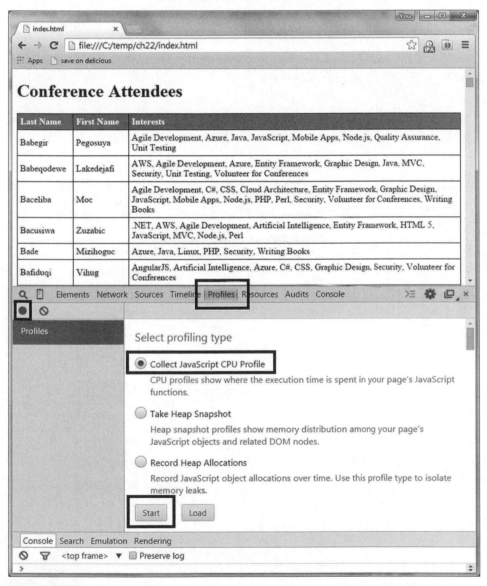

FIGURE 22-9

Scanning down Figure 22-11, notice that a lot of time is spent in the `addInterest` function, particularly where it sets the `innerHTML` property of the `<td>` element devoted to the attendee's interests. (`innerHTML`'s accessor functions are the "anonymous functions" in Figure 22-11.) Here is the relevant part of Listing 22-9:

```
var tdInterests = document.createElement('td'),
    isFirstInterest = true;

/*** Snipped for clarity. ***/

tdInterests.innerHTML = '';
attendee.getInterests().forEach(function addInterest(interest) {
  if (!isFirstInterest) {
    tdInterests.innerHTML += ', ';
  } else {
    isFirstInterest = false;
  }
  tdInterests.innerHTML += interest;
});
```

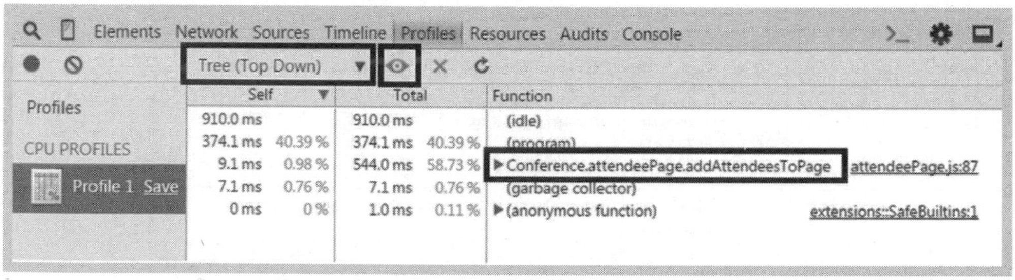

FIGURE 22-10

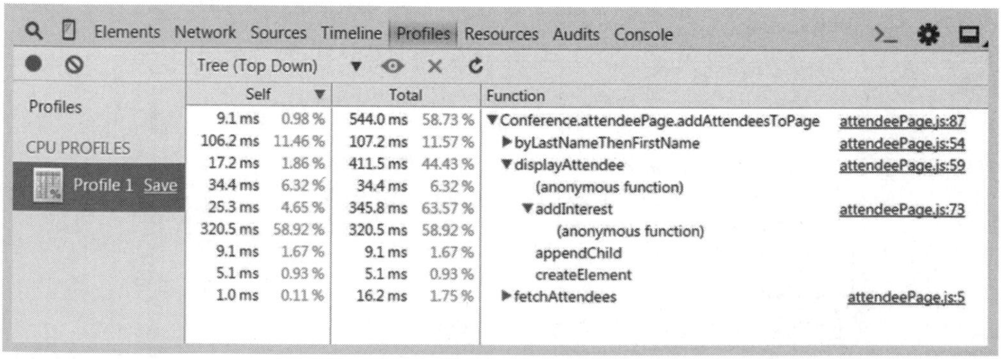

FIGURE 22-11

What could have come over you? This is exactly the sort of plodding, overly procedural code that a beginner with limited JavaScript vocabulary would write. Now that the profiler has drawn your attention to your profligate use of `innerHTML` in this region of code, you realize that the whole mess could be replaced with the following:

```
tdInterests.innerHTML = attendee.getInterests().join(', ');
```

Incidentally, while it was safe to assume that the interests contained no cross-site scripting attacks because they came from a set of choices under the application's control, the code that directly inserted the attendee's names into the HTML plays fast and loose. If this were more than a proof-of-concept exercise, you would protect against a cross-site scripting attack as explained in `https://www.owasp.org/index.php/XSS_(Cross_Site_Scripting)_Prevention_Cheat_Sheet`.

You make the switch (attendeePage_Improved.js in this chapter's downloads) and run the profiler again. This time, the story is quite different (see Figure 22-12).

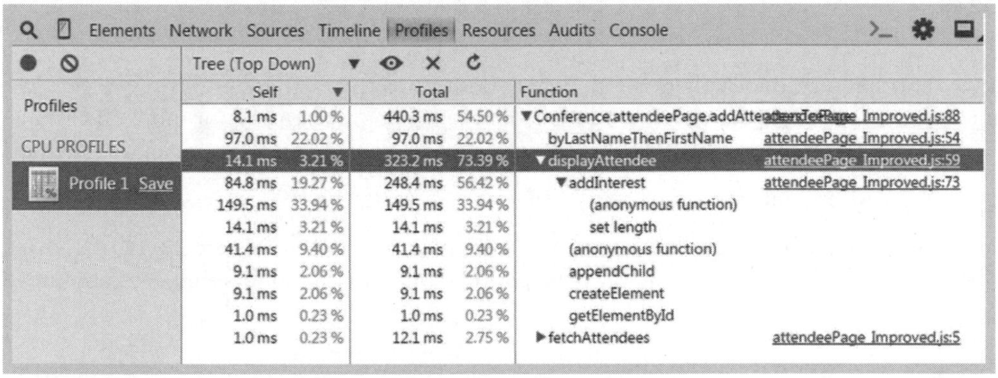

FIGURE 22-12

Total time in `displayAttendee` has decreased from 411.5 milliseconds to 323.2. You achieved a reduction in response time of 21 percent with that one simple change. You make a note to yourself to minimize DOM access, especially in loops. (Incidentally, DOM updates that cause the page's layout to be recomputed are often the most costly.)

> **NOTE** *Optimize for speed by minimizing DOM access, especially to update it, and especially inside loops.*

You decide to reward yourself by taking a moment to look at the other options in the profiler.

With the Tree (Top Down) view, you were able to drill down the call stack. The Heavy (Bottom Up) view is the reverse. It shows how much time was spent in each function and lets you drill *up* to see from where it was called. Figure 22-13 shows this view for the original version of the code, drilling up from uses of the `innerHTML` property.

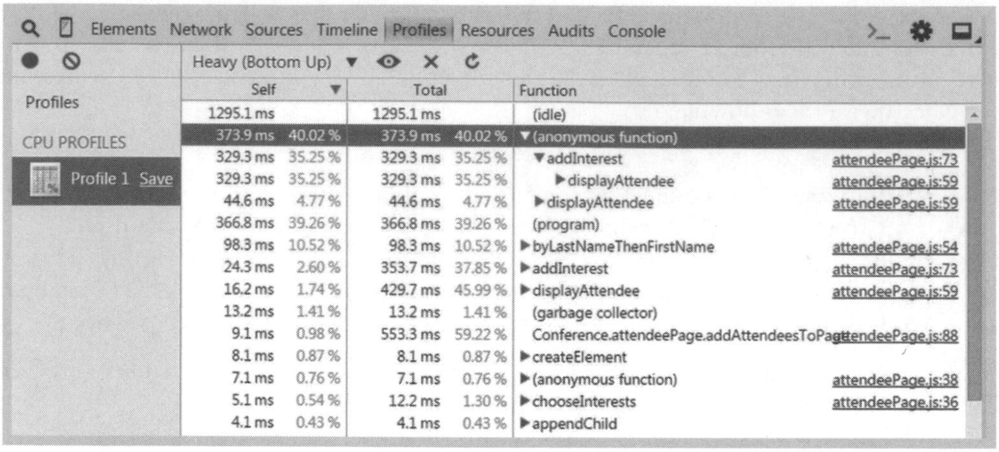

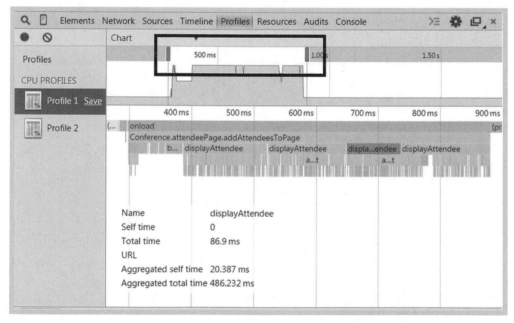

FIGURE 22-13

You can see that the immediate callers of the `anonymous function that sets innerHTML` were `addInterest` and `displayAttendee`, with calls from the former accounting for more CPU time than calls from the latter. Thus, the Heavy view would also have led you to focus on `addInterest`.

Finally, Figure 22-14 presents the Chart view.

The Chart view is handy because it lets you zoom in on a time period. In Figure 22-14, the lower, downward-pointing flame graph reflects only the period chosen by the sliders (indicated by the heavy rectangle).

FIGURE 22-14

The lower graph shows the execution sequence in the horizontal direction and the call stack in the vertical. Thus, it shows `onload` calling `Conference.attendeePage.addAttendeesToPage`, which calls `displayAttendee`, and so on. You can hover over any block in this graph and get details about it. In Figure 22-14, the mouse was over one of the `displayAttendee` blocks, triggering the display of statistics in the lower left.

Avoiding Premature Optimization

You're feeling pretty good about your victory, but something is bothering you. When you coded `displayAttendee`, you began the function with:

```
var table = document.getElementById('attendeeTable')
```

Because `displayAttendee` is called for every one of the 5,000 attendees, you have an uneasy feeling that the repeated call to get the same element might slow things down. Would it be better to do this once, in the calling function, and pass the table element to `displayAttendee` as a parameter? You thought the function's interface was cleaner without the extra parameter, but what price have you paid for this nicety?

Here's where the profiler can set your mind at rest. Figure 22-15 shows that the time spent in `getElementById` amounts to only 2.0 milliseconds of the over 400 milliseconds spent in `displayAttendee`. If someone wants to persuade you to consolidate the calls to `getElementById`, performance can't be the reason.

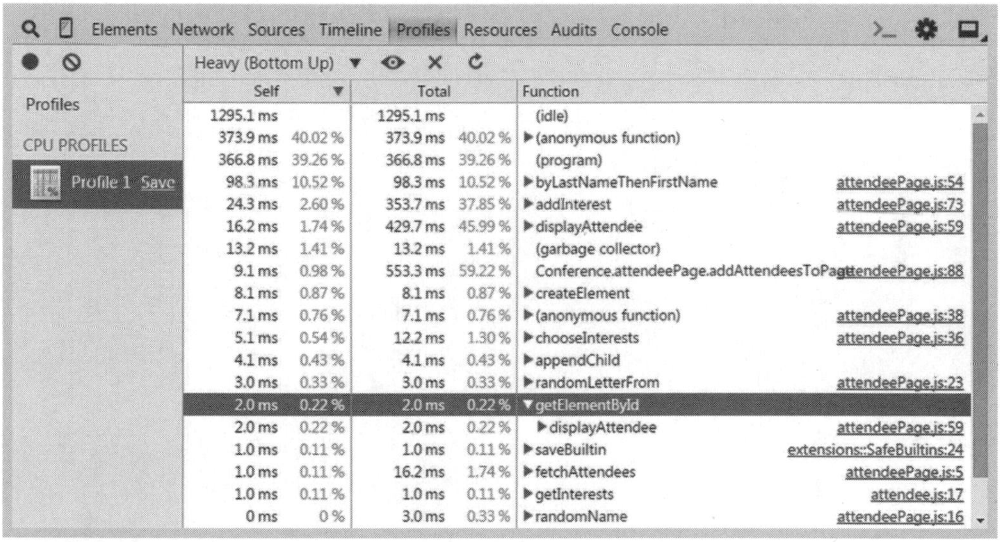

FIGURE 22-15

SUMMARY

In this chapter, you saw how writing JavaScript directly in an HTML file and using inline event handlers can reduce the reusability and testability of your application's UI manipulation code. You used TDD to develop a loosely coupled UI component that you can use throughout your application. Additionally, you saw how to avoid creating brittle UI unit tests. You also saw how to use Chrome's profiler to identify where performance bottlenecks are—and where they aren't. In browser-based programs, performance problems can arise if you access the DOM too frequently, especially for updates.

The next chapter dives deeper than we have so far into tools that help you follow your organization's coding standards, not to mention your own good intentions.

23

Ensuring Conformance to Standards

WHAT'S IN THIS CHAPTER?

➤ Installing, configuring and running ESLint

➤ Creating custom ESLint rules

➤ Enforcing architectural layers

WROX.COM CODE DOWNLOADS FOR THIS CHAPTER

You can find the wrox.com code downloads for this chapter at www.wrox.com/go/ reliablejavascript on the Download Code tab. The files are in the Chapter 23 download and are individually named according to the filenames noted throughout this chapter.

In his article *Frequently Forgotten Fundamental Facts about Software Engineering* (IEEE Software, May/June 2001), Robert L. Glass posits that ongoing maintenance accounts for, on average, 60 percent of software development costs. We're sure any developer that has worked on a long-term software project would feel that Mr. Glass isn't far from the mark.

Inconsistent use of the capabilities of JavaScript that make it powerful, such as method-sharing and monkey-patching, can make JavaScript code more difficult to maintain in the long-term.

When JavaScript was only being used for ad-hoc form validation, long-term maintenance likely wasn't a prime concern. Now that entire applications, both on the client and the server, are built with JavaScript, maintenance must be at the forefront of the developer's mind.

An important way to make sure everyone on your team can maintain a body of code is to promote coding standards. This is true on both the small scale of syntax and the large scale of architecture. This chapter explores ways to do just that.

USING ESLINT

The section "Using a Code-Checking Tool" in Chapter 2 showed how the linting tool JSHint may be used to identify JavaScript code with questionable syntax and structure. JSHint also enforces many code style standards, such as consistent use of double quotes for strings.

While JSHint allows users to turn its built-in rules on and off, it doesn't provide support for custom rules. Does this mean that you must resort to manual code reviews to enforce coding standards not supported by JSHint? Thankfully, no.

ESLint, a linter that was mentioned in the section "Alternatives to JSHint" in Chapter 2, *does* support custom rules. ESLint also implements all of the built-in rules that JSHint supports, making it a suitable replacement for JSHint.

In this section, we show how to install and configure ESLint, how to run it from the command line, and how to write and execute a custom ESLint rule.

Installing ESLint

ESLint is distributed as a Node.js package. As such, before you can install ESLint you must first install Node. Node is available as precompiled binaries for many platforms including Mac OS X and Windows. We'll cover the installation of the binary package on Windows.

If you already have Node and npm, a package manager for Node, installed on your computer, you may jump ahead to "Installing ESLint Using npm."

> **NOTE** *You may also install Node using package managers such as Homebrew and MacPorts on OS X and Chocolatey and Scoop on Windows.*

Installing Node and npm

The following steps describe the process of installing Node and npm on Windows 8.1.

1. Open `http://nodejs.org/download/` in your browser, as shown in Figure 23-1, and download the binary package appropriate for your operating system. We're installing on Windows 8.1, so we chose the 64-bit Windows Installer (.msi).

2. Launch the installer, accept the terms of the license agreement, and then select the installation location on the installer's initial few screens.

3. On the Custom Setup screen, shown in Figure 23-2, make sure that the npm package manager and Add to PATH installation features are selected to be installed.

4. Confirm installation on the final screen of the installer and wait a moment or two while the installer does the heavy lifting.

5. When the installer finishes, launch a command prompt and type **node** and press Enter. You should be presented with a > prompt awaiting your input. If you don't see a prompt, or you receive an error, you should troubleshoot your Node installation before continuing.

6. At the > prompt, type `console.log("Reliable JavaScript!");` and press Enter. You should see output similar to that in Figure 23-3.

7. Press Ctrl+C twice to exit Node.

8. Type **npm** at the command prompt and press Enter. You should see output similar to that in Figure 23-4. If the output you see isn't similar to that shown in Figure 23-4, you should troubleshoot your npm installation before continuing. The npm GitHub repository provides troubleshooting instructions at `https://github.com/npm/npm/wiki/Troubleshooting`.

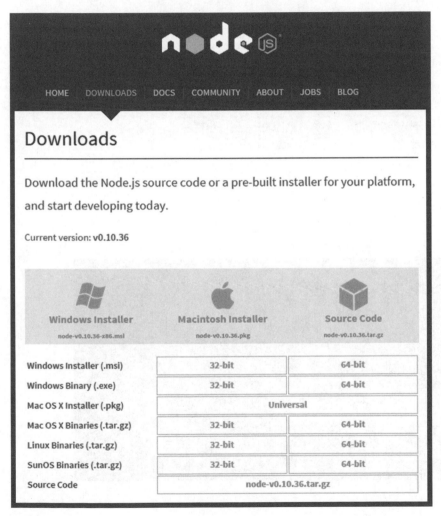

FIGURE 23-1

If you've successfully completed all eight of the Node installation steps, you're ready to continue on to installing ESLint.

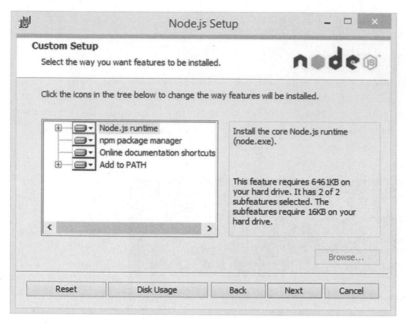

FIGURE 23-2

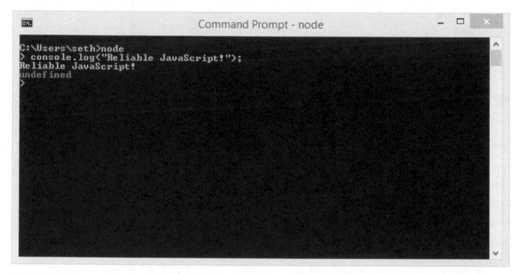

FIGURE 23-3

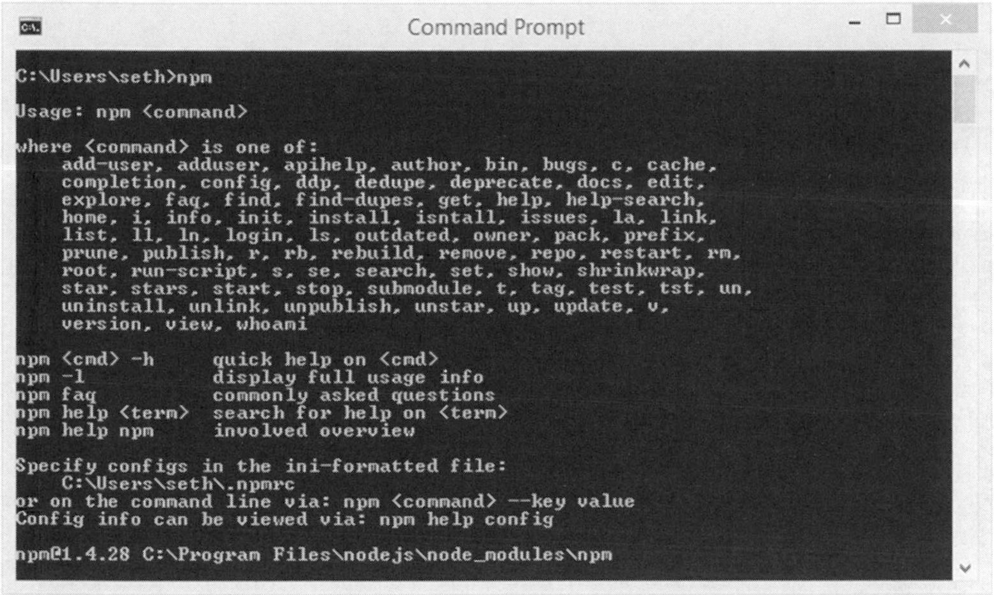

FIGURE 23-4

Installing ESLint Using npm

The following steps describe the process of installing ESLint using npm.

1. Launch a command prompt.

2. Type `npm install -g eslint` and press Enter. Npm will download and install ESLint and all of its dependencies.

   The `-g` option provided to the install command tells npm that ESLint should be installed globally, meaning that it may be executed within any path on your computer. Omitting the `-g` option would cause npm to install ESLint into the path where the command was executed, limiting your ability to execute ESLint only while at that path.

   When installation is complete, your command prompt should look similar to the one shown in Figure 23-5.

3. At the command prompt, type `eslint` and press Enter. You should see output similar to that in Figure 23-6. If the output you see isn't similar, you should troubleshoot your ESLint installation before continuing.

Running ESLint

With ESLint installed, you're ready to begin using it to improve your code's structure, syntax, and adherence to standards. Listing 23-1 provides a sample JavaScript file that's the basis of the examples in this section. For the purposes of samples, how the JavaScript is written is far more important than the actions the JavaScript performs.

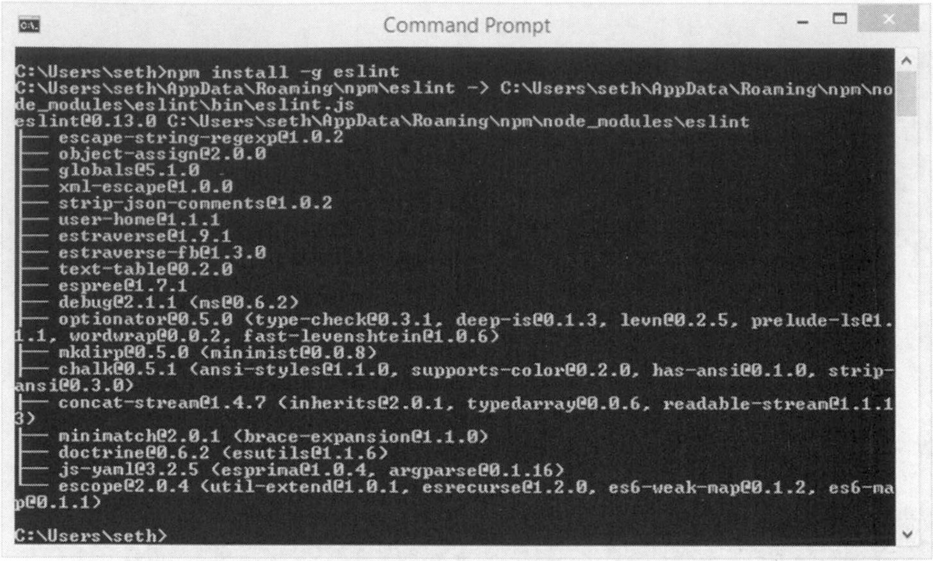

FIGURE 23-5

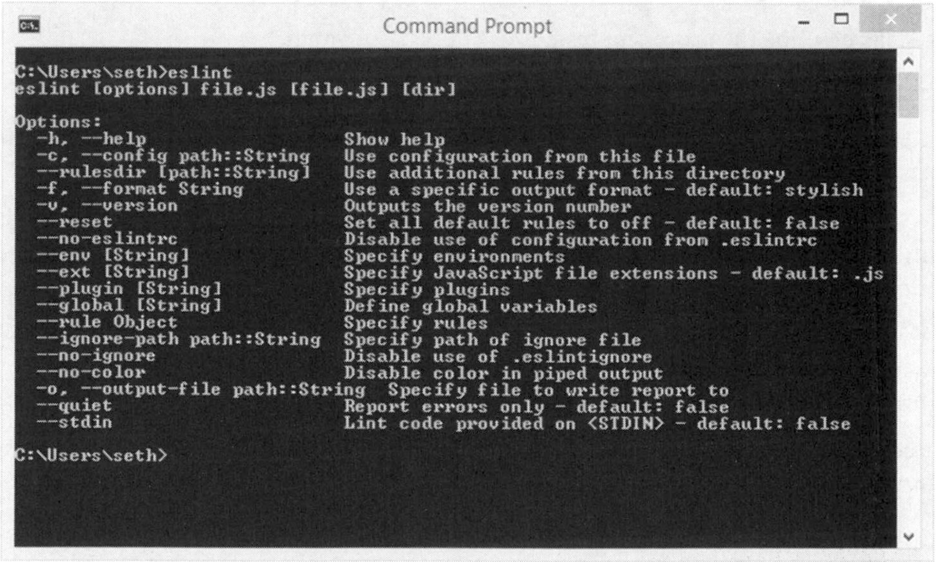

FIGURE 23-6

LISTING 23-1: JavaScript that will be improved using suggestions from ESLint (code filename: ESLint\Example1\DOMUpdater.js)

```javascript
var ReliableJavaScript = ReliableJavaScript || {};

ReliableJavaScript.DOMUpdater = (function DOMUpdater(){

  return {

    appendToElement: function appendToElement(appendToID, elementString){
      if(appendToID == null || appendToID == undefined)
        appendToID = "";

      if(elementString == null || elementString == undefined)
        elementString = "";

      inputsValid = (elementString != "" && appendToID != "");

      if(inputsValid) {
        $('#' + appendToID).append(elementString);
      }
    }

  }
})()
```

The module defined in Listing 23-1, `ReliableJavaScript.DOMUpdater`, defines an object with a single method: `appendToElement`. The function accepts two arguments:

➤ `appendToID`: The ID of the DOM element to which the new element should be appended

➤ `elementString`: The string representation of the DOM element that should be appended to the element with ID `appendToID`

The function creates a DOM element from `elementString` and appends it to the element specified by `appendToID`. The function does some basic checks to ensure that the expected arguments have been provided.

Listing 23-2 provides an HTML page that uses `ReliableJavaScript.DOMUpdater` to add an element to the page.

LISTING 23-2: An HTML page that uses ReliableJavaScript.DOMUpdater (code filename: ESLint\Example1\index.html)

```html
<!DOCTYPE html>
<html>

  <head>
    <script src="http://cdn.jsdelivr.net/jquery/2.1.3/jquery.min.js"></script>
    <script src="DOMUpdater.js"></script>

    <script type="text/javascript">
```

continues

LISTING 23-2 *(continued)*

```
    $(function(){
      ReliableJavaScript.DOMUpdater
        .appendToElement("DocumentBody",
          "<h1>Hello from Reliable JavaScript!</h1>");
    });
    </script>
  </head>

  <body id="DocumentBody">
  </body>

</html>
```

Figure 23-7 shows that the `appendToElement` function does, in fact, add the specified element to the DOM.

Hello from Reliable JavaScript!

FIGURE 23-7

Executing ESLint on a Single File

You may have noticed a few ways that Listing 23-1 may be improved structurally and syntactically. To find out what changes ESLint suggests, you can have ESLint evaluate the file by following these steps:

1. Open a command prompt.

2. Change directories into the directory that contains the file from Listing 23-1.

3. Type `eslint DOMUpdater.js` at the command prompt and press Enter.

Step 3 illustrates that the `eslint` command accepts the name of the file that it should analyze. In the case of the example, the name of the file is `DOMUpdater.js`, the name of the file from Listing 23-1.

The output from executing the command `eslint DOMUpdater.js` is shown in Figure 23-8.

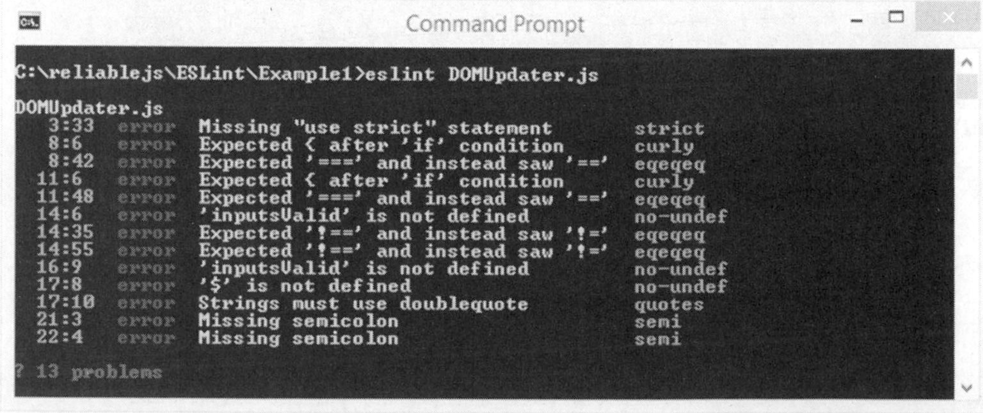

```
C:\reliablejs\ESLint\Example1>eslint DOMUpdater.js

DOMUpdater.js
   3:33   error   Missing "use strict" statement         strict
   8:6    error   Expected { after 'if' condition        curly
   8:42   error   Expected '===' and instead saw '=='    eqeqeq
  11:6    error   Expected { after 'if' condition        curly
  11:48   error   Expected '===' and instead saw '=='    eqeqeq
  14:6    error   'inputsValid' is not defined           no-undef
  14:35   error   Expected '!==' and instead saw '!='    eqeqeq
  14:55   error   Expected '!==' and instead saw '!='    eqeqeq
  16:9    error   'inputsValid' is not defined           no-undef
  17:8    error   '$' is not defined                     no-undef
  17:10   error   Strings must use doublequote           quotes
  21:3    error   Missing semicolon                      semi
  22:4    error   Missing semicolon                      semi

? 13 problems
```

FIGURE 23-8

ESLint found 13 problems in a file that's less than 30 lines long! Charlotte would not be impressed with the code in Listing 23-1, would she?

Each line in the output shown in Figure 23-8 corresponds with an individual issue identified by ESLint.

The ESLint output lines start with the line number and column number, separated by a colon, of the location in the processed file where the issue was identified. Next, the severity of the issue is displayed. All of the issues in Figure 23-8 are errors. Following the issued severity is a brief text description of the rule that was violated, and finally the ESLint code for the violated rule is displayed.

Executing ESLint on All the JavaScript Files in a Directory

ESLint undoubtedly provides valuable feedback, but we probably wouldn't run it very often if we had to feed it files one by one, and we don't expect you would either. To make it easier to run against many files at once, ESLint also accepts a directory name as a command-line argument. To run ESLint against all of the files in the ESLint\Example2 directory of this chapter's downloads, follow these steps:

1. Open a command prompt.

2. Change directories into the *parent* of the directory Example2.

3. Type **eslint Example2** at the command prompt and press Enter.

The Example2 directory contains the files DOMUpdater_1.js and DOMUpdater_2.js. Both files contain the code shown in Listing 23-1.

As the name of a directory has been provided as a command-line argument to ESLint, ESLint will process all of the files with the extension .js in the directory specified. The output of the command entered in Step 3 appears in Figure 23-9.

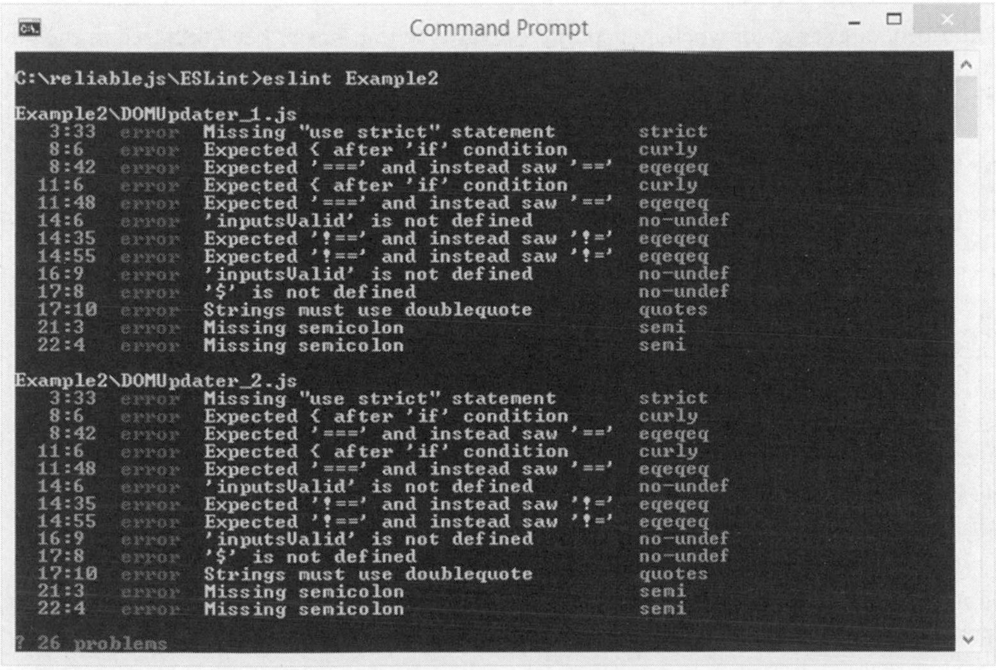

FIGURE 23-9

As an added convenience, ESLint also processes subdirectories automatically. If you have a directory structure in which your JavaScript files are contained in numerous subdirectories, ESLint will recursively process all subdirectories if you provide the root directory as a command-line argument.

> **NOTE** *Node task-execution packages such as Grunt and Gulp may be configured to watch for changes in your JavaScript files and automatically execute ESLint when a change is detected.*

Enforcing Coding Standards with ESLint

ESLint identified quite a few issues with the code in Listing 23-1, among them:

> ➤ Missing "use strict"

> ➤ Multiple missing semicolons

> ➤ Omission of curly braces surrounding single-statement if bodies

> ➤ Use of the undeclared variable $

All of these could be legitimate issues, but they may also be acceptable based on your team's coding standards or additional files included in your solution.

If your coding standard allows the omission of curly braces when the body of a conditional or loop statement has only a single line, must you slog through lines and lines of warnings from ESLint about the braces being missing? Certainly not.

Also, ESLint generates an error when it encounters a variable that hasn't been declared in the file being processed. In some cases, such an error will alert you to the use of an undeclared variable, but in other cases you may be referencing a global variable that's declared in some other file, such as jQuery's $ global variable. Does that mean you have to declare all your variables in every file that references them? Again, not at all.

Like JSHint, ESLint allows rules to be relaxed from error to warning, or to be turned off completely. Rules may be relaxed or turned off on a file-by-file basis via comments in the file. You may also inform ESLint of global variables that are declared in a separate file, reducing the incidence of false positives.

For instance, adding the comment /*eslint curly:0*/ to the top of a JavaScript file turns off the check for curly braces around single-statement conditional or loop bodies. Adding the comment /*global $*/ alerts ESLint that the $ is a global variable defined in another file and the use of $ need not generate an undefined variable error. ESLint may also be notified that jQuery is in use via the comment /*eslint-env jquery*/.

Adding comments to the top of all your JavaScript files is not optimal for projects consisting of any more than one JavaScript file; it's a violation of the DRY principle. To address this, ESLint also supports the use of configuration files. If a folder contains a file named .eslintrc (note the leading period), ESLint will load configuration values from the file. The .eslintrc file, among other settings, may contain directives to enforce, relax, or disable the rules it uses when processing JavaScript files in the directory containing, or subdirectories of the directory containing, the `.eslintrc` file. Listing 23-3 shows an `.eslintrc` file that disables the `curly` rule (missing curly braces around single-statement conditional or loop blocks), relaxes the `semi` rule (missing semicolon) to a warning rather than an error, and informs ESLint that jQuery is in use.

LISTING 23-3: .eslintrc file that disables the curly rule, relaxes the semi rule, and enables the jQuery environment (code filename: ESLint\Example3\.eslintrc)

```
{
    "rules": {
      "curly": 0, // 0 disables the rule
      "semi": 1   // 1 treats violations of the rule as a warning
    },
    "env": {
      "jquery": true
    }
}
```

As Listing 23-3 shows, the `.eslintrc` file is structured as a JavaScript object literal, something you're certainly familiar with by this point in the book.

Figure 23-10 shows the output when ESLint is executed against the `DOMUpdater.js` file in the `Example3` directory. That directory also holds the `.eslintrc` file from Listing 23-3.

```
C:\reliablejs\ESLint\Example3>eslint DOMUpdater.js

DOMUpdater.js
   3:33   error    Missing "use strict" statement          strict
   8:42   error    Expected '===' and instead saw '=='     eqeqeq
  11:48   error    Expected '===' and instead saw '=='     eqeqeq
  14:6    error    'inputsValid' is not defined            no-undef
  14:35   error    Expected '!==' and instead saw '!='     eqeqeq
  14:55   error    Expected '!==' and instead saw '!='     eqeqeq
  16:9    error    'inputsValid' is not defined            no-undef
  17:10   error    Strings must use doublequote            quotes
  21:3    warning  Missing semicolon                       semi
  22:4    warning  Missing semicolon                       semi

? 10 problems
```

FIGURE 23-10

Notice that ESLint no longer emits any errors related to the missing curly braces, nor is it complaining that $ is undefined. Also, it's displaying warnings rather than errors when it encounters a line missing a semicolon.

Creating a Custom ESLint Rule

Listing 23-4 shows a revised version of `DOMUpdater.js`, cleaned up to remove all of the issues reported by ESLint (including the issues reported due to missing curly braces and semicolons).

LISTING 23-4: DOMUpdater.js revised to remove the issues reported by ESLint (code filename: ESLint\Example4\DOMUpdater.js)

```
var ReliableJavaScript = ReliableJavaScript || {};

ReliableJavaScript.DOMUpdater = (function DOMUpdater(){
  "use strict";

  return {

    appendToElement: function appendToElement(appendToID, elementString){
      if(appendToID === null || appendToID === undefined){
        appendToID = "";
      }

      if(elementString === null || elementString === undefined){
        elementString = "";
      }

      var inputsValid = (elementString !== "" && appendToID !== "");

      if(inputsValid) {
        $("#" + appendToID).append(elementString);
      }
    }

  };
})();
```

Figure 23-11 shows that ESLint generates neither errors nor warnings when executed against the revised file.

FIGURE 23.11

Suppose that your team has the standard that any identifier that references the ID of an entity should end with Id rather than ID or id. Instead of relying on humans to catch deviations from the rule in code reviews, you can write a custom ESLint rule to enforce the Id suffix standard. A rule that does just that follows in Listing 23-5.

LISTING 23-5: Implementation of the id-suffix custom ESLint rule (code filename: ESLint\Example4\rules\id-suffix.js)

```
"use strict";

module.exports = function(context) {
```

```
    return {
        "Identifier": function(node){
            var suffix = node.name.length > 1 ? node.name.slice(-2) : "";
            if (suffix === "id" || suffix === "ID"){
                context.report(node, "Identifier ref should end with 'Id'.");
            }
        }
    };
};
```

The `id-suffix.js` file follows the format prescribed by the ESLint rule developer documentation, which may be viewed at `http://eslint.org/docs/developer-guide/working-with-rules.html`.

The custom rule's name is `id-suffix`, which is determined by the name of the file containing the rule. The ESLint website has a comprehensive list of best practices to use when naming your custom rules.

The rule module is provided a `context` argument, through which relevant properties of the JavaScript file may be accessed. The `context` variable also provides a mechanism that the rule can use to report failures: the `report` function.

There are numerous functions that a rule may define to analyze different portions of the JavaScript abstract syntax tree (AST) that ESLint is processing. For instance, a rule may define a `ReturnStatement` function that will be invoked when ESLint encounters a return statement while processing a JavaScript file's abstract syntax tree. ESLint rules may define a function named the same as any node type used by the SpiderMonkey JavaScript parser, and the function will be executed whenever nodes of that type are encountered. A full list of the node types is available at `https://developer.mozilla.org/en-US/docs/Mozilla/Projects/SpiderMonkey/Parser_API`.

The custom `id-suffix` rule is only concerned with identifiers, so it defines a function named `Identifier` that will be invoked each time ESLint encounters an identifier. The AST node of the identifier is provided to the function via the `node` argument.

The custom rule examines the last two characters of the names of the identifiers that are provided to it and reports an issue to ESLint when an identifier ending with `ID` or `id` is encountered. ESLint, in turn, notifies the user that an issue has been found, along with the line and column, text description, and rule name.

To enable the rule, ESLint must be told whether the errors generated by the rule should be ignored, treated as warnings, or treated as errors. Listing 23-6 provides an updated `.eslintrc` file that configures ESLint to treat violations of the `id-suffix` rule as errors.

LISTING 23-6: Updated .eslintrc file that enables id-suffix rule (code filename: ESLint\ Example4\.eslintrc)

```
{
    "env": {
      "jquery": true
    },
```

continues

LISTING 23-6 *(continued)*

```
    "rules":{
        "id-suffix":2   // 2 indicates violations should be treated as errors
    }
}
```

Running ESLint with Custom Rules

ESLint accepts an additional command-line argument, `--rulesdir`, that allows the user to specify a folder from which ESLint should load custom rules.

Follow these steps to execute ESLint against the updated sample file in Listing 23-4, including the custom `id-suffix` rule:

1. Open a command prompt.

2. Change directories into the `Example4` directory.

3. Type `eslint --rulesdir ./rules DOMUpdater.js` at the command prompt and press Enter.

Before the custom `id-suffix` rule was being enforced, ESLint reported no issues with the code in Listing 23-4. Now that the `id-suffix` rule is being enforced, ESLint is reporting a few violations, as Figure 23-12 shows.

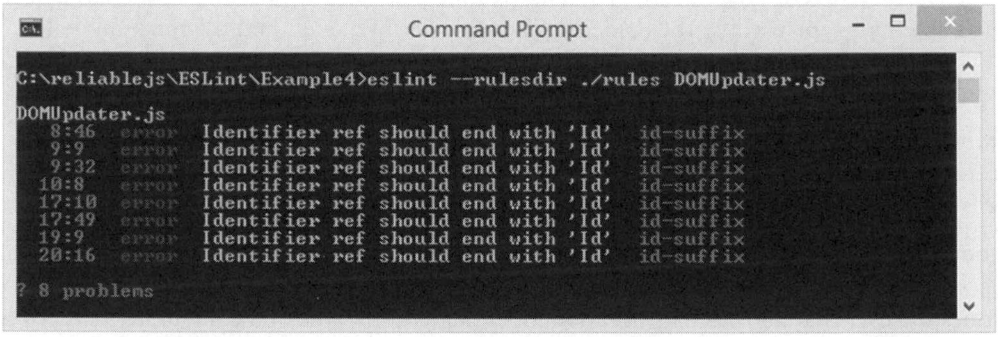

FIGURE 23-12

A majority of the violations ESLint reports are related to the argument `appendToID`, which is named contrary to the standard being enforced by the rule. Notice, however, that ESLint is also reporting an error on line 19, where `appendToID` doesn't appear.

The variable `inputsValid` is used on line 19, however. The `inputsValid` variable *does* end in "id," which violates the rule as it's written, but it doesn't reference the ID of an entity. This means that although the *rule* has been violated, the *standard* has not.

If variables ending in "`valid`" are common, the rule could be updated so that it doesn't report issues with identifiers that end in a lowercase "`id`" when those characters are part of the word "valid." On the other hand, if the rule doesn't result in many false positives, it may be better to add inline exceptions to the rule. Listing 23-7 shows an updated version of Listing 23-4 that addresses the reported violations of the `id-suffix` rule.

LISTING 23-7: Updated DOMUpdater.js that addresses violations of the id-suffix rule (code filename: ESLint\Example5\DOMUpdater.js)

```
var ReliableJavaScript = ReliableJavaScript || {};

ReliableJavaScript.DOMUpdater = (function DOMUpdater(){
  "use strict";

  return {

    appendToElement: function appendToElement(appendToId, elementString){
      if(appendToId === null || appendToId === undefined){
        appendToId = "";
      }

      if(elementString === null || elementString === undefined){
        elementString = "";
      }

      /*eslint-disable id-suffix*/
      var inputsValid = (elementString !== "" && appendToId !== "");

      if(inputsValid) {
      /*eslint-enable id-suffix*/
        $("#" + appendToId).append(elementString);
      }
    }

  };
})();
```

Figure 23-13 shows that the alterations highlighted in Listing 23-7 makes the code comply with the id-suffix rule.

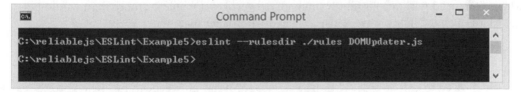

FIGURE 23-13

ENFORCING ARCHITECTURAL DIVISIONS

Your software project is like a show dog. Your deep affection for her may render her minor imperfections invisible to you, but at the show she will be judged as objectively as possible according to how well she conforms to the standard for her breed, and how well she presents.

ESLint and its cousins can take care of the presentation, ensuring that her coat is silky and nails trimmed, but what about the structural issues that can't be cleaned up at the last minute? How well do her body proportions meet the standard, for example? The techniques in this section will address those larger issues of how well software is put together so your program can be more than a pet project.

A theme of this book has been that as your JavaScript programs grow larger, you will want to find ways to mitigate the complexity. This is true when developing in any language, but it is especially true of JavaScript with its idiomatic, diverse, and untraceable ways of getting things done. (We're looking at you, Mr. `call` and Ms. `apply`. Also at you, Mr. `object['property_as_subscript']`.)

Software becomes more complex when more parts of it communicate with each other. A way to mitigate the complexity, then, is to lock down the communication to known channels.

This is especially important when you have designed your application in some sort of layering scheme. For example, consider the game based on the Mediator Pattern in Chapter 21. According to the architecture, only the `mediator` was supposed to call the important functions in the other objects. For example, when a `player` moves, it is not supposed to inform the `gameLogic` object directly. Instead, it should call `mediator.onPlayerMoved`, which in turn calls `gameLogic.onPlayerMoved`.

When programming such a pattern, it is dicey enough to rely on one's own good behavior, but even more problematic to rely on future developers who will maintain your code. They may not know what you intended, and even if they do, they may be under the sort of deadline pressure that has turned the best of us into slash-and-burn coders. What's needed is a way to enforce your intentions in the code. Or, if not *enforce* your wishes, at least make them so abundantly clear that the future developer is unlikely to make an end-run around them.

You will now see several techniques to accomplish this. Each illustrates a way of ensuring that only `mediator` can call `gameLogic.onPlayerMoved`.

The Family-Secret Technique

Does your family have a private language? Maybe it's a made-up word or a quirky phrase that has meaning only among your family members. Perhaps it's a phrase from a movie you saw together that, when referenced within your family, immediately evokes a whole lot more than would be apparent to an outsider. The phrase is a secret key to a broader meaning.

Objects can come in families, too, and objects born in the family can know the family secret.

If `mediator` and `gameLogic` belong to the same family, they can share a secret such that only `mediator` is allowed to call `gameLogic.onPlayerMoved`. What do we mean by "belong to the same family?" We mean that `gameLogic` lives in `mediator`'s house—`gameLogic` is a function enclosed completely in `Game.mediator`. This allows them to share a secret, namely a private variable in `mediator`. When `mediator` calls `gameLogic.onPlayerMoved`, it can pass the secret as an argument. `gameLogic` agrees that the secret is the right one and lets the move proceed.

Nothing prevents `mediator` from letting an instance of `gameLogic` out of the house—passing it to `Game.player`, for example. However, `player` cannot see the private variable and so can get nowhere with the protected function. If it wants to inform the `gameLogic` object of its movements, it must do so through the `mediator`. Your architecture is thus enforced.

Listing 23-8 illustrates the technique.

> **NOTE** *For clarity in this section, we present only abridged forms of the objects. You may refer to the downloads from Chapter 21 if you want to see all that they do.*

LISTING 23-8: A family secret (code filename: FamilySecret\mediator.js)

```javascript
var Game = Game || {};

Game.mediator = function mediator() {
  'use strict';

  // The magicKey is a secret shared in the mediator family.
  // It is a private reference to a private, non-reproducible object.
  var magicKey = {},

    // Encapsulates the logic (rules) of the game.
    // In this version, gameLogic is embedded in mediator so it can
    // see the magicKey.
    gameLogic = function gameLogic(mediator, rows, columns) {

      return {

        // Reflect a player's movement to his current node,
        // and end the game if appropriate.
        onPlayerMoved: function onPlayerMoved(key, player) {
          if (key !== magicKey) {
            throw new Error('Only the mediator may call this function.');
          }
          // Make the logical representation of the game
          // respond to player's move.
        }

        /*** Other function omitted for clarity. ***/
      };
    },

    // The mediator, which will be returned.
    med = {

      // Player calls this when he moves. Mediator informs other components.
      onPlayerMoved: function onPlayerMoved(player) {
        logic.onPlayerMoved(magicKey, player);
        display.onPlayerMoved(player);
      },

      /*** Other functions omitted for clarity. ***/
    },

    svgElement = document.getElementById('gameSvg');

  logic = Game.gameLogic(med, 6, 7);
```

continues

LISTING 23-8 *(continued)*

```
    display = Game.svgDisplay(med,svgElement,logic);

    return med;
};
```

In the listing, the *magicKey* variable serves as the secret. The beautiful thing is that it does not have to have a particular value. As long as it is private and refers to an object that nobody else can reproduce, your secret is safe.

Toward the end of the listing, when the onPlayerMoved function calls logic.onPlayerMoved, it passes *magicKey* as the first parameter. GameLogic.onPlayerMoved verifies that this is the right key before proceeding.

The Family Secret Technique works well and is easy to implement. However, it suffers two drawbacks.

First, things get awkward if there is more than one secret to be kept. You may have noticed in the preceding listing that mediator calls display.onPlayerMoved as well as logic.onPlayerMoved. What if mediator wanted to bring display into the house in the same way? display would now be in on the secret and thereby able to make calls to gameLogic—precisely what we wanted to avoid.

Second, you would probably prefer that mediator and gameLogic live in their own source files. This is not directly possible with this technique.

For those reasons, the pattern is most useful in very tight-knit families of objects. For example, we have used it to allow nodes of a tree structure to call protected functions on each other. The nodes were spawned by a common object that held the secret. This benefitted consumers of the tree by simplifying their interface, and benefitted the tree by ensuring that the outside world could only manipulate it in tightly controlled ways.

The next technique gives all the benefits of the Family Secret, but avoids its limitations.

The Imprinting Technique

Baby geese are famous for imprinting on the first living being they see upon pecking their way out of their shells. Usually, it's Mommy Goose and life goes as planned. Sometimes, however, it might be a human researcher. In that case, the goslings will follow the person around as if she is their mother.

In a similar way, you can imprint one object on another.

With gameLogic, it happens that the object that should get special privileges, namely the mediator, is a parameter to gameLogic's constructor—the first object gameLogic sees. You can make gameLogic imprint on this object so that when the "mommy" is passed as an argument to gameLogic.onPlayerMoved, gameLogic obeys. When anyone else calls it, it refuses.

Easy enough, right? Ready to code it?

Of course not! To code without writing a test first would be to admit that you had continued to invest hour upon hour reading the preceding 22 chapters with no intention of putting their most basic tenet into practice. May it never be!

Listing 23-9, then, details the tests (two are necessary, actually) for this new feature. Once again, only the essential features of the objects are shown. In real life, this code would be filled with spies on *player* and *mediator*, but that would only clutter the example.

LISTING 23-9: Unit tests for the Imprinting Technique (code filename: Imprinting\gameLogic_tests.js)

```
describe('gameLogic', function() {
  'use strict';

  var mediator = 'Pretend this is a mediator',
      player = 'Pretend this is a player',
      gameLogic = Game.gameLogic(mediator,6, 7);

  describe('onPlayerMoved(caller, player)', function() {

    it('throws if caller is not the original mediator', function() {
      expect(function() {
        gameLogic.onPlayerMoved('wrongKey', player);
      }).toThrowError(Game.gameLogic.messages.callerMustBeOriginalMediator);
    });

    it('does not throw if caller is the original mediator', function() {
      expect(function() {
        gameLogic.onPlayerMoved(mediator,player);
      }).not.toThrow();
    });

  });
});
```

The first test ensures that if the `mediator` passed to the constructor is not presented as the `caller` of `gameLogic.onPlayerMoved`, then `onPlayerMoved` throws an exception. The second test is the happy path.

The implementation is completely straightforward (see Listing 23-10).

LISTING 23-10: Implementation of the Imprinting Technique (code filename: Imprinting\gameLogic.js)

```
var Game = Game || {};

// Encapsulates the logic (rules) of the game
Game.gameLogic = function gameLogic(mediator, rows, columns) {
  'use strict';

  var mommy = mediator;

  return {

    onPlayerMoved: function onPlayerMoved(caller, player) {
```

continues

LISTING 23-10 *(continued)*

```
      if (caller !== mommy) {
        throw new Error(Game.gameLogic.messages.callerMustBeOriginalMediator);
      }
      // Make the logical representation of the game respond to player's move.
    }

    /*** Other function omitted for clarity. ***/
  };
};

Game.gameLogic.messages = {
  callerMustBeOriginalMediator: 'The caller parameter must be the mediator ' +
    'supplied when the object was instantiated.'
};
```

As usual, the unit tests' results provide a concise description of the functionality (see Figure 23-14).

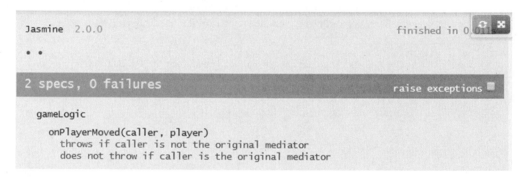

FIGURE 23-14

Your first reaction to the preceding might be skepticism. You may well ask, "What is to prevent another component that also possesses a reference to the `mediator` from calling `gameLogic`.onPlayerMoved? The `player` is an example. It, too, was constructed with a `mediator` instance and could easily call `gameLogic.onPlayerMoved`.

And you would be right. The only response this pattern has to your argument is a lowly variable name.

The first parameter to `onPlayerMoved` was named *caller* rather than *mediator* in the hope that if the `player` developer were to call `gameLogic.onPlayerMoved`, he would see the name *caller* and dutifully pass the `player` instance. He would then get the exception and say, "Oh, I guess I wasn't supposed to do that."

Still, this is only a hope and you might feel it is misplaced. If so, the next technique might interest you.

The Mission Impossible Technique

This technique is a little more trouble to implement, but it truly ensures that the `mediator` is the only one that will be able to call `gameLogic.onPlayerMoved`.

Did you ever see the old TV show *Mission Impossible*? Each episode began with Jim Phelps, the Director of the Impossible Missions Force (Hey, it was the 1960s and TV was cheesy, okay?), listening to a cassette tape that gave his instructions: "Your mission, should you choose to accept it, is … ." The message would usually conclude, "This tape will self-destruct in five seconds," after which the device would go up in smoke. Jim didn't get a second chance, but he was a very smart guy and didn't need one. And there was no way the privileged information would fall into the wrong hands after he had listened to it.

You can do the same thing with a read-once magic key. The idea is that as soon as the `mediator` is constructed, it asks for `gameLogic`'s magic key. `gameLogic` gives it, and the key-granting function self-destructs, as it were, so no other component can get the key. Meanwhile, `mediator` puts the key in a private variable, safe from that overly creative `player` developer.

The read-once magic key is a pattern that deserves to be encapsulated in its own object. The unit tests that describe it are in Listing 23-11.

LISTING 23-11: Unit tests for the readOnceKey (code filename: MissionImpossible\ readOnceKey_tests.js)

```javascript
describe('readOnceKey', function() {
  'use strict';

  var readOnceKey;
  beforeEach(function() {
    readOnceKey = Game.readOnceKey();
  });

  describe('getKey()', function() {

    it('returns something with the first call', function() {
      expect(readOnceKey.getKey()).not.toBeUndefined();
    });

    it('throws on the second call', function() {
      readOnceKey.getKey();

      expect(function() {
        readOnceKey.getKey();
      }).toThrowError(Game.readOnceKey.messages.onlyOnce);
    });

    it('cannot be replaced with an impostor', function() {
      expect(function() {
        readOnceKey['getKey'] = function() { return 'Fake!'; }
      }).toThrow();
    });
  });

  describe('assertMatches(key)', function() {

    it('throws if "key" is not the correct one', function() {
```

continues

LISTING 23-11 *(continued)*

```
      expect(function() {
        readOnceKey.assertMatches('badKey');
      }).toThrowError(Game.readOnceKey.messages.badKey);
    });

    it('does not throw if "key" is correct', function() {
      var magicKey = readOnceKey.getKey();
      expect(function() {
        readOnceKey.assertMatches(magicKey);
      }).not.toThrow();
    });

    it('cannot be replaced with an impostor', function() {
      expect(function() {
        readOnceKey['assertMatches'] = function() { }
      }).toThrow();
    });
  });
});
```

The readOnceKey object has two methods: getKey and assertMatches. The first two unit tests verify that getKey succeeds on the first call but fails after that. The reason for the third test will become clear shortly. The second block of tests verifies that throws if and only if the wrong key is supplied, and cannot be replaced. Listing 23-12 shows the implementation.

LISTING 23-12: Implementation of readOnceKey (code filename: MissionImpossible\ readOnceKey.js)

```
var Game = Game || {};

Game.readOnceKey = function readOnceKey() {
  'use strict';
  var magicKey = {},
      alreadyRead = false,
      ret = {}; // The read-once key that will be returned

  function getKey() {
    if (alreadyRead) {
      throw new Error(Game.readOnceKey.messages.onlyOnce);
    }
    alreadyRead = true;
    return magicKey;
  }
  function assertMatches(key) {
    if (key !== magicKey) {
      throw new Error(Game.readOnceKey.messages.badKey);
    }
  }

  Object.defineProperty(ret, 'getKey', { value: getKey });
```

```
      Object.defineProperty(ret, 'assertMatches', { value: assertMatches });
      return ret;
    };

    Game.readOnceKey.messages = {
      onlyOnce: 'The readOnceKey may only be read once.',
      badKey: 'The supplied key was incorrect. ' +
              'Have you violated an architectural constraint?'
    };
```

Note the use of `Object.defineProperty` to install the methods in the returned object. By default, `Object.defineProperty` makes the defined property read-only. This is important here because we want to guarantee that no developer who is a bad citizen can bypass the intent of `readOnceKey` by replacing the `assertMatches` function with one that never throws an `Error`.

Finally, Figure 23-15 is proof that the tests pass.

Now you'll want to embed a `readOnceKey` in `gameLogic`. If there were more than one `gameLogic` instance, they should share a common key, which you would attach directly to the `gameLogic` *function* rather than to each `gameLogic` *object*. Why not do so in this case, too? That also means the key can be obtained before the first `gameLogic` is instantiated (see Listing 23-13).

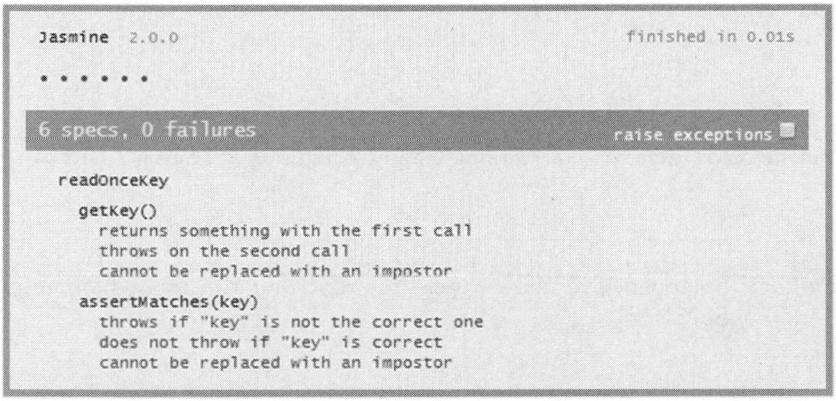

FIGURE 23-15

LISTING 23-13: The readOnceKey installed on the gameLogic function (code filename: MissionImpossible\gameLogic.js)

```
// Encapsulates the logic (rules) of the game
Game.gameLogic = function gameLogic(mediator, rows, columns) {

  /*** Function body omitted. ***/
};

Game.gameLogic.keyToProtectedFunctions = Game.readOnceKey();
```

How would you test `gameLogic.onPlayerMoved`'s use of the key? This is a matter of taste. Do you need to verify that `gameLogic.onPlayerMoved` succeeds when called with the correct key and fails if the wrong key is passed? You could, but that would duplicate the tests of `readOnceKey`. We would argue that it's enough to verify that `gameLogic.onPlayerMoved` calls the `massertMatches` method of `readOnceKey` appropriately. If so, then you can be sure that `onPlayerMoved` will throw an exception if the key fails to match. This test is in Listing 23-14.

LISTING 23-14: Verifying that gameLogic.onPlayerMoved checks the readOnceKey (code filename: MissionImpossible\gameLogic_tests.js)

```javascript
describe('gameLogic', function() {
  'use strict';

  var mediator = 'Pretend this is a mediator',
      player = 'Pretend this is a player',
      gameLogic = Game.gameLogic(mediator,6, 7);

  describe('onPlayerMoved(magicKey, player)', function() {

    it('asserts that "magicKey" is the correct one', function() {
      expect(function() {
        gameLogic.onPlayerMoved('bad key', player);
      }).toThrowError(Game.readOnceKey.messages.badKey);
    });

  });
});
```

The test fails initially but succeeds after you add the single highlighted line of Listing 23-15 to `gameLogic`.

LISTING 23-15: GameLogic.onPlayerMoved now checks the readOnceKey (code filename: MissionImpossible\gameLogic.js)

```javascript
var Game = Game || {};

// Encapsulates the logic (rules) of the game
Game.gameLogic = function gameLogic(mediator, rows, columns) {
  'use strict';

  return {

    onPlayerMoved: function onPlayerMoved(magicKey, player) {
      Game.gameLogic.keyToProtectedFunctions.assertMatches(magicKey);
      // Make the logical representation of the game respond to player's move.
    }

    /*** Other function omitted for clarity. ***/
  };
};

Game.gameLogic.messages = {
```

```
      callerMustBeOriginalMediator: 'The caller parameter must be the mediator ' +
         'supplied when the object was instantiated.'
   };

   Game.gameLogic.keyToProtectedFunctions = Game.readOnceKey();
```

Figure 23-16 is the happy result.

To review, `mediator` is now able to call `Game.gameLogic.keyToProtectedFunctions.getKey()` before it even creates `gameLogic`. In fact, if `mediator` is really paranoid, it will call `getReadOnceKey` before it creates `player` or any other object that might co-opt the key. (Of course, if such an event were to occur, `mediator` would know about it the moment *it* tried to get the key!) The `mediator` will store the key in a private variable and then pass it as the first argument to `gameLogic.onPlayerMoved(`*magicKey, player*`)`.

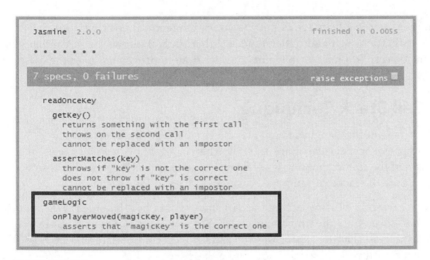

FIGURE 23-16

The Magic Wand Technique

The Mission Impossible Technique is secure, but only if Director Phelps listens to the tape before anyone else does. Maybe it makes sense for a higher authority to confer the proper privileges to the proper agents. If so, you could consider the Magic Wand Technique.

This pattern also uses `readOnceKeys`, but as orchestrated by a top-level object. Continuing in a whimsical spirit, suppose it is called `fairyGodmother`.

In this variation, `fairyGodmother` obtains a `readOnceKey` from `gameLogic` and then bestows it on `mediator`, which must have a method to receive it, `receivePlayerKey`. As in the Mission Impossible Technique, `receivePlayerKey` sequesters the key in a variable that is private to `mediator`. The rest of the story is the same as in Mission Impossible (the software pattern, not the TV show).

The application will ask the `fairyGodmother` to wave her wand over the appropriate objects at the appropriate moments. This snippet shows how she might give `mediator` the special power we have been discussing.

```
Game.fairyGodmother = function fairyGodmother() {

  return {
    waveWand: function waveWand(mediator, gameLogic, otherObjectsToo) {
      var gameLogicKey = Game.gameLogic.keyToProtectedFunctions.getKey();

      // Give mediator access to gameLogic's protected functions.
      mediator.receiveKeyToGameLogic(gameLogicKey);

      // Wave wand over other objects, too....
    }
  };
};
```

The Magic Wand Technique has the advantage of putting your architectural layering decisions in one place, where they are easy to inspect and understand. Furthermore, it allows a `readOnceKey` to be given to more than one object. You may or may not consider it an improvement over the Mission Impossible Technique.

Do Not Use the Call Stack Technique

If you come to JavaScript from another language, you may be wondering why `gameLogic` `.onPlayerMoved` can't simply inspect the call stack to verify that a `mediator` is doing the calling. There are several reasons, but the immediate one is sufficient: JavaScript has no cross-browser–compatible way to inspect the call stack. Period.

Even if it did there are other reasons why inspecting the call stack would be a bad idea. First among them, it would not suffice to check only the immediate caller. What if `gameLogic.onPlayerMoved` had been wrapped in an aspect, so that the aspect was the caller? To accommodate this case, you'd have to continue up the stack until you did (or did not) find a `mediator`.

Second, suppose you did find a `mediator` and it was five levels up. How would you know that the intervening levels are harmless aspects and not bad actors like `player`? You can't check for every possible bad case.

Other Techniques

In this section, you have seen several ways to enforce architectural decisions by restricting the communication between objects. Each technique used a private variable as a key to a protected function or group of functions. You can probably think of more variations on this idea. As usual with JavaScript, your imagination is the only limit.

Other Architectures

The Mediator Pattern is an example of layered architecture. There are others. No doubt you have organized many applications in the classic layers of user interface, business logic, and data access. In AngularJS applications, we have found it useful to collect all HTTP calls in a service layer.

In every case, the key to avoiding chaos is to adhere to the layering standards. This can be difficult on a team where not everyone is aware of them or properly appreciates them. The techniques in this section may be useful in communicating and enforcing your intent.

SUMMARY

This chapter covered how to enforce your standards at both the syntactic and architectural levels.

The open-source JavaScript linting tool, ESLint, was presented as an aid to detect violations of standards at the line-of-code level. A prerequisite for ESLint is Node.js, so you saw how to install Node and npm on a Windows-based PC. A demonstration of installing ESLint followed.

Next, you saw how to run ESLint, both on a single file and multiple files at the same time. Also, you saw that ESLint supports multiple configuration mechanisms, such as in-code directives and configuration files.

ESLint has built-in rules and also lets you write your own. The chapter included demonstrations of both.

Architectural standards often turn on which objects are allowed to communicate with which. The chapter followed the Mediator Pattern as an example. In this pattern, the Mediator is supposed to manage all important communication between colleague objects. Although JavaScript does not have the assemblies and access modifiers of C# or Java, you saw how it is possible to exert very precise control over communication between objects.

As your JavaScript applications grow, you will find it increasingly important to be conscientious about standards large and small.

We have covered a lot of ground in these twenty-three chapters. Perhaps it will be helpful to review where we've been. The next chapter summarizes the principles of test-driven development.

PART V
Summary

24

Summary of the Principles of Test-Driven Development

WHAT'S IN THIS CHAPTER?

➤ Writing unit-testable code

➤ Mastering the mechanics of test-driven development

➤ Testing common patterns in software engineering

There used to be a TV show called *This Is Your Life*. First aired in 1948, it enjoyed several revivals and specials through the 1980s. A fairly ordinary person would be surprised to find himself on the show, where his life would be reviewed. The subject's long-lost childhood friends might make an appearance; his elementary school teacher, now in her nineties, would say how she still remembers what a good boy he was; and so on. Needless to say, the show would have quite an effect on the surprised subject, and the audience, too, would be deeply moved.

As you review the portion of your life spent in the preceding 23 chapters, you will see one friend who was always there for you: test-driven development. Over and over again, it has played an important role in making your software more reliable. In this chapter, let's look back on that friendship. Although you may not be moved to tears as the subjects of *This Is Your Life* often were, we hope you will be inspired to keep test-driven development by your side.

RECALLING WHY TEST-DRIVEN DEVELOPMENT IS WORTHWHILE

Like an old friend, the unit tests of test-driven development are with you from the very beginning. They help you think through a problem ahead of time by clarifying how your program should behave, rather than merely verifying that it runs as you have written it.

Unit tests have got your back. If you want to refactor the code, the complete code coverage that is the inevitable result of test-driven development will alert you if the result is not quite right.

Counterintuitively, test-driven development's insistence that functionality be added in small increments does not lead to *ad hoc* code. We've all worked on applications that have grown worse and worse over time because all the developers on the team are afraid to touch what's there. Refactoring is out of the question because it would be tantamount to a rewrite. With test-driven development, your unit tests inevitably cover nearly 100 percent of your code, enabling the refactoring that keeps it clean and DRY. This is true from the very beginning of the development process. "Test, code, refactor, repeat" is not only the mantra of test-driven development but the key to making your code elegant.

In Chapter 2, you saw how one of the most elegant pieces of code we have ever encountered, the `Aop.js` library, could be built up in a test-driven approach.

Not only that, but you saw that it was possible to use test-driven development to *understand* and code that little gem.

When test-driven development has helped you reach your goal of a working program, it continues to be your friend. The output of the unit tests (Jasmine's, in this book) reads like a functional specification, helping future developers understand and appreciate what you have done…and keeping them from messing it up.

PRACTICING TEST-DRIVEN DEVELOPMENT

As you review the role test-driven development has played in this book, a few general principles will stand out. First among them is to write code that is unit-testable.

Writing Unit-Testable Code

It's simple: To make a program that is unit-testable, write your program in units. By this, we mean modules with small interfaces (see Chapter 3) and a single responsibility (see Chapter 1).

When one unit must use the services of another, dependency injection is your SOLID (see Chapter 1) buddy. If you supply one unit's services to another through the latter's constructor function, you can supply a mock in unit tests, thereby limiting the actual code under test to one unit, not two.

Mastering the Mechanics of Test-Driven Development

The following is the basic cycle of test-driven development:

1. Write a test. Ideally, it will fail, and fail in such a way that you are assured it is testing what it should.

2. Write the code to make the test pass.

3. Refactor to keep your code DRY and beautiful.

4. Repeat until your program is complete.

Writing the Test Before the Code

The most important step, and the one we have found developers have the most trouble with, is the first one: writing the test *before* writing the code. Maintaining this discipline is incredibly difficult but is absolutely the key to reliability. Never let your code get ahead of your tests.

A test that is written *after* the code will initially pass rather than fail. How can you know that it passes because the code is correct, and not because the test is faulty?

Keeping Your Tests DRY

Often, your tests will contain more lines of code than their subjects. This is a very broad hint that it's just as important to keep your tests DRY as to keep your code in good shape. Jasmine's nested structure, with the possibility of using `beforeEach` at each level, makes this easy (see Chapter 2).

Testing Error Conditions First

The first tests you write should be for error conditions. The reason is more psychological than technical. If you delay these tests until you've done all the "real" tests, you're more likely to be tired of the subject under test, and more likely to cut corners so you can move on to other things. If, on the other hand, you save the most interesting and important tests for last, you have something to look forward to and will maintain enthusiasm until the end.

Beyond that, writing the error- and boundary-checking tests first will help you think through the parameters of the problem and may bring some additional positive tests to mind.

Testing the Simple Before the Complex

When testing the happy paths, start with the simplest. This will cause the subject under test to grow in the smallest possible increments. Which do you think is likely to be better-tested: a small increment written to fulfill a single test, or a larger increment that also fulfills one test? The answer is clear.

Starting with the simplest tests will tend to make your tests simple, too.

Being Specific

It is surprisingly easy to write tests that fall just short of testing what they're supposed to test. For example, when testing an error condition, don't be satisfied with the following:

```
expect(something).toThrow();
```

If the subject being tested does throw an error, how will you know it's the right one? Maybe it threw the error before it even got to the part you're trying to test. Instead, do this:

```
expect(something).toThrow(aSpecificError);
```

The specific error will often be a message that the subject exposes to the outside world for just this unit-testing purpose.

On the positive-testing side, don't be content with this:

```
expect(something).toHaveBeenCalled();
```

How will you know it was called *correctly*? Instead, insist on the following:

```
expect(something).toHaveBeenCalledWith(the,proper,arguments);
```

For an example, see Listing 14-7 in Chapter 14.

Testing Just One Thing

Each test should verify just one thing. To be realistic, however, the one thing might be an array of conditions. You saw an example in Listing 11-3 in Chapter 11, where there was a test that `new WidgetSandbox(toolsArray, widgetFcn)` threw an exception if `widgetFcn` was not a function. Rather than writing a separate test for each kind of argument that is not a function, an array of non-functions was run through some test logic with a `forEach`.

Thinking of your Jasmine output as a functional specification, you want it to be as detailed as possible. However, your policy should also be reasonable enough that developers don't just give up.

Your Test Data Are Just as Important as the Test

Avoid test data that may do unintended favors for the subject under test. That means avoiding special numbers like 0 and 1 (unless those specific numbers pertain to the point of the test) and using different numbers for each piece of data. When testing a `sort`, be sure to use data that sorts differently as strings than as numbers. (See the discussion following Listing 14-8 in Chapter 14.) If the real-life data are in a one-to-many relationship, be sure the test data are, too, and be sure to test the one-to-many behavior.

Most programmers are more interested in writing code than writing data. Don't let a lack of interest make you lazy!

Using Jasmine Effectively

The Jasmine functions `describe` and `it` each take a string as a first argument. If you word the strings in each nested set of `describes` and `its` in such a way that their concatenation produces a sentence, the output of the unit tests will read like a functional specification. This discipline will also clarify in your own mind what you are trying to test.

We have seen many cases where a test passes when run by itself but fails when run as part of the whole suite. Invariably, this is because something is initialized once when it should be initialized in a `beforeEach`.

Also, be sure to use `afterEach` to clean up after your tests where necessary. For example, if each test creates an element on the DOM, use `afterEach` to remove the element so subsequent tests will not confuse it with the elements *they* create.

Testing the Patterns in This Book

The preceding principles apply wherever you use test-driven development, but a large section of this book was devoted to test-driven development of specific software-engineering patterns.

Testing Aspect-Oriented Programming

Aspect-oriented programming has made many appearances on these pages, and we hope you will find just as many uses for this powerful pattern in your code. When you write aspects, keep the following things in mind.

A library like `Aop.js` is guaranteed to pass the proper arguments to the decorated function and capture the return value. However, if you use aspect-oriented techniques without the library, those are things you should test.

If it is important to spy on a function that is decorated with an aspect, be sure to capture a reference to the undecorated function *before* the aspect is applied. Then, spy on the undecorated version, as we did in Chapter 8 when testing the `returnValueCache` memoization aspect.

Testing Object Construction

In Chapter 3, you saw many ways to construct objects in JavaScript. Some of them warrant special care in testing.

Object literals are so easy to make in JavaScript that they tend to creep into a code base untested. The reliable way to make them is to use a factory method that is subject to all the usual rigors of test-driven development.

If an object is designed to be constructed with `new`, be sure to include a test for what happens if it is not. An improper use of the constructor should throw an exception and the test should verify that this exact exception was thrown.

When you make an object with monkey-patching, the *donor* should manage the patching. It should verify that the recipient meets whatever requirements may exist, and unit tests should verify that the donor does this properly.

Testing Callbacks

Callbacks are everywhere in JavaScript code and demand special unit-testing, as Chapter 5 explained. When testing the code that is doing the callback, the usual procedure in Jasmine is to spy on the callback function and ensure that it is called with the right arguments (see Listing 5-2 in Chapter 5).

When testing the callback functions themselves, take special care that the `this` within the function is what you expect. See the section "Minding this" in Chapter 5. Avoid writing inline callbacks that can't be unit-tested. The worst case is the "callback arrow" (see Listing 5-6, also in Chapter 5).

Testing Promise-Based Code

As Chapter 6 showed, `Promises` can be tricky, both to write and to test.

If you're not careful, the `Promise` you're testing may be unresolved when your test finishes. If the code inside the `Promise` is faulty, you won't know about it. Listing 6-4 in Chapter 6 showed how to use Jasmine's `done()` mechanism to solve this problem.

Be aware that if one of the callbacks in `Promise.then(resolveCallback, rejectCallback)` is called and does not return anything, what you actually get is a `Promise` resolved as `undefined`. Often, it's sufficient in a test to construct a `Promise` in an already-settled state (either fulfilled or rejected), but sometimes you need the `Promise` to settle at a particular moment during a test. For these occasions, use a `Promise`-wrapping library such as `AngularJS`'s `$q`.

Chained promises can surprise you. For example, if the code follows the rejection branch of a `Promise` but if that branch returns a fulfilled `Promise`, the result of the chain will be a fulfilled

`Promise` (which you might not expect, considering that a rejection had happened). Be sure to test your execution flow in all cases.

Testing a Partial Function Application

As Chapter 7 made clear, a unit test of a partial function application should only consist of ensuring that the underlying (full) function gets called with the correct arguments. There is no need to write tests for the underlying function in this context in addition to the tests that have *surely* been in place since *before* that function was written!

Testing Memoization

Similarly, your tests of the Memoization Pattern (see Chapter 8) need not concern themselves with the memoized function *per se*. They just have to ensure that multiple calls through the memoizer with the same arguments result in just one call, with the correct arguments, to the underlying function, and that the underlying function's return value is passed through the memoizer. For this purpose, you can replace the underlying function with a spy.

Memoization can be turned into an aspect, at which point all the usual principles of testing an aspect apply. See the example in Chapter 8.

Testing a Singleton

As you saw in Chapter 9, a Singleton brings a special consideration to the game in that every time you create an instance of it, usually with a function like `getInstance()`, you are in fact getting the same instance. The test can be as simple as this:

```
expect(firstInstance).toBe(secondInstance);
```

Unlike C# or Java, you don't need to worry about multiple threads accessing a Singleton because JavaScript is single-threaded.

Testing a Factory Method

In the Factory Pattern (see Chapter 10), the factory's single responsibility is to construct and return another object. The single responsibility of its tests, therefore, is to verify that the correct arguments are passed to that object's constructor, and the object thus constructed is returned. A Jasmine spy, with its ability to track arguments and return a value as commanded, should therefore be a stand-in for the real underlying object.

Testing a Sandbox

If you use the Sandbox Pattern (see Chapter 11), you will probably have help from a third-party product. However, if you're writing your own sandbox component (and it's not difficult), here are some things to consider in your tests.

The function to create a sandbox for a widget might look something like this:

```
function WidgetSandbox(toolsArray, widgetFcn)
```

Its unit tests can verify that `widgetFcn` is indeed a function, that the function is executed, and that the sandbox is the first argument in the call (if that's how your sandbox is designed).

Test the provision of tools to the sandbox by verifying that each tool's constructor is called with the sandbox as an argument (again assuming that's your design), and that each tool can be fetched by name.

To test an individual tool, verify that it adds itself to the sandbox. The sandbox does not have to be a real one for this test; it can be an empty object literal (see Listing 11-9 in Chapter 11). Of course, this is in addition to whatever tests are appropriate for the tool's basic functionality.

Special tests for the widget that is sandboxed include one to verify that it throws the correct `Errors` if the tools it requires are not available, and does not throw if they are. Again, a simple object literal that stands in for the real sandbox will keep your tests isolated to their real subject (see Listing 11-11 in Chapter 11).

Testing the Decorator Pattern

It's tempting to let the object being decorated, with whatever faults it may contain, become an unwitting subject of a decorator's tests. To avoid this potential exposure, consider writing a simplified fake for the decorated object. Another advantage of a fake is that it's usually easier to make it produce an error than to make the real object do so.

Speaking of which, your first test should be that errors in the fake are propagated through the decorator. With that done, you can verify that successful return values make their way up the call stack as planned. We recommend testing the actual functionality of the decorator as a last step. Chapter 12 has all the details.

Testing the Strategy Pattern

The Strategy Pattern in Chapter 13 employed a factory to produce the right kind of object (the strategy) based on the needs of the moment. The implementation of the Strategy Pattern itself, as distinct from the factory, needed to be tested for error-handling only, for calling the factory properly to obtain the desired strategy, for calling the required function on the strategy, and for returning the strategy's result. As you might guess by now, it's best to mock everything but the subject under test (that is, mock the factory and the object it produces). The mock consists of fakes, spies, or most likely both.

Testing the Proxy Pattern

You will recall from Chapter 14 that the Proxy Pattern consists of one object that serves as an expert in the use of an underlying object. What you want to test is how the proxy handles that object. This is easiest when the proxy receives the object by dependency injection, rather than constructing the object on its own. That lets you inject a spy instead, which can report to your tests how it was called and what it returned.

The proxy should concern itself with as little of its subject's semantics as possible. Often this is very little indeed, which can result in very few tests. See the discussion following Listing 14-10 in Chapter 14.

Testing Chainable Methods

A chainable method is usually nothing more than a method that returns `this`. That's something to test in addition to whatever other tests the method requires.

Sometimes, a method becomes chainable because it returns an object that has the same *type* or the same *shape* as this. The then method of the Promise object is an example. It does not return the Promise on which it was called, but a new Promise. This, too, should be the subject of a test.

Testing Conformance to an Interface

In Chapters 16 and 17, you saw how JavaScript, a language without interfaces, can benefit from the philosophy behind them. If you write code along those lines, something like the ContractRegistry can help. It verifies that an object has the expected methods, and that those methods are called with the expected arguments. You can easily make the ContractRegistry active during testing but vanish completely during production.

Testing the Use of call and apply

As explained at length in Chapter 18, the call and apply functions each take a parameter that becomes this inside the invoked function. If that argument is not supplied, how do you want the code to behave? Remember that if the argument is absent in strict mode, this will be undefined and in non-strict mode it will be the window object. An occasion for a test, surely!

Testing the Method-Borrowing Pattern

When one object borrows a method from another, the chief danger is that the borrowed method might require something from its new host object. The safest course is to install code in the borrowed method to make it check for requirements. Much was said about this in Chapter 19, including the advisability of using an extra level of indirection and maybe an aspect.

As with other patterns that bring objects together in novel arrangements, consider using something like the ContractRegistry.

Finally, be aware that it is surprisingly possible for the borrowed method, called from its new home, to affect even the private variables of its original home.

Testing Mixins

In Chapter 20, you saw how a general-purpose extend function can facilitate the Mixin Pattern. When developing such a function, consider whether you want to copy only the donor's "own" properties or its inherited properties as well. Then, write the appropriate tests.

Also consider what you want to do if the target object already has a property that is about to be imported from the mixin. Do you overwrite what's there, leave it alone, or throw an Error?

Test the mixin on an object that has the minimum requirements to receive it.

A *functional mixin* is one that contains a method to *add itself* to a host. This method is invoked with call or apply, with a context argument (the *this* inside the method) that is the object being extended. The example from Chapter 20 was a mixin that added an id property to any object thus:

```
Conference.mixins.addId.call(newAttendee);
```

If your mixin employs this pattern, the suggestions for call and apply pertain.

Testing Mediators and Observers

The Mediator and Observer Patterns of Chapter 21 both rely on "interfaces" between actors. You'll want to ensure that the requirements of the interfaces are met. The `ContractRegistry` can help.

In the Observer Pattern, you can use a fake, simplified version of the subject. Likewise, when testing a Mediator, you can use fake stand-ins for the real colleagues. As usual, the idea is to keep the focus on the subject under test, isolating your tests from the behavior of other objects.

Testing DOM Access

The first rule of testing DOM access (see Chapter 22) is to avoid it. Put as much of your code as possible in functions that have nothing to do with the DOM. Then, your tests have to concern themselves only with simple questions like, "If I click this button, does this [already tested] function get called?"

Your Jasmine tests can add the DOM element in a `beforeEach` and remove it in an `afterEach`. Consider using `jasmine-jquery` as an aid to interact with the DOM element from there.

Avoid unit tests that are concerned with appearance only; they can be brittle.

Tests to Enforce Architectural Divisions

In Chapter 23, you saw several variations of the Magic Key Technique, which ensured that a component can only be called from other components as your architecture allows. In each variation, unit tests ensured that the key had the desired effect.

SUMMARY

This chapter presented the principles of test-driven development you've encountered in this book, including the general mechanics of test-driven development and specific suggestions for many common patterns in software engineering.

If you came to JavaScript from another language, you might find it somewhat quirky—in a good way. The next chapter summarizes many of the idioms that give JavaScript its charm.

25

Summary of JavaScript Idioms in This Book

WHAT'S IN THIS CHAPTER?

➤ Reviewing the unique aspects of JavaScript objects, variables, and functions

➤ Reviewing other JavaScript idioms

There are enough syntactic similarities between JavaScript and C# or Java that many developers don't think twice about jumping in and writing JavaScript using the same concepts and constructs that they've used to build C# or Java programs.

Taking such an approach, however, invariably leads to unwieldy JavaScript code that has neither the type safety of C# and Java nor the elegance of good JavaScript. In order to create truly reliable JavaScript applications, you must understand the quirks that make JavaScript what it is: a flexible, powerful, and elegant programming language.

While this book explicitly is not a JavaScript primer, there are some features of the JavaScript language that are worthy of explicit review. This chapter highlights some of the unique, idiomatic aspects of JavaScript that were used in the preceding chapters.

REVIEWING OBJECTS

JavaScript has only five primitive types: String, Number, Boolean, Undefined, and Null. Everything else, including functions, is an `object`. This section revisits some of the idiomatic aspects of JavaScript objects that we've used in the book.

Object Properties May Be Added and Removed

A JavaScript object's dynamic nature means it may be manipulated in interesting ways. Generally speaking, once an object has been created in C# or Java, that object's properties are set in stone; it isn't possible to add or remove properties at will. JavaScript objects usually aren't bound by the same restriction. In fact, it's common to add properties to and remove properties from an object after it has been created.

For example, Listing 11-5 in Chapter 11 leveraged the dynamic nature of JavaScript objects to add and remove tools for use within a `Conference.WidgetSandbox`. The following example highlights the relevant portions of Listing 11-5.

```
describe("Conference.WidgetSandbox", function(){
  describe("Constructor function", function(){
    var widgetFcnSpy;

    beforeEach(function(){
      // Add test tools so the tests aren't dependent upon
      // the existence of actual tools
      Conference.WidgetTools.tool1 = function(sandbox){
        return {};
      };
      Conference.WidgetTools.tool2 = function(sandbox){
        return {};
      };

      // create a spy that may be used as the widget function
      widgetFcnSpy = jasmine.createSpy();
    });

    afterEach(function(){
      // remove the test tools
      delete Conference.WidgetTools.tool1;
      delete Conference.WidgetTools.tool2;
    });

    // *** Code omitted for brevity ***
  });
```

Objects May Be Used as a Dictionary

The properties of a JavaScript object may be accessed using dictionary syntax. For example, the following assignment statements are functionally equivalent:

```
var obj = { };

obj.myProperty = 'Property value';
obj['myProperty'] = 'Property value';
```

The capability to access their properties in dictionary fashion make JavaScript objects natural candidates for use as caches, as the following excerpt from Listing 14-6 in Chapter 14 illustrates:

```
Conference.attendeeProfileProxy = function(
attendees, profileService, prefetchLimit) {

  var ix,
      prefetched = {};

  function prefetch(attendeeId) {
    prefetched[attendeeId] = profileService.getProfile(attendeeId);
  }
  // *** Code omitted for brevity ***
};
```

REVIEWING VARIABLES

There are some key idiomatic aspects of variables in JavaScript that must be understood in order to create reliable JavaScript code. This section reviews two of those aspects: hoisting and scoping.

Variable Declarations Are Hoisted

What will the output of the following C# code sample be?

```
static void WriteValue()
{
  value = "this is my value";
  string value;
  System.Diagnostics.Debug.WriteLine(value);
}

WriteValue();
```

If you said: "Nothing, it won't even compile," you're correct. In C#, a variable can't be used before it has been declared. In fact, the C# compiler refuses to create an executable for you because attempting to assign a value to a variable before the variable has been declared generates an error.

Suppose, however, that the C# compiler didn't protect you from referencing a variable before it's declared. When the previous sample executed, you'd expect it to generate some sort of error when it attempted to execute the first line, which references the as yet undeclared variable *value*.

Now consider the following analogous JavaScript example. What do you expect its output to be?

```
function writeValue(){
  value = "This is my value";
  var value;
  console.log(value);
}

writeValue();
```

Though it may be counterintuitive, "This is my value" is written to the console. What type of magic is this?

The preceding sample successfully executes because the JavaScript interpreter hoists all variable declarations to the top of the function that they're contained in. Because of hoisting, that sample is functionally equivalent to the following one:

```
function writeValue(){
  var value;
  value = "This is my value";
  console.log(value);
}

writeValue();
```

It's important to note that only the declaration of a variable is hoisted. If a variable is declared and initialized in the same step, as in this example:

```
function writeValue(){
  console.log(value);
  var value = "This is my value";
}

writeValue();
```

application of hoisting yields the following:

```
function writeValue(){
  var value;
  console.log(value);
  value = "This is my value";
}

writeValue();
```

The declaration of *value* is hoisted to the top of the function, but initialization of *value* is left in its original location. As such, this example will output "undefined," the value of a declared but uninitialized variable.

Many of the examples in the book gather all variable declarations at the top of their containing function, such as this example from Listing 20-15 in Chapter 20:

```
var Conference = Conference || {};
Conference.attendee = function(firstName, lastName){

  var checkedIn = false,
    first = firstName || 'None',
    last = lastName || 'None',
    checkInNumber;

  //*** Code omitted for brevity ***
}
```

Adopting the practice of declaring variables at the top of functions will eliminate hoisting-related surprises.

Variables Have Function Scope

A discussion of JavaScript variables wouldn't be complete without a discussion of scoping. Unlike C# and Java, in which variables are scoped to the block they're declared in, JavaScript variables are scoped to the function they're declared in.

The following example illustrates block scoping in C#:

```
static void BlockScope()
{
    string variable1 = "Outer scope";
    // Only variable1 is in-scope

    if (!string.IsNullOrEmpty(variable1))
    {
        string variable2 = "Inner scope";
        // both variable1 and variable 2 are in-scope
        System.Diagnostics.Debug.WriteLine(variable1 + " " + variable2);
    }

    // Only variable1 is in-scope
    System.Diagnostics.Debug.WriteLine(variable1);
}
```

In the preceding example, *variable2* is only accessible within the if block in which it is declared and *variable1* is available within the entire function block.

The following example illustrates a similar function written in JavaScript:

```
function functionScope(){
    var variable1 = "Outer scope";

    if(variable1){
        var variable2 = "Inner scope (not really)";

        // variable2 is scoped to the function, not the if block
        console.log(variable1 + " " + variable2);
    }

    // both variable1 and variable2 are in-scope
    console.log(variable1+ " " + variable2);
}
```

Although the preceding example declares *variable2* within an if block, *variable2* is scoped to the entire function, not just the containing if block. In fact, the JavaScript interpreter hoists the declaration of *variable2* out of the if block to the top of the function.

Another place C# and Java developers may be surprised by function versus block scoping is for loops. It's common in C#, for example, to write for loops with the indexing variable declared within the for statement:

```
for(int index = 0; index < 100; index++){
    // index is scoped to the for block
}
```

Declaring the indexing variable within the for statement in JavaScript—as in for(var index = 0; index < 100; index++)—doesn't scope the *index* variable to the for block. Instead, *index* is scoped to the function, and its declaration is hoisted to the top of the function. As such, it's common to see the indexing variable declared (and often initialized) outside of the for statement.

Separate declaration of a for loop's indexing variable is illustrated in Listing 18-13 from Chapter 18:

```
var Conference = Conference || {};
Conference.polyfills = Conference.polyfills || {};

Conference.polyfills.arrayForEach = function(callbackFcn, thisObj){
  var i;

  if (typeof callbackFcn !== "function") {
    throw new Error(callbackFcn + ' is not a function');
  }

  for(i = 0; i < this.length; i++){
    callbackFcn();
  }
};
```

Linting tools such as ESLint and JSHint include rules that alert you when they detect JavaScript code that looks like it's attempting to use block scoping.

JavaScript's function scoping is also useful because it allows data to be protected from access, providing functionality similar to private and protected class variables in C#.

The `Conference.simpleCache` module from Listing 9-4 in Chapter 9 illustrates the data-hiding capabilities provided by function scoping:

```
var Conference = Conference || {};

Conference.simpleCache = function(){
  var privateCache = {};

  function getCacheKey(key){
    return JSON.stringify(key);
  }

  return {

    // Returns true if key has an entry in the cache, false if
    // it does not.
    hasKey: function(key){
      return privateCache.hasOwnProperty(getCacheKey(key));
    },

    // Stores value in the cache associated with key
    setValue: function(key, value){
      privateCache[getCacheKey(key)] = value;
    },

    // Returns the cached value for key, or undefined
    // if a value for key has not been cached
    getValue: function(key){
      return privateCache[getCacheKey(key)];
    }
  };
};
```

The variable `privateCache` is declared within the `Conference.simpleCache` function and thus is only in scope within that function. By returning an object that defines functions that access privateCache, the `Conference.simpleCache` has provided an interface to interact with privateCache while disallowing direct manipulation of *privateCache*.

REVIEWING FUNCTIONS

Functions in JavaScript are different beasts than functions in languages such as C# and Java. This section summarizes some of the key features and capabilities of JavaScript functions.

Functions Are Objects

Functions in JavaScript are objects, meaning they have all the capabilities of "regular" objects, and they can be executed. Functions may be assigned to variables and passed as arguments to other functions.

Use of functions as arguments was demonstrated in numerous examples in this book, including many in Chapter 5.

As objects, functions may also have properties. Many of the module functions in this book used this capability to expose a `messages` property. An example, taken from Listing 10-7 in Chapter 10, is shown here:

```
var Conference = Conference || {};
Conference.presentationFactory = function presentationFactory() {
  'use strict';

  return {
    //*** Code omitted for brevity ***
  };
};

Conference.presentationFactory.messages = {
  unexpectedProperty: 'The creation parameter had an unexpected property '
};
```

Functions Declarations Are Hoisted

As it does with variables, the JavaScript interpreter hoists function definitions. There's a bit of additional detail to be aware of, however.

When a function is defined via a function declaration, the function's definition is hoisted along with the declaration. This hoisting behavior means the following code will output "myFunction body":

```
myFunction();

// function declaration and definition is hoisted
function myFunction(){
    console.log("myFunction body");
}
```

When a function is defined via a function expression, however, only the declaration of the function variable is hoisted. The following will result in an error:

```
myFunction();

var myFunction = function(){
    console.log("myFunction body");
}
```

That's because hoisting makes the previous statement equivalent to this

```
var myFunction;

myFunction();

myFunction = function(){
    console.log("myFunction body");
}
```

which attempts to execute `myFunction` when its value is `undefined`.

Functions Don't Have Return Types

You must specify a return type when defining a function in C# or Java, or you need to indicate that the function doesn't return a value. In C#, a function that doesn't return a value to its caller may be defined like so:

```
void NoReturnValue()
{
    // this function doesn't return anything
}
```

JavaScript, on the other hand, doesn't provide a mechanism by which the return type of a function may be specified. The definition of a function in JavaScript doesn't even indicate whether a value will be returned from the function.

A JavaScript function without a `return` statement, or a `return` statement without value, will always return a value of `undefined`:

```
function noReturn(){

};
var fromNoReturn = noReturn();
console.log(fromNoReturn === undefined);    // true

function bareReturn(){
    return;
}
var fromBareReturn = bareReturn();
console.log(fromBareReturn === undefined);  // true
```

Functions May Be Anonymous

Anonymous functions, especially those without a reference by which they may be invoked, are a staple of idiomatic JavaScript. One of the most common uses of anonymous functions is as callbacks participating in the Callback Pattern.

Listing 5-6 in Chapter 5, repeated in the following sample, shows an extreme case of anonymous functions being passed as callback functions.

```
CallbackArrow = CallbackArrow || {};

CallbackArrow.rootFunction = function(){
  CallbackArrow.firstFunction(function(arg){
    // logic in the first callback
    CallbackArrow.secondFunction(function(arg){
      // logic in the second callback
      CallbackArrow.thirdFunction(function(arg){
        // logic in the third callback
        CallbackArrow.fourthFunction(function(arg){
          // Logic in the fourth callback
        });
      });
    });
  });
};
CallbackArrow.firstFunction = function(callback1){
  callback1(arg);
};
CallbackArrow.secondFunction = function(callback2){
  callback2(arg);
};
CallbackArrow.thirdFunction = function(callback3){
  callback3(arg);
}
CallbackArrow.fourthFunction = function(callback4){
  callback4(arg);
};
```

If you're a C# programmer, you may see that anonymous functions in JavaScript are similar to lambda expressions in C#.

Functions May Be Nested

Defining one function inside of another is a common and useful practice in JavaScript. Consider this excerpt from Listing 21-1 in Chapter 21:

```
var Conference = Conference || {};

Conference.recentRegistrationsService = function(registrationsService){

var service = {
   //*** Code omitted for brevity ***
 },

  getNewAttendees = function getNewAttendees(){
    // calls the server and retrieves and returns a promise of an
    // array of the attendees that registered since the last time it
    // polled.
    return new Promise(function(reject, resolve){
      resolve([]);
    });
  },
```

```
        pollingProcess = setInterval(function pollForNewAttendees(){
          getNewAttendees().then(function processNewAttendees(newAttendees){
            newAttendees.forEach(function updateWithNewAttendee(newAttendee){
              service.updateObservers(newAttendee);
            });
          });
        }, 15000);

        return service;
      };
```

In the example, the function `getNewAttendees` is defined within the function `Conference`
`.recentRegistrationsService`. Given JavaScript's scoping rules, `getNewAttendees` is scoped
to `Conference.recentRegistrationsService`. As such, `getNewAttendees` may only be invoked
from within `Conference.recentRegistrationsService`. Leveraging JavaScript's nested functions
and scoping rules allow the creation of functions (and variables) that are private to the function in
which they're defined.

Functions May Be Invoked with Any Number of Arguments

When interviewing developers for our team, one of the questions we regularly ask is: "What happens if you execute a JavaScript function with more arguments than the function expects?" We also
ask the inverse: "What happens if you execute a JavaScript function with fewer arguments than the
function expects?"

Interviewees answer with: "errors are generated" more often than either of us expected. Had we
been asking about C#, the answer wouldn't be far from the mark; code that calls a C# function with
too many or too few parameters won't even compile.

JavaScript, however, happily executes a function with whatever arguments you give it. Within the
body of the function, any extra arguments are ignored, and omitted arguments have a value of
`undefined`.

This flexible argument handling allows for functionality similar to function overloading in C#. In
C#, multiple functions specifying different numbers of parameters are defined:

```
void OverloadedFunction(int argOne)
{
    // function body
}
void OverloadedFunction(int argOne, int argTwo)
{
    // function body
}

void OverloadedFunction(int argOne, int argTwo, string argThree)
{
    // function body
}
```

In JavaScript, overloading may be simulated by defining a function that defines the maximum
number of expected parameters, and then checking to see if the arguments provided have a
value:

```
function simulatedOverloading(var argOne, var argTwo, var argThree){
  if(argOne !== undefined){
    // argOne provided
  }

  if(argTwo !== undefined){
    // argTwo provided
  }

  if(argThree !== undefined){
    // argThree provided
  }
}
```

JavaScript also provides the special array-like variable `arguments`, which contains all of the arguments provided to the function by the caller. The `arguments` special variable is what enabled the `WidgetSandbox` constructor function developed in Chapter 11 to accept any number of tool name arguments.

Functions May Be Invoked Immediately

Immediately invoked function expressions (IIFEs) are, as their name implies, JavaScript functions that are defined and immediately executed. Use of an IIFE ensures that a function is executed only once, and also has the benefit of establishing function-local variables.

Listing 14-8 in Chapter 14 uses an IIFE to both ensure the function named `prefetchAll` is executed only once and the variable `sortedAttendees` is isolated from the outer scope. An excerpt from Listing 14-8 follows:

```
var Conference = Conference || {};

Conference.attendeeProfileProxy = function(
attendees, profileService, prefetchLimit) {

  //*** Code omitted for brevity ***

  (function prefetchAll() {
    var sortedAttendees = //*** omitted ***
  })();

};
```

IIFEs are also used to avoid variable naming collisions. For example, IIFEs are commonly used to ensure that $ is bound to the `jQuery` global variable in this manner:

```
(function($){
  // Function is immediately invoked, providing jQuery as the argument
  // for the $ parameter.
  // Guarantees that $ bound to the jQuery global variable within this
  // function, even if $ is bound to another value elsewhere.
})(jQuery);
```

Also, IIFEs may be used to create static modules, as the following code from Listing 3-2 in Chapter 3 illustrates:

```
var MyApp = MyApp || {};

MyApp.WildlifePreserveSimulator = (function() {
  var animals = [];

  return {
    addAnimal: function(animalMaker,species, sex) {
      animals.push(animalMaker.make(species,sex));
    },
    getAnimalCount: function() {
      return animals.length;
    }
  };
}()); // <--Immediate execution!
```

Because `MyApp.WildlifePreserveSimulator`'s module function is immediately executed, `MyApp` `.WildlifePreserveSimulator` becomes a singleton object. The object exposes two methods, `addAnimal` and `getAnimalCount`, which manipulate the `animals` variable. Because the `animals` variable is defined within the scope of the module function, it's protected from direct access.

REVIEWING BOOLEAN OPERATIONS

This section reviews two important aspects, type coercion and truthy and falsy values.

Types May Be Coerced When Testing Equality

What is the output of the following JavaScript sample?

```
var v1 = 1;
var v2 = "1";

console.log(v1 == v2);
```

If you have a background in C# or Java, you might have said "false." That answer, while logical, is incorrect.

Unlike C# and Java, JavaScript applies automatic *type coercion* to the operands of the `==` and `!=` operators. It "helpfully" converts one of the operands to be the same type as the other before comparing the values of the operands. In the case of the preceding sample, the output is, perhaps unexpectedly, `true`.

In *JavaScript: The Good Parts* (O'Reilly Media, 2008), Douglas Crockford calls the `==` and `!=` operators the evil twins of their non-coercing siblings: `===` and `!==`. The non-coercing operators don't perform any automatic casting, so in order for two values to be equal, the values must have the same type. Altering the example to use `===` rather than `==` yields the answer you likely anticipated: `false`.

From the standpoint of reliability, we favor explicit over automatic. We used `===` and `!==` equality and inequality comparisons throughout the samples in this book to avoid automatic type coercion, and we recommend that you adopt the same practice. As Chapter 23 illustrated, linting tools such as ESLint can help you adhere to the practice.

Values May Be Truthy or Falsy

Many of the examples we presented contained conditional statements such as the following:

```
if (!registry[contractName]) {
    throw new Error(this.getMessageForNameNotRegistered(contractName));
}
```

Is the preceding example, extracted from Listing 16-8 in Chapter 16, checking to see if `registry[contractName]` is `false`? No, it isn't.

The extracted conditional's purpose is to determine if the `registry[ContractName]` is `undefined`, which JavaScript considers to be *falsy*. Falsy values evaluate as `false` when used within a conditional expression, and truthy values evaluate to `true` when used within a conditional expression.

JavaScript considers these values falsy:

➤ `false`

➤ `0`

➤ `''` (empty string)

➤ `null`

➤ `undefined`

➤ `NaN`

and all other values as truthy. An understanding of truthy and falsy values is important when writing—and reading—idiomatic, reliable JavaScript.

SUMMARY

While JavaScript may have been derided as a toy language in the past, it is now considered to be just as suitable for large-scale projects as its strongly-typed compiled cousins.

In order to harness the capabilities of JavaScript, the language's quirks and idioms must be understood and appreciated. Behaviors such as hoisting and type coercion, and capabilities such as dictionary property access and immediate function execution make JavaScript different from C# and Java, but no less powerful.

INDEX

U